Anglo-Saxon Studies
in Archaeology and History

20

# EARLY MEDIEVAL MONASTICISM IN THE NORTH SEA ZONE

Proceedings of a conference held to celebrate the conclusion of the Lyminge excavations 2008–15

Edited by
Gabor Thomas and Alexandra Knox

General Editor: Helena Hamerow

Oxford University School of Archaeology

Published by the Oxford University School of Archaeology
Institute of Archaeology
Beaumont Street
Oxford

*Distributed by*
Oxbow Books
The Old Music Hall, 106–108 Cowley Road, Oxford, OX4 1JE, UK
*Tel: 01865 241249 Fax: 01865 794449*

*Distributed in North America by*
Casemate Academic
1950 Lawrence Rd, Havertown PA 19083, USA

www.oxbowbooks.com



ISBN 978 1 905905 39 3
ISSN 0264 5254

A CIP record for this book is available from the British Library

*Cover image: view of the 2014 excavations on Tayne Field, Lyminge, looking south-west with the parish church captured in the background*

Designed and typeset by Oxford Book Projects
Printed in Great Britain by
Short Run Press, Exeter

*In memoriam*

Nicholas Brooks

# Editor's Foreword

*Anglo-Saxon Studies in Archaeology and History* is a series concerned with the archaeology and history of England and its neighbours during the Anglo-Saxon period.

ASSAH offers researchers an opportunity to publish new work in an inter- and multi-disciplinary forum that allows for a diversity of approaches and subject matter. Contributions placing Anglo-Saxon England in its international context are as warmly welcomed as those that focus on England itself.

Papers submitted to ASSAH must be comprehensible to non-specialist readers. They must, furthermore, conform to the journal's house style. A copy of the style-sheet is available on-line, at: **http://www.arch.ox.ac.uk/assah**. A hard copy can be obtained from the Editorial Assistant, Dr. Laura Morley (Laura.morley@arch.ox.ac.uk). All papers are peer-reviewed.

The Editor is grateful to the contributors to this volume for their prompt and efficient responses, and to those peer reviewers who have taken the time to read and comment upon submissions.

All papers for consideration for future volumes should be sent to the Editor.

Professor Helena Hamerow
(Helena.hamerow@arch.ox.ac.uk)
Institute of Archaeology
34–6 Beaumont Street
Oxford OX1 2PG

# Contents

**Part III: From tribal centre to royal monastery: Anglo-Saxon Lyminge explored through its archaeology**

# Contributors

*Rose Broadley*
UCL Institute of Archaeology, 31–34 Gordon Square, London, WC1H 0PY UK

*Barbara Yorke*
Department of History, University of Winchester, Sparkford Road, Winchester, SO22 4NR UK

*Rosemary Cramp*
Department of Archaeology, Durham University, Dawson Building, South Road, Durham, DH1 3LE UK

*Zoe Knapp*
Department of Archaeology, University of Reading, Whiteknights, Reading, RG6 6AB UK

*Elisabeth Lorans*
Département d'histoire et d'archéologie, Université de Tours, 3, Rue des Tanneurs 37041 TOURS CEDEX 1 France

*Mark McKerracher*
Flat 9 Chatfield House, 428 Southampton Road, Eastleigh, Hampshire, SO50 5QJ UK.

*Tomás Ó Carragáin*
Department of Archaeology, University College Cork, College Road, Cork, T12 YN60 Republic of Ireland

*David Petts*
Department of Archaeology, Durham University, Dawson Building, South Road, Durham, DH1 3LE UK

*Gabor Thomas*
Department of Archaeology, University of Reading, Whiteknights, Reading, RG6 6AB UK

*Tony Wilmott*
Senior Archaeologist, Historic England, Fort Cumberland, Fort Cumberland Road, Portsmouth, Hampshire, PO4 9LD UK

*Ian Wood*
Institute for Medieval Studies, University of Leeds, Leeds, LS2 9JT UK

# Foreword

The conference at which these papers were presented arose from excavations at the early medieval site of Lyminge, Kent (described below by Gabor Thomas), and a wish to contextualize the startling discoveries made there. Launched to investigate the documented Anglo-Saxon royal nunnery, and its background in elite fifth- to sixth-century secular activity suggested by well-furnished burials, the project unexpectedly encountered a major intermediate phase: a seventh-century 'great hall complex', comparable to those already well known from such sites as Yeavering in Northumberland and Cowdery's Down in Hampshire.

Despite the inevitable shift of focus from the monastic to the royal, it was quickly realized that the discovery offered unique perspectives on the secular background to religious foundation during the seventh-century 'monastic boom', and on points of comparison and contrast. Were the two complexes sequential or co-existent? Did the aristocratic nuns genuinely follow a new lifestyle, or maintain their old one while paying lip-service to monastic discipline? And was there – a contentious point – a real difference between the layout, buildings and archaeological signatures of these two different kinds of elite establishment? The papers given at the conference – nearly all of them published here – offer contexts by exploring similar themes on a much wider front, the monastic culture of the North Sea zone between the early seventh and mid-ninth centuries.

If there is one theme that unites these papers, it is the social and cultural relationships between monastic sites and the elite secular world in which they were all, in one way or another, embedded. The most encouraging aspect of the conference was an atmosphere in which everyone seemed willing and eager to talk to each other. For some decades, there has not always been a meeting of minds between the historians and the archaeologists of early medieval monasticism. Historians have tended to take seriously the strong contrasts between secular and religious modes of life assumed by written sources, and to interpret excavated settlements in that light. Archaeologists, very reasonably insisting on autonomy of interpretation within their own field, have rejected such contrasts as over-rigid and inadequately nuanced, putting forward alternative models that historians have in turn criticized as ahistorical, or based on simplistic and over-selective use of historical frameworks.

It is time to get beyond all that. These papers demonstrate the abundant variety of monastic settlement modes, which elude rigid classification and – at one end of the spectrum – were clearly influenced by aristocratic ones. Equally, they show that the forms, organization and rhythms of monastic sites really did have substantial and decisive differences from those of the occupants' aristocratic relatives. Nowhere, perhaps, is this clearer than at Lyminge, with its late-pre-Christian residential and ritual complex giving way to the seventh-century great halls, themselves abandoned within at any rate a few decades of the nunnery's foundation. The dietary evidence, above all, leaves no doubt that life changed radically during the late seventh and eighth centuries. Was monastic Christianity in the driving-seat? Or was it so spectacularly successful because it chimed with a broader shift of preferences in culture and lifestyle?

That interface between religious commitment, secular ambition, everyday life, material culture and socio-economic change was immensely complex, and achieving a fuller understanding of it should now be the main goal. For some years to come, evolving interpretations of Lyminge will be at the heart of that more sophisticated dialogue. Meanwhile, we should celebrate the achievements of Gabor Thomas and his Lyminge team, whose spectacular discoveries have so revitalized and enriched the debate.

John Blair
The Queen's College, University of Oxford

# Introduction: early medieval monasticism in the North Sea zone: recent research and new perspectives

Gabor Thomas
Director of the Lyminge Project

This volume is based upon a conference convened at the University of Kent in April 2015 to celebrate the conclusion of a major programme of archaeological excavation targeting the Anglo-Saxon royal centre and monastery of Lyminge, Kent. The aim of the conference was to contextualize the principal findings of the Lyminge Project by drawing upon a range of historical and archaeological perspectives on early medieval monasticism in north-west Europe, with a geographical emphasis (though not exclusive focus) on Kent and neighbouring regions of the continental North Sea basin. In planning the conference, the organisers were conscious of following close on the heels of a number of high-profile academic networks and initiatives examining the Christianization of the 'Insular' British Isles with the spread of monastic culture forming one of its pivotal themes and institutional contexts.[1] On the other hand, it was felt that the initiative had something genuinely distinctive to offer by shifting the spotlight of attention from Northumbria and the Celtic-speaking regions of the British Isles to Kent, a geographical zone which has been somewhat neglected in recent evaluations of Insular monasticism.[2] This refocusing, it was hoped, would offer an opportunity for scholars to come together to look afresh at Kent as an early medieval monastic province, to re-evaluate the external (in particular) Frankish influences that shaped it and its own shaping influence on the expansion of monastic culture in the Insular British Isles.

One of the key objectives of the current volume is to provide a fresh and current overview of the Lyminge Project and its contribution to early medieval studies at the end of the data-gathering phase and before the initiation of a large and complex programme of post-excavation analysis which lies ahead. For this reason, with the exception of Broadley's contribution on the Anglo-Saxon glass, the editors decided against soliciting additional – or, in the case of the three speakers who were unable to offer their papers for publication, replacement – contributions on the grounds that it would have resulted in an undue prolongation in the publication process. If the end product falls some way short of a comprehensive state-of-the-art review of recent historical and archaeological scholarship on early medieval monasticism in north-west Europe, then it is hoped that it provides a useful entry-point into some of the key debates and research agendas shaping the field as outlined in the rest of this introduction.

The structure of the volume largely follows that of the conference, albeit with some minor modifications and changes in emphasis. Part I brings together two papers which explore the Franco-Kentish nexus as a context for the foundation of royal nunneries in Kent. Historians have long appreciated that the channels of external influence absorbed into the eclectic body of Insular monasticism were diverse and interacting. Yet, as this pair of contributions ably demonstrate, we have much still to learn about the Frankish contribution as 'an insufficiently emphasized' strand within Anglo-Saxon monasticism. Providing a richly informative account of royal women as agents in the consolidation of the early medieval church, Yorke's paper argues that the 'monastic policy' of the Frankish queen, Balthild, had a significant, and hitherto under-appreciated, influence on the development of monasticism in southern England. Yorke's analysis has significant implications for the dating of nunneries in Anglo-Saxon Kent for, if accepted, none of these institutions are likely to have existed prior to the 660s, in the case of Lyminge and nearby Folkestone, nearly a generation later than their traditionally ascribed foundation dates. Wood's paper argues that in order to understand the true nature of Frankish influence on the early Anglo-Saxon church we need to recognize that Merovingian monasticism was far more complex and variegated than a monolithic 'Columbanian' tradition. His more subtle reading of the Frankish background points towards other strands of Merovingian monasticism (including the 'Caesarian') which enjoyed international spheres of influence and as such deserve to be considered as active models for monastic life in Anglo-Saxon England. Wood also critiques the standard view that the institution of the 'double monastery' – a label long synonymous with the early Kentish church and widely reproduced in the relevant scholarly literature – was a widespread and uniform monastic idiom within northern Frankia. A more critical reading of the historical sources indicates that such institutions were invariably female-dominated and thus more appropriately described as nunneries: the same is very likely to be true of Kent.

Part II draws together a suite of five papers offering comparative archaeological perspectives on the character and definition of early medieval monastic space. This section is opened by two synthetic surveys, the first by Cramp providing an up-to-date examination of the physical structure of monastic institutions across pre-Viking England, followed by a more geographically focused examination of Northumbrian sites by Petts. Three individual case-studies of recent monastic excavations then follow. The contributions of Lorans (Marmoutier) and Ó Carragáin (Toureen Peakaun) put spotlights on the extreme edges of north-west European monasticism, the Loire valley and south-central Ireland respectively, while Tony Wilmott's paper draws upon the results of a renewed programme of archaeological investigation at Whitby Abbey to re-evaluate one of the most iconic monastic sites in Anglo-Saxon England. While the focus and underlying content of these contributions is relatively diverse, viewed collectively they provide a vivid demonstration of the fundamental contribution which archaeology has made towards a more nuanced understanding of the character, texture and behaviour of monastic space as an embedded dimension of early medieval cultural landscapes. In particular, three cross-cutting strands of methodological and conceptual relevance can be highlighted to help frame and foreground this section of the volume.

1. *Scale and defining the edges of monastic space.* The fact that monasteries were very often located at the interface between land and water, whether rivers or oceans, for the purposes of seclusion and worldly detachment, can sometimes create formidable methodological challenges for determining scale. As highlighted by Lorans' paper on Marmoutier, our ability to delineate the inhabitable extent of these dynamic 'borderland' sites is often dependent upon peeling back complex biographies of geomorphological and landscape change over the *longue durée.*[3] Similarly, by highlighting the denuding effects of coastal erosion on the early medieval topography, recent archaeological work at Whitby has enabled us to appreciate as never before the massive scale and spatial complexity of the monastery during its 'Anglian' heyday. Defining the edges of monastic space through the identification of man-made boundary features introduces further problems and complexities. As Cramp, Petts and Wilmott highlight, it can be all too easy to confuse external '*vallum monasterii*' for internal boundaries and the danger of underestimating scale becomes particularly acute on monastic sites encroached by subsequent phases of medieval and modern settlement where map regression must invariably be relied upon to provide a sense of the early medieval topography. One of the key contributory factors leading to such confusion (and a poor comprehension of layout more generally) is the 'keyhole' scale at which monastic sites are frequently sampled archaeologically: the task of relating the part under investigation to the whole in such cases is fraught with difficulties and often invites unacceptable levels of speculation.

2. *The dynamics of monastic space.* Several of the papers highlight evidence for change and mutability in the trajectory of monastic precincts, especially with regards to peripheral zones of occupation and activity, but also within and immediately around monumentally permanent cores. A change in the functional use of space, for example encroachment of burial into former domestic zones and vice versa, is evidenced at numerous sites. This pattern has its corollary in the changing use of buildings, a persistent pattern being the transformation of formerly domestic/habitation structures (including structures of sometimes considerable monumental pretensions) into settings for specialist craftworking. As highlighted by Ó Carragáin's paper, once formalized in the landscape, the spatial cohesion of ecclesiastical precincts might be threatened or disrupted by the process of compartmentalization, in this case illustrated by the insertion of a subsidiary habitation enclosure to house a senior ascetic. Finally, as exemplified by the Northumbrian data in particular (e.g. Whitby, Hartlepool and Whithorn), the restructuring of monastic precincts was frequently accompanied by the adoption of new constructional styles, whether in connection with domestic buildings or boundary features: on such evidence it is clear that monastic communities not only assimilated changing vernacular architectural traditions but also adapted them to suit their own needs and requirements.

3. *Identifying monastic space.* As Cramp reminds us, archaeologists working with British evidence have long grappled with the thorny issue of the extent to which it is possible to distinguish monastic sites from other types of contemporary settlement, particularly the residences of lay aristocrats, on the basis of archaeological criteria. She very usefully reviews the various twists and turns within the debate and arrives at the conclusion that, notwithstanding a high degree of regional and localized diversity, it is possible to recognize distinctively 'monastic' characteristics in the built environment of larger, more important, establishments featuring monumentally elaborate cores.[4] Of course, as highlighted by conflicting interpretations over the paradigmatic English site of Flixborough (Lincolnshire), the distinction becomes much finer and more difficult to make when one's view is restricted to excavated

windows within the outlying portions of settlements, although in such cases material culture and bioarchaeological signatures derived from finds-rich midden deposits may sometimes offer an added means of characterizing lifestyle. While such problems are well rehearsed in an Anglo-Saxon context, it is significant to note that an identical debate is now being replayed on the other side of the Irish Sea under the impetus of a massive expansion in early medieval settlement data generated by commercial excavation projects undertaken during the 'Celtic Tiger Boom'. Ó Carragáin makes a series of important observations based upon a review of the Irish situation, arguing that we need to extend our analysis to how buildings and complexes were used, rather than limiting our view to how they looked. Drawing upon Toureen Peakaun evidence, he asserts that it is not the buildings themselves, but subtle variations in their form, use-patterns and interrelationships with bounded space that provide vital evidence for their 'monastic' character, stressing that we need to direct attention towards understanding how vernacular traditions were adapted to 'create a material context for monastic practice'. Anglo-Saxon archaeologists have clearly much to gain from engaging with such an agenda and the more general call for an archaeology of medieval monasticism and belief which pays closer consideration to the embodied experience and ritual actions of religious expression and personal devotion.[5]

Part III focuses attention squarely on the Lyminge Project and its various contributions to contemporary research agendas in early medieval archaeology. Key among them is enriched understanding of the relationship between monastic institutions and pre-existing centres of royal power in Anglo-Saxon England, a relationship which has hitherto been difficult to address directly through the archaeological record, yet which was of fundamental importance in the Christianization of early medieval cultural landscapes. In contrast to other excavated monastic sites of the pre-Viking period, Lyminge has yielded a wealth of antecedent settlement activity encapsulating an unbroken sequence of occupation stretching back from the cusp of the Anglo-Saxon conversion deep into the pre-Christian era. Lyminge's significance as a theatre of power during this ancestral period was brought spectacularly to light in the most recent phase of excavations (2012–15) with the identification of a previously unidentified seventh-century 'great hall complex', one of a small and geographically dispersed group of sites representing the earliest recognizable stratum of royal residence in Anglo-Saxon England. The first of the papers in this section provides a detailed appraisal and interpretation of this discovery situated in the longer-term context of Lyminge's evolution as a regional centre of power culminating in its transformation into a royal monastery.[6] This is followed by three specialized papers on the Anglo-Saxon glass, palaeobotanical and zooarchaeological remains which together highlight the research potential of the rich material and bioarchaeological assemblages recovered from the excavations and their ability to highlight transformations in cultural identity and social behaviour over Lyminge's 400-year occupation sequence.[7]

In concluding this introduction I would like to express my gratitude to a number of individuals who made the conference such an inspirational and memorable occasion. First and foremost thanks go to my co-editor, Alexandra Knox, who bore most of the heavy organizational load of planning and delivering an international conference with alacrity and calm efficiency, ably assisted over the two days by a cohort of University of Reading PhD students comprising Zoe Knapp, Simon Maslin and Matt Austin. Special thanks must also go to Helen Gittos whose contributions as a congenial host, academic adviser and discussant are warmly acknowledged. The conference benefited immeasurably from the Lyminge Project's partnership with the Kent Archaeological Society, particularly through the support and encouragement of its former Chairman, the late Ian Coulson, and Andrew Richardson and through the presence of the many delegates drawn from its membership. The conference formed the culmination of a three-year programme of excavation funded by the Arts and Humanities Research Council.

## Notes

1 Previous relevant initiatives include a 2004 conference on the archaeology of the early medieval Celtic church (published as Edwards 2009), the 'Making Christian Landscapes' symposium (University College Cork, 2012) and the Leverhulme Trust-funded 'Converting the Isles Research Network' which organized a series of workshops and symposia over 2012–14 to examine the social, economic and cultural dimensions of conversion in the early medieval Insular world (the first volume of which is published as Flechner and Mhaonaigh 2016).

2 The spotlight was last turned on Kent in 1997 on the occasion of the 1400th anniversary of the landing of St Augustine's mission, which was celebrated by a series of academic events culminating in an international conference. With the notable exception of a paper on ecclesiastical architecture, the published proceedings of this conference (Gameson 1999) contain relatively little of direct relevance to the monastic archaeology of Anglo-Saxon Kent and its continental background. For reference to the northern and western geographical bias in the monastic archaeology of the pre-Viking era see Cramp 2008, although this bias has to some extent been ameliorated by recent publications on Glastonbury Abbey (Gilchrist and Green 2015) and the Suffolk site of Brandon (Tester, Anderson, Riddler and Carr 2014). It is notable that the early Christian/monastic landscape of Anglo-Saxon Kent has yet to benefit from a systematic analytical attention of the type exemplified by recent archaeological examinations of East Anglia (Pestell 2004) and south-west England (Turner 2006). The closest that exists is a chapter on the 'ecclesiastical testimony' in Everitt's seminal text, *Continuity and Colonization* (1986).

3 As also illustrated by recent attempts to reconstruct the early

medieval monastic landscapes of Wearmouth and Jarrow (Turner, Semple and Turner 2013).

4 See various contributions in De Rubeis and Marazzi 2008 for the international parameters of this debate in early medieval monastic archaeology.

5 Gilchrist 2014; see Dey (2011, 25) for a very similar observation.

6 This contribution should be read in conjunction with Thomas 2013 which provides an account of the monastic-period archaeology excavated in an earlier (2008–10) phase of the project.

7 All three contributions are based on the research of current or recently completed PhD students working either under the direct auspices of, or in collaboration with, the Lyminge Project.

## References

Cramp, R. 2008. 'Monastic settlements in Britain in the 7th–11th centuries', in F. De Rubeis and F. Marazzi (eds.), *Monasteri in Europa occidentale (secoli VIII–XI): topografia e strutture*, 113–34, Rome: Viella.

Dey, H. 2011. 'Bringing chaos into order': new approaches to the study of early western monasticism', in H. Dey and E. Fentress (eds.), *Ante Litteram: The Spaces of Monastic Observance in Late Antiquity and the Early Middle Ages*, 19–42, Turnhout: Brepols.

Edwards, N. (ed.) 2009. *The Archaeology of the Early Medieval Celtic Churches: Proceedings of a Conference on The Archaeology of the Early Medieval Churches*, Society for Medieval Archaeology Monograph, 29, London: Maneys.

Everitt, A. 1986. *Continuity and Colonization: The Evolution of Kentish Settlement*, Leicester: Leicester University Press.

Flechner, R. and Mhaonaigh, M. (eds.) 2016. *Converting the Isles: The Introduction of Christianity into the Early Medieval Insular World*, Cultural Encounters in Late Antiquity and the Middle Ages (CELAMA, 19), Turnhout: Brepols.

Gameson, R. (ed.) 1999. *St Augustine and the Conversion of England*, Stroud: Sutton Publishing.

Gilchrist, R. 2014. 'Monastic and church archaeology', *Annual Review of Anthropology*, **43**, 235–50.

Gilchrist, R. and Green, C. 2015. *Glastonbury Abbey Archaeological Excavations 1904–79*, London: Society of Antiquaries of London.

Pestell, T. 2004. *Landscapes of Monastic Foundation*, Woodbridge: Boydell.

Tester, A., Anderson, S., Riddler, I. and Carr, R. 2014. *Staunch Meadow, Brandon, Suffolk: A High Status Middle Saxon Settlement*, East Anglian Archaeology Report, no. 151, Bury St Edmunds: Suffolk County Council Archaeological Service.

Thomas, G. 2013. 'Life before the minster: the social dynamics of monastic foundation at Anglo-Saxon Lyminge, Kent', *Antiquaries Jnl*, **93**, 109–45.

Turner, S. 2006. *Making a Christian Landscape: The Countryside of Early Medieval Cornwall, Devon and Wessex*, Exeter: Exeter University Press.

Turner, S., Semple, S. and Turner, A. 2013. *Wearmouth and Jarrow: Northumbrian Monasteries in an Historic Landscape*, Hatfield: University of Hertfordshire.

# Part I

## Continental connections: re-examining the Frankish background to monasticism in Anglo-Saxon Kent

# Queen Balthild's 'monastic policy' and the origins of female religious houses in southern England

Barbara Yorke

*Abstract*
*This paper explores the proposition that the famous Frankish queen Balthild, who seems likely to have been an Anglo-Saxon by birth, both directly and indirectly stimulated the foundation of nunneries in southern England as part of an ecclesiastical policy that underpinned her period of regency for her son Chlothar III between 657 and 665. Kent is one of the kingdoms that seems to have been touched by her influence, and the paper ends with a consideration of the chronology of the foundation of the Kentish nunneries, including Lyminge.*

## Balthild and English nunneries: evidence from Frankish sources

Balthild can be said to be one of the Merovingian queens who has made a lasting impression. Not only does a *Vita* survive for her which seems to have been written soon after her death,[1] but there is the cache of some of her luxurious clothes preserved at the nunnery of Chelles which she founded and where she was living at the time of her death in 680.[2] Also preserved at Chelles was her elaborately plaited blonde hair though it appears that she had been dyeing it in her older age, presumably to keep its original appearance.[3] Balthild appears in a number of other Frankish sources, and even some Anglo-Saxon ones, but with some very varying judgements of her character and motives.[4] Collectively, the sources present us with one of the most apparently three-dimensional figures of the early Middle Ages.

The basic facts of Balthild's life can be briefly presented here.[5] Balthild is identified as being of Saxon birth,[6] and this – partly owing to the form of her name and her later interest in Anglo-Saxon England – is usually taken to mean she was an Anglo-Saxon. Some sources suggest she was of high birth,[7] but whether this was so or not she apparently had the misfortune in her adolescence to be sold as a slave to Francia where she was purchased 'for a low price' by Erchinoald, mayor of the palace of Neustria.[8] Erchinoald seems to have had his own connections with Anglo-Saxon England,[9] and some recent interpretations have favoured the idea of Balthild as a well-born hostage rather than a slave, but there is no explicit statement to this effect in the earliest sources.[10] Apparently, Balthild was very attractive, and Erchinoald brought her to the attention of the young Frankish king Clovis II who came of age in 648 and married her soon after. They had three sons in quick succession before Clovis died in 657. Balthild then ruled as regent for their eldest son, Chlothar III, while in 662 her second son Childeric II became ruler in Austrasia under the regency of Queen Chimnechild, his mother-in-law.[11] Balthild and her closest supporters struggled to keep on top of the different factions among the Frankish nobility, and in 665 or 666 Balthild was forced to step down and retire to the nunnery she had founded at Chelles. Here she lived in retirement until her death in 680 and apparently with little opportunity to exercise any of her previous influence. Her *Vita*, written soon after her death, very unusually, as Sarah Tatum has shown, rests her claims to sanctity on her active period as queen and queen-regent, and has virtually nothing to say on her period of monastic seclusion.[12] Its purpose was no doubt to protect her legacy in which the foundation and promotion of favoured religious houses had a key role.

Like other queen-regents of the early Middle Ages,[13] Balthild had the problem of relating to secular nobles when her female status debarred her from many of the activities that might bind together men at the royal court. Any whiff of scandal by too close an association with a secular male could fatally have undermined her position. Balthild's solution, which some subsequent queen-regents would also find expedient,[14] was to work closely with bishops and to ring-fence her reputation by founding and endowing religious houses. Ewig memorably described her strategy as *Klosterpolitik*, hence the 'monastic policy' of this paper's title.[15] It has been very fully studied and it would be inappropriate, and take too long, to go into details of all aspects of it here.[16] But it should be noted that it was a policy that operated on a number of different levels, and can be seen in many ways as a continuation, or even intensification, of policies followed previously by her husband and his father, Dagobert I, to ensure that the royal interest in religious foundations was not allowed to lapse, and that foundations and their founding families were obliged to recognize inherent royal rights and demands.[17]

Nunneries were part of Balthild's 'monastic policy'. Apparently, one of her first actions on becoming regent in 657 was to found a nunnery at the royal vill of Chelles where there was already a small church dedicated to St George founded by Queen Clothild, the wife of King Clovis, who had retired there when widowed.[18] Balthild also took an interest in two major nunneries, Jouarre and Faremoutiers, which had been founded earlier in the seventh century by prominent members of the nobility, with the help of royal patronage, and initially inspired by the example of Columbanus.[19] These foundations can be considered to have been on the royal watch-list, that is, royal interest in them would need to be constantly reasserted if they were not to become independent power-bases for their founding families. From Jouarre Balthild requested nuns for her foundation,[20] and, in particular, acquired Bertila, originally from Soissons, who became abbess of Chelles and whose *Vita* provides important additional insights into Balthild's policies.[21] The *Vita Bertilae* contains an unusual passage in which Abbess Theodechild is said 'to have hesitated for a long time' before complying with Balthild's request.[22] Different interpretations have been offered, but I would agree with Paul Fouracre that Theodechild's reluctance is likely to have been because the request could be seen as an issue about authority over the nunnery.[23] That it should be seen as an aggressive action against Jouarre's founding family, the Authari, to which Theodechild belonged, is supported by the apparent exile of Theodechild's brother Agilbert to Ireland and England in the period of Balthild's regency, during which time he served as bishop in Wessex and attended the synod of Whitby.[24] The hostility of the Authari to Balthild seems to have played a part in her downfall; after she had retired to Chelles, Agilbert returned and became bishop of Paris.[25]

Faremoutiers was the equivalent foundation of another leading noble group, the Faronids, who had family links with the Authari.[26] Its founding abbess Burgundofara/Fara had been blessed by Columbanus himself, and a series of miracle stories involving her and her nuns form one of the sections of the *Vita Columbani* written by Jonas between 639 and 643.[27] Faremoutiers also seems to have been within Balthild's orbit. Her *Vita* stresses her *larga munera* 'generous gifts' to the foundation.[28] Of course, in the early Middle Ages the bestowal of gifts was rarely a disinterested act.[29] Gifts implied countergifts and obligations; the greater the gifts the more a foundation was obligated towards its patron.[30] We do not know when Fara died; it was after Jonas wrote in 639x43, and her will had been drawn up somewhat earlier in 633/4.[31] She may well have been dead by the time of Balthild's regency. Although the Faronids had been a dominant power at the royal court in the first half of the seventh century, they are not heard of after that date (unlike the Authari) and may have died out, thus aiding Balthild's bringing of Faremoutiers more fully into her own monastic empire.[32]

One less well-known aspect of Balthild's monastic policy was its Anglo-Saxon dimension. Both the *Vita Balthildis* and the *Vita Bertilae* refer to the bestowal of patronage on Anglo-Saxons.[33] To have any reference at all to Anglo-Saxon England in Merovingian sources is very unusual. Stephen has several chapters referring to Bishop Wilfrid in Francia and his involvement with prominent individuals and significant political events, yet Wilfrid is not referred to in any Frankish source.[34] As Bertila was abbess of Chelles, a major beneficiary of the patronage of Balthild and the promoter of Balthild's cult after her death, we are probably safe in assuming that the interest in promoting monasticism among the Anglo-Saxons that appears in the *Vitae* of both women was a common enterprise. The *Vita Bertilae* says that Bertila was promoting policies pleasing to Balthild,[35] and we can accept the Anglo-Saxon dimension, referred to in the same chapter, as an example of this. Balthild's own Anglo-Saxon origins have usually been seen as lying behind her involvement, but it cannot be ruled out that Bertila may have had her own links to England and that she was somehow related to Bertha, the daughter of King Charibert of Paris, who married King Æthelbert of Kent, as Paul Fouracre has suggested.[36]

A passage in the *Vita Bertilae* refers to requests for help from 'the faithful kings of the Saxons' and that she sent books, 'chosen women and devout men' to them to build communities of men and women in their lands.[37] This passage is relatively well known because of its discussion by Patrick Sims-Williams who linked it with a reference to an abbess with the Frankish name Bertha (potentially a relative of Bertila?) in the foundation charter of Bath in the kingdom of the Hwicce in 675 or 676.[38] A second charter in the same cartulary, but which Susan Kelly has argued must refer to a different foundation in the Oxford area, perhaps at Eynsham, refers to a nun called Folcburg, a name attested only in Francia.[39] These areas may seem at first surprising places for Bertila's patronage, but trade routes along the Thames and then north into Hwiccian territory can be demonstrated from the sixth century onwards.[40] These areas were very much part of the southern English interface with Neustrian Francia.

A prior passage in the *Vita Bertilae* refers, presumably at a slightly earlier date, to men and women coming from England to learn of the monastic way of life from her.[41] This can possibly be linked with a passage from the *Vita Balthilde* which describes how Balthild purchased and freed slaves in Francia and installed some of them, especially fellow Anglo-Saxons, in her foundations.[42] The *Vita* goes on to say 'however many she was able to attract, these she entrusted to the holy monasteries'.[43] Does this refer back only to the freed Anglo-Saxon 'men and girls' or did the author wish to indicate that she encouraged other men and women to come directly from England to join her? It would seem that part of Balthild's monastic policy was to bind her chosen monasteries more closely to her authority by including in them fellow Anglo-Saxons, perhaps thereby loosening their ties with Frankish elite families. Can we see any reflex in Anglo-Saxon sources of such a policy?

## Balthild and Anglo-Saxon nunneries: the Anglo-Saxon evidence

Arguably, we can link Balthild's policies with an oft-quoted, but in many ways problematic, chapter in Bede's *Historia ecclesiastica*:

> [King Eorcenberht's] daughter Eorcengota, a child worthy of her parent, was a most virtuous maiden who served the Lord in a monastery founded in the land of the Franks by a noble abbess named Fara in a place called Brie. At that time, because there were not yet many monasteries founded in England, numbers of people from Britain used to enter the monasteries of the Franks or Gauls to practise the monastic life; they also sent their daughters to be taught in them and to be wedded to the heavenly bridegroom. They mostly went to the monasteries of Brie, Chelles and Andelys-sur-Seine; among these was Saethryth, stepdaughter of Anna, king of the East Angles … and Æthelburh his own daughter. Both of these though foreigners were, by the merit of their virtues, made abbesses of the monastery at Brie. The eldest daughter of the king was Seaxburh, wife of King Eorcenberht of Kent, whose daughter deserves special mention.[44]

One of the problems with the passage is that no clear indication is given of the date at which Eorcengota and her East Anglian aunts joined the Frankish nunneries.[45] The passage has clearly moved beyond the chronological positioning of the opening sentence of the chapter which recorded the death of King Eadbald of Kent in 640 and the succession of his son Eorcenbert (d. 664). Bede then described Eorcenbert's outlawing of pagan worship in Kent and imposition of Lenten fasting with heavy punishments for non-compliance which Bede saw as a significant stage in the Christianization of the kingdom. A sign of how divinely blessed Eorcenbert was for his actions was the manifestations of heavenly approval at the death of his daughter Eorcengota in the nunnery of Faremoutiers-en-Brie (with which the section cited above opens). There then follows the digression on Anglo-Saxons entering monasteries in Francia. The chapter concludes with the account of Eorcengota's death at Faremoutiers which has a number of unusual features that can be paralleled in Jonas's accounts of holy deaths of nuns at Faremoutiers in his *Vita Columbani*.[46] It seems likely that all the information on Eorcengota and the other connections with the Frankish nunneries came through the Anglo-Saxon links with Faremoutiers.

There is no indication from the *Historia ecclesiastica* or any other reliable source of when Eorcengota died.[47] The only possible indication from Bede of a date for the journeys of any of the Anglo-Saxon princesses to Francia comes from a later chapter in which the Deiran princess Hild is said to have planned to join her sister Hereswith as a nun at Chelles, but was persuaded by Bishop Aidan to follow her religious vows in Northumbria instead.[48] The chronology of Hild's life would place these events in 647,[49] but, as several commentators have pointed out, the accuracy of the dating is questionable as Chelles does not seem to have been functioning as a nunnery before Balthild's foundation in *c.* 657.[50] Régine Le Jan has argued that the East Anglian princesses went to Francia even earlier and were installed as abbesses of Faremoutiers by their kinsman, the Neustrian mayor Erchinoald during a crisis at the convent in 641.[51] However, it is by no means certain that Fara, foundress and first abbess of Faremoutiers, was dead or had relinquished control by 641. Nor is there any firm evidence that Erchinoald was related to the East Anglian princesses or that he had any demonstrable connection with Faremoutiers.

In fact, all of the interconnections of the Deiran and East Anglian princesses with the Frankish nunneries fit better into a context in the late 650s rather than in the late 640s. The late 650s was the period of Balthild's regency when she is known to have founded Chelles and developed control of Faremoutiers and Jouarre, aided by the recruitment of Anglo-Saxons. Dates in the late 650s also make sense in an English political context in the aftermath of the battle of the River Winwaed of 655. The East Angles fought on the losing side, which had been led by Penda of Mercia. The East Anglian king Æthelhere had been killed in the battle;[52] he was probably Hereswith's brother-in-law, though some later sources make him her husband.[53] The Bernician dynasty had already liquidated many of Hereswith's male relatives, and the ambivalent behaviour of the Deiran contingent at the battle of the Winwaed (albeit under the command of a Bernician prince) probably dealt a further blow to the status of the province. It is therefore understandable that Hereswith might have preferred to retire to Francia rather than to her home province (as would have been the regular Anglo-Saxon pattern),[54] and that her sister Hild would have sought to join her. In this scenario, the offer that made Hild change her mind, and return to her Northumbrian monastery of Hartlepool from East Anglia where she was waiting to travel to Chelles, would have been the invitation from King Oswiu of Northumbria in 657 to take charge of his baby daughter Ælfflaed, who was also a cousin of Hild's, and who had been vowed to a religious life should he be victorious in the battle.[55] Two years later both moved to Whitby which subsequently became a major mausoleum for the Northumbrian royal house as well as a centre of Christian learning.[56] Oswiu's entrustment of his daughter to Hild can be seen as a means of reconciling the women of the defeated royal house of Deira to which Hild and Hereswith belonged.[57] Behind it we may suspect the advice of Bishop Finan, Aidan's successor at Lindisfarne, who would have had experience from his background in Ireland of how positions in the church could be used to neutralize defeated royal lines.[58] Bede, or his informant, may simply have been mistaken about which decisive intervention by Northumbrian authorities recalled Hild from East Anglia.[59] Saethryth and Æthelthryth, who were Hereswith's nieces by marriage, may have sought to follow her example, but were diverted by Balthild to the nunnery of Faremoutiers as one of her 'gifts' to that foundation. However, East Anglia had a long tradition of its own of links with Francia.[60]

One might note here possible evidence that Balthild was in communication with East Anglia, during the period of her regency, in the form of the seal-matrix from a gold signet ring in the name of 'Baldehilde' that was found by a metal-detector in a field near Norwich in 1998. The design appears to be an imitation of a Byzantine betrothal ring for which Frankish parallels are known.[61] There can be no objections to the identification because of the spelling of the name. 'D' and 'T' can be seen as interchangeable in early medieval text and the form 'Baldehildis' on the ring is therefore cognate with 'Baltechildis', the version of the queen's name that was used in the *Vita Bertilae*.[62] As Tim Pestell has observed, 'there is only one Balthild known to history', and he has provided strong arguments for the depictions on the ring as appropriate for the period of Queen Balthild's regency when she was at the height of her powers[63] – and, one might add, known to have been in communication with England, inviting Anglo-Saxons to join her monastic foundation. He proposes that the portrait beneath the name 'Baltehildis' should be seen not as a depiction of Balthild herself, but of her young son who was the source of her power as regent. The interpretation of the reverse side of the seal-matrix is more problematical. Pestell has seen it as a crude representation of sexual congress, which not surprisingly has raised doubts about whether this could be appropriate for a queen-regent nurturing her reputation by patronage of religious houses.[64] But exactly what is being shown is far from certain because the marks in question are quite faint, and it may be no more than a crude rendering of a couple clasping hands in a Byzantine original,[65] which would be far more suitable for a ring associated with Queen Balthild.

The collective evidence has been seen as suggesting that Balthild had an unusual interest in East Anglia, even that she was from the province and a member of its royal house.[66] If she was connected with a prominent Anglo-Saxon royal house, perhaps one with which the Neustrian mayor Erchinoald who brought her to Francia had his own connections, that could help explain the circumstances of her marriage to Clovis.[67] A connection with the Deiran or Kentish royal houses would be another possibility. The second element of Balthild's name could possibly link her with Hild of Whitby,[68] but there is nothing in the known naming-patterns of the Kentish or East Anglian dynasties to connect her to them. The only known Anglo-Saxon ruler who does share a first name-element with Balthild is Baldred,[69] a local ruler in northern Somerset and Wiltshire in the last two decades of the seventh century, within the orbit of the West Saxon kings whose overlordship he recognized.[70] This area adjoins the territories discussed previously where Frankish nuns were active in the late seventh century, possibly linked with interventions by Abbess Bertila of Chelles. But it must be stressed that, however appealing the idea of a royal Anglo-Saxon descent for Balthild might be, it is not something that is definitely known. Only the second version of Balthild's life, written in the ninth century when Chelles was closely associated with women of the Carolingian royal house, claims that she was of royal descent.[71] Her status as a Merovingian queen would have been sufficient to ensure that connections with her would have been welcomed by Anglo-Saxon royal houses.

## The foundation of earliest royal nunneries in Kent

But what of Kent? Kent was the Anglo-Saxon province that seems to have had the closest links with the Merovingian royal house, including the marriage in the late sixth century of Æthelbert of Kent to the Frankish princess Bertha.[72] We might therefore expect the kingdom to have been targeted by Balthild when she sought to extend her influence in England. Do its early royal nunneries fit with the suggested pattern of encouragement by Balthild and Bertila in the late 650s and 660s, leading to the first nunnery foundations in southern England in the 670s or a little before (Table 1)? Unfortunately, none of the Kentish nunneries features in Bede's *Historia ecclesiastica* or any other contemporary narrative source. Charters suggest that a number of royal Kentish nunneries were in existence by the end of the seventh century, but do not show us their foundation. The main guide to when foundation might have occurred is the series of related texts collectively known as the *Mildrith Legend* which was in circulation in the later Anglo-Saxon and early Norman periods.[73]

**Table 1** Early nunnery foundations in southern England.

| Dated | Kent (Undated) |
|---|---|
| • Ely 673 | 660s? 670s? |
| • Barking 675 | • Folkestone |
| • Bath 675/6 | • Milton/Minster-in-Sheppey |
| • Abingdon 670s | 680s |
| • Bradfield 670s | • Minster-in-Thanet |
| • Gloucester 679 | • Lyminge |
| • ?Eynsham 680 | |

**Table 2** The Kentish royal house and its nunneries.

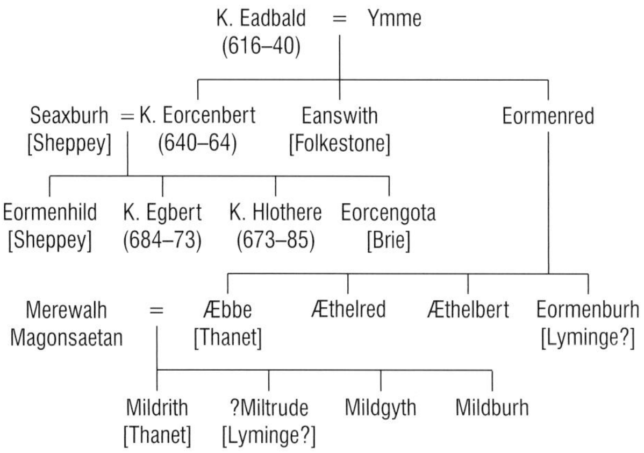


David Rollason and Stephanie Hollis have argued that the core text with the sensational events surrounding the foundation of Minster-in-Thanet may be of eighth- or ninth-century date, and that a number of accretions were made as the text was adapted for different uses in the late tenth and eleventh centuries.[74] Competition between male religious communities in Canterbury which acquired the former royal nunneries and the bodies of their saints in the eleventh and twelfth centuries seems to have led to distortion of their earlier histories.[75] Nineteenth-century clerics such as Canon Jenkins at Lyminge muddied the waters further in their desire to push back origins as far as possible.[76] Nevertheless, if one picks one's way carefully through potential minefields one can see enough to suggest that the Kentish nunneries fit in with a pattern of foundation in the late seventh century, and some evidence for links with Chelles or Faremoutiers can also be recovered.

According to some of the later medieval accretions to the *Mildrith Legend* core text, Lyminge was the earliest nunnery in Kent founded by Eadbald for his sister Æthelburh when she fled back to Kent after the death of her husband Edwin of Northumbria in 633 (as Bede records, but without saying where she settled in Kent).[77] As a royal estate, Lyminge could well have been provided as a place of retirement for Æthelburh. As she was undoubtedly a Christian, it might be an expectation that she would found a church there, and one could also suggest that she lived the life of a pious widow at Lyminge, as Clothild did at Chelles after the death of her husband Clovis.[78] All these things could constitute a reasonable hypothesis, but the claim that she founded a nunnery there does not carry the same degree of plausibility. As Susan Kelly has argued in her study of the early history of Lyminge nunnery, it is very unlikely that this later tradition can be true as it would put the foundation of a nunnery at Lyminge decades before any other nunneries are known to have existed in southern England (see Table 1).[79] As these traditions stress that Æthelburh was buried at Lyminge,[80] what may have lain behind the claim could have been a tomb at Lyminge bearing the name 'Æthelburh'. If so, this could well have been Edwin's widow, but one should also note the existence of a slightly later Queen Æthelburh who was one of the wives of King Wihtred of Kent (690–725) and jointly named with him in a grant to Lyminge.[81] If a Queen Æthelburh was buried at Lyminge it could well have been her.

The next possible candidate in the *Mildrith Legend* texts for earliest royal nunnery in Kent is more promising for it takes us into the time of Eorcenbert whose reign was considered by Bede to be the point that the Kentish royal house fully committed itself to Christianity. The founding of nunneries led by women of the royal house can be seen as a sign of that commitment and of the creation of royal centres of Christian cult.[82] The house in question is Folkestone founded according to some versions of the *Mildrith Legend* by Eorcenbert's sister, Eanswith.[83] A lead reliquary believed to have contained Eanswith's remains was discovered in the north wall of the parish church of Folkestone in 1885.[84] Unfortunately, there seem to be no reliable accounts of Eanswith's life or death, or when Folkestone might have been founded.[85] It was not necessarily before her brother Eorcenbert's death in 664. Michael Metcalf has drawn attention to the intriguing possibility of evidence for a link between Folkestone and the Faremoutiers area.[86] Three out of five Merovingian gold coins found in England from the mint of *Loco Sancto*, identified as Lieusaint-en-Brie, are recorded as being from Folkestone (unfortunately early stray finds). In Bede's account of the death of Eanswith's niece Eorcengota at Faremoutiers-en-Brie, an angel is made to refer to her as 'that gold coin (*nomisma*) which had come from Kent'.[87] It would seem that literal gold coins may have travelled between Brie and Kent as well.

Other early Kentish nunneries also show connections with the family of Eorcenbert and his East Anglian wife Seaxburh, the sister of the Faremoutiers abbesses and mother of Eorcengota (Table 2). Minster-in-Sheppey (also known as Milton) according to some of the later *Mildrith Legend* texts was founded by Seaxburh and her daughter Eormenhild. Seaxburh moved back to East Anglia to take over her sister Æthelthryth's foundation at Ely on her death in 679, and subsequently orchestrated the promotion of her sister as a saint.[88] Eormenhild too subsequently moved to Ely to become its abbess.[89] The texts say that Seaxburh founded Minster-in-Sheppey when she was acting as regent for one of her sons (Ecgbert and Hlothere) after their father's death in 664, but do not agree on which son's reign (though that of the eldest Ecgbert (664–73) might seem the more likely).[90] If that were to be the case, there would be a striking parallel with Balthild's career just a few years earlier and it would be tempting to see Seaxburh modelling herself on Balthild – but the tradition unfortunately has no support in texts other than those connected with the *Mildrith Legend*. Recent excavations at Minster-in-Sheppey have provided some evidence for late-seventh- and eighth-century use of the site, including finds of Ipswich ware that are not otherwise common in

Kent, but could fit potentially with the East Anglian connections of its founders.[91]

The foundation of Minster-in-Thanet is the centrepoint of the *Mildrith Legend* texts.[92] According to these the nunnery was founded in compensation for the murder in the reign of Eorcenbert's and Seaxburh's son Ecgbert (664–73) of two cousins in the royal hall at Eastry (Table 2). In the *Legend*, Ecgbert's chief minister Thunor is made responsible for their deaths, but we need not doubt that this was a removal of rivals for the throne. In compensation for the murder, their sister Æbbe (known as Domne Eafe in the texts of the *Mildrith Legend*), who had been married into the royal house of the Magonsaetan of Herefordshire, was granted a large estate on Thanet where the souls of all involved in the violent story could be prayed for. There are parallels with the foundation of Whitby and Gilling in Yorkshire as religious houses, as places of reconciliation between rival royal lines.[93] Æbbe was succeeded by her daughter Mildrith who had been sent previously for a spell in the nunnery of Chelles.[94] The abbess is said to have been one Wilcoma perhaps successor to Bertila. Both Æbbe and Mildrith are recipients of surviving charters for Minster-in-Thanet which has more surviving evidence than any of the other early nunneries because it came into the possession of St Augustine's abbey, Canterbury.[95]

Can Lyminge be fitted into this pattern of nunnery foundation in Kent in the reigns of Eorcenbert and his sons? As Susan Kelly remarked in her study of Lyminge, 'there is no clinching evidence that Lyminge had previously been a double monastery, apart from much later tradition'.[96] Charters granted by King Wihtred, grandson of Eorcenbert (690–725), do not specify that they are being made to a nunnery, and another of 732 was made to a priest-abbot, perhaps evidence by this stage of a separation of male and female elements – if the latter had ever existed.[97] However, by the mid-eighth century, and into the ninth century, Lyminge was apparently being administered jointly as a nunnery by the abbesses of Minster-in-Thanet, and one of these, Eadburh, seems to have been buried at Lyminge and became the community's main saint.[98]

That there were four major royal nunneries by the end of the seventh century in Kent is suggested by a 699 grant of privileges by King Wihtred to the churches and monasteries of Kent made in the presence of the abbesses Eormenhild, Eormenburh, Æbbe and Nerienda.[99] As we have seen, Eormenhild was abbess of Minster-in-Sheppey and Æbbe was abbess of Minster-in-Thanet, leaving Folkestone and potentially Lyminge for Nerienda and Eormenburh. As Eormenburh was according to the *Mildrith Legend* material a sister of Æbbe,[100] and Lyminge and Minster-in-Thanet were later joined together, it might reasonably be suggested that she was abbess of Lyminge, and, rather more speculatively, that Lyminge too had been founded in compensation for their murdered brothers – perhaps one minster for each brother. It could be further suggested that control of both Lyminge and Minster-in-Thanet was then inherited in the eighth century by one person, perhaps Mildrith of Thanet, daughter of Æbbe and niece of Eormenburh. In this connection, one can note an eleventh-century report of the excavation of a tomb of one 'Militrudis' at Lyminge.[101] The unusual first name-element might suggest that she was one of several daughters said to have been born to Æbbe and her Magonsaetan husband Merewalh, and thus a sister of Mildrith, or some other close relative (see Table 2).[102]

Table 1 shows the earliest nunneries to which a foundation date can be put belong to the 670s. There is the potential that some for which no actual date exists, such as Folkestone, could be a little earlier – perhaps in the late 660s. Archbishop Theodore in his *Penitential* alludes to double houses as an established feature in England – of which he does not fully approve.[103] Does this mean that there were already such houses in southern England by the time of his arrival in England in 669? There were certainly some in Northumbria by that date which was part of his province, but in the south the major period of royal foundation seems to have been after his appointment. Nevertheless, one might expect that the period following the great plague outbreak of 664, which seems to have severely reduced the number of bishops and other clergy in England,[104] could have been a fruitful time for kings to have had a relatively free hand in founding their own minsters. For this is surely how the early nunneries should be seen, that is, not just as religious communities but as minsters especially serving royal interests.[105] It is conceivable that at this early stage kings hoped to control the churches of their kingdom, and the foundation of nunneries at key royal estate centres as in Kent may be a sign of that intention. At the synod of Bapchild in the early eighth century King Wihtred of Kent granted privileges to the eight major churches of Kent; at least four out of the eight were nunneries (a strikingly high percentage seeing as it also included the two bishoprics).[106]

## Conclusion

There are several potential narratives concerning Frankish influence on monastic foundation in late-seventh-century southern England, and one should expect interaction of several different channels of influence.[107] One could make more, for instance, of the possible connections of the Kentish royal house with Erchinoald, the mayor of Neustria, that have been inferred from shared naming-patterns.[108] But it is hoped that a convincing case has been made here for a substantial stimulus coming from Balthild's regency between 657 and 665/6 when she seems to have made a conscious decision to introduce Anglo-Saxons to the monastic life. At Chelles and Faremoutiers she provided an opportunity for Anglo-Saxon women, including some of royal birth, to experience the religious life at first hand and thus stimulated the foundation of similar communities in England in the next couple of decades. In addition, Balthild in her monastic policies also showed the potential to royal patrons of monastic patronage for underpinning royal power as well as a model for widowed queens on how status in widowhood and regency might be supported. Recognition of the importance of Balthild's interventions enhances appreciation of her monastic policy and what made it distinctive. Balthild was, as her first *Vita* suggests, an unusually interventionist and innovative ruler during the period of her regency.[109] How she sought to use her Anglo-Saxon background to underpin her power, and in turn became a major influence in her native land, has perhaps not been appreciated fully in previous assessments of her eventful life. Balthild's interventions and example help to explain why religious communities controlled by royal women became such a distinctive feature of the period of Christian consolidation in Kent and in other areas of southern England.

## Acknowledgements

I am very grateful to Gabor Thomas and Alexandra Knox for the invitation to contribute to the conference and the volume, and for all they have done to make both happen. Special thanks are due to Paul Fouracre for reading and commenting on the text, and to Leslie Webster for providing advice on the Balthild ring.

## Notes

1 *Vita Sanctae Balthildis*, Krusch 1888a, 475–508. Version 'A' is translated with detailed commentary in Fouracre and Gerberding 1996, 97–132, Version 'A' was revised in the late eighth or early ninth century, but without any substantial additions, and this version 'B' has been translated in McNamara and Halborg 1992, 264–78. Krusch's edition prints the revised account 'B' alongside the 'A' version in parallel columns.

2 Laporte 1988; 2013.

3 Laporte 1988, 56–7.

4 Fouracre and Gerberding 1996, 97–114. The main Anglo-Saxon source to refer to her is Stephanus, *Vita Wilfridi* ch. 6, Colgrave 1927, 14–15, from which a reference was probably taken by Bede in his *Historia ecclesiastica* v.19, Colgrave and Mynors 1969, 520–1. The reason for Stephanus's condemnation of her as a Jezebel, which may have discouraged later authors from exploring her links with Anglo-Saxon England, is discussed further below (n. 45).

5 Fuller discussions can be found in Nelson 1978; Wood 1994, 197–201; Fouracre and Gerberding 1996, 97–118; Tatum 2009 (the latter with a useful review of other literature on Balthild on p. 4).

6 'Ex genere Saxonum': *Vita Sanctae Balthildis* ch. 2, Krusch 1888a, 483; 'de genere Saxonorum': *Liber Historiae Francorum* ch. 43, Krusch 1888b, 315.

7 The 'A' version of her life stresses her low birth, though this could be a hagiographical topos. In version 'B' she has become 'ex regali progeniae': *Vita Sanctae Balthildis*, Krusch 1988a, 485. See further Nelson 1978, 46; Fouracre and Gerberding 1996, 98, 102.

8 'Vili pretio venundata': *Vita Sanctae Balthildis* ch. 2, Krusch 1888a, 483.

9 This has been suggested by the occurrence of his first name-element Erchin/Eorcen in the Kentish royal house and from Bishop Eorcenwald of London bearing the same name as the Neustrian mayor (d. *c.* 659). However, it has not proved possible to demonstrate exactly what the connection was. Werner 1985, 42 seems to have been the first to suggest that Ymme/Emma who married King Eadbald of Kent (616–40) and was the mother of King Eorcenbert (640–64) was Erchinoald's daughter. It is, in fact, impossible chronologically for Emma to have been Erchinoald's daughter though she could conceivably have been his sister.

10 Laporte 2013, 127. Although slavery could be explained as a topos or metaphor in a hagiographical text, in the early Middle Ages it could be the fate of even the well-born as a result of warfare or slave-raiding; see further Pelteret 1995.

11 Wood 1994, 222–3.

12 Tatum 2009. The author was probably one of the brothers at Chelles who claims experience of the events he describes; Fouracre and Gerberding 1996, 114–18.

13 Stafford 1983, 143–74.

14 MacLean 2010.

15 Ewig 1973.

16 For useful summaries, see Nelson 1978, 60–72; Wood 1994, 197–202; Tatum 2009.

17 Fouracre 1995; Rosenwein 1999, 59–96.

18 *Vita Sanctae Balthildis* chs. 7–8, Krusch 1888a, 489–90; Laporte 2013, 128–30.

19 Le Jan 2001; Fox 2014, 50–81.

20 *Vita Sanctae Balthildis* ch. 8, Krusch 1888a, 489–90.

21 *Vita Bertilae*, Levison 1913, 95–109; translated in McNamara and Halborg 1992, 279–88.

22 'percunctata diu': *Vita Bertilae* ch. 4, Levison 1913, 104.

23 Fouracre 2013, 192–3; for a different reading, see Hammer 2011–12, 70–1.

24 Bede, *Historia ecclesiastica* iii.7 and 25, Colgrave and Mynors 1969, 234–6, 298–300; Stephanus, *Vita Wilfridi* chs. 9–10, Colgrave 1927, 18–23; Hammer 2011–12, 61–77; Fouracre 2013, 191–4.

25 Fouracre 2013, 192–3.

26 Fox 2014, 63–81.

27 Jonas, *Vita Columbani* II.11–22, Krusch 1902, 130–43; there have been suggestions that the section including the miracles of Faremoutiers was a later addition to the text, but against this see Stancliffe 2001, 189–201. Jonas seems actually to have been at Faremoutiers at the time of the death of the nun Gibitrude, perhaps in 633 or 634 (II.12).

28 *Vita Sanctae Balthildis* ch. 8, Krusch 1888a, 489–90; Fouracre and Gerberding 1996, 125.

29 Davies and Fouracre 2010.

30 Fouracre 1995; Rosenwein 1999, 74–96.

31 Guérout 1965; Fox 2014, 196–200.

32 Fox 2014, 63–81, 206–17.

33 See discussion following for references.

34 Fouracre 2013; Wood 2013.

35 *Vita Bertilae* ch. 5, Levison 1913, 105; McNamara and Halborg 1992, 285. Bertila is said to have strived 'so that she was pleasing to God and to the holy queen in all things'. It would seem a likely hypothesis that it was Bertila who commissioned the *Vita Sanctae Balthildis* to protect not only Balthild's reputation, but the monasteries she had founded and patronized, and Chelles above all.

36 Fouracre 2013, 192–3.

37 *Vita Bertilae* ch. 6, Levison 1913, 106–7; McNamara and Halborg 1992, 285.

38 Sims-Williams 1975; 1990, 111–13; Kelly 2007, 53–62.

39 Kelly 2007, 66–8.

40 Metcalf 1994, 380–1; Harrington and Welch 2014, 183–201.

41 'Even more men and women hastened to her, not only from neighbouring provinces but even from across the seas': *Vita Bertilae* ch. 5, Levison 1913, 105; McNamara and Halborg 1992, 285.

42 *Vita Sanctae Balthildis* ch. 9, Krusch 1888a, 493–4.

43 Fouracre and Gerberding 1996, 126: 'quantas enim adtrahere poutit, eas per sancta coenobia commendavit'.

44 Bede, *Historia ecclesiastica* iii.8, Colgrave and Mynors 1969, 236–9.

45 Bede does not refer to Balthild in this context and has only the one critical reference to her (Bede, *Historia ecclesiastica* v.19, Colgrave and Mynors 1969, 520–1) which was taken from Stephen's *Vita Wilfridi* ch. 7 (Colgrave 1927, 14–15) where she is described as a second Jezebel. Wilfrid was involved on more than one occasion with men in opposition to Balthild and her supporters, and that may be sufficient to explain Stephen's critical assessment of her, followed by Bede, and so the absence of any reference to her in III.8. The Bernician establishment generally, unlike their Deiran rivals and the southern Anglo-Saxon kings, do not seem to have been part of the Neustrian royal court nexus.

46 Distinctive features of Eorcengota's death are given below with references to the parallels in relevant chapters in the second part of Jonas's *Vita Columbani* (Krusch 1902, 130–43) provided in brackets. Date and hour of death revealed (chs. 11, 12, 18, 20); angelic visitors to cell can be seen only by dying nun (chs. 11, 17, 18); cell fills with light at time of death (chs. 11, 13, 15, 20); angelic choirs heard at the time of death (chs. 11, 13, 14, 17, 20); smell of balsam (chs. 12, 16, 21). The account of Eorcengota's death preserved by Bede thus has almost the full set of blessed death experiences shared among several different nuns in Jonas's account of deaths at Faremoutiers.

47 Bede does not say that Eorcengota was at Brie before Fara died as suggested by Le Jan 2001, 255, and reiterated in Fox 2014, 211; he only says that she entered the monastery that had been founded by Fara: 'quod in regione Francorum constructum est ab abbatissa nobilissima uocabulo Fara in loco qui dicitur In Brige'; Bede, *Historia ecclesiastica* iii.8, Colgrave and Mynors 1969, 236–7.

48 Bede, *Historia ecclesiastica* iv.23, Colgrave and Mynors 1969, 406–7.

49 Plummer 1896, II, 244; Hunter Blair 1985, 4–8. In IV.23 (see previous note) Bede says Hild died in 680 aged sixty-six and spent thirty-three years in secular habit and thirty-three as a religious which gives 647 for her entry into religion (though as thirty-three was the age of Christ at his death one does wonder if there has been some tidying up of dates to achieve such a significant figure).

50 Wallace-Hadrill 1988, 163, 232; McClure and Collins 1994, 389, 407; Fouracre forthcoming.

51 Le Jan 2001, 254–5; the dating is influenced by her mistaken belief (see above, n. 47) that Eorcengota was already at Faremoutiers before the death of Fara. Discussion here corrects Yorke 2003, 24–5 which supported the 640s dates.

52 Bede, *Historia ecclesiastica* iii.24, Colgrave and Mynors 1969, 290–1.

53 Stenton 1970.

54 Yorke 2003, 28–36, 145–59.

55 Bede, *Historia ecclesiastica* iii.24, Colgrave and Mynors 1969, 290–3. In this chapter Bede refers to Oswiu endowing twelve small monasteries after the battle, but it would appear from IV.23, Colgrave and Mynors 1969, 406–9, that Hartlepool was not one of these, and that it had been founded and given to Hild before Bishop Aidan's death in 651.

56 Fell 1981; Hunter Blair 1985.

57 Yorke 2003, 162–5. Oswiu's wife and Æthelflaed's mother was Eanflaed, the daughter of the former Deiran king Edwin (d. 633) and Æthelburh, the daughter of King Æthelbert of Kent (d. 616 or 618) (on whom see further below).

58 Ó Corráin 1971. Finan himself seems to have been of royal descent, and a sister or other female relative was the mother of Oswiu's son Aldfrith: Ireland 1991.

59 However, it was undoubtedly the case that Bede for his own reasons wished to make the most of Bishop Aidan's influence on the Northumbrian church and its early leaders; see Yorke forthcoming.

60 Fouracre and Geberding 1996, 102–6.

61 Webster 2000; I am very grateful to Leslie Webster for discussing the problems in interpretation of the ring with me.

62 Fouracre forthcoming; I am most grateful to Paul Fouracre for making this text available to me in advance of publication.

63 Pestell 2013.

64 Fouracre forthcoming.

65 Leslie Webster, pers. comm. The couple embrace beneath a cross as in Byzantine exemplars.

66 Pestell 2013, 148.

67 Fouracre and Gerberding 1996, 102–4.

68 Fell 1981, 78, for possible dithematic names with 'hild' in the Durham *Liber Vitae*, one of which might be that of the Whitby abbess.

69 As discussed above, the elements 'Balt' and 'Bald' can be considered interchangeable in this period.

70 Baldred made grants to Aldhelm of Malmesbury in 688 (S 1170) and to Glastonbury in 681 and, probably, 693 (S 236 and 1165). He was also a witness to Osric's foundation charter for Bath (Kelly 2007, 61). See further discussion and texts in Kelly 2005, 147–50, and Kelly 2012, 219–26, 234–9.

71 In version 'B' she has become 'ex regali progeniae': *Vita Sanctae Balthildis*, Krusch 1988a, 485. See further Nelson 1978, 46; Fouracre and Gerberding 1996, 98, 102; Laporte 2013, 127–30.

72 Wood 1983; Brooks 1989; Brookes and Harrington 2010, 45–9, 60–8.

73 The variant texts are discussed and calendared in Rollason 1982, 15–31, 73–87, and with printed texts of two versions at 89–143.

74 Rollason 1982, especially 33–68; Hollis 1998.

75 Rollason 1982, 58–68; Kelly 2006, 101–3.

76 Publications on his excavations at Lyminge include Jenkins 1874 and 1889, but more generally he influenced how the remains at Lyminge were interpreted and displayed. As Witney 1984, 4, has remarked his assumption, that wherever the name Eadburga (an eighth-century abbess) occurred in connection with Lyminge that of Æthelburh was intended, was 'a reversal of the truth'.

77 Bede, *Historia ecclesiastica* ii.20, Colgrave and Mynors 1969, 204–5.

78 Laporte 2013, 128–9.

79 Kelly 2006, 101–4; see also Brooks and Kelly 2013, 28–35.

80 The fullest account is that of Goscelin written in the late eleventh century which says that she died on 13 December and was buried in a northern porticus of the minster church: Kelly 2006, 101–2. There is no evidence though that she was ever celebrated as a saint, which one might have expected to be the case if she had really been the foundress of Lyminge. A date of 647 for her death appears in later medieval chronicles, but is unlikely to be reliable: Witney 1984, 3.

81 Yorke 2003, 23; S 19; Brooks and Kelly 2013, 286–93.

82 Yorke 2003, 17–46.

83 Rollason 1982, 80–6.

84 Robertson 1886; Crook 2011, 68–70. The original minster church may have been lost to the sea: Richardson 2013, 72–3.

85 Dates of 640 and 673 for the foundation of Folkestone, claims that the nunnery was founded for her by her father Eadbald (d. 640), and that Eanswith was aged twenty-six at the time of her death only surface in late accounts and are unlikely to have any validity (although 673 would be a very acceptable date): Witney 1984, 3; Richardson 2013; Blanton 2014.

86 Metcalf 2003, 37–8.

87 Bede, *Historia ecclesiastica* iii.8, Colgrave and Mynors 1969, 236–7.

88 Bede, *Historia ecclesiastica* iv.19, Colgrave and Mynors 1969, 392–5; Rollason 1982, 30–1, 82, 85, 87; Ridyard 1988, 50–8, 176–81.

89 Rollason 1982, 84, 87.

90 Rollason 1982, 30–1; Ridyard 1988, 89–92.

91 Blinkhorn 1999, 9–10.

92 Rollason 1982; Hollis 1998.

93 Yorke 2003, 31–5, 109–10, 162–5.

94 Rollason 1982, 98, 120.

95 Kelly 1995, xxv–xxxi, 139–82.

96 Kelly 2006, 110.

97 Kelly 2006, 105–12; Brooks and Kelly 2013, 28–35, 286–97, 326–38.

98 Rollason 1982, 21–4, 142–3; Crick 1988; Kelly 1995, xxv–xxxi, 175–82; Kelly 2006, 102–3, 112.

99 S 20; Brooks and Kelly 2013, no. 7, 297–303.

100 In some texts Æbbe and Eormenburh are presented as the same person, but in others they are clearly distinguished and made sisters: Rollason 1982, 39–40, 93, 114.

101 Kelly 2006, 102–3.
102 Rollason 1982, 114–15.
103 McNeill and Gamer 1979, VI, 8, 204.
104 Maddicott 1997.
105 Yorke 2003.
106 S 22; Brooks and Kelly 2013, no. 8, 303–13. An apparent fifth abbess has the name Wilnoth which is masculine and so the identification as an abbess is probably an error made in copying. Ward 1935 made the case for a fifth Kentish nunnery at Hoo, but there seems little evidence that this was ever a nunnery: Kelly 2009, 197–8.
107 Wood, this volume.
108 Fouracre and Gerberding 1996, 102–5.
109 Tatum 2009.

## Bibliography


Blanton, V. 2014. 'The lost and (not) found sources for female saints' legends in John of Tynemouth's *Sanctilogium*', in R. DeMaria, H. Change and S. Zacher (eds.), *A Companion to British Literature*, Vol. 1. *Medieval Literature 700–1450*, 65–80, Oxford: John Wiley and Sons.

Blinkhorn, P. 1999. 'Of cabbages and kings: production, trade and consumption in middle-Saxon England', in M. Anderton (ed.), *Anglo-Saxon Trading Centres. Beyond the Emporia*, 4–23, Glasgow: Cruithne Press.

Brookes, S. and Harrington, S. 2010. *The Kingdom and People of Kent AD 400–1066. Their History and Archaeology*, Stroud: The History Press.

Brooks, N. 1989. 'The creation and early structure of the kingdom of Kent', in S. Bassett (ed.), *The Origins of Anglo-Saxon Kingdoms*, 55–74, Studies in the Early History of Britain, Leicester: Leicester University Press.

Brooks, N. and Kelly, S. (eds.) 2013. *Charters of Christ Church, Canterbury*, Part I, Anglo-Saxon Charters, 17, London: British Academy, Oxford University Press.

Colgrave, B. (ed. and trans.) 1927. *The Life of Bishop Wilfrid by Eddius Stephanus*, Cambridge: Cambridge University Press.

Colgrave, B. and Mynors, R. A. B. (ed. and trans.) 1969. *Bede's Ecclesiastical History of the English People*, Oxford: Clarendon Press.

Crick, J. 1988. 'Church, land and nobility in early ninth-century Kent', *Bull. of the Inst. of Hist. Research*, **61**, 251–69.

Crook, J. 2011. *English Medieval Shrines*, Woodbridge: Boydell.

Davies, W. and Fouracre, P. (eds.) 2010. *The Languages of Gift in the Early Middle Ages*, Cambridge: Cambridge University Press.

Ewig, E. 1973. 'Das Privileg des Biscofs Berthefrid von Amiens für Corbie von 664 und die Klosterpolitik der Königin Balthild', *Francia*, **1**, 63–114.

Fell, C. 1981. 'Hild, abbess of Steonaeshalch', in H. Bekker Nielsen, P. Foote, J. H. Jørgensen and T. Nyberg (eds.), *Hagiography and Medieval Literature: A Symposium*, 76–99, Odense: Odense University Press.

Fouracre, P. 1995. 'Practical aspects of the development of Frankish immunities', in W. Davies and P. Fouracre (eds.), *Property and Power in the Early Middle Ages*, 53–81, Cambridge: Cambridge University Press.

Fouracre, P. 2013. 'Wilfrid on the continent', in N. J. Higham (ed.), *Wilfrid. Abbot, Bishop, Saint*, 186–99, Donnington: Shaun Tyas.

Fouracre, P. forthcoming. 'Balthild and "her" seal ring: text and artefact', in *Festscrift for Shoichi Sato*.

Fouracre, P. and Gerberding, R. A. 1996. *Late Merovingian France. History and Hagiography 640–720*, Manchester: Manchester University Press.

Fox, Y. 2014. *Power and Religion in Merovingian Gaul. Columbanian Monasticism and the Frankish Elites*, Cambridge: Cambridge University Press.

Guérout, J. 1965. 'Le testament de Sainte Fare: matériaux pour l'étude et l'edition critique de ce document', *Revue d'Histoire Écclésiastique*, **60(3–4)**, 761–821.

Hammer, C. I. 2011–12. '"Holy Entrepreneur": Agilbert, a Merovingian bishop between Ireland, England and Francia', *Peritia*, **22–3**, 53–82.

Harrington, S. and Welch, M. 2014. *The Early Anglo-Saxon Kingdoms of Southern Britain AD 450–650*, Oxford: Oxbow Books.

Hollis, S. 1998. 'The Minster-in-Thanet foundation story', *Anglo-Saxon England*, **27**, 41–74.

Hunter Blair, P. 1985. 'Whitby as a centre of learning in the seventh century', in M. Lapidge and H. Gneuss (eds.), *Learning and Literature in Anglo-Saxon England*, 3–32, Cambridge: Cambridge University Press.

Ireland, C. 1991. 'Aldfrith of Northumbria and the Irish genealogies', *Celtica*, **22**, 64–78.

Jenkins, R. C. 1874. 'The basilica of Lyminge: Roman, Saxon and medieval', *Arch. Cantiana*, **9**, 205–23.

Jenkins, R. C. 1889. 'Observations on the remains of the basilica of Lyminge', *Arch. Cantiana*, **18**, 46–54.

Kelly, S. (ed.) 1995. *Charters of St Augustine's Abbey, Canterbury and Minster-in-Thanet*, Anglo-Saxon Charters, 4, London: British Academy, Oxford University Press.

Kelly, S. (ed.) 2005. *Charters of Malmesbury Abbey*, Anglo-Saxon Charters, 11, London: British Academy, Oxford University Press.

Kelly, S. 2006. 'Lyminge minster and its early charters', in S. Keynes and A. P. Smyth (eds.), *Anglo-Saxons. Studies Presented to Cyril Roy Hart*, 98–113, Dublin: Four Courts Press.

Kelly, S. (ed.) 2007. *Charters of Bath and Wells*, Anglo-Saxon Charters, 13, London: British Academy, Oxford University Press.

Kelly, S. (ed.) 2009. *Charters of Peterborough Abbey*, Anglo-Saxon Charters, 14, London: British Academy, Oxford University Press.

Kelly, S. (ed.) 2012. *Charters of Glastonbury Abbey*, Anglo-Saxon Charters, 15, London: British Academy, Oxford University Press.

Krusch, B. (ed.) 1888a. *Vitae Sanctae Balthildis*, Hanover: MGH SS rer. Merov. II, 475–508.

Krusch, B. (ed.) 1888b. *Liber Historiae Francorum*, Hanover: MGH SS rer. Merov. II, 215–328.

Krusch, B. (ed.) 1902. *Jonas, Vita Columbani Abbatis Discipulorumque euis*, Hanover: MGH SS rer. Merov. IV, 65–152.

Laporte, J.-P. 1988. *Le Tresor des Saints de Chelles*, Chelles: Société Archéologique et Historique de Chelles.

Laporte, J.-P. 2013. 'Grab und Reliquien der Königin Balthilde in Chelles-sur-Marne', in E. Wamers and P. Périn (eds.), *Königinnen der Merowinger. Adelsgraber aus den Kirchen von Köln, Saint-Denis, Chelles und Frankfurt am Main*, 126–44, Regensburg: Schnell und Steiner.

Le Jan, R. 2001. 'Convents, violence, and competition for power in seventh-century Francia', in M. De Jong, F. Theuws and C. Van Rhijn (eds.), *Topographies of Power in the Early Middle Ages*, 243–70, The Transformation of the Roman World, 6, Leiden: Brill.

Levison, W. (ed.) 1913. *Vita Bertilae Abbatisae Calensis*, Hanover: MGH SS rer. Merov. VI, 95–109.

McClure, J. and Collins, R. (trans.) 1994. *Bede; The Ecclesiastical History of the English People, The Greater Chronicle, Bede's Letter to Egbert*, Oxford: Oxford University Press.

MacLean, S. 2010. 'Monastic reform and royal ideology in the late tenth century; Ælfthryth and Edgar in continental perspective', in D. Rollason, C. Leyser and H. Williams (eds.), *England and the Continent in the Tenth Century. Studies in Honour of Wilhelm Levison (1876–1947)*, 255–74, Turnhout: Brepols.

McNamara, J. A. and Halborg, J. E., with Whatley, E. G. (ed. and trans.) 1992. *Sainted Women of the Dark Ages*, Durham, NC: Duke University Press.

McNeill, J. T. and Gamer, H. M. (trans.) 1979. *Medieval Handbooks of Penance. A Translation of the Principal* Libri Poenitentiales *and Selections from Related Documents*, New York: Octagon Books.

Maddicott, J. R. 1997. 'Plague in England in the seventh century', *Past and Present*, **156**, 7–54.

Metcalf, M. 1994. *Thrymsas and Sceattas in the Ashmolean Museum*, Vol. 3. *Secondary Sceattas*, Oxford: Royal Numismatic Society, Ashmolean Museum.

Metcalf, M. 2003. 'Variations in composition of the currency at different places in England', in T. Pestell and K. Ulmschneider (eds.), *Markets in Early Medieval Europe. Trading and 'Productive' Sites, 650–850*, 37–47, Macclesfield: Windgather Press.

Nelson, J. L. 1978. 'Queens as Jezebels: the careers of Brunhild and Balthild in Merovingian history', in D. Baker (ed.), *Medieval Women*, 31–77, Ecclesiastical History Society, Oxford: Basil Blackwell.

Ó Corráin, D. 1971. 'Irish regnal succession: a reappraisal', *Studia Hibernia*, **11**, 7–39.

Pelteret, D. A. E. 1995. *Slavery in Early Mediaeval England. From the Reign of Alfred until the Twelfth Century*, Woodbridge: Boydell Press.

Pestell, T. 2013. 'Das Baldehildis-Siegel', in E. Wamers and P. Périn (eds.), *Königinnen der Merowinger. Adelsgraber aus den Kirchen von Köln, Saint-Denis, Chelles und Frankfurt am Main*, 145–8, Regensburg: Schnell und Steiner.

Plummer, C. 1896. *Venerabilis Baedae Opera Historica*, 2 vols., Oxford: Clarendon Press.

Richardson, A. 2013. 'Late Roman and Anglo-Saxon Folkestone (*c.* AD 300–900)', in I. Coulson (ed.), *Folkestone to 1500. A Town Unearthed*, 55–76, Ashford: Canterbury Archaeological Trust.

Ridyard, S. J. 1988. *The Royal Saints of Anglo-Saxon England. A Study of West Saxon and East Anglian Cults*, Cambridge Studies in Medieval Life and Thought, 9, Cambridge: Cambridge University Press.

Robertson, S. 1886. 'St Eanswith's reliquary in Folkestone church', *Arch. Cantiana*, **16**, 322–6.

Rollason, D. W. 1982. *The Mildrith Legend. A Study in Early Medieval Hagiography in England*, Studies in the Early History of Britain, Leicester: Leicester University Press.

Rosenwein, B. H. 1999. *Negotiating Space. Power, Restraint, and Privileges of Immunity in Early Medieval Europe*, Manchester: Manchester University Press.

Sims-Williams, P. 1975. 'Continental influence at Bath monastery in the seventh century', *Anglo-Saxon England*, **4**, 1–10.

Sims-Williams, P. 1990. *Religion and Literature in Western England, 600–800*, Cambridge Studies in Anglo-Saxon England, 3, Cambridge: Cambridge University Press.

Stafford, P. 1983. *Queens, Concubines and Dowagers. The King's Wife in the Early Middle Ages*, London: Batsford Academic and Educational Ltd.

Stancliffe, C. 2001. 'Jonas's *Life of Columbanus and his Disciples*', in J. Carey, M. Herbert and P. O'Riain (eds.), *Saints and Scholars. Studies in Irish Hagiography*, 189–220, Dublin: Fours Courts Press.

Stenton, F. M. 1970. 'The East Anglian kings of the seventh century', in D. M. Stenton (ed.), *Preparatory to Anglo-Saxon England. The Collected Papers of Frank Merry Stenton*, 394–402, Oxford: Clarendon Press.

Tatum, S. 2009. '*Auctoritas* as *sanctitas*: Balthild's depiction as "queen saint" in the *Vita Balthildis*', *European Rev. of Hist.*, **16(6)**, 809–34.

Wallace-Hadrill, J. M. 1988. *Bede's Ecclesiastical History of the English People. A Historical Commentary*, Oxford: Clarendon Press.

Ward, G. 1935. 'The forgotten Saxon nunnery of Saint Werburg at Hoo', *Arch. Cantiana*, **47**, 117–25.

Webster, L. 2000. 'Norwich area, Norfolk: gold swivelling bezel from a Frankish seal-ring', *Treasure Annual Report* 1998–9.

Werner, K. 1985. 'Les rouages de l'administration', in P. Périn and L.-C. Feffer (eds.), *La Neustrie. Les Pays au Nord de la Loire, de Dagobert á Charles le Chauve (VII–IX siecle)*, 41–6, Rouen: Les Musées et Monuments départementaux de Seine-Maritime.

Witney, K. P. 1984. 'The Kentish royal saints; an enquiry into the facts behind the legends', *Arch. Cantiana*, **101**, 1–21.

Wood, I. N. 1983. *The Merovingian North Sea*, Occasional Papers on Medieval Topics, 1, Alingås: Viktoria Bokförlag.

Wood, I. N. 1994. *The Merovingian Kingdoms 450–751*, London: Longman.

Wood, I. N. 2013. 'The continental journeys of Wilfrid and Biscop', in N. J. Higham (ed.), *Wilfrid. Abbot, Bishop, Saint*, 200–11, Donnington: Shaun Tyas.

Yorke, B. 2003. *Nunneries and the Anglo-Saxon Royal Houses*, London: Continuum.

Yorke, B. forthcoming. 'Bede's preferential treatment of the Irish', in S. DeGregorio and P. Kershaw (eds.), *Cities, Saints and Communities in Early Medieval Europe: Essays in Honor of Alan T. Thacker*, Turnhout: Brepols.

Anglo-Saxon Studies in Archaeology and History 20, 2017

# Merovingian monasticism and England

Ian Wood

*Abstract*

*The earliest monastic foundation in England was that of SS Peter and Paul at Canterbury, which obviously followed the traditions of Gregory the Great. In Northumbria, by contrast, the initial impetus for monasticism came from Iona for Lindisfarne and its dependencies, as is well known from the writings of Bede. In contrast to these two traditions, the influence of Merovingian monasticism has been rather less considered, and yet in Western Europe, in general, the Gallo-Roman and Merovingian monastic tradition was much more substantial than that of either Rome or Ireland, at least in terms of the number of early foundations, the wealth which they gained, and the surviving documentation, in terms of charters, rules and hagiography. Not surprisingly, the influence of Merovingian monasticism in England was considerable, reaching to Hexham, Ripon, Wearmouth and Jarrow. It is also well attested for more southern centres such as Bath and Barking, and it can be easily inferred for the Kentish houses, including Lyminge. This contribution examines the evidence for Merovingian influence on the monastic houses of southern England, and stresses the extent to which the foundations of the south need to be seen in the context of the religious history of Francia.*

The earliest monastic foundation in the Anglo-Saxon world was that of SS Peter and Paul at Canterbury, which was in origin the community of the followers of Saint Augustine. It was surely modelled on Gregory the Great's foundation of St Andrew on the Coelian in Rome. The second oldest monastic foundation in an Anglo-Saxon kingdom was probably that of Aidan on Lindisfarne, where the model was undoubtedly that of Iona. Because of the richness of the evidence for Northumbria, historians of monasticism have tended to concentrate on the great northern houses of Lindisfarne, Ripon and Hexham, Wearmouth and Jarrow, and Whitby, although Kent, East Anglia and Wessex all came to boast significant monastic foundations, many of which looked neither to Rome nor to Ireland for inspiration, but rather to Francia, whose contribution to Anglo-Saxon monastic history has, arguably, been insufficiently emphasized, and which certainly deserves renewed investigation. It is this Frankish influence with which this paper is concerned.

It is worth beginning with a statement about chronology: Merovingian monasticism evolved considerably over the course of the sixth and seventh centuries. Its precise significance for the monastery founded at Lyminge depends therefore to a considerable extent on the date of the Anglo-Saxon foundation. If one gives any credence to a foundation in the 630s, then the likely Continental influences would be very different from those that one would expect in the 650s or later. The discussion that follows, therefore, deliberately says little about Lyminge itself, but concentrates rather on the Continental connections of houses that are more certainly dated.

## 'Hiberno-Frankish' influence on Anglo-Saxon monasticism

That there was considerable Merovingian influence on early Anglo-Saxon monasticism is well known. Above all there is Bede's comment in Book III chapter 8 of the *Historia ecclesiastica*, where we learn that Eorcenberht's daughter Eorcengota

> was a most virtuous maiden who served the Lord in a monastery founded in the land of the Franks by a noble abbess named Fara in a place called Brie. At that time, because there were not yet many monasteries founded in England, numbers of people from Britain used to enter the monasteries of the Franks or Gauls to practise monastic life; they also sent their daughters to be taught in them and to be wedded to the heavenly bridegroom. They mostly went to the monasteries at Brie, Chelles, and Les Andelys; among these was Sæthryth, stepdaughter of Anna, king of the East Angles … and Æthelburh his own daughter. Both of these (Sæthryth and Æthelburh) though foreigners were … made

> abbesses of the monastery at Brie. The eldest daughter of the king was Seaxburh, wife of Eorcenberht of Kent, whose daughter Eorcengota deserves special mention.[1]

Bede goes on to provide a unique account of the nunnery of Brie, better known as Faremoutiers, in the time of Sæthryth and Æthelburh, which essentially continues the narrative provided by Jonas of Bobbio in Book II of the *Vita Columbani.*

Bede's list of Brie, Chelles and Les Andelys has been thought to suggest that we are dealing with the influence of a group of nunneries usually categorized as 'Columbanian'. By 'Columbanian' we mean a cluster of monasteries associated with Columbanus' foundation of Luxeuil (founded *c.* 595), and with a group of families which came into contact with the Irish saint, and, more significantly, with his successor as abbot of Luxeuil, Eustasius. Brie, or Faremoutiers, and Fara, or Burgundofara, can certainly be characterized as 'Columbanian' as early as the 630s, and Chelles and Les Andelys can be so described in the second half of the seventh century. Arguably, however, the term 'Luxovian' is more accurate as a descriptor than 'Columbanian', in that these houses were inspired by the community of Luxeuil after Columbanus' departure for Italy and death. Unlike Columbanus' foundation of Bobbio, Luxeuil did not boast many strikingly Irish features, nor did it share some of the distinctively Irish learning that can be found in the Italian monastery.[2] Equally significantly, while Péronne, the burial place of another Irish saint, Fursa, was remembered as *Peronna Scottorum*,[3] Luxeuil was not thought of as a house of *Scotti.* A further term, 'iro-frankish', is also problematic, because it is used to cover a variety of traditions, which, although they can be linked ultimately to Irishmen, including both Columbanus and Fursa, are rarely specifically Irish. Both 'Columbanian' and 'iro-frankish' should thus be regarded as no more than terms of convenience.

Adding to Bede's statement on the importance for the Anglo-Saxons of the Île-de-France nunneries, historians have pointed to the *Life* of Bertilla of Chelles who is said to have sent books to England, in the years after 659 – and a strong case has been made for seeing Bath as one of the houses to gain from her beneficence.[4] There are also inferences to be drawn from Bede's account of the nuns of Barking (founded around 660), which suggests that his source, a *libellus* which does not survive, was modelled on Book II of the *Vita Columbani*, and especially on its account of Burgundofara and Faremoutiers.[5] Yet more indications of contact with 'Columbanian' communities in the region, this time with male houses, might be discovered in Wilfrid's sojourn at Meaux, which boasted a 'Columbanian' house:[6] Wilfrid may have spread the traditions of Luxeuil to the whole network of monasteries with which he is associated.

In other words, the standard picture of Frankish influence on Anglo-Saxon monasticism is dominated by what is known as 'Columbanian monasticism', and this picture can be seen to link neatly with the work of Friedrich Prinz, in his mapping of patterns of monastic development,[7] and of Eugen Ewig and Hans Hubert Anton in their work on monastic privileges – episcopal, royal and papal.[8] And the fact that one of the major figures associated with the jurisdictional changes in the world of Merovingian monasticism in the 650s and 660s was Queen Balthild, of Saxon, which is probably to say Anglo-Saxon, origin, has further strengthened this particular view of early Frankish influence on England.[9]

There are two significant additions to this picture of monastic ties between Francia and England that are relatively well known. First, there is the history of the Irish saint Fursa, who settled initially in East Anglia, but then having left for the Continent set up a monastery at Lagny; his brothers Foillan and Ultan, who followed him, subsequently established Péronne.[10] Initially Fursa's patron was Erchinoald, who also happened at one stage to have been the master of Balthild. The Irishman left East Anglia for Neustria in around 648, roughly the time that Balthild married Clovis II (who came to the throne as an infant in 639 and died in 657/8). A little more might be deduced of the context in which Fursa left East Anglia for Francia if one keeps in mind the histories of Felix, bishop of the East Angles, a Burgundian, perhaps from the Luxeuil orbit,[11] who is supposed to have died in 647/8, and also of Botulf, who is said to have founded Icanho in 653, perhaps after travelling to Francia.[12] Felix may well help explain Fursa's decision to leave England for the Continent, while Botulf perhaps adds to the picture of ecclesiastical connections between East Anglia and the Frankish world.

## The continental associations of Benedict Biscop

The other major addition to our knowledge of Frankish influence on Anglo-Saxon monasticism comes from the career of Benedict Biscop, who is said to have drawn on the Rules of seventeen monasteries in formulating his own Rule for Wearmouth.[13] Biscop made his first visit to the Continent together with Wilfrid, but they soon parted company.[14] Although the latter was an important monastic founder, and is credited (oversimplistically) by his hagiographer with the introduction of the Benedictine Rule into England,[15] it was Biscop who had the monastic career. The one monastic house in Francia that he is known to have spent time in, Lérins, was not obviously a 'Columbanian' house when he was based there – although at the time it may have been in the process of adopting the Benedictine Rule, since it is probable that the abbot during his stay in the island monastery was Aigulf, who seems to have been the thief who removed the body of Benedict from Montecassino.[16] Biscop is also known to have had close links with Vienne, another major monastic centre,[17] and again one that does not seem to have been dominated by Luxeuil. One additional point may suggest that Biscop did not draw directly on 'Luxovian' tradition: Bede only talks of Columbanus as a heretic and not as a monastic founder.[18] As we have already noted, he does, however, know a good deal about the Columbanian house of Faremoutiers in the generation following the death of the founding abbess Burgundofara, when the community was led by the Anglo-Saxons Sæthryth and Æthelburh.[19]

## Faremoutiers and England

What has been described as 'Columbanian' influence on early Anglo-Saxon monasticism has been relatively well explored, not least by Patrick Wormald in his study of Benedict Biscop.[20] Before we accept the standard view as it stands, however, we need to look again both at Bede's statement about the daughters of King Anna, and also at the evidence for non-Columbanian elements in the history of Merovingian monasticism, in the late sixth and seventh centuries.

Bede's comment on the presence of Anglo-Saxon princesses in nunneries of the Île de France follows the mention of the death of Eadbald of Kent in 640.[21] He notes that Sæthryth and Æthelburh, the step-daughter and daughter of Anna of East Anglia, in turn became abbess of Faremoutiers. Anna himself died in 654, but the chronology for Sæthryth and Æthelburh is less than secure. The former succeeded Burgundofara as abbess of Faremoutiers, but all we can say of the date of Burgundofara's death is that it occurred between 642/3 and 664.[22] The nineteenth-century historian Fontaine de Resbecq thought there were reasonable grounds for placing it in 655, and if Bishop Landericus of Paris was present at the funeral, as later tradition claimed, he must be correct.[23] However, given the uncertainties of the chronology we cannot be sure that Sæthryth and Æthelburh had even entered Faremoutiers before the 650s. The only Anglo-Saxon nun that we can place in the nunnery at an earlier date is Willesuinda, *ex genere Saxonum*, who, according to Jonas of Bobbio, died in *c.* 641[24] – in all probability she was an Anglo-Saxon, although Adalbert de Vogüé asserted that she was a Continental Saxon.[25] As for Eorcengota, the niece of Sæthryth and Æthelburh, although it has been claimed that she entered Faremoutiers while Burgundofara was still alive, this is not directly stated by Bede, who provides us with our earliest and best evidence.[26] In other words, although Bede places his comments on the presence of Anglo-Saxon princesses in the context of the 640s, he is referring more generally to the middle and later seventh century, by which time there were a number of monasteries in England including Canterbury, Ikenhoe, Tilbury and Bradwell. The question of female houses is more problematic, and depends on whether one accepts early dates for the foundations of Folkestone and Lyminge.[27] From the early 660s, however, there was a marked increase in both male and female foundations, including Minster in Sheppey, Barking, Chertsey and Reculver, as well as Minster in Thanet in 670.[28] The monastic movement was firmly under way by the same period in both Wessex and Northumbria.[29]

## Cross-channel communication

Once we reach the foundations of the north Kentish minsters we are, of course, in well-charted waters when it comes to considering relations between Anglo-Saxon and Frankish monasteries, not least because of the surviving charter evidence.[30] Later Merovingian coastal monasteries, like their Kentish counterparts, can be shown to have had a role to play in cross-Channel communication. Although it can scarcely have influenced Anglo-Saxon, as opposed to British, monasteries, because its heyday antedated the mission of Augustine to England, it is worth noting that the model for the great riverine and coastal monasteries of the seventh century may well have been Pentale.[31] This was the major foundation of the British saint Samson, almost certainly much more important in the mid-sixth century than his more famous base at Dol. Samson attracted a great deal of support and attention from the Merovingians, even, it would seem, providing one Merovingian prince with his name. The importance of Pentale has to be assessed by its commanding position on the Lower Seine. This was no out-of-the-way community, but a monastery that was established near one of the major viewpoints of the most important riverine route to the heart of the Merovingian kingdom. Why it declined we do not know, but it may well have been eclipsed by the seventh-century foundations of St Wandrille and Jumièges, both of them established by 'Columbanian' patrons.

## Variety within the 'Columbanian' movement

In order to understand Frankish monastic influence on England, we need to reconsider the 'Columbanian' movement, and its status within Francia. The simple point is that the 'Columbanian' movement as currently understood is a modern construct. Certainly a number of monasteries are presented by Jonas as being the foundations of Columbanus' disciples.[32] In addition, several houses are stated in their diplomas as following the Rule of Columbanus, along with those of Benedict and Caesarius – by my count there are four such authentic charters (Pardessus 275, 350, 351, 596), which relate to Rebais, S. Amand and Strasbourg, although the forgeries may, of course, have been based on genuine originals.[33] Further, there are three surviving Rules, which combine elements of Columbanus' monastic legislation with that of Benedict and Caesarius: one can be associated directly with Donatus of Besançon and the nunnery he founded there,[34] while a second *Regula ad virgines*, which de Vogüé argued was compiled by Waldebert of Luxeuil, and has been linked to Faremoutiers, has more recently been ascribed to Jonas of Bobbio, and might have been composed for the community of Marchiennes.[35] The third of these Rules is for an unidentified male monastery.[36]

There is other evidence that allows us to talk about a 'Columbanian' or 'Luxovian' tradition. In addition to the diplomatic and regular evidence, a cluster of Merovingian houses can be seen to have had copies of Jonas' *Life of Columbanus*, which can be read as a model, and therefore as a Rule.[37] We find citations of the *Vita Columbani* in the *Lives* of Germanus of Grandval, Praeiectus of Clermont,

Sadalberga, Segolena and Wandregisel, as well as, perhaps, the *Vita Wilfridi* of Stephen of Ripon.[38]

Yet the differences to be found within the so-called 'Columbanian' tradition need to be emphasized as much as the movement's coherence. Even within the three Rules that combine Columbanus, Benedict and Caesarius, there are markedly different emphases, which suggest widely divergent views inside what is usually regarded as a relatively tight-knit movement.[39] Further, from Jonas' narrative, it is clear that the cohesion of the 'Columbanian' tradition is something of a mirage. For instance, Remiremont, which is generally seen as a 'Columbanian' house because its first abbot, Amatus, trained at Luxeuil, adopted the complex liturgy known as the *laus perennis*, which places it rather more firmly in the tradition of the spirituality of the monastery of Agaune (the first community to which Amatus was attached) than in that of Columbanus himself.[40] Indeed, it is difficult to see how a Rule devoted to the ceaseless performance of the liturgy can be squared with pure 'Columbanian' tradition, with its emphasis on labour.

## The problem of the 'double monastery'

Since Remiremont is usually described as a double monastery, it is worth at this point pausing over the question of such institutions, not least because a number of Anglo-Saxon houses (including Lyminge) have been described as double monasteries, and they are supposed to conform to a model borrowed from the Continent.[41] According to Bede there were both monks and nuns at Faremoutiers, where Sæthryth and Æthelburh held the position of abbess, and where Eorcengota, daughter of Eorcenberht of Kent, was an inmate.[42] He records that, on Eorcengota's death, 'many of the brothers of the monastery who were in other buildings related that they clearly heard choirs of angels singing'. Similarly, he notes that when Æthelburh died the brothers put off the completion of the building works that she had begun. If, however, we turn to Jonas of Bobbio's lengthy account of the community of Faremoutiers, completed in 642/3, almost ninety years before Bede set down his information, there is nothing to suggest the existence of a house of monks. We are told that the community was initially put under the oversight of Burgundofara's clerical brothers,[43] no doubt because of her age, but since Chagnoald was bishop of Laon and Waldebert abbot of Luxeuil, it is clear that they were not physically present at Faremoutiers. The monastery was ruled by an abbess, in the person of Burgundofara and her Anglo-Saxon successors. We do learn, however, that Jonas himself was present in the community at a commemorative mass held thirty days after the death of the saintly Gibitrudis.[44] Yet there is nothing in Jonas to suggest the existence at Faremoutiers of a male community equivalent to that of the nuns. One has to wonder whether Bede has extrapolated from the existence of male informants, to conclude that the monastery also housed a community of monks.

It needs to be stressed that the term 'double monastery' is not derived from any Merovingian phrase – and its application to Merovingian monasteries has been inconsistent. Even Friedrich Prinz, in what is the standard manual for the history of early Frankish monasticism, used the word *Doppelkloster* to refer to a variety of different types of association, including twinned male houses, as for instance Stablo-Malmédy, which was a community of monks, based in two separate locations.[45] He also applied the same term to male and female houses occupying adjacent space,[46] and (as in the case of Bèze and Brégille) to male and female houses founded by a single patron.[47] So, too, he used the word *Doppelkloster* to describe Montier-en-Der, a monastery that was responsible for the foundation of the nunnery of Puellemontier six kilometres away.[48]

Perhaps closer to what is suggested by the evidence for Faremoutiers, Jouarre is said to have been a community of men as well as women, but again there is no early evidence for a male house,[49] and if it existed it may have been no more than a group of priests who served the female community. All that can certainly be said is that the leading male members of the founder's family retained an interest in the nunnery, which was under the control of an abbess.[50] One might deduce a similar situation at Nivelles, where the presence of a group of men has been identified in the years shortly after the foundation of the nunnery.[51]

There is, however, evidence for what were essentially female communities directed by men. Thus, Marchiennes, intended by Amandus to be a foundation for monks, and apparently set under an abbot Jonatus (perhaps to be identified with Jonas of Bobbio), was turned into a convent, whose first abbess was Rictrudis.[52] Unfortunately, the evidence for this somewhat complex chain of events comes from the tenth-century *Vita Rictrudis* by Hucbald of St Amand, and it does not allow us to construct a model of Merovingian double houses. The clearest image of a double community relates to Remiremont, where both the founder (Romaric) and the first abbot (Amatus) were male, although the main community was female: the *Vita Amati* talks specifically of a *monasterium puellarum*.[53] Amatus himself, however, subsequently retired to a cell on the other side of the hill where he had contact with monks, *fratres*.[54] In the narrative of his death we hear of both *fratres* and *sorores*.[55] In the subsequent *Vita Romarici* again we are told that the foundation was a community of nuns,[56] but once more we hear of *fratres* when the hagiographer reaches the narrative of the saint's death.[57]

In other words, although he is not supported by Jonas, Bede, in his account of Faremoutiers, provides us with the best early evidence for the existence of a double monastery in Merovingian Gaul, if by that one means a house where there were both male and female religious within a single, albeit compartmentalized, space, although there are examples of adjacent communities of men and women, which surely shared some resources, and there are examples of female communities being directed by abbots. We seem to be faced with a variety of arrangements, dependent on the wishes of founders and patrons, but nothing that suggests an established pattern of a combined house for men and women. Whatever the nature of the Anglo-Saxon double monastery, it was not based on a widespread Merovingian model.

## The continuing influence of Lérins

To return to the broader issue of Columbanian influence: the problem with the standard model of the role played by Columbanus and his disciples in the spread of monasticism in Francia and beyond is not that there is no evidence that they were influential, but rather that it downplays the evidence for other influences. It is necessary to begin with the obvious: in the sixth and seventh centuries, Gaul, subsequently Francia, was the centre of western monasticism. Historians often compare the known number of monasteries in late-sixth-century Francia, around 220, with the known number a century and a half later, when around 550 are attested, and ascribe the increase to the impact of Columbanus.[58] What they fail to stress is the fact that 220 is more than twice the number of monasteries known for Italy before the mid-eighth century (100), and over two and a half times what is known for Spain (eighty-six).[59] In other words, western monastic history is predominantly Gallo-Roman and Frankish even before the arrival of Columbanus on the Continent.

The second point to consider, when thinking of influences other than Luxeuil, is the continuing importance of Lérins, the unquestioned centre of western monasticism in the late fifth century. There is an assumption that it fell into a decline in the late sixth century, in part because Athala, one of Columbanus' disciples, left the Mediterranean house to join the Irish holy man,[60] though one should remember here that dissatisfaction with monastic standards was one of the few reasons for moving to a new monastery according to some monastic legislators,[61] and that the comment on the laxity of Lérins might be no more than a way of absolving Athala from criticism. In addition to the supposed dissatisfaction of Athala with the standards at Lérins, historians have noted the opposition to and murder of the reforming abbot Aigulf at some point in the 660s.[62] One should, however, beware of making too much of this late tradition: one needs to remember that Biscop was at Lérins in Aigulf's time.[63] In fact, a group of texts, including letters of Gregory the Great, and a poem by the patrician Dynamius, as well as the *Life* of John of Réomé by Jonas of Bobbio, make it clear that Lérins and the Lérinian tradition were well respected in the early and middle years of the seventh century.[64]

## The influence of Caesarius of Arles

Third, and less well known, is the importance of Caesarius of Arles, himself a product of Lérins. That 'Columbanian' houses combined the Rule of Caesarius with those of Benedict and Columbanus, in the mid-seventh century, is well enough known – as indeed is the fact that the early dissemination history of the Rule of Benedict is Frankish and not Italian.[65] Yet whereas historians have paid some attention to the transmission of Benedict's Rule, they have scarcely noted the importance of that of Caesarius. In fact, some of the most famous aspects of 'Columbanian' monasticism that are usually regarded as Irish in origin, like the monastic *saepta*, or enclosure, come from the Caesarean tradition.[66] If Columbanus had a firm notion of monastic enclosure, even though the idea is not central to his Rule, that notion may have been Irish in origin (and archaeology certainly suggests that enclosures were important in Ireland).[67] Yet we should also recognize that the idea of monastic enclosure was well established on the Continent, especially in the legislation for some nunneries, before the Irishman's arrival. It is, of course, possible that the Irish derived some of their monastic ideas in the late sixth and early seventh centuries from Caesarius. Texts from Arles might have been available to Columbanus before his departure for the Continent, if Michael Lapidge is right to ascribe to him one of the poems in the Antiphonary of Bangor.[68]

The extent to which Columbanus' own religious writings, and indeed those of Jonas, were dependent on Caesarius has only just started to become apparent – in part because the identification of the bishop of Arles' sermons was not made until the mid-twentieth century, and here one has to admit that the creation of a Caesarean corpus of sermons, which is partly based on style, is not without problems. As a result, the dependence of Columbanus and Jonas on the homilies that have been ascribed to Caesarius was not apparent either to Krusch, the editor of Jonas' work, or to that of Columbanus, Walker. Even the classic description of Columbanus' concern with the 'medicines of penitence', *medicamenta paenitentiae*, in Jonas is probably derived from Caesarius, since the phrase appears in over twenty of the sermons ascribed by Morin to the bishop of Arles.[69]

In addition to the circulation of the sermons, there is also the matter of knowledge of Caesarius' Rules, for monks and above all for nuns. These were already cited in the sixth century by a string of Gallo-Roman Rules, including that of Caesarius' successor in the see of Arles, Aurelian, and by the anonymous *Regula Tarnatensis*.[70] As we have already noted, the bishop of Arles' Rule for nuns was also used, in combination with those of Benedict and Columbanus, in two anonymous Rules, as well as that of Donatus of Besançon. One could even argue that his nunnery might as accurately be called 'Caesarean' as 'Columbanian', which is scarcely a surprise, because Caesarius wrote specifically for women: indeed, he is the earliest author of a surviving Rule for nuns in the West.

Further, in the decades before Columbanus' arrival in Gaul, the Thuringian princess and Frankish queen Radegund decided to model her monastery of the Holy Cross in Poitiers on the community of nuns in Arles, and to adopt the Rule of Caesarius.[71] The importance of the Rule of Caesarius for the royal nunnery of the Holy Cross in Poitiers may indicate that its dissemination was less dependent on Columbanus' disciples, than was that of the Rule of Benedict.

In addition to his Rules, Caesarius' foundations in Arles were also centres of inspiration, and not just to Radegund. His nunnery was still a place of importance in the early seventh century, as is clear from the contemporary *Vita Rusticulae*[72] – the *Life* of the abbess who was an exact contemporary of Columbanus, which was composed at precisely the moment that Jonas was writing the *Vita Columbani*. And it is surely worth remembering that travellers moving between Rome and Kent, from Augustine onwards, were highly likely to pass through Arles.

## Merovingian royal foundations

In addition to the dissemination of Caesarius' writings and reputation, there is another possible line of influence which needs to be considered. Among the female houses in Francia other than Faremoutiers listed by Bede, Chelles was said to have been founded by Chrotechildis, wife of Clovis, in the opening decades of the sixth century. It was supposedly refounded by Balthild in 659.[73] As for Les Andelys, like Chelles it, too, was claimed to have been a foundation of Chrotechildis; its refoundation was supposedly by Audoin of Rouen, and thus belongs to the 630s or 640s.[74] Because of the refoundations by Balthild and Audoin, these houses are usually categorized as 'Columbanian', yet we should perhaps pay a little more attention to their earlier existence, especially if we are looking for monastic influence on England before the second half of the seventh century. Equally important here is the fact that Chrotechildis died in the vicinity of the cathedral of Tours, which may imply that she had entered an ascetic establishment associated with the tomb of Martin.[75] More certainly, another female member of the royal house, Ingitrude, founded a community in the atrium of the church of St Martin, and it may have been there that Ingoberga, widow of Charibert and mother of Bertha, wife of Æthelberht of Kent, died.[76] The dedications of St Martin's at Canterbury and of St Martin in the Fields in London suggest an interest in the Loire city and its religious institutions that we might well trace back to Bertha. If we are looking for possible monastic influence on England before the 640s, we would be well advised to bear these early Merovingian foundations in mind.

The exact nature of these houses founded by Chrotechildis in the early sixth century is unclear. Although Gregory of Tours was well aware of the presence of pious female members of the ruling dynasty who had established themselves in the vicinity of his cathedral, and indeed comments on their behaviour from time to time,[77] he says nothing about the regular arrangements to which they were subject. They might well have been a good deal closer to the sorts of houses for women that we can see in Rome in the late fourth and early fifth centuries, and in the Rhône valley a century later. That is, they might have been little more than the town houses of rulers or aristocrats, turned into havens where widows and spinsters could follow their own version of the religious life. Such places of religious retreat must have been appealing to many an aristocratic widow. If Lyminge boasted a religious community before the middle of the seventh century, it may have been no more than this; and if it were to such a house that Æthelburh, daughter of Æthelberht of Kent, and widow of Edwin of Northumbria, retired, she might well have had her grandmother's example in mind. Archaeologically, of course, it would be indistinguishable from an aristocratic residence.

## Conclusion

I would suggest, then, that if we are looking for Merovingian influence for an early foundation at Lyminge we should be looking to the early-sixth-century traditions of Merovingian Francia, to Caesarius' nunnery at Arles, to the Holy Cross at Poitiers, and to the foundations of Chrotechildis. The 'Columbanian' houses could not have been a model for foundations established before the middle of the seventh century, and even then we should bear in mind that they only provided one model among the several available.

The standard reading of Merovingian monastic history as one that begins in a period of a declining Gallo-Roman tradition, which was reversed by the arrival of the Irish, is one which neglects far too much of the evidence. So, too, the reading of Frankish influence on Anglo-Saxon monasticism as being largely a spin-off of the impact of Columbanus oversimplifies the complex world indicated by our sources. To get a full sense of the riches of monastic culture in the mid-seventh century, it is worth remembering the seventeen monasteries from which Biscop drew his monastic ideas. These would have included houses in Rome, but must for the most part have been Gallo-Roman and Frankish: among them Lérins, and probably Arles and Vienne. And it is worth remembering Biscop's time as abbot of SS Peter and Paul in Canterbury, while Hadrian was detained in Francia.[78] Canterbury, of course, looked back to Augustine, and to Gregory the Great's foundation on the Coelian, but it most certainly had strong links with Francia (as can be seen from the Canons of the Council of Paris),[79] and Biscop must have reinforced these. So, too, in earlier generations Bertha and Æthelburh were surely aware of developments at Tours.

Columbanus has provided a useful line of research, which has helped us to understand monastic developments of the seventh century, but it is time to look further afield, and above all to investigate the influence of Caesarius and the 'Caesarean' tradition not just in Francia, but also in England. If we are going to accept an early date for houses at Folkestone and Lyminge they must take us back to a period before 'Columbanian' influence was significant. Yet even if we confine our searches to the later seventh century, we should remember the divisions within the so-called 'Columbanian' tradition, as well as the continuing influence of such centres as Lérins and Arles.

## Notes

1 Bede, *Historia ecclesiastica* III.8.
2 Richter 2008.
3 Traube 1900.
4 Sims-Williams 1990, 110, 204; Foot 2000, I, 36.
5 Bede, *Historia ecclesiastica* IV.6–10; Wood 1982, 68–9.
6 Prinz 1965, 125; Stephanus, *Vita Wilfridi* 56; Wood 2013a, 203.
7 Prinz 1965.
8 Ewig 1979, 411–583; Anton 1975.
9 Nelson 1978.
10 *Transitus beati Fursei*; Bede, *Historia ecclesiastica* III.19.
11 Bede, *Historia ecclesiastica* II.15.
12 West, Scarfe and Cramp 1984.
13 Bede, *Historia abbatum* 11; Grocock and Wood 2013, xxv.
14 Stephanus, *Vita Wilfridi* 4.
15 Stephanus, *Vita Wilfridi* 47; Álvarez López 2013, 44–7.
16 Grocock and Wood 2013, 26–7, n. 22; Wood 2014, 306.
17 Bede, *Historia abbatum* 4.
18 Bede, *Historia ecclesiastica* II.4.
19 Bede, *Historia ecclesiastica* III.8.
20 Wormald 1976.
21 Bede, *Historia ecclesiastica* III.8.
22 Fox 2014, 212.
23 de Fontaine de Resbecq 1863, 13.
24 Jonas, *Vita Columbani* II.17.
25 de Vogüé 1988, 216.
26 Fox 2014, 211–12; Ridyard 1988, 60–1.
27 Foot 2000, II, 89–91, 111–15.
28 Bede, *Historia ecclesiastica* IV.6, V.8; Foot 2000, II, 27–33, 121–3, 125–32.
29 Bede, *Historia ecclesiastica* IV.23.
30 Kelly 1992; Lebecq 2000; Wood 2011a.
31 Le Maho 2008.
32 Besançon (Jonas, *Vita Columbani* I.14), Jouarre, Rebais (I.26), Faremoutiers (II.7), Remiremont, Solignac, Paris, Bourges, Isle, Charenton (II.10).
33 Pardessus 1843–9, II, 40, 133, 134, 409.
34 de Vogüe 1978.
35 *Regula cuiusdam patris ad virgines.*
36 *Regula cuiusdam patris ad monachos.*
37 Wood 1982, 66–8.
38 Wood 1982, 68–9; O'Hara 2009, 126–7.
39 Diem forthcoming.
40 Prinz 1965, 105.
41 Foot 2000, I, 36–7, 49–56.
42 Bede, *Historia ecclesiastica* III.8.
43 Jonas, *Vita Columbani* I.7.
44 Jonas, *Vita Columbani* II.12.
45 Prinz 1965, 169.
46 Prinz 1965, 66, 127–8, 132.
47 Prinz 1965, 179; Fox 2014, 102.
48 Prinz 1965, 182; Bouchard 2004, 15–16.
49 Prinz 1965, 125, with n. 19.
50 de Maillé 1971, 33.
51 Dierkens 2004, 73.
52 Ugé 2005, 98–109.
53 *Vita Amati* 7, 10; Prinz 1965, 142.
54 *Vita Amati* 10–11.
55 *Vita Amati* 12, 14.
56 *Vita Romarici* 5, 7.
57 *Vita Romarici* 9.
58 Atsma 1976, 168.
59 Wood 2013b, 46, 49.
60 Jonas, *Vita Columbani* II.1.
61 Gildas, fragment 4.
62 *Vita Aigulfi* 2.
63 Bede, *Historia abbatum* 2.
64 Dumézil 2009, 186–8.
65 Prinz 1965, 263–92.
66 Wood forthcoming.
67 Stalley 2005, 716–18.
68 Lapidge 1997; Stevenson 1995, 96–7.
69 Wood forthcoming.
70 Prinz 1965, 75–84.
71 *Epistolae aevi Merowingici collectae* 11.
72 Florentius, *Vita Rusticulae.*
73 Prinz 1965, 174–5.
74 Prinz 1965, 296–7.
75 Gregory of Tours, *Decem libri historiarum* IV.1; Prinz 1965, 153.
76 Gregory of Tours, *Decem libri historiarum* IX.26, 33.
77 Gregory of Tours, *Decem libri historiarum* IX.33.
78 Bede, *Historia abbatum* 3; *Historia ecclesiastica* IV.1.
79 Wood 2011b, 453–4.

## Bibliography

### *Primary sources*


Bede, *Historia abbatum*, ed. and trans. C. Grocock and I. N. Wood, 2013. *Abbots of Wearmouth and Jarrow*, Oxford: Oxford University Press.

Bede, *Historia ecclesiastica*, ed. and trans. B. Colgrave and R. A. B. Mynors, 1969. *Bede's Ecclesiastical History of the English People*, Oxford: Oxford University Press.

*Epistolae aevi Merowingici collectae*, ed. W. Gundlach, 1892, MGH, Epist. III, Berlin: Weidmann.

Florentius, *Vita Rusticulae*, ed. B. Krusch, 1902, MGH SS rer. Merov. IV, 339–51, Hannover: Hahn.

Gildas, ed. and trans. M. Winterbottom, 1978. *The Ruin of Britain and Other Works*, Arthurian Period Sources, Chichester: Phillimore.

Gregory of Tours, *Decem libri historiarum*, ed. B. Krusch and W. Levison, 1951, MGH SS rer. Merov. I.1, Hannover: Hahn.

Jonas, *Vita Columbani*, ed. B. Krusch, 1905, MGH, Scriptores rerum Germanicarum in usum scholarum, Hannover: Hahn.

Pardessus, J.-M. 1843–9. *Diplomata, Chartae, Leges aliaque instrumenta ad res gallo-francicas spectantia*, Paris: Typogr. Regio.

*Regula cuiusdam patris ad monachos*, ed. F. Villegas, 1973. 'La "Regula cuiusdam Patris ad monachos". Ses sources littéraires et ses rapports avec la "Regula monachorum" de Colomban', *Revue d'Histoire de la Spiritualité*, **49**, 3–36.

*Regula cuiusdam patris ad virgines*, PL 88, cols. 1053–70.

Stephanus, *Vita Wilfridi*, ed. and trans. B. Colgrave, 1927. *The Life of Bishop Wilfrid by Eddius Stephanus*, Cambridge: Cambridge University Press.

*Transitus beati Fursei*, ed. and trans. O. Rackham, 2007, Norwich: Fursey Pilgrims.

*Vita Aigulfi*, *Acta Sanctorum*, September I, 743–7.

*Vita Amati*, ed. B. Krusch, 1902, MGH SS rer. Merov. IV, 215–21, Hannover: Hahn.

*Vita Romarici*, ed. B. Krusch, 1902, MGH SS rer. Merov. IV, 221–5, Hannover: Hahn.


### *Secondary literature*


Álvarez López, F. J. 2013. 'The Rule of St. Benedict in England at the time of Wilfrid', in N. J. Higham (ed.), *Wilfrid, Abbot, Bishop, Saint. Papers from the 1300th Anniversary Conferences*, 40–53, Donington: Shaun Tyas.

Anton, H. H. 1975. *Studien zu den Klösterprivilegien der Päpste im frühen Mittelalter*, Berlin: De Gruyter.

Atsma, H. 1976. 'Les monastères urbains du Nord de la Gaule', *Revue d'Histoire de l'Église de France*, **62**, 163–87.

Bouchard, C. (ed.) 2004. *The Cartulary of Montier-en-Der, 666–1129*, Toronto: Medieval Academy of America.

de Fontaine de Resbecq, E. 1863. *L'abbaye royale de Faremoutiers au diocèse de Meaux*, Paris: Furne et Cie.

de Maillé, Marquise 1971. *Les cryptes de Jouarre*, Paris: Picard.

de Vogüé, A. 1978. 'La règle de Donat pour l'abbesse Gauthstrude', *Benedictina*, **25**, 219–313.

de Vogüé, A. (trans.) 1988. *Jonas de Bobbio, Vie de saint Colomban et de ses disciples*, Bégrolles-en-Mauges: Abbaye de Bellefontaine.

Diem, A. forthcoming. 'Columbanian monastic rules: dissent and experiment'.

Dierkens, A. 2004. 'La sculpture sur pierre du très haut moyen âge dans l'ancien diocese de Tongres-Maastricht-Liège', in M. Lodewijkx, *Bruc Ealles Well: Archaeological Essays Concerning the Peoples of North-West Europe in the First Millennium A.D.*, 73–86, Leuven: Leuven University Press.

Dumézil, B. 2009. 'Le patrice Dynamius et son réseau', in Y. Codou and M. Lauwers, *Lérins, une île sainte de l'Antiquité au Moyen* Âge, 167–94, Turnhout: Brepols.

Ewig, E. 1979. *Spätantikes und Fränkisches Gallien*, Vol. 2, Munich: Artemis.

Foot, S. 2000. *Veiled Women*, 2 vols., Aldershot: Ashgate.

Fox, Y. 2014. *Power and Religion in Merovingian Gaul. Columbanian Monasticism and the Frankish Elites*, Cambridge: Cambridge University Press.

Grocock, C. and Wood, I. N. 2013. *Abbots of Wearmouth and Jarrow*, Oxford: Oxford University Press.

Kelly, S. 1992. 'Trading privileges from eighth-century England', *Early Medieval Europe*, **1**, 3–28.

Lapidge, M. 1997. '"Precamur patrem": an Easter hymn by Columbanus?', in M. Lapidge (ed.), *Columbanus: Studies on the Latin Writings*, 255–63, Woodbridge: Boydell.

Lebecq, S. 2000. 'The role of the monasteries in the systems of production and exchange of the Frankish world between the seventh and the beginning of the ninth centuries', in I. L. Hansen and C. Wickham (eds.), *The Long Eighth Century: Production, Distribution and Demand*, 121–48, Leiden: Brill.

Le Maho, J. 2008. 'Ermitages et monastères bretons dans la province de Rouen au haut Moyen Âge (VIe–IXe siècle)', in J. Quaghebeur and B. Merdrignac (eds.), *Bretons et Normands au Moyen Âge. Rivalités, malentendus, convergences*, 65–95, Rennes: Presses universitaires de Rennes.

Nelson, J. L. 1978. 'Queens as Jezebels: Brunhild and Balthild in Merovingian history', in D. Baker (ed.), *Medieval Women: Essays Dedicated and Presented to Professor Rosalind M. T. Hill*, 31–77, Ecclesiastical History Society, Studies in Church History, Subsidia 1, Oxford: B. Blackwell.

O'Hara, A. 2009. 'The Vita Columbani in Merovingian Gaul', *Early Medieval Europe*, **17**, 126–53.

Prinz, F. 1965. *Frühes Mönchtum im Frankenreich*, Kempten: Ferdinand Oechelhäuser.

Richter, M. 2008. *Bobbio in the Early Middle Ages. The Abiding Legacy of Columbanus*, Dublin: Four Courts Press.

Ridyard, S. 1988. *The Royal Saints of Anglo-Saxon England: A Study of West Saxon and East Anglian Cults*, Cambridge: Cambridge University Press.

Sims-Williams, P. 1990. *Religion and Literature in Western England, 600–800*, Cambridge: Cambridge University Press.

Stalley, R. 2005. 'Ecclesiastical architecture before 1169', in D. Ó Cróinín (ed.), *A New History of Ireland*, 1. *Prehistoric and Early Ireland*, 714–43, Oxford: Oxford University Press.

Stevenson, J. 1995. 'Irish hymns, Venantius Fortunatus and Poitiers', in J. M. Picard, *Aquitaine and Ireland in the Middle Ages*, 81–110, Black Rock: Four Courts Press.

Traube, L. 1900. '"Peronna Scottorum": ein Beitrag zur Überlieferungsgeschichte und zur Palaeographie des Mittelalters', *Sitzungsberichte der philos. philol. und histor. Klasse der k. bayer. Akademie der Wissenschaften*, 419–537.

Ugé, K. 2005. *Creating the Monastic Past in Medieval Flanders*, Woodbridge: York Medieval Press.

West, S. E., Scarfe, N. and Cramp, R. 1984. 'Iken, St. Botolf and the coming of East Anglian Christianity', *Proc. of the Suffolk Inst. of Arch. and Hist.*, **35**, 279–301.

Wood, I. N. 1982. 'The Vita Columbani and Merovingian hagiography', *Peritia*, **1**, 63–80.

Wood, I. N. 2011a. 'Monastères et ports dans l'Angleterre des VIIe–VIIIe siècles', in A. Gautier and C. Martin (eds.), Échanges, *communications et réseaux dans le haut Moyen* Âge, 89–100, Turnhout: Brepols.

Wood, I. N. 2011b. 'The Continental connections of Anglo-Saxon courts from Æthelberht to Offa', *Le relazione internazionali nell'alto medioevo*, 443–80, Settimane di Studio, 58, Spoleto: CISM.

Wood, I. N. 2013a. 'The Continental journeys of Wilfrid and Biscop', in N. J. Higham (ed.), *Wilfrid, Abbot, Bishop, Saint. Papers from the 1300th Anniversary Conferences*, 200–11, Donington: Shaun Tyas.

Wood, I. N. 2013b. 'Entrusting Western Europe to the Church, 400–750', *Trans. of the Royal Hist. Soc.*, **23**, 37–73.

Wood, I. N. 2014. 'Between Rome and Jarrow: papal relations with Francia and England, from 597–716', *Chiese locali e chiese regionali nell'alto medioevo*, Vol. 1, 297–320, Settimane di Studio, 61, Spoleto: CISM.

Wood, I. N. forthcoming. 'Columbanus, the Columbanian tradition and Caesarius'.

Wormald, P. 1976. 'Bede and Benedict Biscop', in G. Bonner (ed.), *Famulus Christi: Essays in Commemoration of the Thirteenth Centenary of the Birth of the Venerable Bede*, 141–69, London: SPCK. Reprinted in Wormald, P. 2006. *The Times of Bede: Studies in Early English Christian Society and its Historian*, 3–29, Oxford: Blackwell.

# Part II

## Re-conceptualizing early medieval monastic space: comparative archaeological approaches

Anglo-Saxon Studies in Archaeology and History 20, 2017

# New perspectives on monastic buildings and their uses

Rosemary Cramp

*Abstract*

*In 1973, a Forum discussed the problems of identifying and characterizing early medieval monastic sites in Britain. It was concluded that there were few distinctive features and no common plan, and this view has since been frequently endorsed. Nevertheless, the sampling by excavation of many more sites over the last forty years has improved the picture for ecclesiastical sites of the seventh to ninth centuries, particularly in the north and east of England, and in the sites with timber buildings. There are still major gaps in knowledge, as for example the lack of excavation of the reformed Benedictine monasteries of the tenth and eleventh centuries, a period when Continental evidence demonstrates substantial change and development in monastic plans.*

*For the earlier period, however, a probable pattern of layout has emerged, with zones of craft and domestic structures at the margins and large hall-like buildings laid out parallel to the churches and separated from them by an open space forming the liturgical heart of the complex. These communal buildings can, like those at Wearmouth and Jarrow, be as well constructed and as elaborately decorated as the churches themselves. There are, however, still problems in identifying the uses of the many smaller excavated structures.*

## Introduction and historiographical background

For more than forty years there has been discussion on what, if anything, distinguishes a monastic settlement from other ecclesiastical or lay settlements in the period from the seventh to the tenth centuries. In the limited scope of this paper, I will consider mainly the areas ruled by the Anglo-Saxons, and will review the more recent evidence for the buildings on such sites, discussing their relationships, form and apparent functions, but I have deliberately left aside sites which are the main subject of other papers.

Nevertheless, at the outset it is educative to recall earlier viewpoints. In 1973, the fifth Scottish Archaeological Forum convened in Edinburgh to discuss the problems posed by monastic settlements,[1] the major issue being that early monastic Rules defined what was expected of the behaviour of their monks, but not the form and disposition of the buildings, so how could one recognize a monastic site? As one of the few survivors from that group of archaeologists from Britain and Ireland, I thought it would be interesting to see what questions had been answered from the new evidence and new approaches which had appeared in the last forty plus years, and what, if any, of the ways forward we discussed then have been followed. I cannot, however, cover here all the issues raised, since we ranged more widely than the evidence for buildings. Topics covered were: identification and characterization; the interaction of the religious and lay worlds; trade, wealth, economy and industry; demographic implications; and new archaeological approaches.

Obviously the form of the buildings is influenced by the nature of the understanding of what constitutes the monastic ideal. The eremitical monastic life can be lived in caves, small structures of any indigenously available material, or indeed in parts of larger houses. A single monk needs only a living space to include perhaps areas for specific tasks, so working space with a focus for prayer, and a sleeping space (and this could all be in one structure), but there is also need of space for waste disposal, perhaps for some food production, and provision outside this private space for visitors. Such provision is well illustrated in the contemporary account of Cuthbert's hermitage on Farne,[2] and at the Forum by O'Kelly's excavation of Church Island.[3]

It was recognized then, as today, that once communal monastic life developed and communities were enlarged, stratified and divided by age, function, and relationship to the secular world, a more complex living system had to be provided and this had already taken many forms before reaching western Europe, with monasteries in the Syrian and Egyptian deserts as large as towns, justifying the term *monastic cities*.[4] In the coenobitical way of life, there had to be communal buildings for worship, eating, sleeping, sometimes duplicated for different parts of the community according to age, sex, and status within the monastic hierarchy, and in addition there had to be buildings to support the community: domestic, agrarian or craft. It was recognized in 1973 that although the building materials could be indigenous, there could also be a hierarchy of material used according to the perceived importance of the buildings; also recognized were differences in scale, and that there could develop formalization in their relationships. In 1973, there were, however, no large-scale excavations of pre-eleventh-century monastic sites in the west.

In all of these sites which continued in western Europe throughout the Middle Ages, the churches and their appendages have received the most intensive consideration and indeed, as often the only structures which survived above ground throughout the history of a site, have attracted the most attention both architectural and archaeological. I am not discussing them here any more than we did in Edinburgh, but it must be remembered that the churches and chapels are the pivotal foci for the daily life of monks and are the buildings which received the greatest elaboration. In fact, in considering monasteries in physical terms, despite the variety of forms, a major indicator seemed to be churches or chapels with cemeteries and other buildings laid out in an orderly way in relation to them. In 1973, we also considered indicators in the finds, such as evidence for literacy in inscriptions, writing implements and ink wells, and we even discussed the evidence provided by animal bones for separating lay and religious lifestyles; monastic sites such as, for example, Hartlepool and Jarrow being distinguished by food waste incorporating mainly riverine fish and shoreline shellfish, as well as fowl – duck and goose – which seemed to be especially large specimens. Also considered was the evidence for craft-working, in particular metalworking, and for trade and outside contacts. Philip Rahtz, in considering the monasteries as settlements, wanted to treat them like prehistoric sites, to use models and take out the Christian bias, to rely on modern scientific aids, and he saw the future need to increase the recovery of environmental evidence, and to excavate better.[5] Worthy aims!

Ralegh Radford, for so long the leading authority on British monastic sites, had to sum up, having heard a young Ian Burrow question whether his identification of Tintagel as a monastery could be sustained, or whether it was really a secular site (a conclusion now reached by more recent excavation).[6] Radford stressed the variations in the forms and how our overall view could be skewed by the fact that so many of the larger monastic settlements were under townscapes today. Despite the lack of support amongst the group for most suggested indicators of the monastic life, he did cling to the monastic ditch or *vallum* as a defining characteristic.[7] I will return to this point.

Since then there has been increasing scepticism as to whether one can distinguish high-status lay from rich ecclesiastical, let alone monastic, sites. In addition, Tim Pestell's conclusion that there are 'no obvious categories of artefacts that can be used to identify a site as purely "monastic" or "religious"' has been shared by others.[8] A useful summary and discussion of this problem are also to be found in John Blair's *The Church in Anglo-Saxon Society*.[9] Yet without some of these items and the continuing religious tradition, one would hesitate to pronounce a site monastic. Some items can be pointers, and have been used as identifiers, like for instance the evidence for vellum production at Portmahomack[10] or for the *monastic phase* at Flixborough,[11] or the ink wells and book mount at Brandon.[12] It has been claimed that minsters show notably rich assemblies of artefacts, but so far this evidence has not been compared comprehensively with elite secular sites, nor has the distinction between male, female and double monasteries been explored. It may be that the secular differences in dress between male and female carried on into the religious life, and so, as in furnished graves, many of the accoutrements which survive are female. Certainly this could explain the many personal possessions discovered at double monasteries such as Whitby, as contrasted with the simple iron buckles and knives found at Jarrow and Wearmouth.

As for distinctive buildings in the period before the tenth century in England, the consensus has been that a monastery cannot be defined by the form and position of its structures, since the wide variations in scale and wealth make any generalizations about their form and economy rather superficial, if not downright misleading.[13] So does this mean that I should stop now and decide we have not progressed much in understanding since the 1970s? I think we can be more hopeful than that if we survey the later scene.

There has been, after all, a considerable increase in the number of sites sampled. In considering the ninety or so seventh- to ninth-century monasteries known from contemporary texts or from aerial photographs, only ten had seen any significant excavation in 1973, and this included two not now considered monastic, namely Tintagel and Burgh Castle. Of later reformed monasteries only Canterbury, Glastonbury and Winchester had been examined by excavation (these were also the only such sites I considered in a general article in 1976).[14] Since then there has been more work at Canterbury, Glastonbury, Wearmouth, Jarrow and Whitby, whilst there have been new campaigns at Bardney, Barking, Beverley, Brandon, Eynsham, ?Flixborough, Glastonbury, Hartlepool, Hoddom, Lyminge, Portmahomack, Repton, Whithorn and Winchester (Fig. 1).

At once it is clear that there is an evidential bias to the north and east of the country for the earlier period. The major development overall, however, has been in better excavation and interpretation of timber buildings, but, even where there has been a quite extensive excavation, we have not the whole picture on any one site and in most places it is difficult to decide how the part excavated

**Fig. 1** Anglo-Saxon sites mentioned in the text, after Daniels 2007, fig. 10.2.

functions in relation to the whole, thus rendering it extremely difficult to compare sites like with like.

Some topographic features have been proposed as determining the choice of sites for monasteries, such as access to the sea, or enclosure in the loop of a river, as well as access to Roman roads, but it would seem that most of the communal monasteries, as opposed to the eremitical, are situated on good routes and near to centres of population. In the initial period, it is also clear that the foundations were sited on royal land, not communal land, where ownership could be expected to rotate, although Blair, in his seminal discussion on the topography of monasteries in 1992, did suggest deliberate reuse of Roman sites and enclosures for monasteries.[15] This has been verified in a limited way at sites like Abingdon, and Kentish sites such as Lyminge, and whilst, from documentation, we know female monasteries were founded in old Roman towns like Carlisle or Gloucester, there is

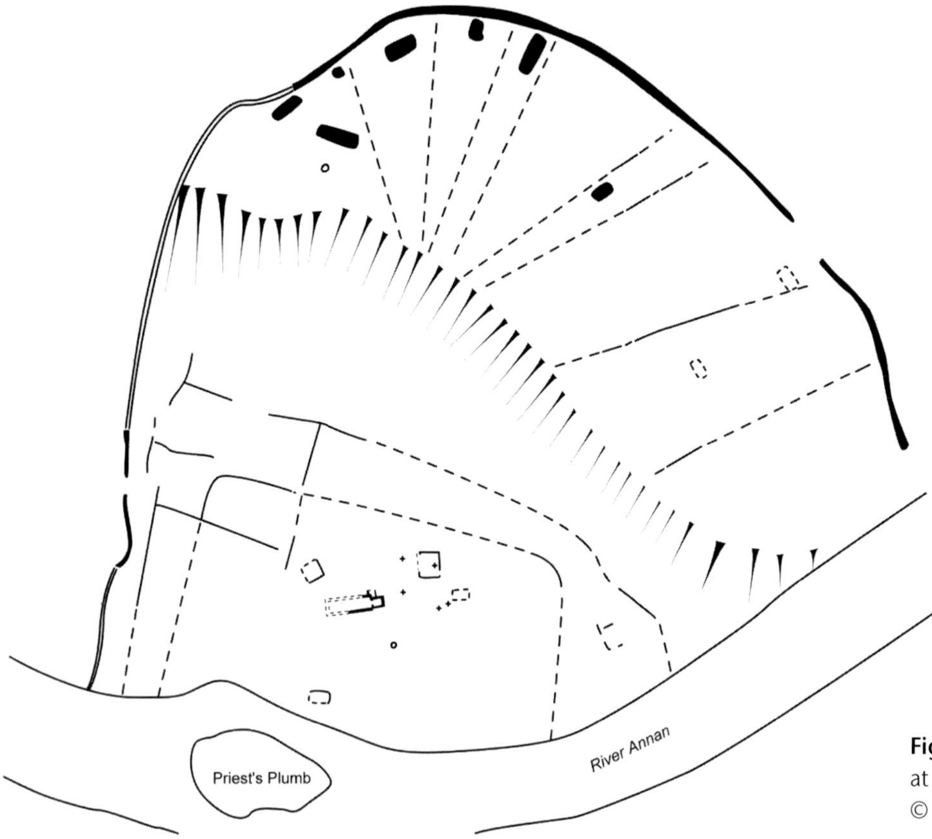


**Fig. 2a** General plan of the site at Hoddom, Dumfriesshire, © C. Lowe.

no evidence for continuity of site use. So far there is no evidence either for the reuse of Roman buildings such as we find in France at St Radegunde's monastery at Poitiers, or the monastery at Marmoutier which developed on the site of a Roman villa.[16] There is also no evidence for building on the same foundations, nor, as has been suggested for San Vincenzo al Volturno in Italy, that a Roman villa layout directly determined the first monastic layout.[17] This does not mean such sites did not exist in Britain, and certainly there is plenty of evidence for the reuse of Roman building materials in the Saxon structures – sometimes creatively as in the reuse of Roman *tegulae* for drains at Jarrow.[18] Nevertheless, although there could be Roman sites nearby, there is so far no evidence except in churches for the monastic reuse of Roman sites.

## Enclosures and boundaries

It is rare in England to find the sort of open site with a delimited enclosure as is more common in Ireland, so the outer boundaries of the sites are usually unknown. We know from literary sources that enclosures, which defined legally and spiritually the sacred space in which monastic life was promulgated, took many forms: high walls, earthworks and ditches, fences and hedges. Enclosure of some type does seem more important for monastic than secular sites in Anglo-Saxon England – at least for the pre-tenth century, although functional subdivisions in secular sites, such as West Heslerton (North Yorkshire), are known. Sometimes an enclosure surrounding a sector of a site can also be found on monastic foundations and this can be mistaken for the outer perimeter. Sometimes older ditches and earthworks have been mistaken for the monastic vallum, as at Brixworth.[19] Sometimes with spaced excavation, different features can be erroneously joined together, as the work of Roberta Gilchrist and her team has now revealed at Glastonbury.[20] Without large-scale excavation these problems will not be solved. Blair, in his work on topography, drew out a large number of enclosed sites which could be monastic; in all, however, there has been later settlement and only the church survives as the representative of the monastic complex, and there are other types of site which include a church and cemetery, for example Sprouston, which is so far unexcavated.[21]

There is, however, one open enclosed site which has been examined by modern excavation and survey: Hoddom, in the Anglo-Saxon-dominated area of southern Scotland, where air photography picked up a large enclosure, which was tested later by resistivity survey and limited excavation in 1991. An area of about 20 acres (8 ha) was enclosed by a ditch and this proved to have often been recut. It varied in width from just over 3 m to just under 1 m and in depth from 1.40 to 0.50 m. In parts, however, this enclosure was more complex and involved an earthen bank, a palisade and a ditch. Interestingly, this major enclosure was not focused on the well-known ruins of the early church and cemetery with a wealth of important stone crosses dating from the eighth to the eleventh centuries (Fig. 2a).[22] In the past, this complex of church and burials sited in the loop of a major river was seen as the monastic site and

THE EXCAVATED STRUCTURES

**Fig. 2b** Detail of buildings adjacent to the Hoddom enclosure, © C. Lowe.

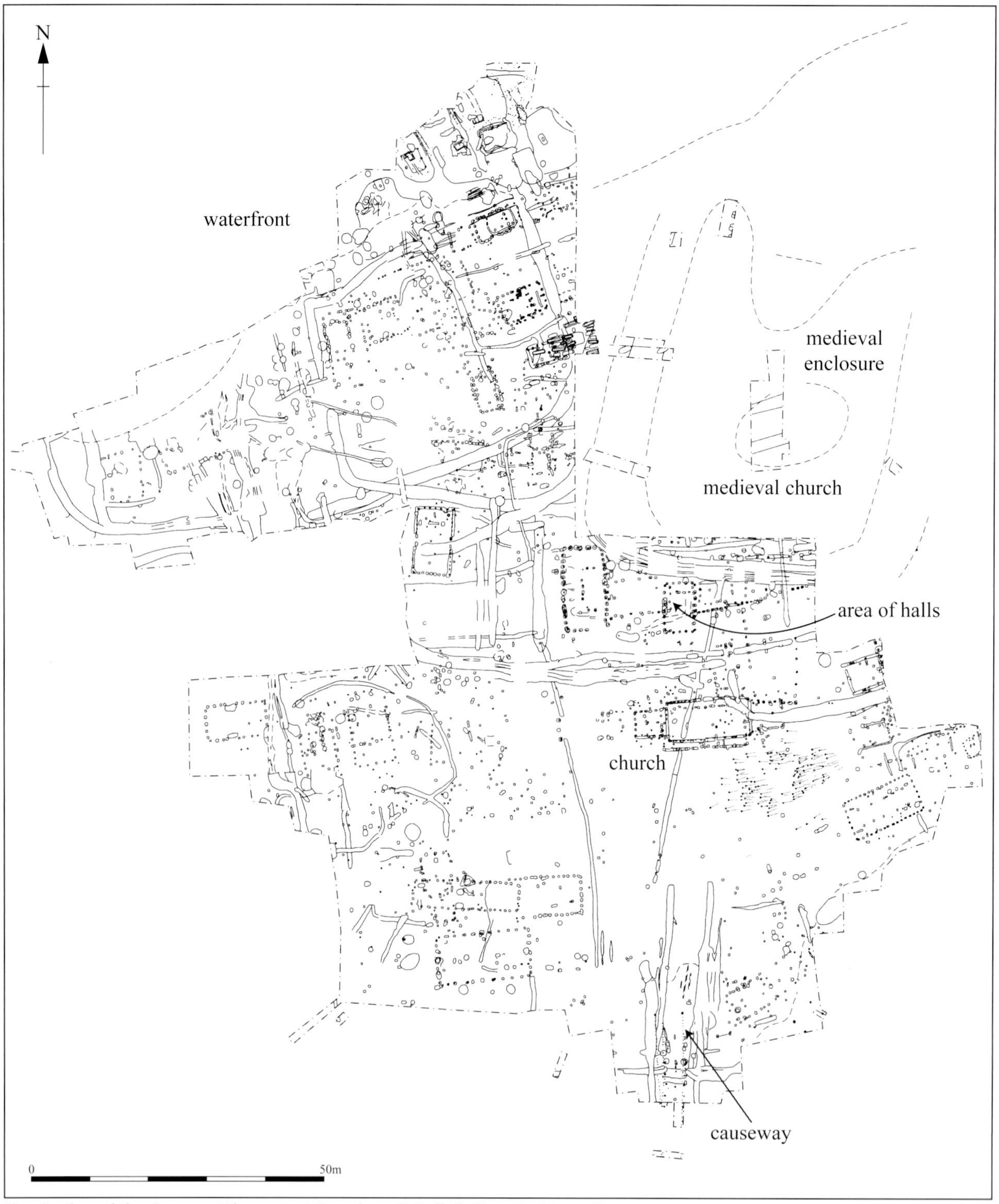


**Fig. 3** Plan of the Saxon settlement at Brandon, © Suffolk County Council.

indeed it may be the primary focus. There is a gap and inner enclosure between it and the enclosure which has more recently been identified and sampled by excavation. Indeed, it is a tragedy that the upper and the lower areas were not sampled and linked together in function and date before the destruction of so much of the site. The upper enclosure had a very planned use of space in which there is evidence for massive crop processing (Fig. 2b). Larger structures, identified as kiln barns, measured 20 × 5–6.1 m, 16.2 × 4.60–6.75 m and 15.2 × 6.0–6.6 m respectively,[23] and associated with them were small buildings interpreted as corn dryers.[24] The proliferation of these structures demonstrates the economic wealth of the site and the link with its supporting estates, just as the production of three great bibles which needed the skins of 1550 animals demonstrates this in another way at Wearmouth/Jarrow.[25]

It is often difficult to identify the functions of the timber buildings sometimes surrounded by their own

**Fig. 4** Aerial photograph of Jarrow with its southern boundary, showing marked out plans of the Saxon and medieval buildings, © R. Cramp.

enclosures as at Brandon (Fig. 3).[26] When the use is clear, as with kilns, hearths for domestic and craft activity or (as at Brandon) domestic ovens, they are often separated from the liturgical heart of monasteries. Dangers of fire and fumes from workshops, as well as the noise no doubt, located such buildings near to boundaries of monasteries. So a hearth for metalworking was found by the boundary ditch at Beverley,[27] and at Jarrow the workshops, with evidence for glass- and metalworking, were hidden by a slope near to the river and at some distance from the church. Fine metalworking and glassworking are often found at monastic sites in Ireland as well as at Jarrow, Brandon and Glastonbury, although sometimes not far distanced from the church,[28] but it is possible that some working sites may have been used on the occasion of specific periods of production and not continuously. This was indicated at Jarrow where the workshop floors were separated by layers of clean sand.[29]

The Hoddom site exemplifies a feature in the layout which may have been more widespread – namely that churches, with associated buildings, need not be central to the major enclosure. This is also demonstrated potentially in some enclosures cited by Blair and by the partial excavation of the Jarrow site.[30] At Jarrow (Fig. 4) it seems that the cult buildings clustered at one end of the site, like Hoddom in the loop of a river, and it is probable that other buildings – domestic, craft or industrial, as well as agricultural – extended to the north up to the

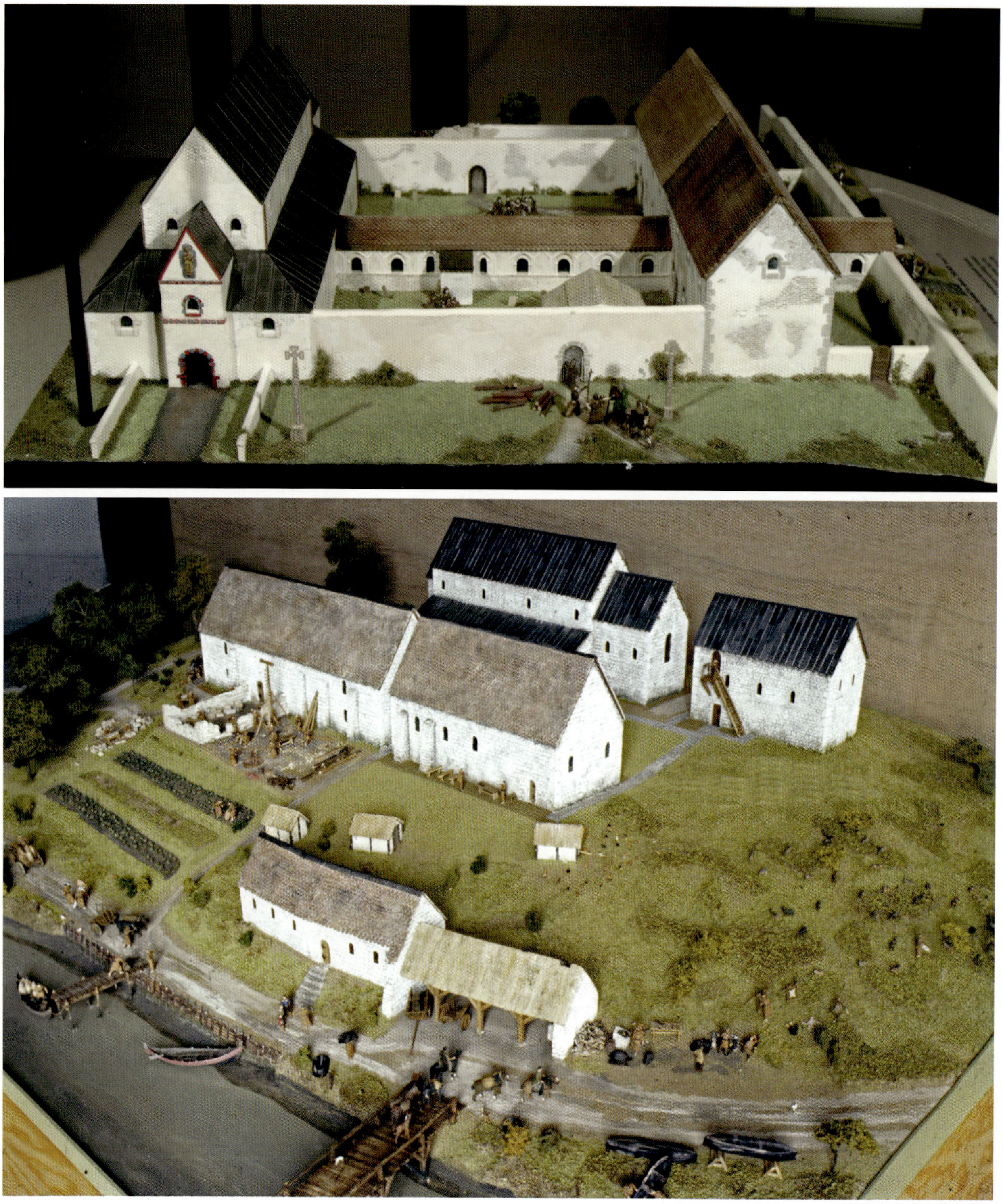

**Fig. 5** Models of the Anglo-Saxon buildings in the area excavated south of the churches of (a) Wearmouth and (b) Jarrow, © R. Cramp.

Tyne, with the tributary as initially the southern boundary. Bede's cell was shown by the monks in the Middle Ages to the north of the church and many small buildings were noted in that area as late as the eighteenth century. None of these structures, however, need have been part of the Anglo-Saxon monastery, and it should be noted that so far attempts to locate them have been unsuccessful,[31] although there must be buildings to complement the large excavated structures.

On all sites it is important to try to work out where entrances to the different functioning parts of the site could have been. At Jarrow (Fig. 5) the most open access is by sea to the north or north-east, whilst on the south the river is tidal, but there is a land route here, with a causeway leading from

**Fig. 6** Imported pottery, possibly eastern Mediterranean, from the 'guest house' at Jarrow, © R. Cramp.

the marshes to a path running up the east side of the church by the lay burial ground. Some access to lay burial grounds and to churches within the enclosures might be expected for the laity and in the seventh and eighth centuries a western entrance for churches is the most common, so that is another potential point of access. A speculative attempt has been made in relation to the double monastery at Hartlepool to define spaces with different access, such as the male and female cemeteries at the core and the craft area for working stone and metal, and the guest house by the boundary, with an entrance to the outer zone, but the evidence is very vestigial.[32] Documentary evidence does, however, support the common sense suggestion that hospices were on the periphery of sites with access to major routes. Cuthbert, when the guest master at Ripon, went out to the hospice *de interioribus monasterii aedibus* and found an angelic visitor, so went back into the interior to see if the bakers had finished their daily stint of bread. The building does not seem to have been very well furnished since he also went to fetch a table, but clearly guest houses could have varied in importance.[33] As opposed to passing travellers, distinguished guests could have expected something more luxurious. Bede quoted with approval of the Lindisfarne community that 'They had no need to provide a dwelling (*domus*), for the reception of powerful seculars'.[34] Building D, sited alongside the river at Jarrow, has been interpreted as a guest house and probably for privileged visitors; it was one of the most highly decorated houses on the site with painted walls, multicoloured glass windows, and included in the debris of the floor, parts of glass vessels and exotic foreign pottery beakers (Fig. 6).[35] It was the only building with evidence for meat-eating. By the ninth century, however, it had turned into a workshop, and this is a salutary reminder that then, as now, buildings could change their use through time.[36] Buildings could also go out of use altogether.

## Internal use of space

Once an outer enclosure has been laid out in any monastic site, then there is inevitably pressure on space, and several sites have shown destruction and rebuilding on the same space, for example Whitby, Brandon and Hartlepool. How space was divided up inside an enclosure could have varied according to topography or local traditions as well as the Rule of life adopted by the communities. There would have been some space which could be defined as public, where interactions with the lay world took place, and this could have included a school or guest house as well as craft and agricultural buildings, then there were communal buildings for the use of the community, for liturgical use,

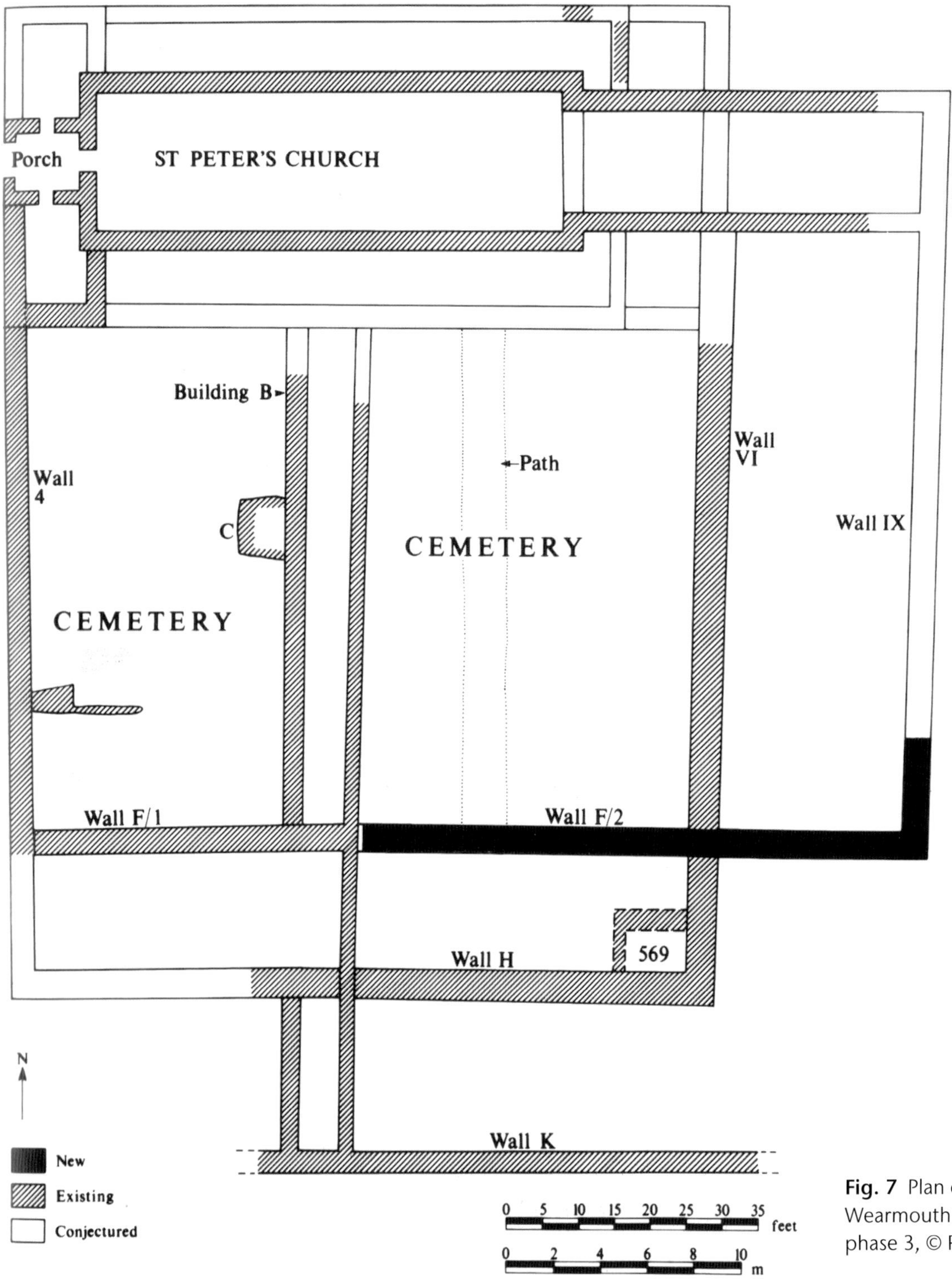


**Fig. 7** Plan of Wearmouth Anglo-Saxon phase 3, © R. Cramp.

for meeting, eating and sleeping, and finally private, with rooms or separate cells for individual use. These spatial zones could have been in concentric circles or segments of a circle, as recorded in some eighth-century Irish Canons, where three zones, *Holy, Holier and Most Holy*, are suggested for ecclesiastical sites.[37] But sites could also have been laid out in linear blocks or within rectangular enclosures, as seems to be the norm in Anglo-Saxon England.

As on the Continent, many sites had several churches and this could be for functional as well as liturgical reasons, so there could be funerary churches, alongside those for more congregational use or, in a double monastery, division by gender. There are also structures within cemeteries which, it has been suggested, are chapels for holding corpses before burial. There also needed to be circulating space around churches and cemeteries for stational processions, and in several excavated sites there seem to be open spaces which serve as foci, as in the Brandon phase 2.1 plan or at Wearmouth (Fig. 7) where an open space with some burials south of the church had surviving patches of

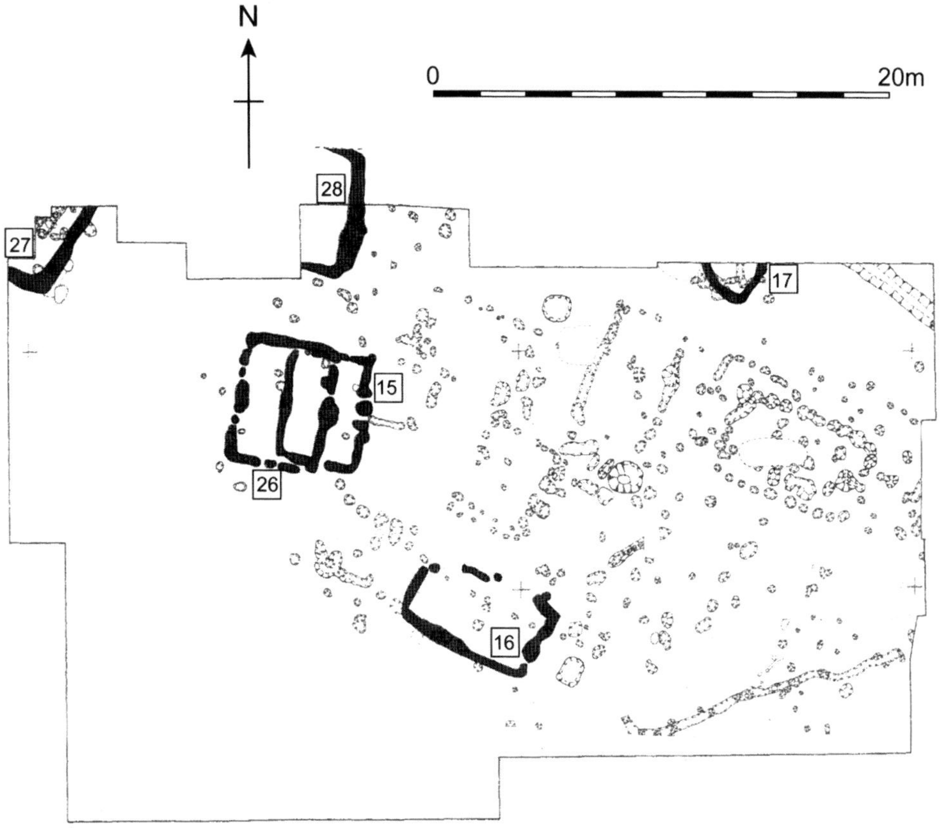


**Fig. 8a** Hartlepool phase 2 buildings, © R. Daniels.

cobbled pathways. At Wearmouth also there is a corridor which crosses the open space between the church and a range of large buildings to the south, and this seems to constitute a division in the burial ground with lay burials to the west and monastic to the east.[38] This assignment of significant space to the community of the dead and a cemetery position between church and monastic buildings seems a clear feature in Britain and Ireland, and its open space is perhaps a pointer towards claustral development as discussed below.

Now what of the dwellings of the living? The old idea that there was a division between monasteries where monks lived individually in cells, or communally as demanded by the Benedictine Rule, is not so far substantiated in England by archaeology, although literary texts indicate that there could have been sites where individual cells surrounded an enclosure, as has been discovered in France for instance at Marmoutier or Angoulême, with its double rooms and a walkway.[39]

A rather dubious documentary source describes a situation in Abingdon's first monastery as surrounded by a wall and within its circuit twelve *habitaculi* with chapels attached and in these buildings the monks ate, drank and slept. They did not have a cloister but for them the high wall was a cloister.[40] Small buildings which could be called *cells* are referred to in contemporary texts, but they seem to exist alongside communal buildings. At Lindisfarne there was a common dormitory in what was in origin an Irish site, whilst alongside the communal buildings at Wearmouth and Jarrow there were also private cells for senior monks. But Bede's description of Coldingham counsels caution as to determining the functions of the small buildings which have been excavated at sites such as Whitby, Hartlepool or Brandon as discussed below. Adamnan, on approaching the double monastery of Coldingham, first perceived the lofty buildings of the monastery, and later prophesied that both public and private buildings would be burnt down. He visited the cells (*singulorum casas*) and beds of the community, but also noted that the little buildings (*domunculae*) built for prayer and reading were being used for eating, drinking, gossip and worse.[41] So there could be two types of small monastic buildings – one as a cell for living, and one for occasional and varied use. The difficulty archaeologically is to identify which is which. These types of buildings were first defined in the 1920s' excavations at Whitby, where stone-footed buildings were divided into two rooms, some with hearths, but others with evidence for craft work.[42]

Robin Daniels' careful re-analysis of the Hartlepool houses has put these in a better context. Beginning in the late seventh century there are small timber buildings, rebuilt on the same site, with changes in architectural style from spaced posts, post in trench to stone footed (Fig. 8a). This last type, set on stone cills, is coin dated to post-AD 700 (coin 735–58). There is variation in size, but they average 4.4 × 2.7 m. Despite the clay moulds and stone and metal waste discovered in the adjacent ditch, the excavator considers, because of the cleanliness of the floors, that they were cells for living, not craft workshops. Certainly when reconstructed (Fig. 8a–b) they are

**Fig. 8b** Reconstruction of Hartlepool building 26 at Bede's World, Jarrow, © R. Daniels.

surprisingly spacious, but there is no hearth, and no indication of division, as with some at Whitby, where similar buildings have a typical measurement of *c.* 5.5 × 3.4 m. There remains a difficulty of judging the functions of these small buildings, here and at sites such as Brandon. I consider that some could be cells for living and working, but others could well be buildings set aside for a variety of uses: for occasional private use and prayer, or for 'clean' craft work such as weaving, sewing or writing, and indeed they need not have been used solely for one type of work.[43]

The nearest parallel to the type of building recorded for Abingdon, with a living space and prayer space, is the small room attached to the east end of Jarrow Building B, which is one of two large buildings set end to end south of the cemetery and parallel with the churches. The main building measures 18.52 × 7.93 m externally and the adjunct 3.35 × 6.40 m. It had a separate entrance and in the south room a stone bench, a partially paved floor and a drain in one corner (Fig. 9). It was apparently divided by a screen from a smaller room to the north with an *opus signinum* floor inset with a stone altar base against the east wall and there is evidence for a window with coloured glass above.[44]

The slight division between the two rooms, interpreted as a low screen, fits the type of building described in the account of Bede's death since, when dying as he lay on the floor of his cell, he asked that he should be lifted up so that he could see the place where he was accustomed to pray. This private space attached to one end of a large communal building is not to be seen as Bede's cell; it could have been for the abbot or another senior monk. But the whole complex of a large building with a private suite at one end is interestingly like the plans of some elite secular *halls* such as at the royal site of Yeavering.[45]

This likeness of the mortared stone buildings A and B at Jarrow to secular halls in timber was remarked on when they were first excavated. It is clear from literary sources not only that kings and aristocrats founded monasteries in the seventh/eighth centuries in which the abbots were of their own status, but also that they used them for visitations, councils or to house their relations or attendants.[46] This link between the aristocratic lay families and the monastic *familia* with the *abba* (father) at its head was then unsurprisingly reflected in the likeness of the main buildings on their sites. The importance of such buildings for assembly and interaction for both groups meant that they were dominant and grandly constructed and there is a tendency to build and rebuild on the same spot, sometimes with architectural change. Secular halls were symbols of companionship, and the interaction of a close

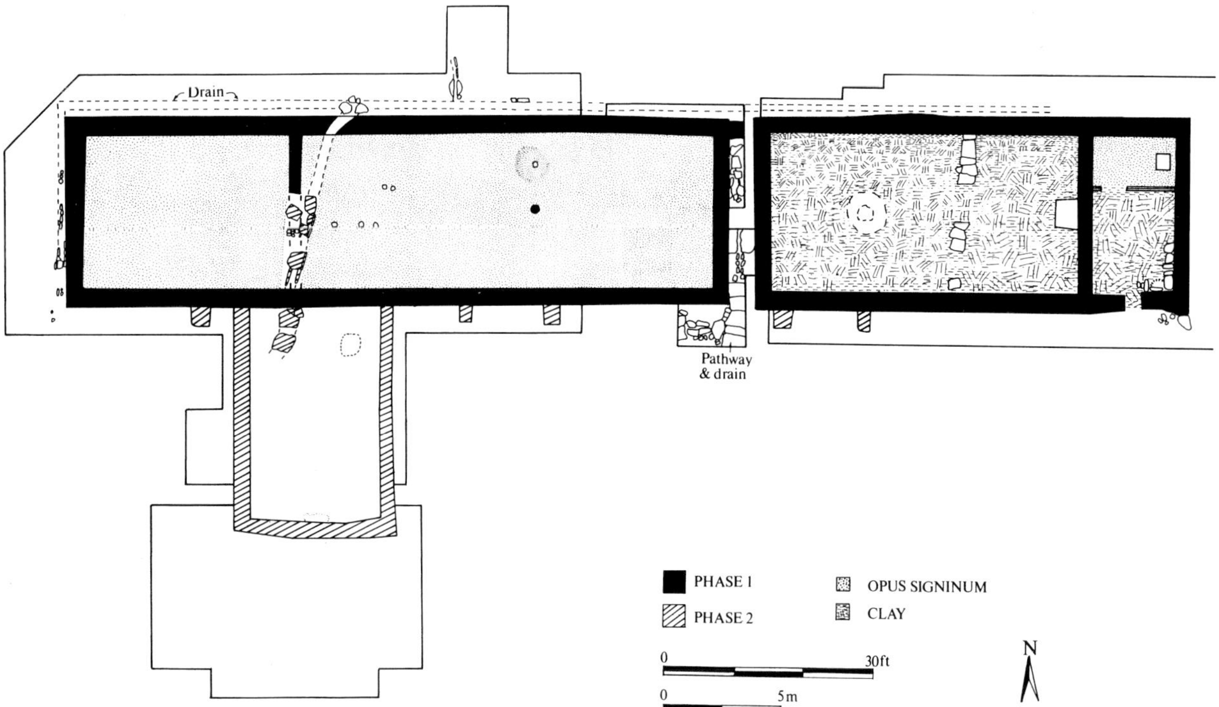


**Fig. 9** Outline plan of Buildings A (refectory) and B (hall) from the Jarrow excavations, © R.Cramp.

group, as well as, after the acceptance of Christianity, a foretaste of the happiness of the heavenly banquet.[47]

The essential need of a few large buildings is reflected on Insular and Continental sites. I have previously compared these Jarrow buildings with monastic buildings described in Irish sources as the *tech mor and proindtech*,[48] but similarly in the seventh to ninth centuries at Continental sites there can be two large buildings near to the church.[49]

If one compares the large hall-like buildings on early medieval sites with the main buildings in a later Benedictine foundation they may be differently disposed, but essentially they are the same: the churches dominate, with an open space between them and a refectory to the south and at a right angle a chapter house with dormitory above and at one end the abbot's lodging. The buildings at Wearmouth and Jarrow are constructed on the same model, but at the earlier monastery at Wearmouth, built in 674 by Gallic masons, the two buildings were not separated but joined in a range in a more *Roman manner* (Fig. 9). So far these are unique in Anglo-Saxon archaeology in that they have been fully excavated down to their existing floor levels and they show the same high quality of decoration as churches in their *opus signinum* flooring, windows with coloured window glass and sculptural decoration.

Building B could be seen as the multipurpose hall, the big house, the chapter house, and it had evidence for its use for assembly with possible benches along the south wall and the setting for a raised seat at the east end, and evidence for writing with a stylus and whetstone.[50]

Building A could be seen as a refectory, elite feasting hall, opposite the church, not as large and grand as some described on the Continent, but with stone plaques and a column carved with plant scrolls which echoes the sculptural decoration of the church. There are no hearths in either building, but a possible place for a brazier in Building A.[51] That building was also subdivided, which may indicate a hierarchy in the seating plan or that the west end was used as a servery. In a subsequent phase, the building was adapted with cruder workmanship by taking away a dividing wall and adding what has tentatively been interpreted as a kitchen. The development of cooking arrangements between the seventh and the ninth centuries is a whole subject in itself, which needs further study. Here there is some evidence for outside hearths to the west, but nothing like the Roman-derived ovens with multiple flues of San Vincenzo or the St Gall plan.[52]

The decline of this site, as others like Brandon, in the ninth century is where the evidence for Anglo-Saxon monasteries diverges from the Continent, where by the Carolingian period there is lavish development of monastic sites and their buildings such as is described elsewhere in this volume. This is especially relevant in considering what is the signifier of monastic life *par excellence* – the cloister with its walks. There is a substantial literature on the origin and development of the cloister in western Europe,[53] and even in the early Anglo-Saxon sites discussed above one can note the significance of open areas between buildings which acted both as barriers and as recreational space. The proto-claustral gallery at Wearmouth possibly had its origin in Roman corridor villas and there is a parallel in the much more elaborate processional corridor which links the churches to other monastic buildings at San Vincenzo al Volturno, but sites such as Chelles, Landevennec or Lorsch all had a fully developed cloister by the mid-ninth century. This is the period in England when so many monastic sites were lost or laicized in the Viking age's wars and settlements, but by the tenth century, with the general acceptance in southern England of the Benedictine Rule, textual evidence suggests that the cloister was an essential part of the monastic building plan.[54] Certainly in the *Regularis Concordia* it is implied that a cloister was a normal part of the monastic layout,[55] but the archaeological evidence is almost non-existent. A re-evaluation of the evidence for a cloister at Glastonbury concludes that there was evidence for free-standing buildings around a central space, but not a developed cloister,[56] at Eynsham a cloister is inferred to the north of some free-standing structures, but is not established,[57] and Potts' findings at Canterbury are open to question.[58] This leaves the small section at Winchester of what has been identified as part of the infirmary cloister.[59] There is an obvious need to excavate one of the reformed houses of Wessex or East Anglia.

## Conclusion

So in summary, new excavation and re-evaluation of earlier interventions have provided a more coherent picture of the large and small structures on ecclesiastical sites, although it has not proved easy to identify their functions and changing use. Some distinctive characterization of building types has emerged, but the interaction of the lay and ecclesiastical worlds is clearly apparent. Clean sites with a regimented and orderly layout of the core buildings can be found on both elite lay and monastic sites, and it has been postulated for example at Flixborough that there can be changing lifestyles, lay to ecclesiastical or vice versa, on the same site, although in this case the buildings excavated are most probably marginal to the whole site and deductions are based on the rich refuse deposits from other unknown buildings.[60] The buildings, grouped spatially as public, communal and private, are better represented in their various forms on our sites than they were in 1973, and there seems an order and purpose behind this, and a gradual movement towards the functional zones in the idealized plan of St Gall.

Of course, there were many contexts in which the *monastic life* was lived, and some may have been nothing but a scruffy enclosure intruded into a secular site. But we should not underestimate the aspirational aspect of many of the buildings on these sites; they could imitate the grandest of secular buildings with changing architectural styles in wood and additionally in stone, and they could also serve as a reminder of a wider world, from Rome to Jerusalem, a world both real and imagined. Alcuin, writing to the monks of Wearmouth/Jarrow in the late eighth century, exhorted them in his schoolmasterly way: 'Look to the treasures of your library, the beauty of your churches and the fineness of your buildings, the order of the religious life. Think how happy is the man who goes from these fine buildings to the joys of the kingdom of heaven.'[61]

## Acknowledgements

I am very grateful to Belinda Burke and Derek Craig for their help with the preparation of this text for publication, and to Jeff Veitch for help with the illustrations.

I am also very grateful to Robin Daniels, Christopher Lowe and Andrew Tester for permission to reproduce illustrations from their site reports.

## Notes

1 *Scottish Archaeological Forum*, **5**, 3 March 1973 (published 1974).
2 Colgrave 1940, 216–17; Cramp 1981.
3 O'Kelly 1974.
4 Chitty 1966.
5 Rahtz 1974.
6 Burrow 1974; Barrowman, Batey and Morris 2007.
7 Radford 1974.
8 Pestell 2004, 46–8.
9 Blair 2005, 206–12.
10 Carver 2008, 120–6; Carver and Spall 2004.
11 Loveluck and Atkinson 2007, 52–81; Evans and Loveluck 2009, 125–37; Loveluck 2007, 8–30. Here Pestell also comments on the lay use of styli.
12 Tester, Anderson, Riddler and Carr 2014, 256–60.
13 Hines 1997.
14 Cramp 1976; 2008, ill. 1.
15 Blair 1992, 235–7.
16 Sapin 2008, 97, fig. 3; Lorans 2012.
17 Hodges and Mitchell 1996, 22–3.
18 Cramp 2005, 197, fig. 16.17.
19 Parsons and Sutherland, with Cramp, Gem, Barnwell and Hall 2013, 143, 276–7.
20 Gilchrist and Green 2015, 124, fig. 5.1.
21 St Joseph 1982; Smith 1991.
22 Lowe 2006, 7–8; Craig 1992, Vol. 2, 128–267.
23 Lowe 2006, 102, table 4.8, figs. 4.16, 4.17.
24 *Ibid.*, figs. 4.32–4.34.
25 Bruce-Mitford 1969, 2.
26 Tester *et al.* 2014, figs. 2.2, 4.1, 12.1, 12.2.
27 Armstrong, Tomlinson and Evans 1991, 246–7.
28 Cramp 2005, 219–41; Ryan 1988; Gilchrist and Green 2015, 131–43, figs. 16.4, 16.5, 22.5.
29 Cramp 2005, fig. 16.87.
30 Blair 1992, fig. 10.2.
31 Turner, Semple and Turner 2013, 121–38.
32 Daniels 2007, fig. 8.12.
33 Colgrave 1940, 78–9.
34 Bede, *Historia ecclesiastica* III.xxvi, Colgrave and Mynors 1969, 310–11.
35 Cramp 2006, 332–5.
36 Cramp 2005, 219–30.
37 Herity 1995; Picard 2008, 70.
38 Cramp 2005, 111–12, fig. 9.33.
39 Lorans 2012; Sapin 2008, 96, fig. 2.
40 Biddle, Lambrick and Myres 1968, 26–69; Cramp 1976, 215–17.
41 Bede, *Historia ecclesiastica* IV.xxv, Colgrave and Mynors 1969, 424–5.
42 Peers and Radford 1943.
43 Daniels 2007, 69–71, fig. 3.2; Tester *et al.* 2014, fig. 12.1.

44 Cramp 2005, fig. 16.36.
45 Hope-Taylor 1977, figs. 59, 60.
46 Foot 2006, 172–85, 326–31.
47 The description of earthly life as given by one of Edwin's counsellors in Bede: *Historia ecclesiastica* II.xiii, Colgrave and Mynors 1969, 182–5, reflected this, and in *The Dream of the Rood* 140–1, Dickens and Ross 1951, the *saved* are seated at a heavenly banquet, and see Cramp 1993.
48 'the great house and the eating house'; Cramp 1986, 196–8.
49 Sapin 2008, 94–5; Zettler 2008, 269, fig. 2; Cramp 2005, fig. 16.37.
50 Cramp 2005, 204–7, fig. 16.36.
51 Cramp 2005, fig. 16.35.
52 Horn and Born 1979, Vol. 2, 249–64; Sogliani 2008, 523–50, plan 1.
53 Horn 1973 and more up-to-date summaries in Lobbedey 2008 and Sapin 2008, 94–5.
54 Cramp 1976, 208.
55 *Regularis concordia*, Symons 1953, 26, 54, 56.
56 Gilchrist and Green 2015, 418–20, fig. 10.7.
57 Hardy, Dodd and Keevill 2003, 69–72.
58 Potts 1934.
59 Biddle 1972, 123, figs. 6, 7.
60 Loveluck 2007, 159–63.
61 Allott 1974, 39–40.

## Bibliography


Allott, S. (trans.) 1974. *Alcuin of York, c. A.D. 732 to 804 – His Life and Letters*, York: William Sessions.

Armstrong, P., Tomlinson, D. and Evans, D. H. 1991. *Excavations at Lurk Lane, Beverley, 1979–82*, Sheffield Excavation Reports, 1, Sheffield: J. R. Collis Publications.

Barrowman, R. C., Batey, C. E. and Morris, C. D. 2007. *Excavations at Tintagel Castle, Cornwall, 1990–1999*, Reports of the Research Committee of the Society of Antiquaries of London, 74, London: Society of Antiquaries.

Biddle, M. 1972. 'Excavations at Winchester 1970: ninth interim report', *Antiquaries Jnl*, **52**, 93–131.

Biddle, M., Lambrick, H. T. and Myres, J. N. L. 1968. 'The early history of Abingdon, Berkshire, and its abbey', *Medieval Arch.*, **12**, 26–69.

Blair, J. 1992. 'Anglo-Saxon minsters: a topographical review', in J. Blair and R. Sharpe (eds.), *Pastoral Care before the Parish*, 226–66, Leicester, London and New York: Leicester University Press.

Blair, J. 2005. *The Church in Anglo-Saxon Society*, Oxford: Oxford University Press.

Bruce-Mitford, R. L. S. 1969. 'The art of the Codex Amiatinus: Jarrow Lecture 1967', *Jnl British Arch. Assoc.*, 3rd series, **32**, 1–25.

Burrow, I. C. G. 1974. 'Tintagel – some problems', *Scottish Arch. Forum*, **5**, 99–103.

Carver, M. O. H. 2008. *Portmahomack: Monastery of the Picts*, Edinburgh: Edinburgh University Press.

Carver, M. O. H. and Spall, C. 2004. 'Excavating a *parchmenerie*: archaeological correlates of making parchment at the Pictish monastery of Portmahomack, Easter Ross', *Proc. of the Soc. of Antiquaries of Scotland*, **134**, 183–200.

Chitty, D. J. 1966. *The Desert a City: An Introduction to the Study of Egyptian and Palestinian Monasticism under the Christian Empire*, Oxford: Basil Blackwell.

Colgrave, B. (ed.) 1940. *Two Lives of Saint Cuthbert: A Life by an Anonymous Monk of Lindisfarne and Bede's Prose Life*, Cambridge: Cambridge University Press.

Colgrave, B. and Mynors, R. A. B. (eds.) 1969. *Bede's Ecclesiastical History of the English People*, OMT, Oxford: Clarendon Press.

Craig, D. J. 1992. 'The Distribution of Pre-Norman Sculpture in South-West Scotland', unpublished PhD thesis, University of Durham.

Cramp, R. 1976. 'Monastic sites', in D. M. Wilson (ed.), *The Archaeology of Anglo-Saxon England*, 201–52, London: Methuen.

Cramp, R. 1981. *The Hermitage and Offshore Island*, Second Paul Johnstone Memorial Lecture, Occasional Lecture, 3, London: National Maritime Museum.

Cramp, R. 1986. 'Northumbria and Ireland', in P. Szarmach with V. D. Oggins (eds.), *Sources of Anglo-Saxon Culture*, 185–201, Studies in Medieval Culture, 20, Kalamazoo: Medieval Institute Publications.

Cramp, R. 1993. 'The hall in Beowulf and in archaeology', in H. Damico and J. Leyerle (eds.), *Heroic Poetry in the Anglo-Saxon Period: Studies in honor of Jess B. Bessinger, Jr.*, 331–46, Studies in Medieval Culture, 32, Kalamazoo: Medieval Institute Publications.

Cramp, R. 2005. *Wearmouth and Jarrow Monastic Sites*, Vol. 1, Swindon: English Heritage.

Cramp, R. 2006. *Wearmouth and Jarrow Monastic Sites*, Vol. 2, Swindon: English Heritage.

Cramp, R. 2008. 'Monastic settlements in Britain in the 7th–11th centuries', in F. De Rubeis and F. Marazzi (eds.), *Monasteri in Europa occidentale (secoli VIII–XI): topografia e strutture*, Atti del Convegno Internazionale, Museo Archeologico di Castel San Vincenzo, 23–26 settembre 2004, 113–33, Rome: Viella.

Daniels, R. 2007. *Anglo-Saxon Hartlepool and the Foundations of English Christianity: An Archaeology of the Anglo-Saxon Monastery*, Tees Archaeology Monograph Series, 3, Hartlepool: Tees Archaeology.

Dickens, B. and Ross, A. S. C. (eds.) 1951. *The Dream of the Rood*, 2nd edit., London: Methuen.

Evans, D. H. and Loveluck, C. (eds.) 2009. *Life and Economy at Early Medieval Flixborough, c. AD 600–1000: The Artefact Evidence*, Excavations at Flixborough, 2, Oxford: Oxbow Books.

Foot, S. 2006. *Monastic Life in Anglo-Saxon England* c. *600–900*, Cambridge: Cambridge University Press.

Gilchrist, R. and Green, C. 2015. *Glastonbury Abbey: Archaeological Investigations 1904–79*, London: Society of Antiquaries.

Hardy, A., Dodd, A. and Keevill, G. D. 2003. *Ælfric's Abbey: Excavations at Eynsham Abbey, Oxfordshire, 1989–92*, Thames Valley Landscapes Monograph, 15, Oxford: Oxford Archaeological Unit.

Herity, M. 1995. *Studies in the Layout, Buildings and Art in Stone of Early Irish Monasteries*, London: Pindar Press.

Hines, J. 1997. 'Religion: the limits of knowledge', in J. Hines (ed.), *The Anglo-Saxons from the Migration Period to the Eighth Century: An Ethnographic Perspective*, 375–401, Studies in Historical Archaeoethnology, 2, Woodbridge: Boydell Press.

Hodges, R. and Mitchell, J. 1996. *The Basilica of Abbot Joshua at San Vincenzo al Volturno*, Miscellanea vulturnense, 2, Cassino: Abbazia di Montecassino.

Hope-Taylor, B. 1977. *Yeavering: An Anglo-British Centre of Early Northumbria*, Department of the Environment Archaeological Report, 7, London: HMSO.

Horn, W. 1973. 'On the origins of the medieval cloister', *Gesta*, **12(1/2)**, 13–52.

Horn, W. and Born, E. 1979. *The Plan of St Gall: A Study of the Architecture and Economy of, and Life in, a Paradigmatic Carolingian Monastery*, 3 vols., Berkeley, Los Angeles and London: University of California Press.

Lobbedey, U. 2008. 'Klosterbau im deutschen Reich vom frühen Mittelalter bis zur Zeit der Ottonen', in F. De Rubeis and F. Marazzi (eds.), *Monasteri in Europa occidentale (secoli VIII–XI): topografia e strutture*, Atti del Convegno Internazionale, Museo Archeologico di Castel San Vincenzo, 23–26 settembre 2004, 103–11, Rome: Viella.

Lorans, É. 2012. 'Aux origines du monastère de Marmoutier: le témoignage de l'archéologie', in B. Judic (ed.), *Les Abbayes Martiniennes*, 178–203, Annales de Bretagne et des Pays de l'Ouest, 119, no. 3, Rennes: Presses Universitaires de Rennes.

Loveluck, C. 2007. *Rural Settlement, Lifestyles and Social Change in the Later First Millennium AD: Anglo-Saxon Flixborough in its Wider Context*, Excavations at Flixborough, 4, Oxford: Oxbow Books.

Loveluck, C. and Atkinson, D. 2007. *The Early Medieval Settlement*

*Remains at Flixborough, Lincolnshire: The Occupation Sequence, c. AD 600–1000*, Excavations at Flixborough, 1, Oxford: Oxbow Books.

Lowe, C. E. 2006. *Excavations at Hoddom, Dumfriesshire: An Early Ecclesiastical Site in South-West Scotland*, Edinburgh: Society of Antiquaries of Scotland.

O'Kelly, M. J. 1974. 'Monastic sites in the west of Ireland', *Scottish Arch. Forum*, **5**, 1–16.

Parsons, D. and Sutherland, D. S., with Cramp, R., Gem, R., Barnwell, P. S. and Hall, D. 2013. *The Anglo-Saxon Church of All Saints, Brixworth, Northamptonshire: Survey, Excavation and Analysis 1972–2010*, Brixworth Archaeological Research Committee, Oxford: Oxbow Books.

Peers, C. R. and Radford, C. A. R. 1943. 'The Saxon monastery of Whitby', *Archaeologia*, **89**, 27–88.

Pestell, T. 2004. *Landscapes of Monastic Foundation: The Establishment of Religious Houses in East Anglia, c.650–1200*, Woodbridge: Boydell Press.

Picard, J.-M. 2008. '*In platea monasterii*: the layout of ecclesiastical settlements in early medieval Ireland (7th–9th C.)', in F. De Rubeis and F. Marazzi (eds.), *Monasteri in Europa occidentale (secoli VIII–XI): topografia e strutture*, Atti del Convegno Internazionale, Museo Archeologico di Castel San Vincenzo, 23–26 settembre 2004, 67–82, Rome: Viella.

Potts, R. U. 1934. 'The plan of St Austin's abbey, Canterbury', *Arch. Cantiana*, **46**, 179–94.

Radford, C. A. R. 1974. 'Summary and discussion', *Scottish Arch. Forum*, **5**, 136–40.

Rahtz, P. 1974. 'Monasteries as settlements', *Scottish Arch. Forum*, **5**, 125–35.

Ryan, M. 1988. 'Fine metalworking and early Irish monasteries: the archaeological evidence', in J. Bradley (ed.), *Settlement and Society in Medieval Ireland: Studies presented to F. X. Martin, o.s.g.*, 33–48, Kilkenny: Boethius.

St Joseph, J. K. S. 1982. 'Sprouston, Roxburghshire: an Anglo-Saxon settlement discovered by air reconnaissance', *Anglo-Saxon England*, **10**, 191–9.

Sapin, C. 2008. 'L'archéologie des premiers monastères en France (Ve–déb. XIe s.), un état des recherches', in F. De Rubeis and F. Marazzi (eds.), *Monasteri in Europa occidentale (secoli VIII–XI): topografia e strutture*, Atti del Convegno Internazionale, Museo Archeologico di Castel San Vincenzo, 23–26 settembre 2004, 83–102, Rome: Viella.

Smith, I. M. 1991. 'Sprouston, Roxburghshire: an early Anglian centre of the eastern Tweed Basin', *Proc. of the Soc. of Antiquaries of Scotland*, **121**, 261–94.

Sogliani, F. 2008. 'Proposte di ricostruzione dell'arredo di alcuni ambienti monastici fra IX e XI secolo sulla base dei nuovi risultati di scavo nel monastero volturnense' in F. De Rubeis and F. Marazzi (eds.), *Monasteri in Europa occidentale (secoli VIII–XI): topografia e strutture*, Atti del Convegno Internazionale, Museo Archeologico di Castel San Vincenzo, 23–26 settembre 2004, 523–50, Rome: Viella.

Symons, T. (trans.) 1953. *Regularis Concordia Anglicae Nationis Monachorum Sanctimonialiumque; The Monastic Agreement of the Monks and Nuns of the English Nation*, London: Nelson.

Tester, A., Anderson, S., Riddler, I. and Carr, R. 2014. *Staunch Meadow, Brandon, Suffolk: A High Status Middle Saxon Settlement on the Fen Edge*, East Anglian Archaeology, 151, Bury St Edmunds: Suffolk County Council Archaeology Service.

Turner, S., Semple, S. and Turner, A. 2013. *Wearmouth and Jarrow: Northumbrian Monasteries in an Historic Landscape*, Hatfield: University of Hertfordshire Press.

Zettler, A. 2008. 'Public, collective and communal spaces in early medieval monasteries: San Vincenzo and the Plan of Saint Gall', in F. De Rubeis and F. Marazzi (eds.), *Monasteri in Europa occidentale (secoli VIII–XI): topografia e strutture*, Atti del Convegno Internazionale, Museo Archeologico di Castel San Vincenzo, 23–26 settembre 2004, 259–73, Rome: Viella.

# Places and spaces: reflections on reconstructing the spatial organization of Northumbrian monasteries

David Petts

*Abstract*
*Anglo-Saxon monastic sites were complex places combining religious and economic functions. They were locations where many different communities, secular and ecclesiastical, high and low status, confronted and engaged with each other. They were also caught in a web of local and long-distance religious, political and economic relationships. This paper explores some of the practical and methodological issues involved in identifying the spatial organization of these sites, both at an inter- and intra-site scale. The practical limitations in reconstructing internal organization and chronological development will be considered.*

## Introduction

There are few parts of Britain that have such a corpus of well-excavated early medieval monastic sites as the region between the Humber and the Forth–Clyde line, an area we might term greater Northumbria. Ecclesiastical sites which have seen significant archaeological excavation include Ardwall Island, Auldhame, Dacre, Hartlepool, Hoddom, Inchmarnock, Isle of May, Jarrow, Kirkdale, Monkwearmouth, Ripon, Whitby and Whithorn, in addition to new projects in progress at Aberlady, Coldingham, Old Melrose and Lindisfarne.[1] This body of research certainly provides a solid basis on which to discuss the spatial arrangement of Northumbrian monastic sites. However, this paper attempts to take a step back and explore how far, despite this substantial corpus of excavation evidence, we are really able to understand these sites.

Figure 1 is a fairly coarse-grained exercise in mapping the distribution of sites that have a claim to be pre-Viking ecclesiastical sites in Northumbria – in total numbering 168 sites. This includes sites with early sculpture, early structural evidence, archaeological excavation or that are mentioned in the works of Bede and the *Life* of St Wilfrid. It does not include potential ecclesiastical place-names (such as *eccles* or *stow*), nor does it attempt to map potentially early dedications. Even without these two more problematic sources of evidence, it provides a good sense of the spatial extent of the early church across the region, although it is certainly possible to debate the inclusion or non-inclusion of specific, individual sites. This impressive spread of sites, whilst not as dense as the distribution of churches in some other parts of the country, is a reminder of the extent of the resource we need to consider when trying to characterize the extent and organization of the early medieval Northumbrian church. Although Northumbria may be well served with excavated sites, this map reminds us that these excavated sites are both only a tiny proportion of the overall number of sites identifiable and geographically unevenly spread. The range of sites which have been excavated is selectively biased towards more famous and more important monastic sites for a variety of reasons owing to both research bias and the

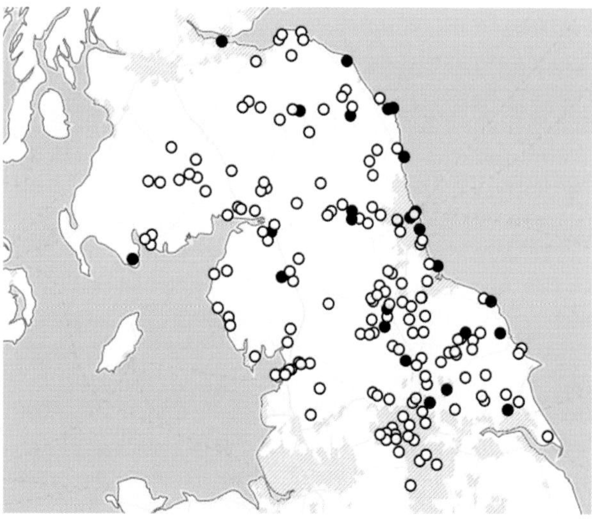

**Fig. 1** Distribution of probable pre-Viking ecclesiastical sites in Northumberland. Black dots are sites mentioned in the works of Bede; open dots are sites not mentioned in the works of Bede. Created using CartoDB.

subsequent historic development of these sites. Whereas only twenty-five out of a total of 168 sites plotted were mentioned by Bede (fourteen per cent), ten of the seventeen excavated sites mentioned in the introduction to this paper appeared in the works of Bede (fifty-eight per cent).

## Identifying sites

The first and most basic question is: how far is this map representative of the actual distribution of early ecclesiastical sites? It is worth thinking about the different types of evidence used to compile this map.

The bulk of the sites plotted were identified solely on the presence of pre-Viking sculpture, drawing on the comprehensive catalogues available via the *Corpus of Anglo-Saxon Stone Sculpture*.[2] It is easy to assume that this kind of sculpture acts as a 'barium meal' for the early church, providing an unproblematic proxy for the distribution of ecclesiastical establishments. The spread and number of sites identifiable through the presence of sculpture do certainly seem to be extensive; however, it is worth boring down into these data. It soon becomes clear that there is a range of sites that are likely to be early church sites that do not produce sculpture. For example, despite the presence of early church buildings at sites such as Ledsham (West Yorkshire), Corbridge (Northumberland) and Seaham (County Durham), to pick three sites at random, no early sculpture has been identified.[3]

Textual evidence can also be adduced for ecclesiastical sites such as Gainford and Sockburn (both in County Durham). Higbald is recorded in the *Anglo-Saxon Chronicle* as being consecrated as Bishop of Lindisfarne in 780,[4] whilst the *Historia regum* records the burial of an abbot at Gainford in AD 801.[5] Both sites have produced extensive assemblages of sculpture of entirely Anglo-Scandinavian date. Would they have been identified as Anglian church sites in the absence of the documentary evidence? It may simply be that, in some cases, this lack of sculpture is due to accidents in discovery and differential recovery levels. There are enough sites, such as Sockburn and Gainford, however, where substantial quantities of later material have been found, to suggest that the lack of Anglian sculpture is a real phenomenon rather than just a factor of survival.[6]

We can identify two different ways in which these church sites lacking sculpture are geographically distributed. First, there are entire regions where sculpture is either entirely lacking or very limited. Most of the obvious gaps in this map relate to major upland areas, particularly the Yorkshire Dales and Northern Pennines, the North York Moors, the Cheviots and the upland areas of southern Scotland. However, there are also other areas where the distribution of sculpture is surprisingly thin. For example, Lancashire south of the sands is almost entirely lacking in Anglian sculpture, with no certain sites south of the Ribble.[7] Although it is an area which saw extensive post-medieval urban and industrial sprawl, this is unlikely to have caused the lacuna in sculptural evidence, as industrial areas of West Yorkshire have produced plenty of sculpture (e.g. Birstall, Dewsbury, Mirfield *et multi alii*).[8]

On the other side of the Pennines, there is also a far thinner spread of sites than might be expected in East Yorkshire between the southern edge of the Vale of Pickering and the Humber. This contrasts with the dense spread of early Anglo-Saxon cemeteries across the Wolds and its northern and southern scarp edges. These were clearly settled areas with wealthy populations, yet this is not reflected in the evidence for sculpture. The contrast with the dense spread of early material along Ryedale and the northern edge of the Vale of Pickering is noticeable. One explanation for these areas of sculptural absence may simply be that there are no or very few pre-Viking ecclesiastical sites in this area. This seems unlikely given there is evidence for an extensive early medieval population in this area and that several ecclesiastical sites are mentioned by Bede. For example, Watton (East Yorkshire), mentioned by Bede, has produced no sculpture, whilst Beverley, also mentioned by Bede, has only produced the unornamented stone seat of possible late-seventh-century date.[9] The lack of good stone is not a satisfactory explanation as there is plenty of Anglo-Scandinavian sculpture from this area.

There are a number of reasons why these patterns might exist. As Martin Carver has noted, in the middle Anglo-Saxon period, there was intense regionality in the strategies of monumentalization used by both church and the secular elites and he has termed these different regions 'intellectual communities'.[10] This brings to mind Peter Brown's notion of 'micro-Christendoms' – localized, relatively small-scale, territorial responses to the emerging church.[11]

Carver's intellectual communities can certainly be recognized through stylistic similarities between groups of sculpted monument – such as the different sculptural traditions seemingly focused on centres such as Lindisfarne, Whitby and York.[12] But we should also perhaps see in some regions, in south Lancashire and East Yorkshire for example, the decision not to use sculpture, or just limited quantities of it, as another example of these intellectual strategies for expressing Christian belief in a local form. Are we seeing here micro-Christendoms in which other materials are turned to as appropriate media for monumentalization of faith? Scholars are comfortable with the notion that the choice of church fabric (stone or wood) can be an ideologically charged decision.[13] It is important to be conscious that such ideological motivations may inform other decisions about the erection of monuments and memorials and that the absence of stone sculpture may be as significant as its presence.

These intellectual communities may not just be expressed in simple territorial terms but also in other ways. For example, Eric Cambridge in his important paper on the distribution of early churches in County Durham also drew attention to the evidence for clustering of known sites in some parts of the county, with a

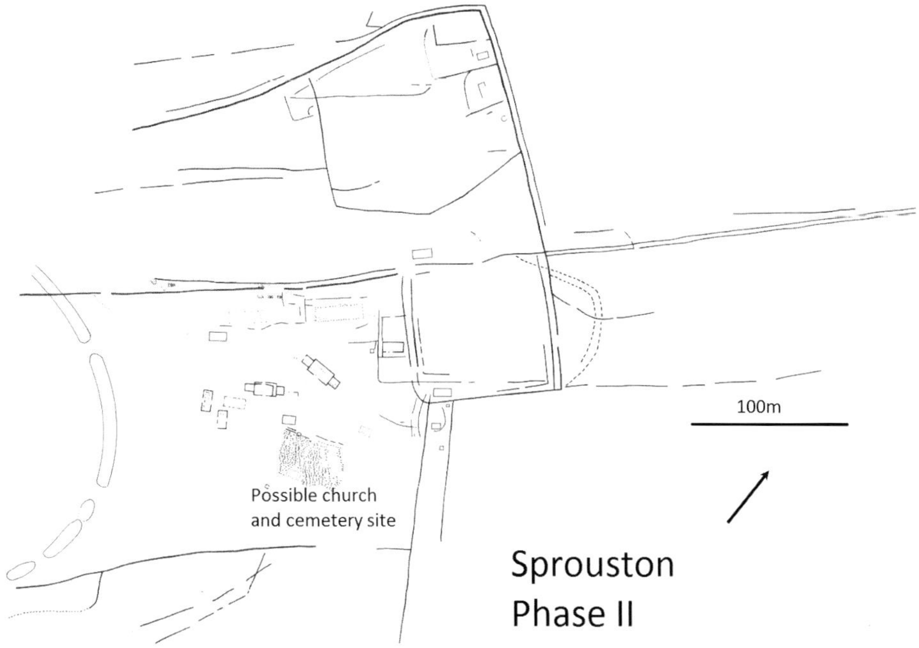


**Fig. 2** Wooden church and associated cemetery and other wooden structures, plot from cropmarks, Sprouston (Borders). Based on Smith 1992.

lack of sites elsewhere.[14] He suggested that these might reflect a difference between secular minsters which produced little sculpture and retained wooden churches until relatively late, and more monastic sites which produced a higher quantity of stone sculpture.[15] He argued that differences in the status and organizational context of a church might be reflected in different patterns of monumentalization – in essence, sculpture is a feature of only certain forms of ecclesiastical foundation. Whether one accepts Cambridge's particular distinction here, the underlying variability is clear. Thus, even in regions where sculpture is liberally distributed, we need to be alive to the fact that within this matrix of archaeologically easily detectable church sites may be a marbling of less visible sites identified through chance textual records, the rare survival of early fabric and fortuitous archaeological discoveries. The extent of unidentified church sites is, of course, an unknown, but it is probably higher on the western side of the Pennines, an area which figures less prominently in the limited textual sources, which tend to focus on churches associated with Monkwearmouth and Jarrow or connected to Lindisfarne.

## Case study: the Tweed valley

Occasionally we have small areas where, for a variety of reasons, a number of church sites without sculpture are identifiable, which gives us an opportunity to better understand the complexity of the patterning of church distributions. A good example is the greater Tweed Valley. The river gravels of this area produce excellent cropmarks, and as a result, particularly in the Milfield basin, there is an extensive distribution of good early/middle Anglian settlements identifiable, several of which have produced cropmark evidence for churches.

Yeavering is the best-known example, where within a complex high-status site identified by Bede as a royal *vill* used by Edwin, there is evidence for a small wooden building situated within a cemetery.[16] It is not possible easily to date this structure on strictly archaeological grounds, but given Bede's statement that Yeavering was replaced by a new estate at Milfield, the entire use-life of this structure probably fits into a period between 627 and perhaps the early eighth century. Interestingly, the estate centre which seemingly replaced it at Maelmin/Milfield appears to be lacking a church; indeed the entire Milfield basin seems to have lacked a church perhaps until the eleventh century, when there is limited sculptural evidence from Kirk Newton and Wooler.[17] There is a need to better understand the cropmark site at Ford Westfield, where a small possible cemetery and putative church enclosure of uncertain date have been identified.[18] At Sprouston, near Coldstream, a similar cemetery and possible wooden church can be seen integrated into a settlement visible as cropmarks which appears very similar to those at Milfield and Yeavering and can broadly be dated to between the sixth to tenth centuries AD (Fig. 2).[19] None of these putative church sites, Sprouston, Philiphaugh, or Ford Westfield (or indeed Yeavering), has produced any sculpture.

Elsewhere in the region, there are ecclesiastical sites which have produced early medieval sculpture, such as Jedburgh, on the Jed Water, a tributary of the River Teviot, and Norham.[20] Not all sites that have produced sculpture appear in the documentary record, although there has been a tendency in the past to try and connect isolated sculptural fragments with better-known ecclesiastical sites in the region. For example, Radford suggested that a fragment of Anglian shrine from Ancrum, and the well-known shrine elements from Jedburgh, were both parts of the original shrine of Boisil and had been taken from Old Melrose six miles away.[21] Cramp

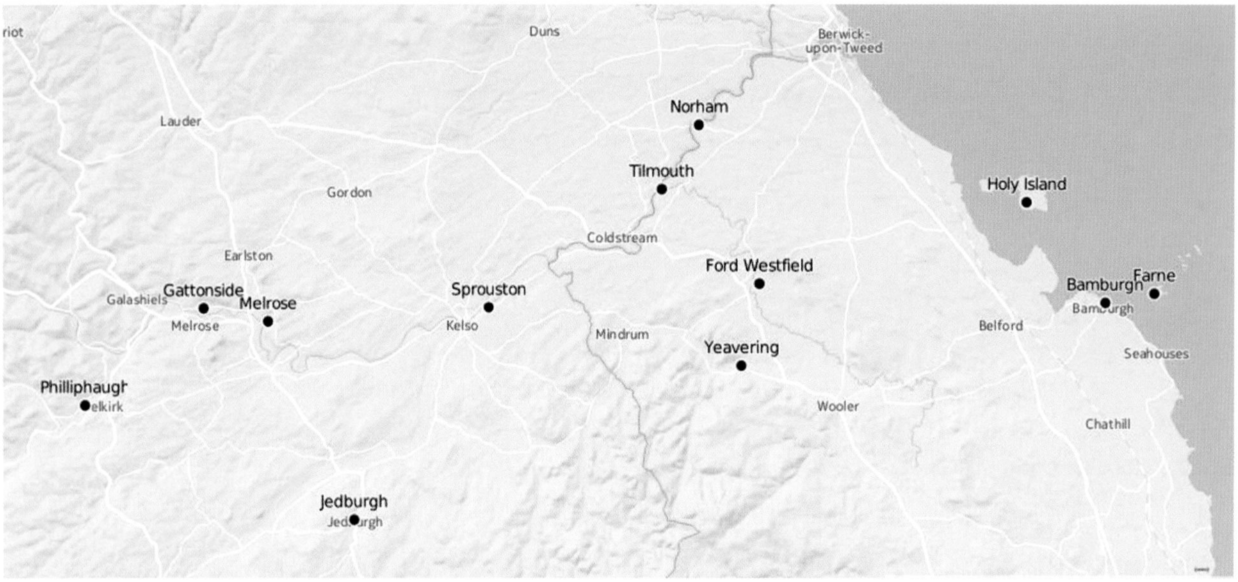


**Fig. 3** Early ecclesiastical sites in the Tweed Valley. Created using CartoDB.

has, however, queried this, noting the very different techniques used on the fragments implying they were not from the same monument.[22] Whether they are from the same monument or not, there is no reason to think that the fragments from either Jedburgh or Ancrum came from anywhere but near their places of discovery. It has also been suggested, on the basis of nothing but relative proximity, that the fragment of stone sculpture from Gattonside also originated from Old Melrose.[23] Given that we know that monasteries such as Hexham and Lichfield had several subsidiary or satellite foundations in their immediate hinterland, when it comes to attributing sculpture the gravitational pull of major foundations should be resisted.[24]

These can be supplemented with sites for which there is good documentary evidence but limited or no sculptural evidence, such as Old Melrose, best known through its association with the early church life of Cuthbert,[25] and which despite clearly being a major monastic establishment has only produced one relatively unimpressive fragment of stone sculpture.[26] In the case of Tillmouth, recorded as one of the northern possessions (*mansiones*) of Lindisfarne,[27] nothing survives at all beyond the probable cropmarks of the enclosure and a medieval chapel (heavily restored).

Along the Tweed Valley and its tributaries in the Anglian period, there are thus developed monastic sites with sculpture (Jedburgh; Norham), developed monastic sites without sculpture (Tillmouth; Old Melrose) and church sites of uncertain function (Yeavering; Sprouston; Philiphaugh) without sculpture (Fig. 3). Whilst some of the churches lacking sculpture might be seen as private, secular or proprietary establishments, others, such as Melrose and Tillmouth, are clearly not. Within a relatively small area, there are thus a variety of responses and approaches to building and adorning religious space which cannot be reduced to a distinction between monastic and secular foundations, and there are other decisions and strategies at play here.

There is also another important conclusion to draw about the possibility of recognizing variability and patterns of influence in the early churches. Whilst Carver is absolutely correct in his identification of zones of monumental variation, we need to remember that ideological affinity in the early medieval church is not simply distributed territorially, with entire zones or landscapes sharing the same monumental strategies. Influence can be capillary, spreading along networks, intermingling, entwining and co-existing with other approaches. One just has to consider the spread of Ionan/Columban influence into Northumbria and Ireland. There was not a simple bow-wave of advance centred on Iona, but instead sites of Columban influence appeared mushroom-like overnight, at Lindisfarne and Hartlepool for example, reflecting particular political contingencies. Returning to the distribution map we can thus assume there are an unknown number of additional sites, and we cannot use sculpture, or indeed any other single source of evidence, to 'read off' unproblematically the extent and nature of early medieval ecclesiastical provision in the region.

Accepting this, looking at the map the overwhelming impression given by these many sites is the sheer diversity and variety in the material and documentary expressions of these sites – small enclosures, large enclosures, minimal levels of sculpture, large quantities of sculpture, standing fabric, no remaining early fabric, extensive documentary evidence to an absence from the historical sources and every stage in between. This presents a very practical challenge to any attempt to categorize or characterize the material record of the pre-Viking church in Northumbria. The council of despair is to see every site as *sui generis*, a unique, creative attempt to create a focus for devotional practice and accommodate religious specialists. However, it is clear that there are some basic consistencies: the presence of a central church, a burial ground and probably some kind of boundary or enclosure. What I want to do now is address how we start to get to grips with pinning down the evidence from these sites in detail and identify some of these key elements.

## Defining the edges

One of the basic elements of planning at ecclesiastical sites is the presence of an external boundary feature or *vallum*. One of the most frequently adduced examples is the substantial bank and ditch that surrounds Iona, still comprising a significant landscape feature at the site. However, the identification of such external boundaries is often a challenging one. Even at sites as well investigated as Monkwearmouth, Jarrow and Hartlepool, excavators have faced challenges in identifying putative external boundaries.[28] In these three cases, the main problem is that there has been a contraction of later activity to a smaller core area around the main church, and the wider area which constitutes the original total area of the site has been heavily redeveloped in the post-medieval period to such an extent that the basic topography of the landscape has been resculpted. Even at sites such as Holy Island, there is a surprising lack of certainty about the precise boundaries of the monastery, despite extensive recent geophysical survey.[29]

The pattern of the contraction around a core, whether this occurred in the Viking period, the medieval period or was even a result of post-Reformation reorganization, is one which can be identified at many ecclesiastical sites. The evidence from a number of other sites can be adduced to demonstrate this contraction; three examples should serve to demonstrate the range of evidence that can be found.

Corbridge, standing on the River Tyne, lies outwith the area of the Roman town. Symeon of Durham records the consecration of Aldulf, Bishop of Mayo, there in AD 786.[30] Despite the monastery's importance, and the excellent preservation of important early church fabric, this is another attested Anglian site that lacks early sculpture, with the only surviving sculpture belonging to the Saxo-Norman overlap.[31] The church today sits in an irregularly shaped enclosure within the heart of the town. However, burials have been observed in chance excavations and limited, more formal archaeological interventions across the town centre (Fig. 4c). It is not possible to relate these convincingly to any other possible medieval burial grounds, and a good case can be made for their being part of either a substantially larger cemetery or perhaps a number of smaller burial areas within a larger early medieval monastic *enceinte*. However, the surviving street system does not appear to preserve any potential earlier boundaries and is instead typical of a medieval borough with burgage plots and a back lane.[32] Whilst it is not possible to define the full extent of the original site, a good case can be made for a site that was originally around 5 ha as opposed to the modern churchyard of *c.* ⅓ ha.

A similar situation can be found at Gainford, attested by Symeon as being the burial place of Abbot Edwin in AD 801.[33] It lacks early sculpture though has produced significant quantities of Anglo-Scandinavian sculpture and again sits in a typical riverine location adjacent to a river and a fording point.[34] Here the later churchyard is again around ⅓ ha, but it sits within a potentially larger semi-circular enclosure defined by roads (Fig. 4a). Unlike Corbridge, however, this area remained empty of any development until the sixteenth or seventeenth century and was set apart from the probable core of the associated village which seems to have grown up around the site of Gainford Hall, 200 m to the north. Like Corbridge, burials have been recovered from outside the existing churchyard, on the site of the village green, and some of the Viking sculpture was also recovered from a paddock adjacent to the church. The putative larger enclosure is around 4.5 ha in extent – and is comparable in shape, if not size, with other riverside monastic sites such as Hoddom.

A final example is Seaham on the Durham coast. Here there is a church containing substantial eighth-century fabric.[35] A series of Anglo-Saxon burials of seventh- to tenth-century date have been found around 200 m to the north in Flower Field near the lodge to Seaham Hall (Fig. 4b).[36] Smaller-scale trenching to the south, between the burials and the church, has also produced some evidence of broadly contemporary agricultural and domestic activity.[37] In this case, we have a slightly different proposition to Gainford and Corbridge, which were both clearly important, if potentially subsidiary, monastic sites. Seaham is first attested in the tenth century when it was granted to the Community of St Cuthbert, but previously it is likely to have been a possession of Monkwearmouth, which may explain the construction of the church.[38] However, there is no suggestion that the site was ever monastic in the fullest sense of the word. We might question whether here we have evidence for a possible estate centre with a church and a separate cemetery, although presumably the church also had an associated burial ground, so we need to think about why a small estate centre might have two cemeteries.

If even relatively small and seemingly unimportant sites such as Seaham can be at the centre of a complex of at least perhaps 5 ha, then we need to go back to visit sites such as Escomb. Here the pleasingly rounded small churchyard has generally been accepted as the authentic boundary of the small early church; however, we need to open up to the idea that it could be part of a potentially significantly larger complex.[39]

Very often, purported reconstructions of ecclesiastical enclosures are based on fairly limited, highly circumstantial evidence, often projecting back from known boundaries often of much later date or extrapolating from very limited archaeological evidence. The use of later boundaries fossilized in road systems is a common strategy. Certainly, in some cases, where there is good early cartographic evidence, combined with fieldwork interventions,

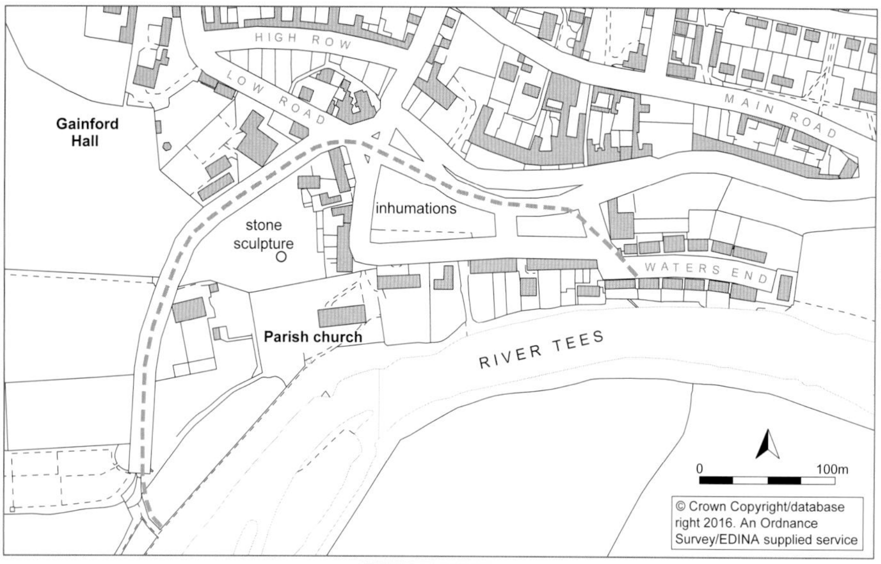


a

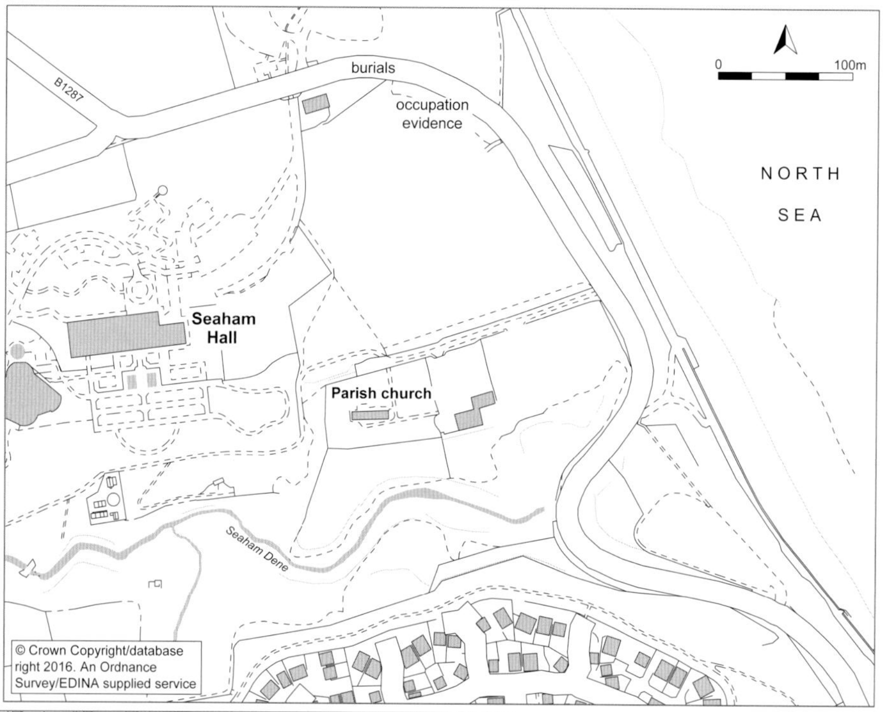


b

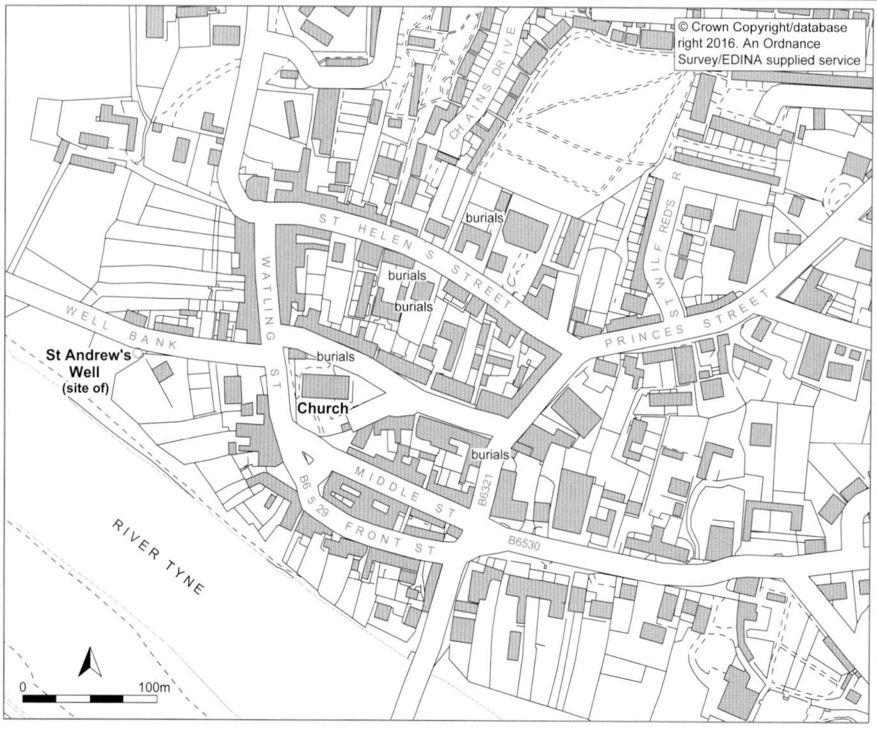


c

**Fig. 4** Burial and other activity around known early medieval ecclesiastical sites: (a) Gainford, County Durham; dashed line shows putative monastic boundary; (b) Seaham, County Durham; (c) Corbridge, Northumberland.

such as at Armagh, the later layout of roads does seem to preserve some of the earlier boundaries.[40]

Road networks, however, can often prove frustratingly intransigent. For example, attempts to map the boundaries associated with Lindisfarne by both Deirdre O'Sullivan and myself have ultimately been unsatisfactory precisely perhaps because we both came at it with the underlying assumption that the road network of the village *would* fossilize some element of the earlier boundary system.[41] Evidence is increasingly demonstrating that much of the surviving village is constructed over a substantial medieval midden, and as such we cannot assume that *any* of the road network is of significant antiquity.

One topic that needs further exploration is the range of factors that may lead to the longer-term preservation of possible boundaries in roads or field boundaries. Two interesting examples are Hoddom, a site that has been extensively excavated, and Tillmouth on the River Tweed west of Norham, lacking in excavation but recorded as *mansiones* of Lindisfarne and combining interesting cropmark evidence with a largely rebuilt chapel dedicated to St Cuthbert.[42] Set in similar riverine contexts, in both cases, the monasteries were defined by broadly semi-circular enclosures recognizable on aerial photographs. Certainly in the case of Hoddom, this boundary appears to have been reasonably substantial.[43] However, in both cases, the boundaries did not survive to be fossilized in the later field systems.[44] Instead, these surviving field boundaries belong entirely to the post-medieval period of field enclosure, which erased any earlier existing field system.

It would be interesting to explore whether there is any regional distinction between areas where earlier boundaries have been entirely removed owing to the laying out of open fields and subsequent enclosure, compared with regions dominated by 'ancient' or 'unplanned' landscapes,[45] where the lack of reworking by first later medieval and then post-medieval landscapes may have preserved potential earlier boundaries. The same applies to the preservation of boundaries in urban contexts and the distinction between towns with formally laid out burgage plots and those which have grown more organically. Whilst it may not be possible to identify hard and fast rules of thumb, a better sense of how subsequent landscape development could influence the survival of earlier enclosures would be useful when trying to unpick regional patterns and tendencies in the substantial surviving resource.

A further challenge is that it is clear a wide variety of techniques were used to create external and internal boundaries at ecclesiastical sites. Whilst the influential image of the substantial bank and ditch at Iona, a reused prehistoric enclosure, encourages us to assume that such external boundaries are monumental in size, this need not always be the case. At Hoddom, the northern boundary comprised a bank, a wooden palisade, a 2-m wide berm and a ditch, although on the western side of the site neither the bank nor ditch could be identified.[46] This might seem to confirm the precedent set by Iona. However, the situation is often more complex. At Sockburn, the loop of the River Tees in which the site sits was likely to have partially defined the site, and the common coastal and riverine contexts of Anglian monastic sites mean that topographic features were regularly incorporated into boundaries, such as the cliff edges at Tynemouth and Whitby and shorelines at Alnmouth.

Deliberately constructed boundaries are also common and a range of other strategies could be used to mark the edge of a monastery. At Whithorn, the evidence for the postulated enclosures is very different. In Period I/1, a short stretch of ditch was certainly uncovered.[47] It only lasts a single phase before disappearing entirely. A second boundary is identified in Period I/2, although this was only 0.15 m deep and again later disappeared,[48] whilst in Period I/11 a further boundary division was identified, consisting first of a simple fence, followed by a small wall-like feature which was replaced by a path.[49] In all cases, an excavated stretch of between only 6 and 10 m was extrapolated by the excavators to form a putative complete circuit that encompassed the entire site. Throughout the excavation report runs the underlying thread that there *must have been* an identifiable boundary feature that encircled the whole complex, even though the archaeological evidence was ephemeral, short-lived and limited in extent. When some of the putative projected courses of the boundaries were tested in subsequent fieldwork, none of the postulated curvilinear boundaries could be recognized at all.[50]

Although in broad terms none of the evidence from subsequent excavations at Whithorn contradicted the original schematic outline of the shifting morphology of the monastic site, the presence of clear boundary features related to it became increasingly tenuous. There is certainly no evidence for substantial banked/ditched features such as those found at Hoddom and Iona. Boundaries at Whithorn were localized, varied and shifting.

Similar evidence for less substantial boundary features was also found at Hartlepool, where the excavators identified three main types of principal boundary features: large timbers set in post-pits (presumably with something less substantial placed in the intervening gaps), palisade trenches, which mainly appear to replace the earlier post-pit alignments, and also a range of smaller ditches. There was no evidence for banks associated with these later ditches; they were only around 0.5 m deep, a little bigger than some of the Whithorn boundaries but clearly significantly less substantial than the Iona *vallum*.[51] Literary evidence suggests that hedges could also be used to define monastic enclosures. The *Life* of Wilfrid refers to the monastery at Oundle as being surrounded by a thorn hedge, and there are later references to hedged boundaries surrounding Evesham Minster (Worcester) and Culross (Fife).[52] Whilst there is good evidence that the notion of a boundary or enclosure may have been a highly significant one, the actual way in which monastic boundaries could be materialized clearly varied widely, ranging from the monumental to the ephemeral.

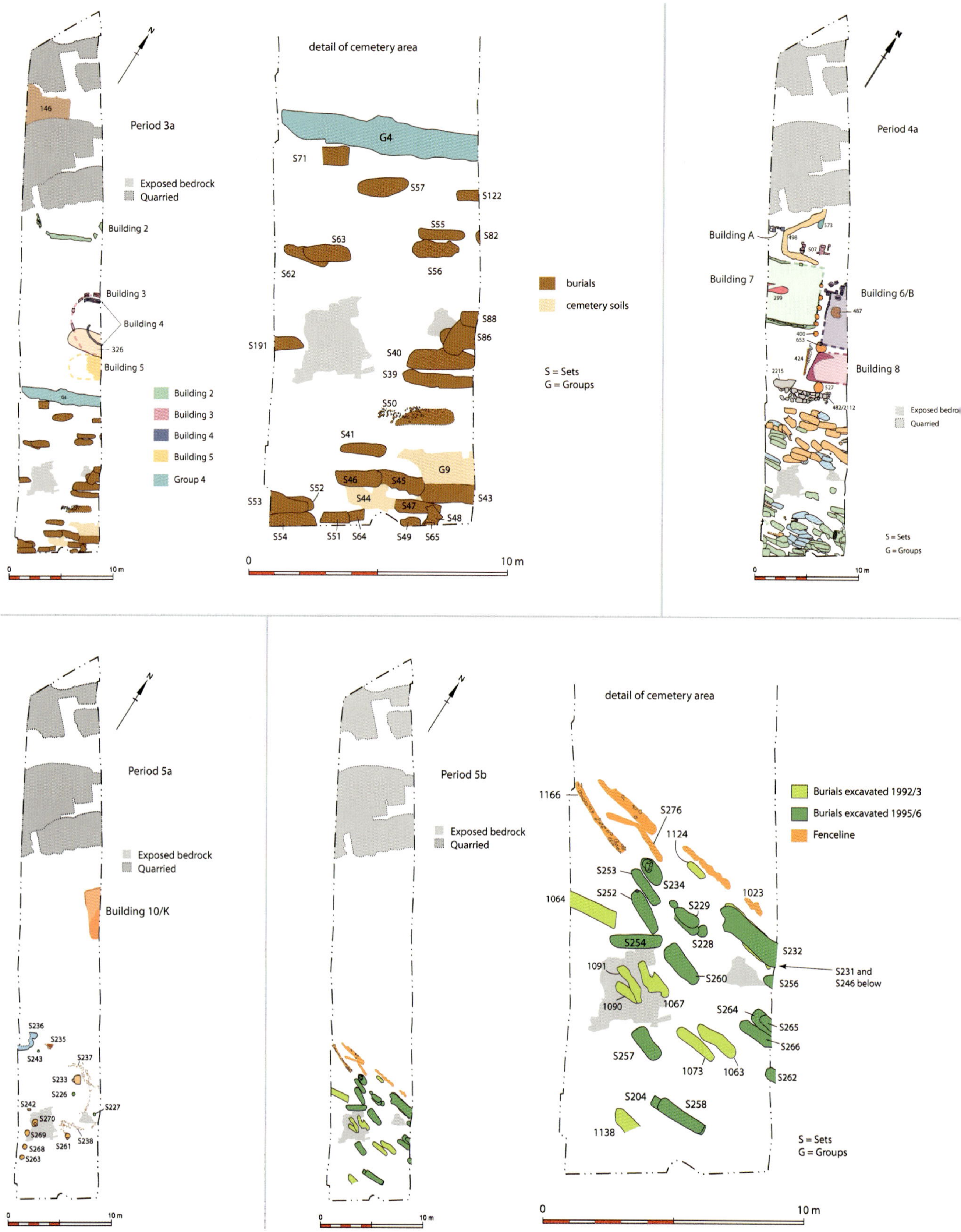


**Fig. 5** Fey Field, Whithorn: phase plan of trench showing rapidly changing activity patterns within one small area of the ecclesiastical site (from McOmish and Petts 2008). © York Archaeological Trust.

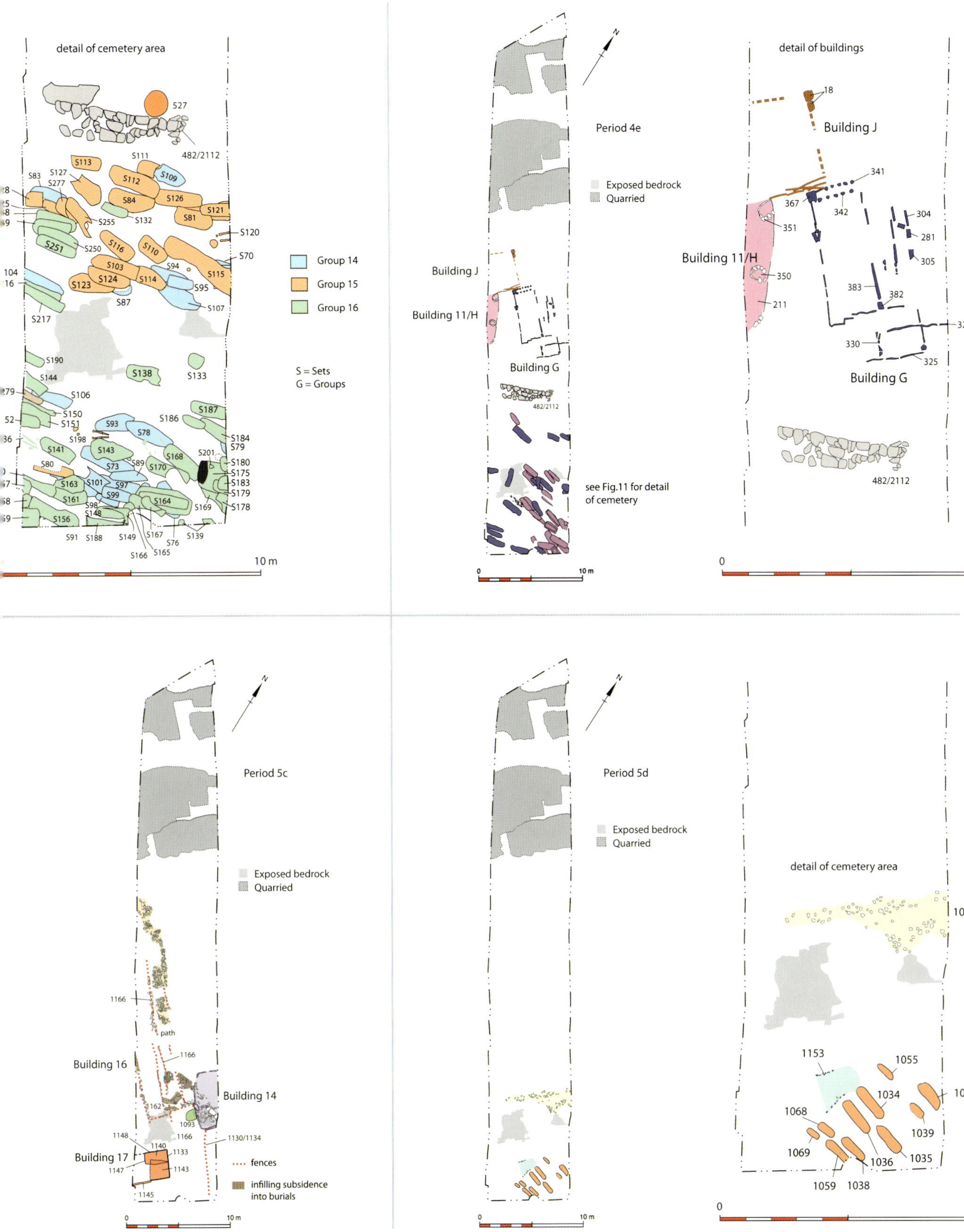
detail of cemetery area
527
482/2112
S111
S113
S109
S83
S127
S277
S112
S84
S126
S121
S81
S255
S132
S120
S251
S250
S116
S110
S70
S103
S94
S115
S123
S124
S114
S95
S87
S107
104
16
S217
Group 14
Group 15
Group 16
S190
S138
S133
S144
S = Sets
G = Groups
S106
S187
S150
S151
S93
S78
S186
S184
S79
S198
S141
S143
S168
S201
S180
S175
S183
S179
S178
S80
S73
S89
S170
S163
S101
S97
S99
S164
S169
S161
S98
S148
S156
S91
S188
S149
S167
S76
S139
S166
S165
10 m
Period 4e
Exposed bedrock
Quarried
Building J
Building 11/H
Building G
482/2112
see Fig.11 for detail of cemetery
10 m
detail of buildings
18
Building J
341
367
342
304
351
281
Building 11/H
305
350
383
382
211
324
330
325
Building G
482/2112
0
10 m
Period 5c
Exposed bedrock
Quarried
1166
path
1166
Building 16
Building 14
1162
1093
1148
1166
1130/1134
1140
Building 17
1133
1147
1143
fences
infilling subsidence into burials
1145
0
10 m
Period 5d
Exposed bedrock
Quarried
detail of cemetery area
1024
1153
1055
1034
1065
1068
1039
1069
1036
1035
1059
1038
0
10 m

## Understanding chronology

The way in which boundaries at Whithorn shifted brings me to my final concern, the challenges of modelling the use of space across sites. Perhaps more than any other site, excavation here has shown the extent to which use of space could change over time. These can perhaps best be seen in the sequence uncovered in the excavations in Fey Field to the west of Hill's major excavations. Here the area excavated went through a complex sequence of changes of use over the sixth to twelfth centuries, with varying periods of settlement, craft and industry and burial use (Fig. 5). Over 600 years, this range of activities was varied and repeated. The area excavated was used as a burial zone on at least three separate periods, with other activities using the area in between.

It is clear that any attempt to model or map clear zones of activity on limited spreads of information is a brave move. Earlier in this paper, we saw plots of distributions of burials around a number of known Anglo-Saxon ecclesiastical centres. These are useful to the extent that they help partially to plot the possible extent of activity at these sites, but it is dangerous to extrapolate this into clear, defined zones of activity that remain unchanging over any lengths of time.

Even where activity shows less variability over time, there are still real practical problems of a type faced in trying to understand the archaeology of any complex site, particularly those that are, relatively speaking, artefactually limited. This can best be seen at Hoddom, where the excavators identified a series of agricultural structures, including several corn driers.[53] Many of these buildings were rebuilt over a period of time, resulting in small islands of complex stratigraphy, with good internal relative chronologies. Yet it is challenging to tie together these complexes of dense stratigraphic relationships, as they share only relatively limited stratigraphic relationships with the main boundary feature. The excavator made a brave stab at trying to create a clear phasing, but in the lack of good quality, fine resolution dating, any such phasing remains highly optimistic.[54] It is interesting to note that the results of the suite of radiocarbon dates from the site suggest that there were no clearly identifiable phases of construction and that building and rebuilding may have taken place on a more *ad hoc* and contingent timetable.[55] A similar situation occurred at Hartlepool, where a series of small excavations across the built-up modern town has again resulted in a sequence of isolated areas of activity or burial – again, the excavator makes a good attempt to try and phase these remains, but is open about the challenges.[56]

This kind of post-excavation challenge is a common one. Precisely the same problems underpin the challenges presented in trying to understand contemporary secular sites, such as Yeavering, where there is exactly the same combination of isolated complex stratigraphy that cannot be easily compared with neighbouring structures.[57] Indeed, these basic problems in interpreting stratigraphy across a site can be found in the archaeology of all periods, but along with the complex and shifting nature of boundaries and the problems with changing patterns of use of particular areas of the site, these wider issues with synchronizing activity across a site are frustrating and limit attempts to compare activity both within individual sites and between sites. This limits our ability to interpret some interesting patterns that appear in the archaeological record. For example, the appearance of stone-founded, wooden buildings during the life of Hartlepool, Hoddom and Whithorn is intriguing, and it is tempting to link this into the spread of a Northumbrian monastic influence across the region.[58] However, we cannot with honesty satisfactorily synchronize their appearance chronologically. There are also interesting differences: Hartlepool shows a sequence of constructional techniques running from post-hole structures, to plank-in-gully, to stone-founded wooden structures, whereas at Hoddom, the middle stage is absent.[59] Does this reflect a chronological distinction or something else? The detail remains frustratingly vague.

One of the underlying problems, a very obvious one, is that despite the excellent range of excavations of Northumbrian ecclesiastical sites, there is not one site where there has been anything like total excavation. Even at sites like Whithorn which have seen large-scale excavation, perhaps less than ⅓ of the site has been investigated. The often small-scale and scattered excavations that characterize much of the work on ecclesiastical sites make it extremely challenging to pull together plans and chronologies. Although it is understandably tempting to extrapolate and simplify, the sheer complexity of the sites themselves should warn us against that. Similar problems have been seen at sites such as Iona, which has suffered excavation by a thousand cuts. The words of Richard Reece reporting on some of his excavations on the island should perhaps be a warning: 'the information extracted in a small trench was not commensurate with the information that was destroyed'.[60] It is, of course, useful to build models. For the sites under discussion, the dominant and complementary models can perhaps be characterized as *concentric* and *polyfocal*. But it is important not to let the model lead too firmly in interpreting often difficult and fragmented remains.

In conclusion, this paper has tried to go back to first principles and assess, if only in broad-brush terms, how much we actually know about the spatial distribution of early medieval ecclesiastical sites in Northumbria, both in terms of geographical spread and also in terms of the immediate extent and internal topography of individual sites. Whilst the presence of stone sculpture may provide a general sense of the extent and intensity of the establishment of early church sites, when we home in on particular areas, such as the Tweed Valley, we can see that the pattern is far more complex and nuanced than a simple mapping of sculpture would allow. Equally, even plotting the basic outline and extent of ecclesiastical sites is surprisingly difficult, whether looking at major, well-attested sites, such as Whithorn or Lindisfarne, or less clearly understood sites, such as Corbridge or Seaham. Finally, our understanding of the spatial organization and chronological development of ecclesiastical sites is based on the excavation of relatively small areas of large sites, with the chronological development often far harder to define than often appreciated. Whilst it is tempting to develop overarching models for spatial organization and development, these are based on a small sample size and limited chronological control. Compared with many areas of early medieval Britain, Northumbria has an excellent corpus of excavated ecclesiastical sites, but it is crucial that this does not allow us to make too many assumptions about the archaeology of a still poorly understood class of sites.

## Notes

1 Cramp 1976; 2005–6; Daniels 2007; Hall and Whyman 1996; Hill 1997; James and Yeoman 2008; Leech 1985; Lowe 2008; McOmish and Petts 2008; Peers and Radford 1943; Rahtz and Watts 1997; Thomas 1967; Watts, Grenville and Rahtz 1996.
2 Cramp 1977; Bailey and Cramp 1988; Lang 1991; 2002; Coatsworth 2008; Bailey 2010.
3 Taylor and Taylor 1965, 172–6, 378–84, 534–6.
4 *ASC* 780, Plummer 1892–9, I, 52–3.
5 Arnold, *Sym. Op.* II, 65.
6 Cramp 1977, 80–90, 135–44.
7 Bailey 2010, 19.
8 Coatsworth 2008, 103–4, 129–48, 214.
9 *HE* 5.2–3; Lang 1991, 224.
10 Carver 2011.
11 Brown 1996, 218; Petts 2011, 27–8.
12 Carver 2011, 190–1; Cramp 1989; Lang 2002, 40; Lang 1991, 18.
13 Cramp 2005–6, 352; Gem 1983, 1; Ó Carragáin 2010, 15, 64; Stalley 1999, 34.
14 Cambridge 1984.
15 *Ibid.*, 81.
16 *HE* 2.14.
17 Cramp 1977, 232–3, 251.
18 Passmore and Waddington 2012, 92.
19 Smith 1992.
20 Cramp 1983; 1977, 208–14.
21 Radford 1955.
22 Cramp 1983, 269, 281–4.
23 Allen and Anderson 1993, 432–3.
24 Blair 2005, 218.
25 E.g. *VCA* 3; *VCB* 6; *HSC* 43–5; *LE* i.3.
26 Allen and Anderson 1993, 435–6.
27 *HR* iii.89.
28 Turner, Semple and Turner 2013, 113–17; Daniels 2007, 172–3.
29 O'Sullivan 1989; Petts forthcoming.
30 *HR* 53.
31 Taylor and Taylor 1965, 172–7; Cramp 1977, 239–41.
32 Finlayson and Hardie 2008, 21; for a wider discussion of the pattern of churchyard shrinkage, see Zadoro-Rio 2003.
33 Arnold, *Sym. Op.* II, 65.
34 Cramp 1977, 80–90.
35 Taylor and Taylor 1965, 534–6.
36 Adamson and Abramson 1998; Parry 2001.
37 Wood and Middleton 2014.
38 *HSC* 26.
39 Pocock and Wheeler 1971.
40 Edwards 1996, 108–11.
41 O'Sullivan 1989; Petts forthcoming.
42 *HSC* 10; Passmore and Waddington 2009, 104, fig. 3.19.
43 Lowe 2006, 34–9.
44 *Ibid.*, 12–18.
45 *sensu* Rackham 2000, 1–5.
46 Lowe 2006, 32–9.
47 Hill 1997, 77, fig. 3.5.
48 *Ibid.*, 90–1, fig. 3.13–14.
49 *Ibid.*, 130–1, fig. 3.42.
50 McOmish and Petts 2008.
51 Daniels 2007, 157–62.
52 *VW* c.67; *VK* c.6.
53 Lowe 2006, 39–99.
54 Lowe 2006, 169–79.
55 Dalland 2006, 161.
56 Lowe 2006, 169–80.
57 Hope-Taylor 1977.
58 Lowe 2006, 180–4.
59 Daniels 2007, 162–8; Lowe 2006, 180–4.
60 Reece 1981, 56.

## Abbreviations

*HR* = *Historia regum*, in Arnold, T. (ed.) 1885. *Symeonis Monachi Opera Omnia*, Vol. 2, 1–283, London: Longman.

*HSC* = Johnson South, T. (ed. and trans.) 2002. *Historia de Sancto Cuthberto*, Woodbridge: Boydell and Brewer.

*LE* = Rollason, D. (ed. and trans.) 2000. *Libellus de exordio atque procursu istius, hoc est Dunhelmensis, ecclesie: Tract on the Origins and Progress of this the Church of Durham*, Oxford: Oxford University Press.

*VCA* = *Vita Sancti Cuthberti Auctore Anonymo*, in Colgrave, B. (ed. and trans.) 1969. *Two Lives of Saint Cuthbert*, 59–139, Cambridge: Cambridge University Press.

*VCB* = *Vita Sancti Cuthberti Auctore Beda*, in Colgrave, B. (ed. and trans.) 1969. *Two Lives of Saint Cuthbert*, 141–310, Cambridge: Cambridge University Press.

*VK* = *Vita Kentigerni*, 'The Life of S. Kentigern by Jocelinus, a monk of Furness', in Forbes, A. P. 1874. *Lives of S. Ninian and S. Kentigern. Compiled in the Twelfth Century*, 29–119, 159–247, Edinburgh : Edmonston and Douglas.

*VW* = Stephen of Ripon ('Eddius Stephanus'), 'Vita Wilfridi', in Colgrave, B. (ed.) 1985. *The Life of Bishop Wilfrid by Eddius Stephanus*, Cambridge: Cambridge University Press.

## Bibliography

Adamson, C. H. and Abramson, P. 1998. *Excavation of a Cemetery at Seaham Hall Lodge, County Durham*, NAA unpublished report 97/47.

Allen, J. R. and Anderson, J. 1993. *The Early Christian Monuments of Scotland*, Vol. 2, Brechin: Pinkfoot Press.

Bailey, R. 2010. *Corpus of Anglo-Saxon Stone Sculpture: Cheshire and Lancashire*, London: British Academy.

Bailey, R. and Cramp, R. 1988. *Corpus of Anglo-Saxon Stone Sculpture*, Vol. 2. *Cumberland, Westmorland, Lancashire-north-of-the-sands*, London: British Academy.

Blair, J. 2005. *The Church in Anglo-Saxon Society*, Oxford: Blackwell.

Brown, P. 1996. *The Rise of Western Christendom*, Oxford: Blackwell.

Cambridge, E. 1984. 'The early church in County Durham, a re-assessment', *Jnl British Arch. Assoc.*, **137**, 65–85.

Carver, M. 2011. 'Intellectual communities in early Northumbria', in D. Petts and S. Turner (eds.), *Early Medieval Northumbria: Kingdom and Communities AD 450–1100*, 185–206, Turnhout: Brepols.

Coatsworth, E. 2008. *Corpus of Anglo-Saxon Stone Sculpture*, Vol. 8. *West Yorkshire*, London: British Academy.

Cramp, R. 1976. 'Analysis of the finds register and location plans of Whitby Abbey', in D. Wilson (ed.), *The Archaeology of Anglo-Saxon England*, 453–7, London: Methuen.

Cramp, R. 1977. *Corpus of Anglo-Saxon Stone Sculpture*, Vol. 1. *County Durham and Northumberland*, London: British Academy.

Cramp, R. 1983. 'The Anglian sculptures from Jedburgh', in A. O'Connor and D. Clarke (eds.), *From the Stone Age to the 'Forty-five, Studies presented to R. B. K. Stevenson*, 264–84, Edinburgh: John Donald.

Cramp, R. 1989. 'The artistic influence of Lindisfarne within Northumbria', in G. Bonner, D. Rollason and C. Stancliffe (eds.), *St Cuthbert, his Cult and his Community to AD 1200*, 213–30, Woodbridge: Boydell.

Cramp, R. 2005–6. *Wearmouth and Jarrow Monastic Sites*, Swindon: English Heritage.

Dalland, M. 2006. 'Statistical analysis of the radiocarbon dates', in C. Lowe, *Excavations at Hoddom, Dumfriesshire: An Early Ecclesiastical Site in South-West Scotland*, 161–8, Edinburgh: Society of Antiquaries of Scotland.

Daniels, R. 2007. *Anglo-Saxon Hartlepool and the Foundations of English Christianity: An Archaeology of the Anglo-Saxon Monastery*, Hartlepool: Tees Archaeology.

Edwards, N. 1996. *The Archaeology of Early Medieval Ireland*, London: Routledge.

Finlayson, R. and Hardie, C. 2008. *Corbridge: Extensive Urban Survey*, unpublished report, Northumberland County Council.

Gem, R. 1983. 'Towards an iconography of Anglo-Saxon architecture', *Jnl of the Warburg and Courtauld Insts*, **46**, 1–18.

Hall, R. and Whyman, M. 1996. 'Settlement and monasticism at Ripon, North Yorkshire, from the 7th to 11th centuries A.D.', *Medieval Arch.*, **40**, 62–150.

Hill, P. 1997. *Whithorn and Saint Ninian: The Excavation of a Monastic Town 1984–1991*, Stroud: Sutton.

Hope-Taylor, B. 1977. *Yeavering: An Anglo-British Centre of Early Northumbria*, London: HMSO.

James, H. and Yeoman, P. 2008. *Excavations at St Ethernan's Monastery, Isle of May, Fife, 1992–7*, Perth: Tayside and Fife Archaeological Committee.

Lang, J. 1991. *Corpus of Anglo-Saxon Stone Sculpture*, Vol. 3. *York and Eastern Yorkshire*, London: British Academy.

Lang, J. 2002. *Corpus of Anglo-Saxon Stone Sculpture*, Vol. 6. *Northern Yorkshire*, London: British Academy.

Leech, R. H. 1985. 'Excavations at Dacre, 1982–4: an interim report', *Trans. of the Cumberland and Westmorland Antiquarian and Arch. Soc.*, new series, **85**, 87–93.

Lowe, C. 2006. *Excavations at Hoddom, Dumfriesshire: An Early Ecclesiastical Site in South-West Scotland*, Edinburgh: Society of Antiquaries of Scotland.

Lowe, C. 2008. *Inchmarnock: An Early Historic Island Monastery and its Archaeological Landscape*, Edinburgh: Society of Antiquaries of Scotland.

McOmish, J. M. and Petts, D. 2008. *Fey Field, Whithorn: Excavations by David Pollock and Amanda Clarke*, Archaeology of York Web Series, York: York Archaeological Trust, http://www.yorkarchaeology.co.uk/wp-content/uploads/2014/08/Whithorn-AYW10-reduced.pdf (accessed 1/10/15).

Ó Carragáin, T. 2010. *Churches in Early Medieval Ireland. Architecture, Ritual and Memory*, New Haven and London: Yale University Press.

O'Sullivan, D. 1989. 'The plan of the early Christian monastery on Lindisfarne', in G. Bonner, D. Rollason and C. Stancliffe (eds.), *St Cuthbert, his Cult and his Community to AD 1200*, 125–42, Woodbridge: Boydell.

Parry, J. 2001. *Excavation of a Cemetery Site at Flower Field, Seaham, County Durham*, NAA unpublished report 01/108.

Passmore, D. and Waddington, C. 2009. *Managing Archaeological Landscapes in Northumberland*, Till-Tweed Studies, 1, Oxford: Oxbow.

Passmore, D. and Waddington, C. 2012. *Archaeology and Environment in Northumberland*, Till-Tweed Studies, 2, Oxford: Oxbow.

Peers, C. and Radford, C. A. R. 1943. 'The Saxon monastery at Whitby', *Archaeologia*, **59**, 27–88.

Petts, D. 2011. *Pagan and Christian: Religious Change in Early Medieval Europe*, London: Bloomsbury.

Petts, D. forthcoming. '"A place more venerable than all in Britain": the archaeology of Anglo-Saxon Lindisfarne', in R. Gameson (ed.), *The Lindisfarne Gospels: New Perspectives*, Leiden: Brill.

Plummer, C. (ed.) 1892–9. *Two of the Anglo-Saxon Chronicles Parallel*, Oxford.

Pocock, M. and Wheeler, H. 1971. 'Excavations at Escomb Church, Co Durham', *Jnl British Arch. Assoc.*, **34**, 11–29.

Rackham, O. 2000. *The History of the Countryside*, London: Phoenix.

Radford, C. A. R. 1955. 'Two Scottish shrines: Jedburgh and St Andrew's', *Arch. Jnl*, **112**, 43–60.

Rahtz, P. and Watts, L. 1997. 'Kirkdale Anglo-Saxon minster', *Current Arch.*, **13**, 419–22.

Reece, R. 1981. *Excavations at Iona 1964 to 1974*, Institute of Archaeology Occasional Publications, 5, London: Institute of Archaeology.

Smith, I. 1992. 'Sprouston, Roxburghshire: an early Anglian centre of the eastern Tweed basin', *Proc. of the Soc. of Antiquaries of Scotland*, **121**, 261–94.

Stalley, R. 1999. *Early Medieval Architecture*, Oxford: Oxford University Press.

Taylor, H. M. and Taylor, J. 1965. *Anglo-Saxon Architecture*, Vol. 1, Cambridge: Cambridge University Press.

Thomas, C. 1967. 'An early Christian cemetery and chapel on Ardwall Isle, Kirkcudbright', *Medieval Arch.*, **11**, 127–88.

Turner, S., Semple, S. and Turner, A. 2013. *Wearmouth and Jarrow: Northumbrian Monasteries in an Historic Landscape*, Hertford: University of Hertfordshire Press.

Watts, L., Grenville, J. and Rahtz, P. 1996. 'Archaeology at Kirkdale', supplement to the *Ryedale Historian*, **18**.

Wood, P. and Middleton, P. 2014. *Seaham Community Excavation, Flower Field, Old Seaham, County Durham*, NAA unpublished archaeological evaluation report 14/06.

Zadoro-Rio, E. 2003. 'The making of churchyards and parish territories in the early-medieval landscape of France and England in the 7th–12th centuries: a reconsideration', *Medieval Arch.*, **47**, 1–19.

# Marmoutier (Tours), a late Roman and early medieval monastery in the Loire Valley (4th–11th centuries)

Elisabeth Lorans

*Abstract*

*Elected as bishop of Tours in 371, St Martin decided to create a hermitage on the northern bank of the River Loire near Tours, and spent part of his time there until he died in 397. The description of the place by Sulpicius Severus in the Vita Sancti Martini conjures up the image of a remote spot, difficult of access, between the cliff and the river. Archaeology reveals a different story, showing an early Roman settlement which was reused by the bishop and his companions without any chronological gap. This paper will present an overview of the morphology and topography of the site using all the evidence provided by recent research undertaken by Tours University. Geophysical and geomorphological surveys allow us to reconstruct the formation, in the seventh–ninth centuries, of an island which gradually became joined to the mainland, and this made possible the extension of the precinct towards the south.*

*Various Roman and early medieval buildings as well as funerary areas are known through excavations and texts, which makes it possible in part to reconstruct the topography of the site during the first millennium, before the major development it underwent between the eleventh and the thirteenth centuries.*

## Introduction

Marmoutier is well known to those interested in the early phases of monasticism in the West. Saint Martin, the centenary of whose birth we celebrate this year (316–2016), was elected as bishop of Tours in 371; however, wishing to escape from his too many visitors he decided, according to his biographer Sulpicius Severus, to spend some of his time in a quieter place than the city of Tours:

> For a time he occupied a cell next to the cathedral. Then, when he could no longer endure the disturbance from his many visitors, he made himself a hermitage about two miles from the city. This place was so secluded and remote that it had all the solitude of a desert. On one side, it was walled in by the rock-face of a high mountain, and the level ground that remained was enclosed by a gentle bend of the River Loire. There was only one approach to it, and that a very narrow one.[1] (*Vita Sancti Martini* X.3–4; Hoare 1954, 24–5.)

This marks the beginning of what eventually became a very powerful and rich Benedictine monastery, owning a large number of priories in western France and England, but for the time being we shall concentrate on the early phases of the long history of this community. It started as a hermitage for Martin and a few companions on the northern bank of the River Loire, a couple of miles away from the newly built *castrum* of Tours where the first cathedral had been erected by Litorius, predecessor of Martin in the episcopal see (Fig. 1).[2]

This beautiful spot enclosed between the chalk cliff and the River Loire (Fig. 2), facing south, had been occupied since the Roman period, as shown by the first excavations conducted by Charles Lelong between 1974 and 1983.[3] In 2005, a new research programme was initiated by the University of Tours. This aims to study the transformation of the site in the *longue durée*, using all available investigative methods such as geomorphology, geology, building archaeology and excavation, and bringing these into dialogue with written sources and iconography when possible.[4] The study of this suburban site is also being conducted in close connection with the long-term archaeological investigations from which Tours itself has benefited since the late Sixties.[5] On a larger scale, the research programme developed at Marmoutier aims to contribute to a better understanding of early monasticism in Gaul and western Europe. This is currently being tackled at a number of very famous fifth- to early-sixth-century monastic sites such as Lérins, an island opposite Canne, l'Ile-Barbe near Lyon, Saint-Claude (Jura) and at

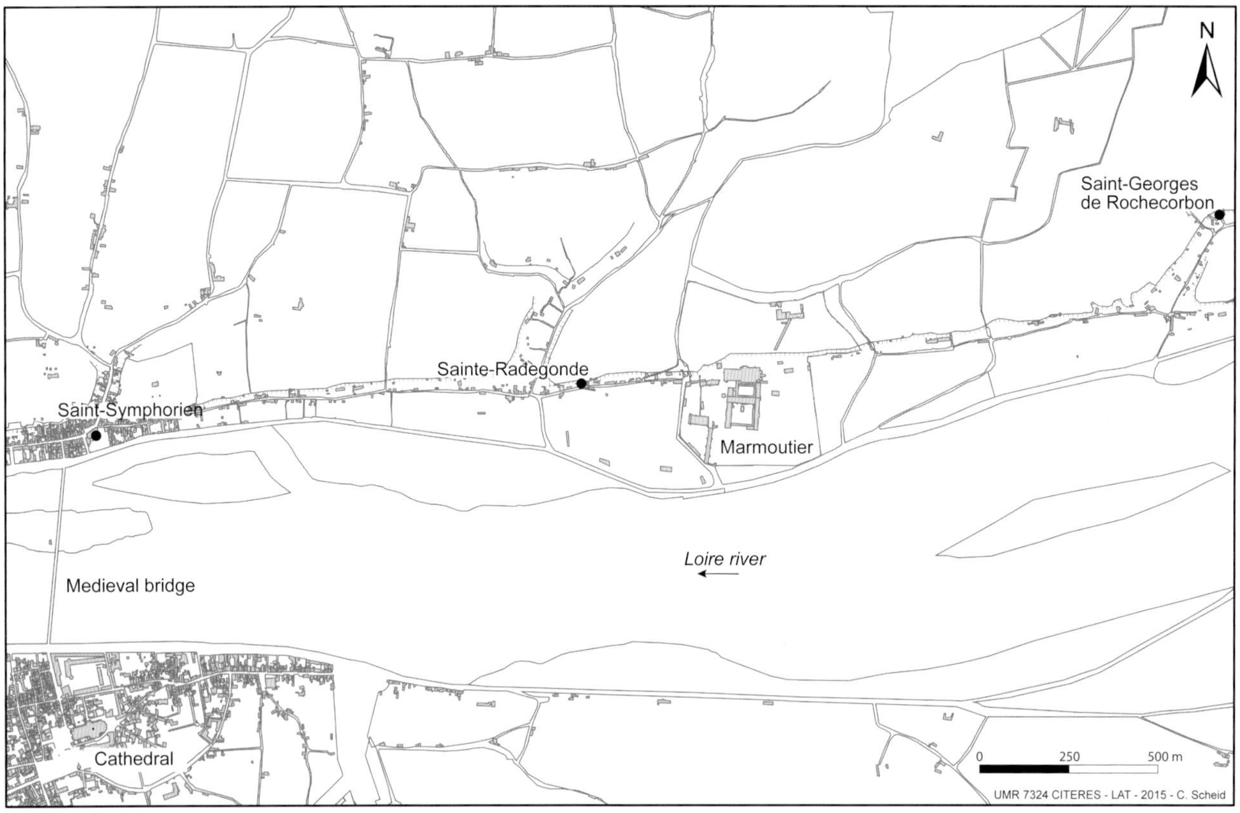


**Fig. 1** Map locating Tours and Marmoutier based on the nineteenth-century Ordnance Survey.

**Fig. 2** Marmoutier, the cliff from the south showing caves turned into chapels that were restored in the nineteenth century and the bell tower built in the second half of the eleventh century.

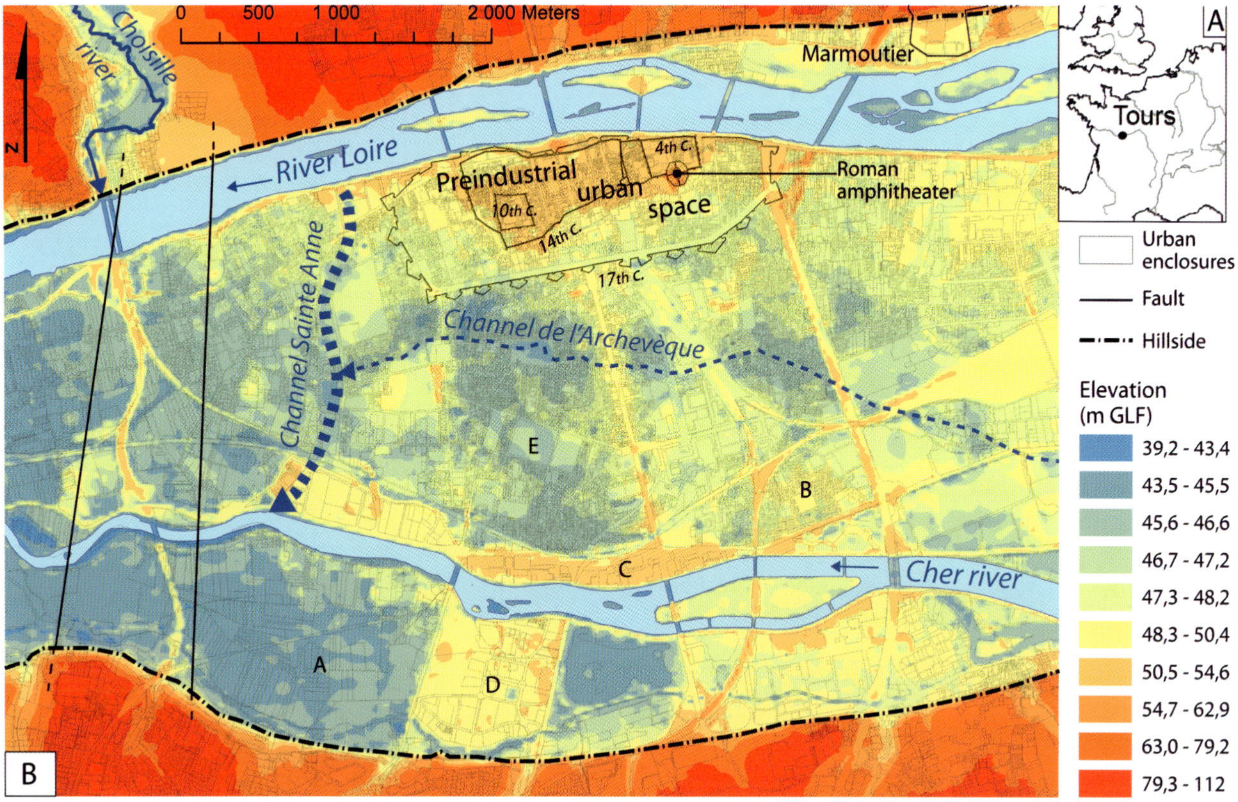


**Fig. 3** Map of the floodplain around Tours.

Agaune (Switzerland), and also at later foundations such as Luxeuil (Haute-Saône) and Bobbio (Italy) established by Columbanus.[6]

In accordance with the main focus of the conference organized in Canterbury in April 2015, this paper will concentrate on the first millennium, and will consider in succession three main topics:

1. the formation of the river bank where Marmoutier was established, which plays an important part in the Roman and early medieval topography;
2. the Roman heritage and the foundation of Marmoutier;
3. the layout of the monastic settlement in the late Roman period and the early Middle Ages.

## From island to terra firma

The impact of the river on the lengthy history of the site is one major target of the research programme developed at Marmoutier. That section of the river flows through a fairly narrow part of the floodplain, with a northern limit marked by a chalk cliff, whereas towards the south, the plain is wider, extending as far as the River Cher (Fig. 3). Several geological and geophysical surveys have been undertaken in the last few years, combined with C14 and Optical Stimulated Luminescence (OSL) analysis. The whole set of data suggests a general evolution divided between five main phases which may be summarized as follows (Fig. 4):

- phase 1: before 5000 BC, the bank was very narrow and the main channel of the River Loire flowed partly over the area which was to become the monastic site;
- phase 2: between 5000 BC and the seventh century AD, an alluvial bar developed within the Loire channel;
- phase 3: during the seventh–ninth centuries, the alluvial bar gradually turned into an island, which was a more established element of the landscape. Thus, a secondary channel separated the island from the mainland;
- phase 4: between the ninth and the eleventh centuries, the formation of the island was completed and it was possible to use this area in a more permanent way. The secondary channel still formed a depressed area but less and less water was flowing through it;
- phase 5: probably as early as the twelfth–thirteenth centuries, anthropogenic deposits accumulated not only in this depressed area but also over the whole site of Marmoutier, which then covered a much larger surface; *c.* 1220, a new gate, which is preserved and stands close to the present course of the river, was erected, showing the greater extension of the precinct at this date.

Thus, a combination of geological and geophysical data set alongside historical and archaeological information shows that the present morphology of the site results, first, from the dynamic evolution of the River Loire up to the end of the first millennium AD, and, secondly, from subsequent human activities.

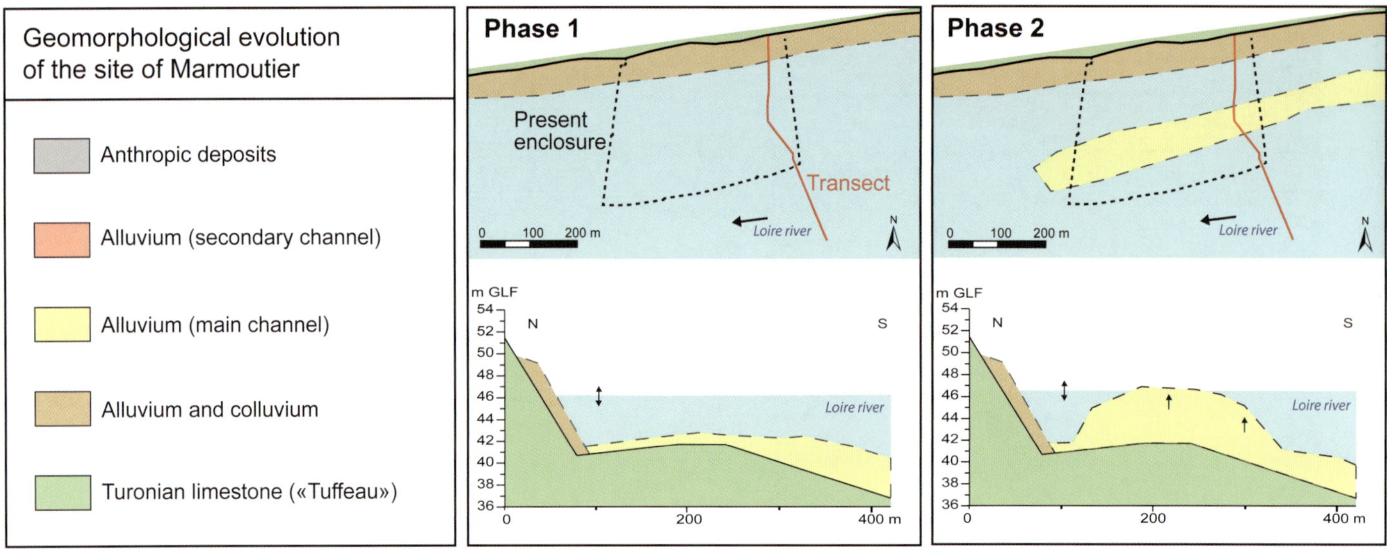


**Fig. 4** Marmoutier, morphological evolution of the area.

## The Roman occupation and the foundation of Marmoutier

Since 2005, three main areas have undergone archaeological recording (Fig. 5):

- the eastern half of the area eventually enclosed in the Gothic church which abutted the cliff in the northern part of the precinct (zone 1);
- to the west, the area where the guest house was built in the late twelfth century; one third of this survived the post-Revolution destruction (zone 3 for the standing remains and zone 4 for the destroyed part);
- the terraces which extend between the western gate

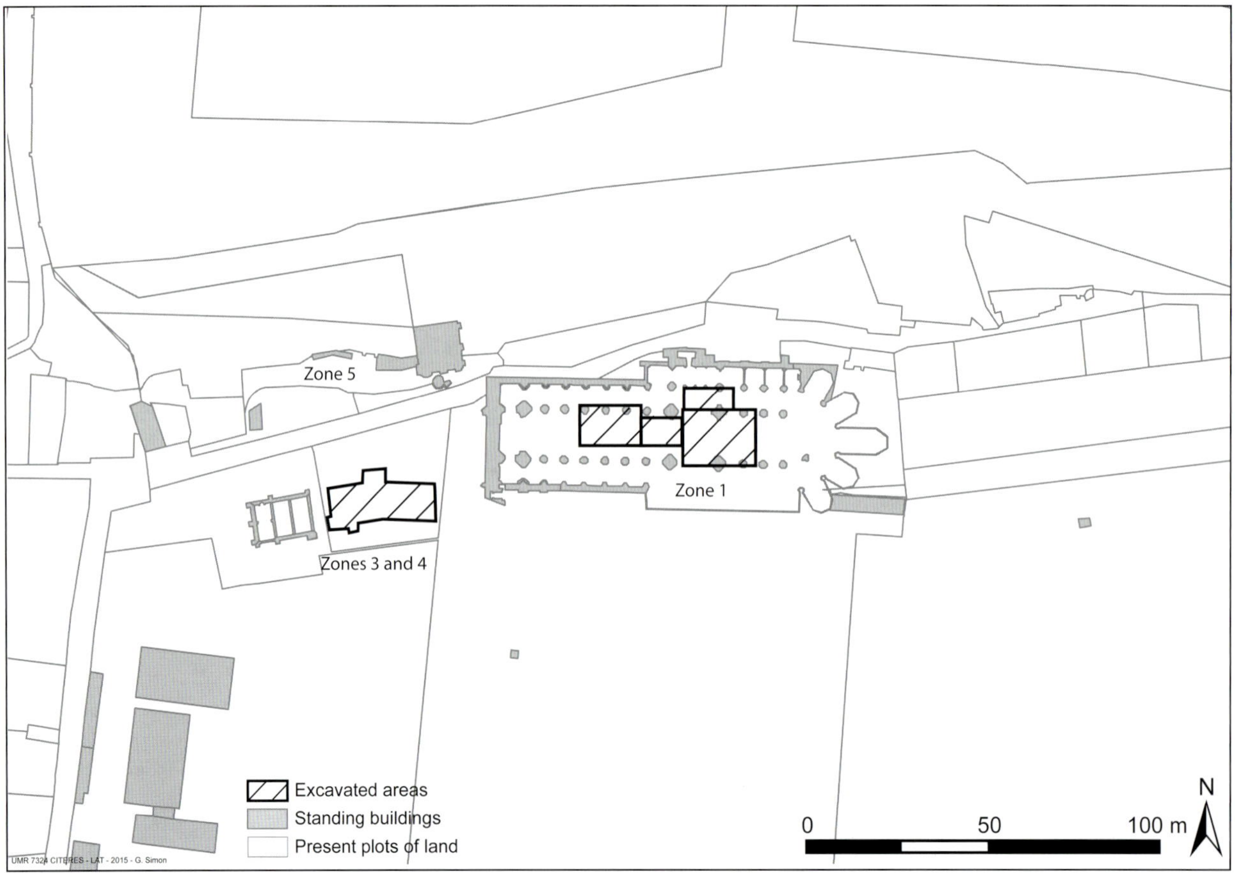


**Fig. 5** Marmoutier, plan of excavated areas. Zone 1, contours of the Gothic church; zones 3 and 4, the former medieval guest house; zone 5, the western terraces with troglodyte chapels and the eleventh-century bell tower.

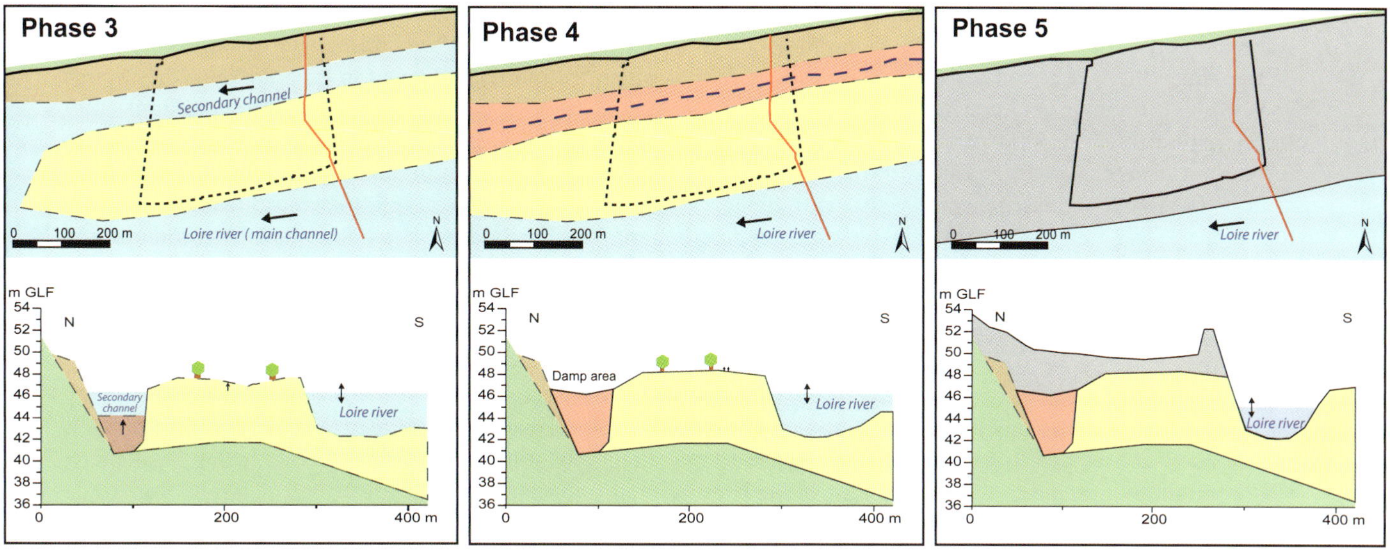


UMR 7324 CITERES - LAT - 2014 - E. Morin

and the bell tower erected in the second half of the eleventh century and which include several caves hollowed out of the chalk cliff; among them are the remains of the Lady chapel associated with a number of graves (zone 5).

As mentioned earlier, occupation on the site which became the *Majus Monasterium*[7] (hence Marmoutier in French), the only name that we know of for this area, started in the first century and has never stopped since. Roman occupation is characterized by a certain number of walls of various types and dates which run parallel or at right angles to the line of the cliff (Fig. 6); one of them, identified over 15 m, is built in '*petit appareil*' alternating with rows of tiles and can be assigned a fourth-century date. Some of these walls were covered with white or coloured plaster and associated with earthen floors which were replaced by concrete ones during the fourth and fifth centuries. Overall, Roman constructions were identified over *c.* 300 m$^2$ in zone 1, but later remains did not allow access to extensive areas of associated occupation levels.

Thus, the difficulty is to assign a function to these different constructions, which may well have fulfilled various purposes between the first and the late fourth centuries. Any interpretation at the moment should be regarded as highly hypothetical and must rely more on general considerations than on archaeological demonstration. We should bear in mind the narrowness of this piece of land in Roman times and the fact that a road – a narrow one says Sulpicius Severus – went through it. Although no

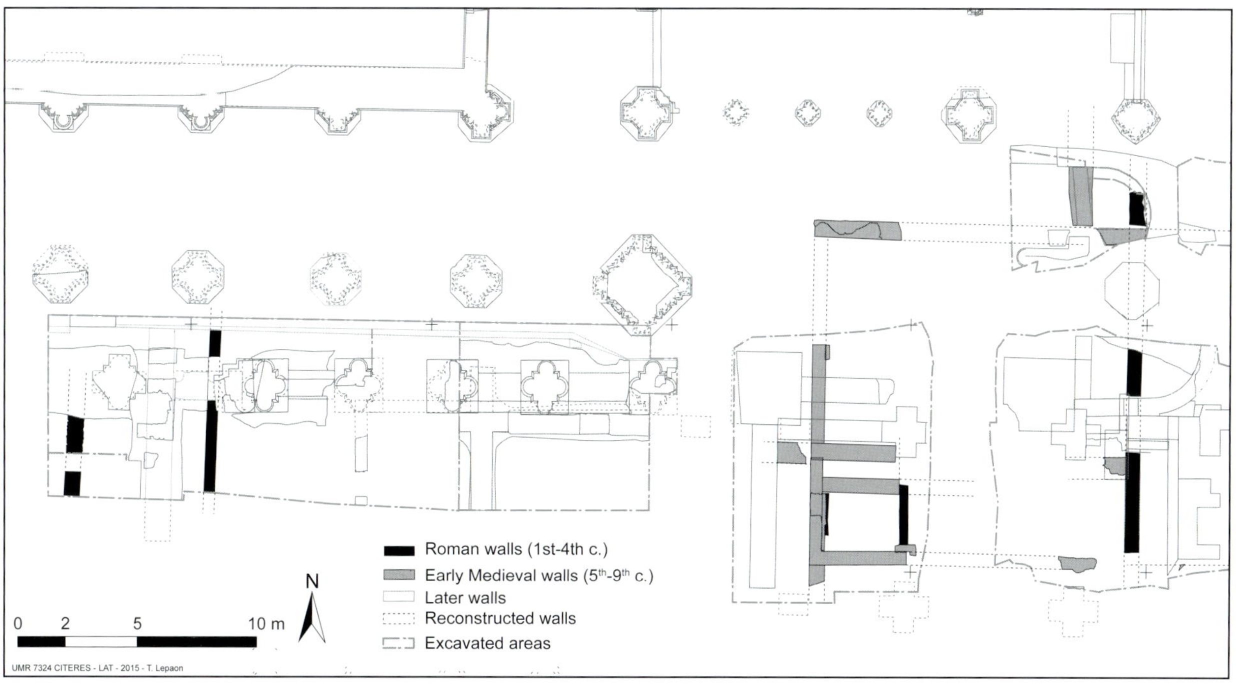


**Fig. 6** Marmoutier, plan of Roman and early medieval walls prior to the construction of the late-tenth-century church.

archaeological trace of it has been recorded so far, we can assume that it did exist and that it ran along the bottom of the cliff. This is where a long-distance road, which goes through the monastic precinct, is mentioned from the eleventh century onwards, and it is clearly drawn on the earliest plans that were produced in the seventeenth century. In view of all these points, together with the fact that Roman *villae* were not associated with long-distance roads and that none of them has been identified so far in the floodplain of the River Loire (as opposed to smaller rivers), we suggest that this place might have been a road station.

Only further excavation over a much larger area will enable us to characterize this Roman site more precisely, but we know at least that Roman stone walls and associated levels did not extend to the western part of the later precinct where a large guest house stood from the late twelfth century onwards (zone 4). Two trial trenches, together covering *c.* 15 sq m, were excavated in 2015. They revealed immediately on top of the natural ground a thick black layer of *c.* 60 cm which contained a fair amount of fifth–sixth-century sherds. A large quantity of Roman pottery in these levels as well as in the upper ones, which can be described as dark earth, shows the proximity of Roman occupation, but zone 4 is clearly on the outskirts of it. Thus, the western limit of the Roman site, strictly speaking, runs somewhere between the area of zone 1 – at least the eastern part of it which was deeply excavated – and zone 4.

One more element should be taken into consideration in order to characterize the site in the late Roman period: the fact that a wooden bridge had been built (probably in the third century) on the same axis as the Roman amphitheatre of *Caesarodunum*, which was fortified in the second half of the century and then incorporated into the *castrum* erected at the beginning of the fourth century.[8] This bridge joined the two sides of the river about 2 km downstream from Marmoutier.[9] As this bridge was substantially rebuilt some time between 487 and 535, it is likely – but not certain – that it was in use in Martin's time. If so, it would provide a different picture of the site, probably chosen by the bishop of Tours as a retreat, from that which is given by Sulpicius Severus. It was, in fact, not as isolated as Sulpicius Severus presents it, but, on the contrary, could easily be reached from the late Roman town.

Obviously, Sulpicius Severus' purpose was not to offer a precise topographical description of the place. While referring to the real landscape of the area, marked by the proximity of the cliff and the river, he also follows the usual 'Desert' *topos* found in many eastern saints' lives: it was important to insist on the solitude of the site in order to amplify the sanctity of Martin and his companions.[10]

By establishing a religious community two miles from Tours, just on the other side of the river, Martin reproduced the pattern he had followed a few years earlier near Poitiers. With the support of the bishop of Poitiers, Hilary, he had then established a hermitage on a site by the River Clain later known as Ligugé, five miles out from Poitiers.[11] The chosen site was a Roman *villa*, which was partly excavated in the middle of the twentieth century.[12] It is important to underline the similarities between both foundations: a few miles from the capital city, by a river, in an inhabited place with major Roman buildings. We know very little about Ligugé in Martin's time; but Sulpicius Severus describes the community at Marmoutier as a gathering of hermits living in wooden cells or (for most of them) in caves hollowed out of the soft stone cliff.[13] After the election of Martin as bishop of Tours in 371, Ligugé's size and prestige decreased, whereas according to Martin's biographer about eighty disciples lived at Marmoutier in the late fourth century. Their way of life was spartan, with only one meal a day; food and clothing were dispensed centrally and trade was prohibited. The only work undertaken by the monks, the young ones, was the copying of manuscripts, which shows the strong connection which existed between this episcopal settlement and the Church, which was being organized in Gaul at the time. From this point of view, and also because of its location close to the capital city of the diocese, the community of Marmoutier is very different from Egyptian monasticism, even if the semi-eremitic way of life of these men, most of them members of aristocratic families, was inspired by the first communities in the desert. Thus, Marmoutier was always closely associated with the city of Tours, even after Martin's death, and it became a place of pilgrimage for the local Christian community who, according to Gregory of Tours, went there at Easter.

## The layout of the monastic settlement in the late Roman period and the early Middle Ages

What do we know from written sources and from archaeological data regarding the layout and functions of the monastic settlement in the first centuries of its existence? Evidence is still rather sparse for the beginning of the community but a few points can be highlighted regarding access, churches, funerary areas and craftwork, which help to reconstruct the landscape and the various activities.[14]

### *Access and precinct*

The very early texts do not explicitly mention a precinct. This is referred to for the first time in the middle of the ninth century with the word *moenia*, which suggests a stone wall. However, on the basis of several pieces of information, we can locate the main access to the monastery on the north-west side, probably in connection with the road running between the cliff and the River Loire. It is impossible to reconstruct the extent of the precinct before the thirteenth century, but the geomorphological analyses revealed the limited extent of the mainland between the river and the cliff until the seventh–ninth centuries, which explains the location of all the identified buildings near or within the cliff for this period.

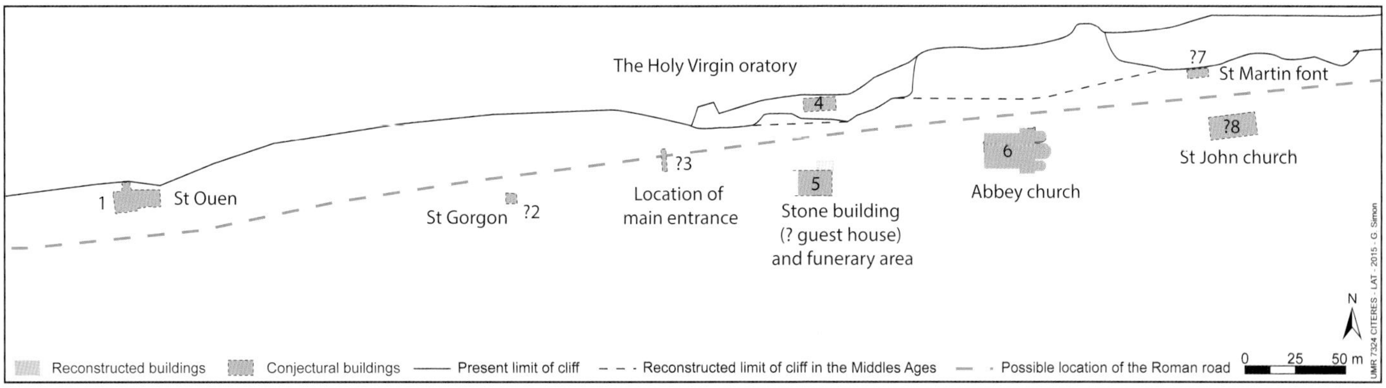


**Fig. 7** Marmoutier, topography of the monastery and its outskirts in the eleventh century.

### *The churches*

Several churches are mentioned by various written sources, some inside the precinct and others outside it, but all closely connected to the monastic community. They must therefore be considered for a better understanding of the sacred landscape of that area during the earliest part of the Middle Ages (Fig. 7).

#### The late Roman *basilicae*

According to Sulpicius Severus, a '*locus orationis*', where the brothers gathered every day, existed in Martin's time. This first church is usually identified with the *basilica* dedicated to SS Peter and Paul mentioned in the late sixth century by Gregory of Tours, who regarded St Martin as the builder. According to the same source, bishop Volusianus (488/9–495/6) built another *basilica* dedicated to St John [the Baptist].[15]

None of these buildings has been identified on the site but it is believed that the first one was in the same area as the later abbey churches and, on the basis of later textual evidence, that the second one was further east, both of them standing at the bottom of the cliff and more or less on the same line, which was a common feature in early Christian topography.

If the first *basilica* was built where the later ones stood, there is no chance of identifying it because of the many reconstructions which occurred. It is also possible that the community reused part of the pre-existing Roman buildings as a *locus orationis* before building a proper church in the following centuries, near the 'Repos'. This is the cave dug into the cliff which is identified by historical tradition as the resting place of St Martin. [16]

#### The late-tenth-century abbey church and associated graves

Although some stone remains, which are surrounded on two sides by a dozen male graves attributed to the ninth century, might correspond to a church, the earliest abbey church which can be clearly reconstructed on the basis of archaeological data was built towards the end of the tenth century. It was a stone building divided into three naves, very likely ending in three apses to the east, of which only part of the northern one survives (Fig. 8).[17] The rectangular contour of a robbed structure which stood very close to the western facade might have been the base of a font such as those identified, also in the western part of the church, at La Madeleine, a suburban *basilica* excavated by Charles Bonnet in Geneva, and on the St Gall plan.[18]

Two graves were uncovered just outside the facade of the church, which should be viewed as high-status graves, either of abbots or members of the family of the count of Blois, who were buried at Marmoutier in the late tenth–early eleventh centuries. In fact, the whole construction of this church was undertaken during the *reformatio* of the monastery, which was supported by the count of Blois, towards the end of the tenth century. Odo asked the famous monastery of Cluny to send a dozen monks who settled in Marmoutier under the supervision of abbot Gilbertus. According to later sources, they did not stay for very long; nevertheless, their coming to Marmoutier was the starting point of the golden age of the monastery expressed both by the many transactions recorded in charters in the eleventh and twelfth centuries and by the construction or reconstruction of a large number of buildings, including a new church, the bell tower and the whole cloister, which were erected before 1100.[19]

As for the second church, the dedication to John the Baptist suggests a possible function as a baptistery, sometimes identified in early monasteries such as Agaune, but this can be no more than a hypothesis. It could also have been a funerary church for the main members of the community, but this is also conjectural as we know almost nothing about this church which is not mentioned in the medieval records that have come down to us after the twelfth century.[20]

#### The oratory dedicated to the Blessed Virgin

An oratory (*oratorium, locellus*) dedicated to the Blessed Virgin is mentioned in the middle of the ninth century and can be located near the entrance to the monastery, on a terrace halfway up the cliff. The text refers to a crypt (*crypta*), in which were deposited the bodies of several disciples of St Martin. This last piece of information is very doubtful as it obviously refers to the cult of the Seven

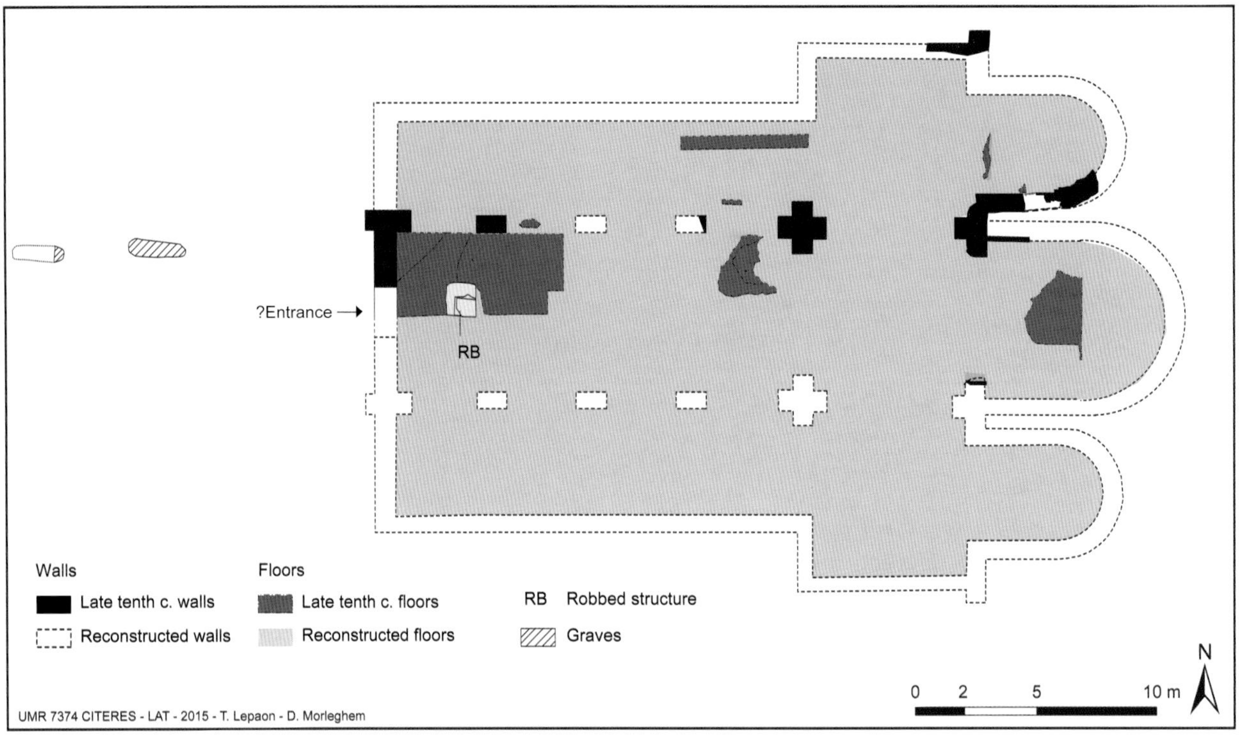


**Fig. 8** Marmoutier, reconstructed plan of the late-tenth-century abbey church. The east end is largely conjectural.

Sleepers of Marmoutier which developed in the twelfth century, drawing on Gregory of Tours' history of the Seven Sleepers of Ephesus.[21]

Several caves dug into the rock and the remains of an apse mainly built in *petit appareil* might be part of this chapel. It was largely destroyed in the second half of the eleventh century when the bell tower was built against the cliff (Fig. 9).

Some tombs dug through the rock were excavated in the past, some as early as the seventeenth century when the monastic community wanted to know more about the origins of the chapel and of the cult of the Seven Sleepers. Today, five of them can be seen on the terrace but they used to be inside the oratory - they could belong to the early Middle Ages, but could also date from the twelfth or thirteenth century when the cult developed. In any case, they express the funerary character of the chapel, which was reconstructed with a double nave probably in the twelfth century as shown on seventeenth-century drawings.

### The *extra muros* churches

The religious topography of Marmoutier before *c.* 1000 included another two churches, which stood outside the precinct, to the west (Fig. 7).

First, a chapel was dedicated to St Gorgon whose relics were brought back from Rome around 946 by Renaldus, abbot of Marmoutier.[22] The narrative of this translation makes it clear that the chapel was built just outside the precinct, close to the main entrance, to enable the laity, male and female, to come and pray to the saint. It shows that the abbot wanted to develop a popular cult but at the same time to protect the community from too much disturbance. This chapel is still mentioned as such in the twelfth century, but then disappears from the records.

The last church to be considered is located about 500 m to the west of the entrance to the monastery and was mentioned at the very end of the first millennium. It became the parish church of the monastic *burgus*, and was mentioned for the first time between 1032 and 1064.[23] The greater part of the church was dug into the cliff, and the south wall and the apse still stand as built in the twelfth century, in spite of heavy restoration in the nineteenth or twentieth century.

As a conclusion to this section, one should point out the large number of separate churches which were erected at Marmoutier before *c.* 1000. Two, built before the end of the fifth century, provided a location for the monastic offices and perhaps baptisms and/or burials. Another two were erected in the middle of the ninth century, one inside and one outside the precinct; these had funerary and commemorative functions. All of them were built either against the cliff or just at the bottom of it, forming a line of sacred buildings along the main road and parallel to the River Loire. That line of churches was even extended at the very beginning of the eleventh century by the church of St George at Rochecorbon, built 1.5 km to the east.[24] This religious topography was preserved at least until the twelfth century when some of these churches disappeared from the records, but not necessarily from the landscape.

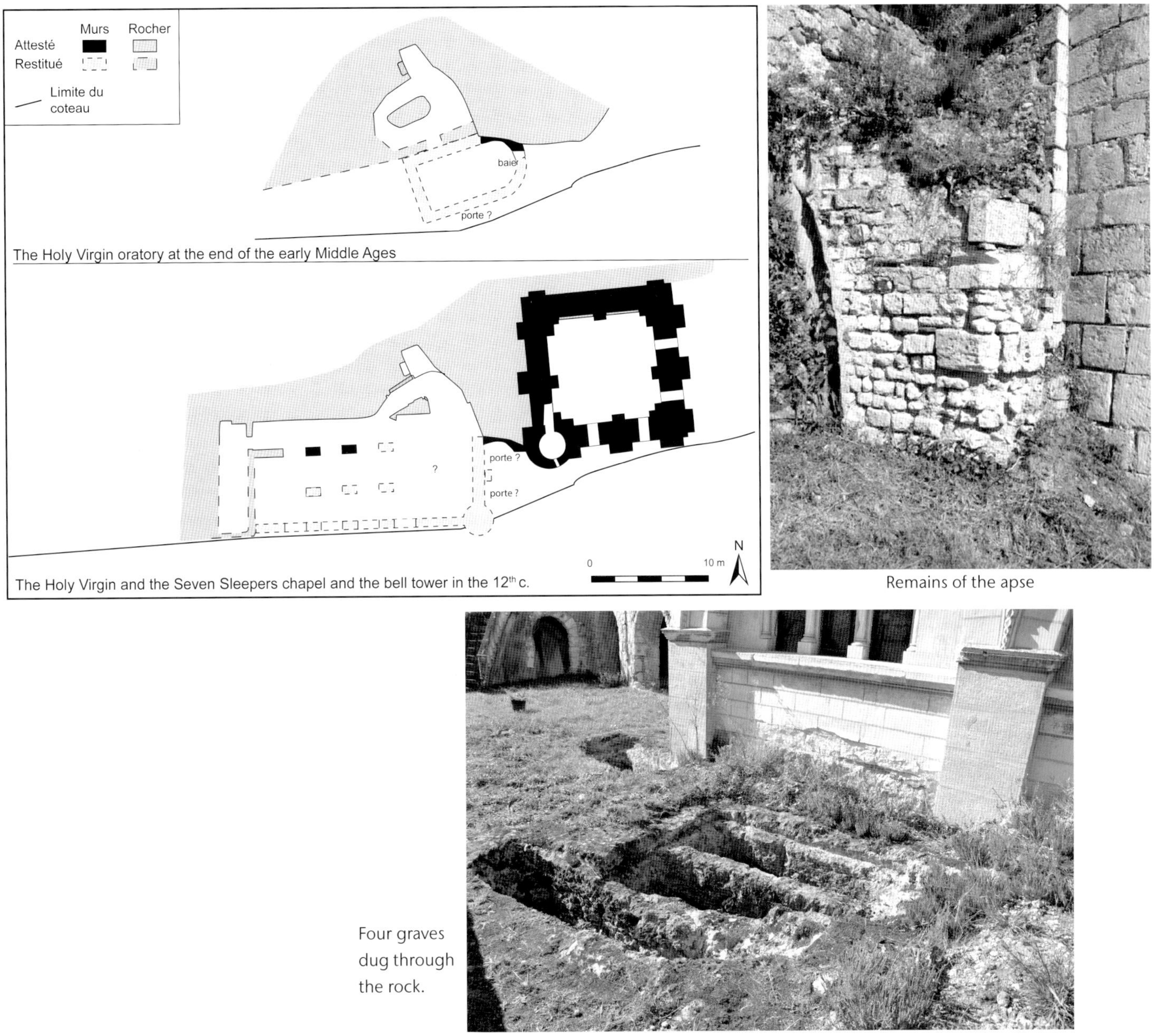


**Fig. 9** Marmoutier, oratory dedicated to the Holy Virgin, conjectural plans and archaeological remains.

### *A working and discard area in the western part of the precinct*

In the north-western part of the site, close to the assumed location of the main access, early medieval levels have been excavated. These lie within the later extension of the large guest house that was built towards the end of the twelfth century. Although excavation is still in progress, one can summarize the stratigraphic sequence which was observed over a surface of *c.* 360 $m^2$.

On top of the black layer attributed to the fifth–sixth centuries already mentioned, a thick backfill was deposited which contained few artefacts. The next deposit, about 60 cm deep, can be described as dark earth and developed roughly between the seventh/eighth and the tenth centuries. Some features such as post-holes and especially pits of various shapes have been identified but no structure could be reconstructed and the functions of most pits are not clear. Micro-morphological analysis of several samples of dark earth revealed that they result from a complex process associated with the accumulation of various kinds of debris, including some connected with metalwork (copper and iron), some with human circulation, and others with natural biological activity. Craftwork in that area or nearby is also confirmed by a few artefacts such as a piece of bone with traces of saw marks or a fragment of antler.

The contrast between this area and zone 1, where stone buildings were standing all through the early Middle Ages, should be underlined. Thus, the whole stratigraphic sequence of zone 4 between the fifth and the tenth centuries suggests a working and discard area at the western periphery of the monastic settlement.

**A cobbled yard at the entrance to the monastery**
Finally, on top of dark earth, a cobbled surface was revealed over about 160 $m^2$. We can, however, assume that it covered a much larger area as it was destroyed to the east in the twelfth century by a large excavation connected with one of the stone buildings preceding the guest house (see below). This cobbled surface, on which traces of ruts were well preserved, can be identified as an open area lying between the gate to the west and the main monastic church to the east. In other words, the former discard area would have been turned into a much cleaner yard, perhaps owing to the construction of the new abbey church in the late tenth century (see above).

*A possible guest house and cemetery*
Finally, the last episode for the time being was the construction, possibly in the eleventh century, of a rectangular stone building which was associated with a funerary area lying to the north of it. Graves of both sexes allow us to identify a lay cemetery, perhaps for people working for the monks.

In view of the location of this building near the main entrance and the fact that a significant guest house was erected in the same place in the late twelfth century, one is tempted to identify a similar function for the first stage of this architectural development, but this cannot be proven.

## Conclusion

It is time to come to a conclusion, emphasizing the main topographical aspects of Marmoutier in the first millennium.

1 We must keep in mind how narrow the river bank was until the island became incorporated into it after the seventh–ninth centuries. Thus, in the very first centuries of monastic settlement, this area could itself be equated to an island, a location often chosen for very early monastic foundations, in Gaul as elsewhere, as a substitute for the oriental desert. Martin himself had his first experience of monastic life on the island of Gallinara, off the Ligurian coast.
2 The association between a Roman city and a suburban monastery which was created by Martin at Ligugé and Marmoutier was reproduced in several other places in Gaul, for example near Lyon, where l'Ile Barbe was established in the fifth century on an island in the River Saône, or in Auxerre, where Bishop Germanus founded a monastery dedicated to SS Cosmas and Damian on the other side of the River Yonne, reproducing Martin's criss-crossing of the river between Tours and Marmoutier.[25]
3 The morphology and topography of the site at Marmoutier are responsible for the location of the oldest main buildings at the bottom of the cliff, or incorporated into it. So far, our knowledge of the monastery in its early phases mainly includes churches and funerary areas of various status, but we hope that the continuation of the work will provide more information regarding daily life. Craftwork is also attested, as in many early medieval monasteries, both in the British Isles and on the Continent, but the main structures connected with these activities remain to be found. Some of the pottery and glass (both vessel and window glass) uncovered in the early medieval levels and some artefacts such as a game piece reveal the high status of the community in comparison with what has been found in Tours at a similar period.

## Acknowledgements
I am most grateful to Dr Clare Stancliffe for correcting my English and for suggesting various alterations which have much improved the quality of my paper.

## Notes

1 (3) Aliquandiu ergo adhaerenti ad ecclesiam cellula usus est: dein cum inquietudinem se frequentantium ferre non posset, duobus fere extra civitatem milibus monasterium sibi statuit. (4) Qui locus tam secretus et remotus erat, ut eremi solitudinem non desideraret. Ex uno enim latere praecisa montis excelsi rupe ambiebatur, reliquam planitiem Liger fluvius reducto paululum sinu clauserat: una tantum eademque arta admodum via adiri poterat (*Vie de Saint Martin*, edited and translated into French by Jacques Fontaine, Paris, 1967, Vol. 1, X.3–4, 274).

2 Pietri 1983 and 1987 provide all the references to early texts regarding Tours between the fourth and sixth centuries.

3 These archaeological investigations were concentrated on the surface covered by the Gothic abbey church which was built on top of the previous ones – at least two of them have been identified – but Roman levels were reached in trial trenches here and there.

4 This programme has been directed by Elisabeth Lorans since 2005 with the collaboration of Thomas Creissen since 2010. It is funded by the City of Tours, the Région Centre-Val de Loire and the State (Ministry of Culture), with the support of the University of Tours and the Centre national de la Recherche Scientifique (CNRS). This site is the main training excavation for students from Tours University and six weeks of fieldwork take place every year. Annual reports can be downloaded from HAL-CNRS. A general view of the main archaeological results is provided by Lorans and Creissen 2013 and 2014.

5 For the most recent synthesis on Roman and medieval Tours, see Galinié 2007, updated for some aspects regarding the first millennium by Lorans, Jouquand, Fouillet and Rodier 2013.

6 Among the most recent publications which include papers on monastic sites in various European countries, see De Rubeis and Marazzi 2008; Codou and Lauwers 2009; Lauwers 2014.

7 'monasterium qui nunc major dicitur', in Gregory of Tours, *Decem libri historiarum* X.xxxi.3, 527 for the first mention; he applies it to Martin's time and later periods.

8 The study of these wooden remains was carried out in 2003 (Seigne

and Neury 2007) and 2011 (Hirn 2013), taking advantage of the very low water-level in the River Loire. The dating of the construction of this bridge and therefore its connection either with the amphitheatre or with the *castrum* is a very difficult matter and is still not entirely resolved. V. Hirn decides in favour of the earlier dating, some time in the third century, on the basis of a higher statistical probability of the dendrochronological results.

9 If we add the length of the bridge itself, based on the present width of the River Loire, i.e. *c.* 540 m (this was different in the late Roman period), the total distance would be roughly 2.5 km.

10 See *Vie de Saint Martin*, ed. J. Fontaine, 667 *et sq.* on the links between oriental ascetic landscapes and the description of Marmoutier by Sulpicius Severus, who produced in the *Vita Martini* the western version of it that was developed so extensively in medieval hagiography.

11 'Cum iam Hilarius praeterisset, Pictavos eum est vestigiis persecutes; cumque ab eo gratissime fuisset exceptus, haud longe sibi ab oppido monasterium conlocavit' (*VM* VII.1); 'Hilary, however, had already passed through the City [Rome], so Martin followed in his track [as far as Poitiers]. He was given a warm welcome by him and made himself a hermitage not far from the town' (Hoare 1954, 20).

12 This very limited investigation revealed two main elements: a horseshoe-shaped yard surrounded by a *porticus*; and a pool which was partly reused as a large room perhaps built for the first monastic community, in Martin's time. Later on this room was converted into a church by the addition of an apse (sixth century?), and all the subsequent monastic churches were built on top of it (Boissavit-Camus 2010). *Porticus* and pool are common features in late Roman *villae* in south-western Gaul.

13 'His own cell was built of wood, as were those of many of the brethren; but most of them had hollowed out shelters for themselves in the rock of the overhanging mountain' (*VM* X.4–5; Hoare 1954, 24). On the beginnings at Ligugé and Marmoutier, see Pietri 1983, especially 421–7; Stancliffe 1983, 22–6; Oudart 1993; Bord 2012; Lorans 2012.

14 For an overview of the monastic topography at Marmoutier in medieval and modern times, see Lorans 2014.

15 '... in monasterio ... basilicam in honore sanctorum apostolorum Petri et Pauli aedificavit ...'; '... hujus tempore ... aedificatus est et basilica sancti Johannis ad majorem monasterium' (Gregory of Tours, *Decem libri historiarum* X.xxxi.3 and 7).

16 For a general view of the questions surrounding the 'Repos', its location and relationships with the successive abbey churches, see Lorans 2014, 311–14.

17 A full description and interpretation are provided in Creissen and Lorans 2014.

18 Bonnet 1977; Sennhauser 2013, 534 underlines the fact that after the production of the St Gall plan, the baptismal font is often placed near the main door of the church, to the left.

19 Lorans 2014, 318–24.

20 Lorans 2014, 313–14. Nearby is located a feature which has been called St Martin's fountain since the eighteenth century. This is a cavity within which a pool, set up in 1897, retains the water accumulating from the water table. The historical tradition associates this with the well which, according to Gregory of Tours, was excavated by the saint himself and provided miraculous water, but obviously this connection cannot be taken for granted.

21 Lorans 2014, 314–18.

22 Lorans 2014, 333–4.

23 Zadora-Rio and Gauthiez 2003; Lorans 2014, 339–40.

24 Lorans 2014, 341.

25 Dessi and Lauwers 2009, 248–9.

# Bibliography

## *Primary sources*


Gregory of Tours, *Decem libri historiarum*, ed. B. Krusch and W. Levison, 1937–51, new edition 1962, MGH, srm, I, 1.

Sulpice Sévère, *Vie de Saint Martin*, ed. J. Fontaine, 1967, 2 vols., Paris: Cerf.

*The Western Fathers: Being the Lives of SS Martin of Tours, Ambrose, Augustine of Hippo, Honoratus of Arles, and Germanus of Auxerre*, trans. and ed. F. R. Hoare, 1954, London: Sheed and Ward.


## *Secondary sources*


Boissavit-Camus, B. 2010. 'Les édifices cultuels de l'abbaye de Saint-Martin de Ligugé (Vienne)', in L. Bourgeois (ed.), *Wisigoths et Francs autour de la bataille de Vouillé (507). Recherches récentes sur le haut Moyen Âge dans le Centre-Ouest de la France. Actes des XXVIII^e Journées internationales d'archéologie mérovingienne, Vouillé et Poitiers (Vienne, France) – 28–30 septembre 2007*, 215–36, Saint-Germain-en-Laye: AFAM.

Bonnet, C. 1977. *Les premiers* édifices *chrétiens de la Madeleine à Genève*, Genève: Société d'Histoire et d'Archéologie de Genève.

Bord, L.-J. 2012. 'Aux origines du monachisme en Gaule : les communautés martiniennes du IV^e siècle', in B. Judic (dir.), *Les abbayes martiniennes. Annales de Bretagne et des Pays de l'Ouest (Anjou, Maine, Poitou-Charente, Touraine)*, **119(3)**, 13–25.

Codou, Y. and Lauwers, M. (eds.) 2009. *Lérins, une* île *sainte de l'Antiquité au Moyen* Âge, Collection d'études médiévales de Nice, 9, Turnhout: Brepols.

Creissen, Th. and Lorans, E. 2014. 'L'apport des dernières fouilles archéologiques à la connaissance des églises abbatiales de Marmoutier antérieures à la reconstruction gothique', *Hortus Artium Medievalium*, **20(2)**, 532–43.

De Rubeis, F. and Marazzi, F. (eds.) 2008. *Monasteri in Europa occidentale (secoli VIII–XI): topografia e strutture. Atti del convegno internazionale, Museo Archeologico di Castel San Vincenzo, 23–26 settembre 2004*, Rome: Edizioni Viella.

Dessi, R. M. and Lauwers, M. 2009. 'Désert, Église, île sainte, Lérins et la sanctification des îles monastiques de l'Antiquité à la fin du Moyen Âge', in Y. Codou and M. Lauwers (eds.), *Lérins, une* île *sainte de l'Antiquité au Moyen* Âge, 231–79, Collection d'études médiévales de Nice, 9, Turnhout: Brepols.

Galinié, H. (ed.) 2007. *Tours antique et médiéval. Lieux de vie, temps de la ville : 40 ans d'archéologie urbaine*, Supplément à la Revue archéologique du Centre de la France, 30; numéro spécial de la collection Recherches sur Tours, Tours: FERACF.

Hirn, V. (ed.) 2013. *Tours, étude archéologique des ponts dits de Eudes et de l'île Aucard*, unpublished report, Service de l'archéologie du département d'Indre-et-Loire.

Lauwers, M. (ed.) 2014. *Monastères et espace social. Genèse et transformation d'un système de lieux dans l'Occident médiéval*, Collection d'Etudes médiévales de Nice, 15, Turnhout: Brepols.

Lorans, E. 2012. 'Aux origines du monastère de Marmoutier : le témoignage de l'archéologie', in B. Judic (dir.), *Les abbayes martiniennes. Annales de Bretagne et des Pays de l'Ouest (Anjou, Maine, Poitou-Charente, Touraine)*, **119(3)**, 177–203.

Lorans, E. 2014. 'Circulation et hiérarchie au sein des établissements monastiques médiévaux : autour de Marmoutier', in M. Lauwers (ed.), *Monastères et espace social. Genèse et transformation d'un système de lieux dans l'Occident médiéval*, 289–352, Collection d'Etudes médiévales de Nice, 15, Turnhout: Brepols.

Lorans, E. and Creissen, T. 2013. 'Marmoutier : archéologie d'un site monastique dans la longue durée', *Bulletin de la Société Archéologique de Touraine*, **59**, 123–47.

Lorans, E. and Creissen, T. (eds.) 2014. *Marmoutier, un grand monastère ligérien (Antiquité–XIX^e siècle)*, Orléans: Ministère de la Culture et de la Communication (Patrimoine en région Centre). http://www.

culturecommunication.gouv.fr/Regions/Drac-Centre/Ressources/Publications/Nos-collections/Patrimoines-en-region-Centre/Patrimoine-protege

Lorans, E., Jouquand, A.-M., Fouillet, N. and Rodier, X. 2013. 'Les rythmes de l'espace urbain à Tours : nouvelles données, nouvelles questions (Ier–Xe siècles après J.-C.)', in E. Lorans and X. Rodier (dirs.), *Archéologie de l'espace urbain*, 209–20, Tours: Presses Universitaires François-Rabelais/CTHS.

Oudart, H. 1993. 'Marmoutier au IVe siècle, un exemple de vie érémitique', *Revue Mabillon*, **65**, 109–32.

Pietri, L. 1983. *La ville de Tours du IVe au VIe siècle, naissance d'une cité chrétienne*, Rome: Ecole française de Rome.

Pietri, L. 1987. 'Tours', in L. Pietri and J. Biarne (eds.), *Topographie chrétienne des Cités de la Gaule des origines au milieu du VIIIe siècle. Province ecclésiastique de Tours (Lugdunensis Tertia)*, 19–39, Paris: De Boccard.

Seigne, J. and Neury, P. 2007. 'Les ponts antiques sur la Loire', in H. Galinié (dir.), *Tours Antique et Médiéval, lieux de vie, temps de la ville, 40 ans d'archéologie urbaine*, 232–8, 30e suppl. à la Revue Archéologique du Centre de la France, Tours: FERACF.

Sennhauser, H. R. 2013. 'A propos de l'architecture monastique, entre Saint-Gall et Cluny II', in D. Iogna-Prat, M. Lauwers, F. Mazel and I. Rosé (eds.), *Cluny : Les moines et la société au premier âge féodal*, 527–47, Rennes: Presses Universitaires de Rennes.

Stancliffe, C. 1983. *St. Martin and his Hagiographer. History and Miracle in Sulpicius Severus*, Oxford Historical Monographs, Oxford: Clarendon Press.

Zadora-Rio, E. and Gauthiez, B. 2003. 'Les fondations de bourgs de l'abbaye de Marmoutier en Anjou-Touraine : ressorts de juridiction ou espaces urbanisés?' in B. Gauthiez, E. Zadora-Rio and H. Galinié (eds.), *Village et ville au Moyen Âge : les dynamiques morphologiques*, 299–348, Tours: Presses Universitaires François-Rabelais.

Anglo-Saxon Studies in Archaeology and History 20, 2017

# Vernacular form, monastic practice in the early Middle Ages: evidence from Toureen Peakaun

Tomás Ó Carragáin

*Abstract*

*A review of recent excavations at ecclesiastical sites in Ireland is presented, and the challenges in distinguishing monastic sites from other ecclesiastical sites on archaeological grounds are considered. While we should be cautious about placing church sites into fixed and sharply defined categories, it is sometimes possible, through contextual analysis, to build up a picture of the specific character of a site, and to identify some that were, to a greater or lesser extent, monastic. Usually, it seems, vernacular building forms encountered at other sites in the landscape were adapted to accommodate and structure monastic practices. It is primarily by analysing the contexts, combinations and use-patterns of buildings and related features that we may be allowed to identify them as monastic. Such analysis can then inform us about the specific ways in which monasticism was practised and experienced in the early Middle Ages. This conclusion is illustrated by the example of Toureen Peakaun, a royal, cosmopolitan foundation with possible Anglo-Saxon links. In particular, a small curvilinear complex excavated at the edge of the site is interpreted as a subsidiary habitation enclosure, possibly for an abbot or another senior ascetic.*

This paper outlines some emerging trends in the archaeology of early monasticism in Ireland, and looks in particular at Toureen Peakaun (Tipperary), which was the subject of a programme of survey and excavation directed by the author and funded by the Royal Irish Academy.[1] Though these investigations were on a relatively modest scale, the site itself, and some of the archaeology uncovered there, provide some interesting points of comparison and contrast with Lyminge (Kent).[2] The chronology of the two sites is very similar: Toureen was founded, probably with the involvement of the kings of Munster, in the later seventh century making it a relatively late foundation in the Irish context but contemporary with Lyminge and with the main wave of monastic foundation in England. Indeed, there is some evidence that Toureen enjoyed contacts with England and that, in its early phases, it was at the forefront of current debates within ecclesiastical circles in Britain and Ireland, such as the Easter question. Rather than attempting a comprehensive treatment of the site, this paper focuses on certain aspects of its archaeology in order to explore a few key themes, such as the dynamic use of space at early monasteries; the balance struck, at such sites, between cohesion on the one hand and compartmentalization on the other; and the ways in which vernacular building forms were adapted to make them suitable for a monastic way of life.

## Recent developments in the archaeology of early monasticism in Ireland

While it used to be believed that most early church sites in Ireland were primarily monastic in character, it is now recognized that this was true of only a minority of them.[3] Over 5000 church sites have been identified, and in many well-studied parts of Ireland early church sites are just 3 or 4 km apart.[4] Of course, these were not all contemporary but, in contrast to England, the majority of them seem to have been founded in the pre-Viking period. Many of them have been characterized as 'family' or 'community' churches served (sometimes, perhaps, only occasionally) by a priest, rather than by a community of monks. At the other end of the spectrum are major sites such as Armagh and Clonmacnoise. In later hagiography, the founders of these sites were usually portrayed as ascetic monastic figures; but whatever their initial character, they later became multi-functional sites with a resident bishop as well as a variety of religious/monastic communities. It is problematic, therefore, to refer to them as monasteries, and in contemporary sources *civitates* is a more common term.[5]

One of the upshots of these changes in our understanding is that both historians and archaeologists have to redefine and rediscover early medieval monasticism. Whereas before, archaeologists interpreted virtually all ecclesiastical remains as monastic, now we must be more discerning.[6] When it comes to the lesser sites, we cannot rely on documentary evidence, which is usually scant and ambiguous. Most sites follow the same basic grammar in terms of architecture, layout and organization (simple rectangular churches, curvilinear enclosures etc.), so distinguishing monastic sites from other churches often has to be done on the basis of quite subtle differences. Potential archaeological indicators of monasticism include: a remote location, such as an island, though not all monasteries were in liminal locations and not all island churches were monasteries;[7] burial segregated according to sex, though this is not confined to monastic or even ecclesiastical sites; faunal remains indicating a distinctive diet;[8] evidence for a high degree of literacy and related craft activities such as vellum production;[9] a preponderance of, or, conversely and yet more tentatively, an absence of, craft activities closely associated with a particular gender, such as textile production;[10] a satellite complex at a short remove from a substantial ecclesiastical site, some of which seem to have been foci for ascetic communities or places of ascetic retreat;[11] and evidence for the cult of relics and for complex liturgies and devotions of a sort particularly, though not exclusively, associated with monastic communities.

The many qualifications appended to each of these potential indicators are telling. While a combination of them may allow us to suggest the presence of a monastic community, such a check-list approach will only bring us so far. More generally, we need to be cautious about assigning church sites to discrete functional categories such as monastic, family, community, episcopal churches and royal chapels etc. Such labels *can* sometimes be useful as shorthand in the context of wider comparative studies, but we must remember they are, to some extent, modern impositions on the evidence that can quickly become anachronistic if used mechanistically to make sharp distinctions between 'types' of site. Like most categorizations, they tend to conceal as much about the messy reality of life as they reveal. Early ecclesiastical sites are best conceptualized as fluid and dynamic places and even modest examples could have more than one function and could change significantly over time. Those with a monastic ethos could vary greatly from eremitic to coenobitic, and various combinations thereof, as well as according to their conception of monasticism and the extent of their engagement with the laity. We should also be ever conscious of likely variations *within* communities as well as between them. Even within highly regulated communities, people's experience of, and commitment to, the monastic way of life must have varied considerably, not least according to factors such as age and seniority. Nor should we see asceticism as being confined entirely to eremitic and coenobitic sites, or indeed to church sites, for all clerics, and some people who had not taken religious orders and who lived at a variety of settlements in the landscape (most notably ecclesiastical tenants known as *manaig*), were expected to engage in ascetic practices, though the extent to which they did doubtless varied considerably.[12]

The challenges and limitations inherent in seeking to distinguish between different sorts of church site should therefore be clear. A recent review of the excavation evidence concluded that there was little point in attempting to do so:

> Whether church settlements had abbots, bishops or parishes or not was something that varied in the past, and in any case is not likely ever to be clearly visible in the archaeological record. In this study, therefore, the terms 'monastery', 'church settlement' and 'ecclesiastical settlement' are used interchangeably and have the same general meaning: a place dating to the early medieval period and containing a church.[13]

On the contrary, while they share many basic tenets, there are significant variations between church sites and the challenges in interpreting such variations do not absolve us from our duty to try: while categorizing them risks reductionism, *characterizing* them, through interdisciplinary contextual analysis, is an objective to which we should aspire. Contrary to traditional archaeological thinking, as exemplified by Hawkes' ladder of inference,[14] there is no compelling reason to think that variations in the material evidence for religion and religious complexes are any less susceptible to archaeological analysis than that relating to other aspects of human life, such as the subsistence economy.[15] For example, such variations have been used tentatively to suggest that some sites had a greater role in pastoral care than others (though the term 'parish' is best confined to the later Middle Ages).[16] Indeed, the study quoted above goes on to put forward several convincing interpretations along these lines. 'Church' and 'ecclesiastical' site/settlement are useful generic terms, especially when the available evidence does not allow, or support, more specific interpretations. The term 'monastery', however, brings with it more specific connotations, as well as the baggage of a discredited historical model of church organization, and is hard to disassociate from images of later medieval cloistered communities. It should be used much more sparingly, therefore, more sparingly even than terms such as 'monastic character' and 'monastic practice'.

Because they tend to leave traces in the landscape, church sites were generally avoided by developers and road builders during the 'Celtic Tiger' boom, so pre-development excavations have not provided us with as much data about them as they have about other early medieval cemeteries and settlements.[17] Most pre-development excavations have been relatively small scale and on the margins of the church sites in question. Some of them have nonetheless provided us with important new insights, though relatively little in the way of archaeology that immediately suggests itself as evidence for specifically monastic practice.[18] Relatively large-scale pre-development excavations took place at a handful of sites, most notably Clonfad (Westmeath), Kilgobbin (Dublin), and the possible church site of Owenbristy (Galway) (Fig. 1).[19] The hugely significant evidence uncovered at these sites

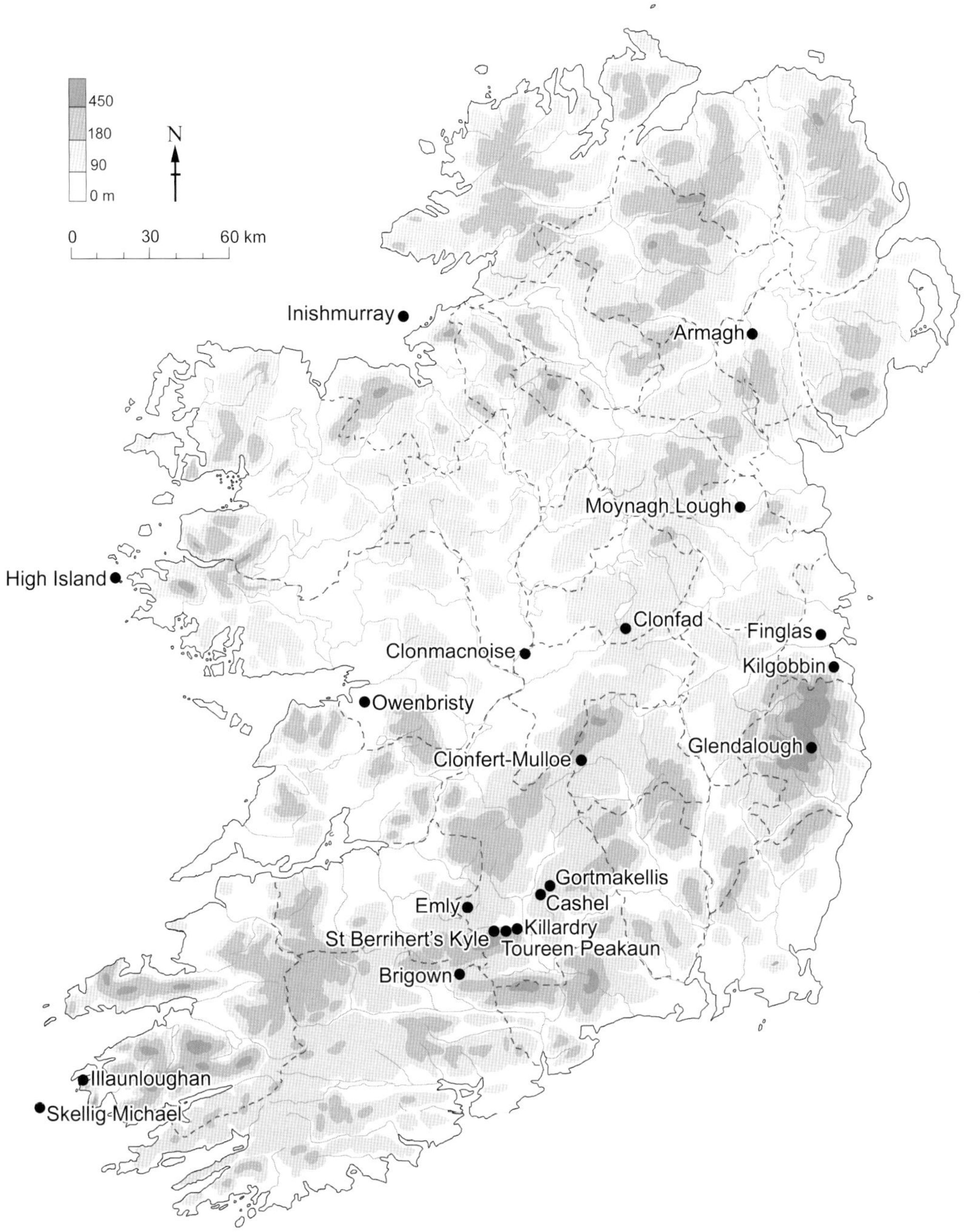


**Fig. 1** Location map showing Irish sites mentioned.

illustrates the importance of open-area excavation when seeking to tackle early ecclesiastical sites. Clonfad produced the most impressive evidence uncovered to date for the production of specifically ecclesiastical metalwork.[20] There was evidence for iron-working at the site from the time of its foundation in the sixth century and it produced one of the biggest deposits of iron-slag from any early medieval Irish site (1.5 tonnes), as well as evidence for a substantial rectangular blacksmith's forge.[21] There was little evidence for smelting. Instead, the iron-working took the form of primary and secondary smithing, especially the manufacture of iron handbells, each of which was produced from a single large sheet of iron. Most importantly, Clonfad has produced some of the best evidence from early medieval Europe for the clay shrouds used to cover the iron bell during the brazing process, whereby a veneer of copper-alloy was added to its surface. The stratigraphic contexts of the shroud fragments suggest that bells were produced at different times over a considerable period, possibly to supply churches across a wide area.[22] The possibility that some or all of this work was undertaken by, or with the involvement of, monks is supported by extensive documentary evidence associating monks with the production of ecclesiastical metalwork including bells.[23]

To date, however, much of the most convincing excavation evidence for specifically monastic communities and practices comes from islands off the west coast, most notably Illaunloughan, Inishmurray, Skellig Michael and

High Island.[24] These excavations have been carried out for the purposes of conservation, sometimes because of erosion by the sea. Apart from their liminal locations, excavations have uncovered evidence for some of the other possible indicators of monasticism mentioned above, including segregated burial (i.e. a preponderance of males at Illaunloughan, Skellig Michael and High Island); the presence of satellite ascetic/eremitical complexes (Inishmurray and Skellig Michael); evidence for the cult of relics (all four sites); complex liturgical and devotional practices (especially Inishmurray and Skellig Michael); and perhaps diet.[25] Because of their location on the western littoral, these sites have extensive, sometimes upstanding, remains of drystone buildings. In most cases it would be impossible to identify these as monastic solely on the basis of their form. Some of them are largely indistinguishable from their equivalents at 'non-monastic' church sites and other settlements such as cashels, though in the light of other evidence, certain aspects of their form can be read as expressions of their monastic character. Primarily, however, it is their *context*, both in relation to each other and to the landscape, as well as the relatively ephemeral evidence for when and how they were used, that allows us to suggest specific monastic purposes for them. For example, the absence of a hearth in or near the cliff-edge house of the satellite complex of Trahanareear on Inishmurray may support its interpretation as a place of ascetic retreat in which such comforts are eschewed.[26] Similarly, based on their placement, as well as subtle differences in form (e.g. size, the presence or absence of hearths, windows, cupboards, benches etc.), Bernadette McCarthy has suggested specific complementary functions for the so-called beehive houses on Skellig Michael: three sleeping quarters for monks, the dwelling of a senior ecclesiastic, a kitchen and refectory as well as a *magna domus* for indoor daytime activities.[27] Though tentative, her analysis demonstrates what is also clear from the textual evidence: that substantial monastic sites were often characterized by a range of buildings with specific functions, used at different times of the day and by different members of the community, in contrast to the multi-functional houses used for sleeping, working, cooking and eating that are perhaps more likely to predominate at non-monastic settlements.[28]

## Insular monasticism at Toureen Peakaun

One of the reasons for the initiation of the Toureen Peakaun project was to provide a counterweight to this emphasis on the west coast. The project aimed to investigate the archaeology of a substantial inland monastic site, and in this regard we were led by documentary and sculptural evidence suggestive of monasticism. Another attraction of the site was its unusually steep decline after the ninth century: unlike more important early churches it did not achieve parish status in the twelfth century, nor did it attract a substantial amount of later settlement. Thus, two of the main factors leading to the disturbance of early ecclesiastical archaeology were not present. Other factors such as the continued use of abandoned church sites for burial, and disturbance by agricultural cultivation, did adversely affect its buried archaeology, however.

The site now known as Toureen Peakaun was Cluain Aird Mo-Becóc, which was founded by an individual called Beccán (Mo-Becóc) who died in 690.[29] It is situated at the east end of the Glen of Aherlow in the northern foothills of the Galtee Mountains, County Tipperary. The remains include the ruins of a small, largely Romanesque stone church, several composite stone crosses, a corner-post shrine, a sundial, and over sixty lesser pieces of sculpture, mostly small stones inscribed with a name and a simple cross, dating to the seventh/eighth century (Fig. 2). In the early-ninth-century Martyrology of Óengus, and in later hagiography, Beccán is portrayed as a monastic leader with a penchant for arduous ascetic practices including cross vigils.[30] Whether or not he was 'Beccán eremita', one of the individuals to whom Cummian addressed his *c.* 633 letter exhorting Irish clerics to follow the Roman method of calculating Easter,[31] it is clear that Beccán of Toureen was linked to this circle of *Romani*. One of the name-stones at the site commemorates both a Cumméne and a Ladcen, most likely Laidcen of Clonfert-Mulloe, one of the other addressees of Cummian's Paschal Letter; both individuals died in 661, though the name-stone may be a little later.[32] The east cross bears the longest inscription of any Irish high cross, and may incorporate the female Anglo-Saxon name Osgyd, a possibility supported by the Anglo-Saxon associations of St Berehert's Kyle, another church site a short distance further up the Glen of Aherlow, with which Toureen must have been closely linked.[33] On the basis of letter forms, the inscription can be dated to around 700, making this one of the earliest datable high crosses in Ireland or Britain.[34] All of this indicates that Toureen was a cosmopolitan establishment at the forefront of contemporary doctrinal debates and an innovator in monumental stone sculpture and potentially manuscript production.

Patrick Gleeson has shown that at the time of its seventh/eighth-century floruit, the territory in which Toureen is situated (later approximating to the tríche cét/local kingdom of Muscraige Breogain[35]) was controlled by the kings of Munster based at Cashel, some 20 km to the north-east.[36] More specifically, there are indications that the subdivision of that territory in which Toureen is sited, later preserved approximately as the parish of Killardry ('Church of the High King'), was outlying royal demesne. Apart from its name, these indications include the fact that it was later an estate of the archbishops of Cashel, who inherited a great deal of royal demesne when Cashel was granted to the church *c.* 1101,[37] as well as the fact that it incorporates a likely assembly site (preserved in the name Drangan, from Drung which derives from the same root as throng), another characteristic of royal demesne.[38] The Glen of Aherlow was heavily wooded into the post-medieval period,[39] and there is a striking paucity of early medieval settlements such as ringforts in the vicinity of

**Fig. 2** The Romanesque chapel at Toureen Peakaun with some of the site's early medieval sculpture, including the shaft of a high cross, on the left.

Toureen, in stark contrast to the royal core-land closer to Cashel.[40] Woodlands, of course, were associated with both kings and ascetic monks: the former prized them for symbolic reasons, as well as for hunting; the latter saw them as ideal desert places in which to stage the spiritual battles that were central to their way of life.[41] Thus, when siting Toureen, Beccán and his patrons apparently sought to strike a balance between ascetic seclusion in a sylvan setting on the one hand and royal associations and wider ecclesiastical links on the other. While our excavations did not uncover any evidence for pre-monastic settlement, it remains possible that, like Lyminge, there was a pre-existing royal settlement nearby, possibly at or near the church of Killardry, on the banks of the Suir a little over a kilometre to the north-east. In contrast to Lyminge, which shifted uphill during its monastic phase, Toureen is quite low lying and spans a little valley (Fig. 3). At the east, the *c.* 170 m diameter curvilinear enclosure that delimited the site runs halfway up the valley side, showing with particular clarity that ecclesiastical enclosures were primarily about identifying a place as sacred, rather than for defence. Owing to acid soils, preservation of bone and plant remains is poor, so the excavations provide few insights on issues such as monastic diet. I will briefly summarize the excavation results, providing a little more detail on Trench D, the evidence from which will form the basis for a final discussion.

As much as possible of the interior of the Romanesque chapel was excavated (20 $m^2$) with the aim of determining if traces of earlier wooden churches and/or early medieval burials survived, and to investigate how the Romanesque chapel was used in the later and post-medieval periods. It was found to have been used for the burial of infants in recent centuries and of a significant number of men, women and children in the later medieval period. Below these were burials pre-dating the mid-twelfth-century Romanesque chapel, the earliest eight of which were on a different orientation (still roughly W–E), suggesting that they were aligned on one or more earlier churches of wood. Owing to poor preservation, the sex of only one – probably male – individual could be determined. The size of one of the grave-cuts suggests it was for a child and while this could indicate a mixed community, children were, of course, also members of monastic communities. These are becoming increasingly visible in the archaeological record, for example in the burial record at Illaunloughan and Skellig Michael,[42] and in the incised slates from what must have been a schoolhouse at Inchmarnock.[43] One of the Toureen name-stones commemorates 'Finánpuer', 'the boy Finán',[44] and the use of Latin may have religious significance, meaning perhaps 'oblate'.[45] While it was not possible to determine the sizes or forms of the buildings on which these burials may have been aligned, substantial intercutting post-holes at the north-east of the trench possibly represent one of the corners of successive wooden churches, one probably dating to the ninth century,[46] the other to the tenth.[47]

The locations of the other trenches were determined on the basis of micro-topography (low earthworks etc.) and geophysical survey (magnetometry and resistivity). Trenches A (30 $m^2$) and E (64 $m^2$) spanned the site's ecclesiastical enclosure and determined that it took the form of a modest *c.* 2 m wide U-shaped ditch with internal bank (the latter much denuded), and that, while it is possible

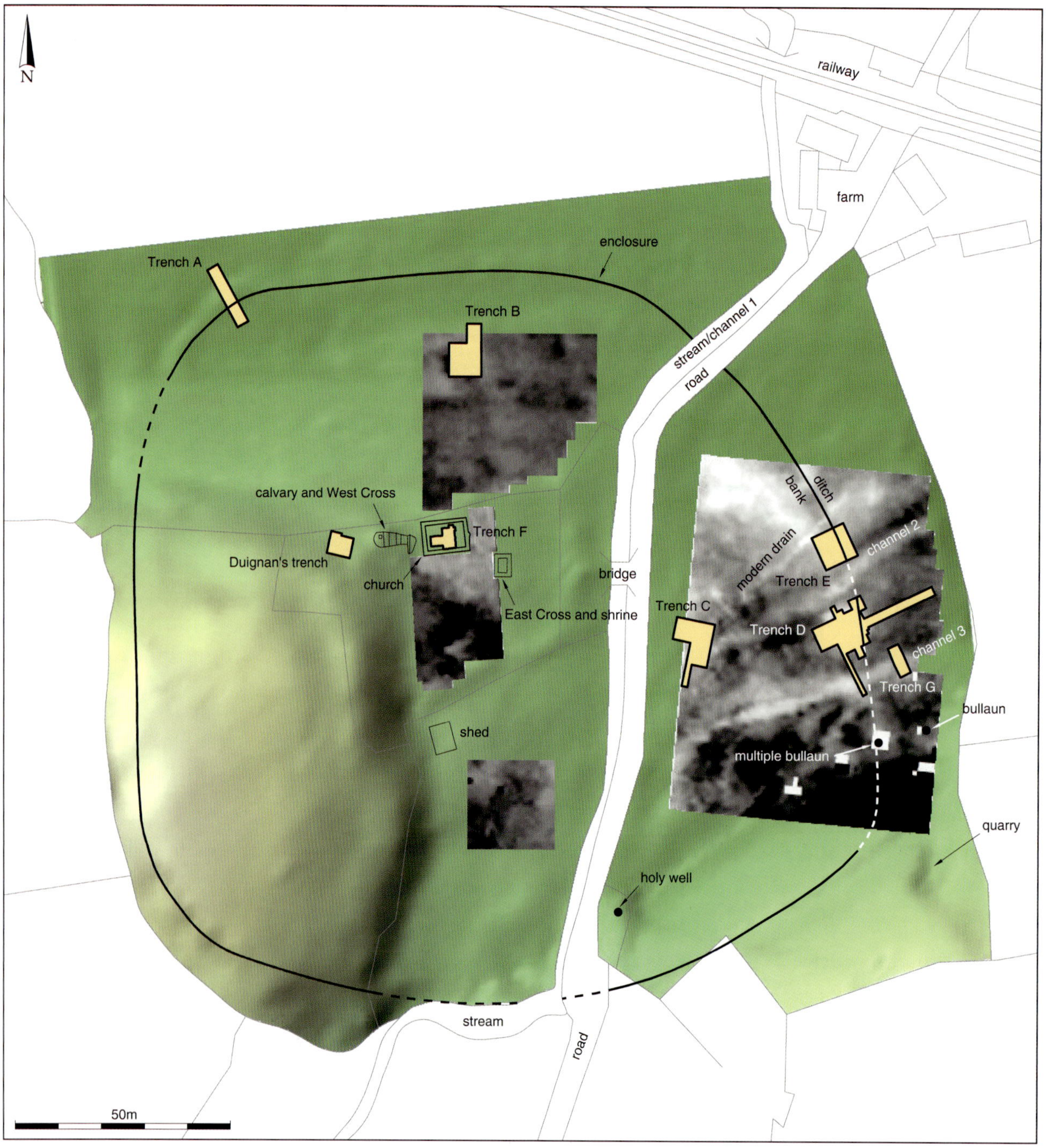


**Fig. 3** Digital terrain model of Toureen Peakaun overlain by earth resistance survey. DTM by Hugh Kavanagh. Geophysics by Earthsound Ltd. Excavation showed that Channel 3 was much wider in the early medieval period (cf. Fig. 5); it was narrowed and straightened in the post-medieval period before being filled in.

that stretches of the ditch were cleaned out, no attempt was made to recut it. Trench E was located at the junction between this enclosure and Channel 2, one of two palaeochannels in the eastern sector of the site, both of which were open during the early medieval period. These were the broadly parallel channels of a braided stream, though it is not clear whether the current channel of the Toureen Stream (Channel 1) was also open at this time. Trench E uncovered a modest levee which had been raised to limit the flow of water from Channel 2 into the enclosing ditch. Nevertheless, and unsurprisingly, this stretch of ditch was waterlogged and produced relatively well-preserved plant remains, including some pieces of worked wood. In Trench C (84 $m^2$), which spanned Channel 2, a series of stepping stones, probably of medieval date, were uncovered. In the area north of the stream, occupation surfaces had been removed by later agricultural disturbance, but several seventh–ninth-century pits were excavated, some of which produced iron-working residues (Fig. 4). Trench B (48 $m^2$) investigated geophysical anomalies in

**Fig. 4** Trench C from the south (before extension) showing Channel 2, stepping stones and iron-working activity on the far bank.

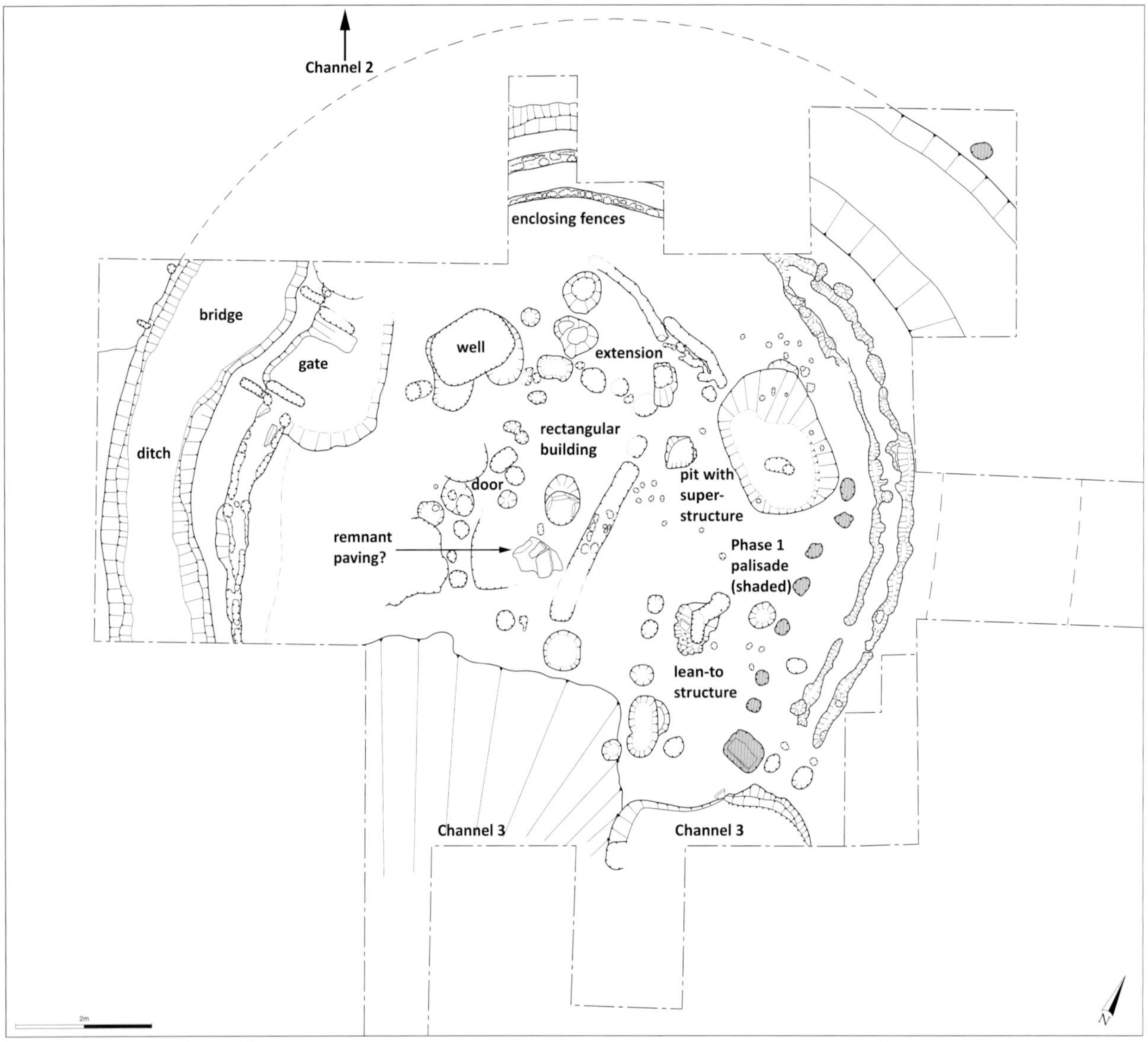


**Fig. 5** Trench D showing Phase 1 palisade running between the two palaeochannels, and Phase 2 curvilinear complex with central building delimited by parallel fences and ditch.

the northern sector of the site, most of which was low lying, waterlogged, and unsuitable for permanent habitation. It uncovered the basal layers of an artificially raised platform delimited by drainage gullies, and the base of a central charcoal-filled pit and a few post-holes, but the occupation layers did not survive.

Finally, Trench D (162 m$^2$ including Trench G, a small addition) investigated the area between Channels 2 and 3 at the eastern perimeter of the site (Figs. 5 and 6). Activity can be divided into three phases. First, instead of an enclosing bank and ditch, in this part of the site the ecclesiastical enclosure comprised a palisade represented by a series of post-holes, terminating at the edge of Channel 3 (and probably Channel 2 also) with a much larger post supported on a post-pad; this was probably erected in the later seventh or early eighth century.[48] Not long after,[49] the fence was removed and a little complex was built which is unique in the Irish archaeological record (Phase 2). Except for the south side, where the north bank of Channel 3 remained accessible, the area was enclosed by a ditch, similar in size to the main ecclesiastical enclosure (Trenches A and E), with an overall diameter of *c.* 13.6 m, inside of which was a pair of parallel curvilinear post-and-wattle fences enclosing an area 8.8 m in diameter. The basal fills of the ditch were alluvial in nature, reflecting the fact that it was filled with water from Channel 3, and probably Channel 2. Access to the enclosure was via a bridge and gate at the north-west: pegs secured the bridge at the exterior, while at the interior the bridge was represented by two identical parallel slots, inside of which was a pair of larger slots for the gate. Very sandy natural in this area made it a challenge to position the gate and bridge in this particular location but this decision was not governed by practical concerns: rather, the gate was positioned to face the church at the centre of the site. At the centre of the enclosure was a very small north–south-oriented rectilinear building, represented by post-holes and slots, with a likely doorway

**Fig. 6** Aerial photo showing Trenches D, E, G and related features.

facing the gateway and the church. It was rebuilt at least once and extended a little to the north, its new north wall represented by two overlapping slots. The interior was heavily truncated by later pits (Phase 3), so if there was a hearth it did not survive, but charcoal-rich deposits with a relatively high number of burnt bone inclusions support the idea that it was for habitation. There was an even smaller structure at the south-east corner, leaning against the perimeter fences, and a large pit at the north-east, originally with a light superstructure over it, which later seems to have been used for cess. Then, probably some time in the eighth century,[50] this area of the site was entirely reorganized. The ditch was filled in and the fences removed, and, though it remained a distinct and bounded area, with new linear fences and a gate, it was now used for industrial/craft activity, most notably smithing: a substantial amount of iron-slag was found, along with at least one smithing hearth and possibly the impression of an anvil base. This marks the end of activity in this part of the site and, apart from the church (Trench F), little evidence was found for activity after the early ninth century. The site was important enough to be raided by Vikings in AD 833,[51] but was probably already in decline by then.

## Discussion

Apart from the problem of agricultural disturbance encountered in many of them, the fact that these trenches were of modest size (408 m$^2$ in total) means that they provide only a partial picture of the density and character of occupation at Toureen. There is a clear need for larger-scale investigations at one or more major ecclesiastical sites in Ireland such as those at Lyminge and Portmahomack. It seems unlikely, though, that Toureen was ever quite as populous as either of these two sites. A substantial proportion of the land both within and immediately outside its enclosure is either too steep and exposed or too waterlogged for permanent occupation. This, combined with its secluded location, suggests that the overriding concern of its founders and patrons was to create a spiritual and intellectual, rather than an economic or political, powerhouse. It was not unheard of for remote sites to gain political power and perhaps to stimulate economic expansion, for example through the accumulation and management of land: Glendalough (Wicklow), in particular, springs to mind. Notwithstanding its royal associations, however, it does not seem ever to have been envisaged that Toureen would control large estates or become the seat of a bishop.[52] While, for a time, it seems to have occupied an important niche in the strategy of ecclesiastical patronage of the kings of Cashel, this was not at the expense of more ancient, more worldly, and increasingly multi-functional establishments within their ambit, most notably Emly (Tipperary). Excavation evidence from sites like Clonfad and Clonmacnoise (Offaly),[53] and landscape analysis, such as that carried out on the estates of Brigown (Cork),[54] are yielding new insights on the role of ecclesiastical 'central places' as drivers of economic intensification; Toureen seems to have had a somewhat different role. In part, its decline after the eighth century may be due to the fact that, at about this time, the kings of Cashel granted control of the territory in which it stood to their vassals, the Muscraige.[55] Notwithstanding these specific circumstances, however, this ninth-century decline is part of a wider pattern. Though few are abandoned entirely, some of the other excavated ecclesiastical sites apparently contract substantially at around this time, indicating very significant changes to their scale and character. This, of course, parallels developments in England to some extent, though some of the factors that led to a decline in English minsters did not pertain in Ireland; for example, there was no great increase in local churches in Viking Age Ireland, for they had already been established in great numbers by AD 800.[56]

Let me conclude be reiterating three points arising from the Toureen excavations. First, the project highlights how dynamically space was used within early medieval monasteries. While the above-ground remains often present quite a static picture, excavations like this show that the use of particular zones was not always fixed. Trench D goes from an open area delimited by the site's enclosure, to a domestic zone, to a craft-working zone all within a relatively short period. Secondly, the balance struck at this site between cohesion on the one hand and compartmentalization on the other is interesting. The ecclesiastical enclosure was established only once. The community did not feel the need to use material culture to reiterate the sacredness of the site as a whole, though they may have done so through other acts such as processions:[57] in physical terms, the always modest and increasingly filled-in ditch seemed to have been sufficient. Instead, within a generation there is an emphasis on compartmentalization: fences, ditches, gullies and screens are used to separate off certain areas (especially in Trenches B and D) for particular purposes. And yet, in both later phases in Trench D, they are careful to link this zone at the edge of the site with the sacred core by facing gateways and bridges in that direction.

Finally, the Phase 2 domestic enclosure in Trench D is worthy of further consideration. While, to date, there are no close parallels for it in the Irish archaeological record,[58] there are documentary references to subsidiary enclosures for habitation: for example the abbot's enclosure at Armagh,[59] and the nun's enclosure in eighth-century Finglas.[60] Some of these are associated with ascetic practices. For example, St Kevin was said to have retreated at times to a small wattle enclosure or house (Cró Coemgen) on the edge of his establishment at Glendalough.[61] We might also think of St Cuthbert's Hermitage on Farne which, at least according to hagiography, was delimited by a high wall to block out the outside world.[62] The design of the Trench D complex also encourages us to consider the possibility that it might be for a senior ascetic and/or an abbot. On the one hand, it is carefully designed and represents considerable investment of labour and materials suggesting that it was built for a purpose, or a person, that the community considered important. On the other hand, the effect of this effort is not to create an environment conducive to a conventionally high-status lifestyle. Rather, the fences, water-filled ditch, gate and bridge all served to cut our putative occupant off – at times, at least – from the wider community, while the tiny central structure (just 6.6 $m^2$ internally) is suggestive of a life, or periods thereof, of frugality and self-denial. Also, while it would be simplistic to suggest a straightforward negative correlation between flashy artefacts and asceticism,[63] it is worth noting that no artefacts relating to personal display (pins, brooches, beads etc.) were recovered from the complex, in contrast, for example, to Trench B.

Whatever its exact purpose, given its context at the edge of a known monastic centre, this little complex is, I would suggest, an example of the phenomenon discussed above in relation to sites such as Skellig Michael, whereby local vernacular building traditions are adapted to create a material context for monastic practice. The only somewhat unusual element is the rectilinear structure at the centre. Rectangular domestic buildings are not entirely absent from pre-Viking Ireland as was once believed,[64] but they are still relatively rare, and the construction of the Toureen structure is more unusual still. Given the evidence that one or more Anglo-Saxons may have spent time at the site (above), we should not rule out the possibility that this structure was a conscious expression of these cultural links. It is reminiscent, for example, of the contemporary diminutive rectangular buildings represented by combinations of discrete post-holes and short trenches excavated at Hartlepool (Durham).[65] These have been interpreted as adaptations of Anglo-Saxon vernacular architecture for monastic purposes: they are considerably smaller than most buildings at secular sites, in several cases just as small as the Toureen building, and it has been argued that they were built for one person, or at most two.[66] Instead of the opposed doorways in most Anglo-Saxon buildings, they generally have one, usually, as in the case of the Toureen building, in one of the long walls.[67] I would not lay too much weight on the possibility of direct influence from Anglo-Saxon monastic architecture, however; and, in any case, the other elements of the Trench D complex *are* commonly found at contemporary Irish sites, though, as far as our evidence goes, they are not usually combined in this way. For example, its mutually supporting parallel fences are reminiscent of the double-skinned insulated walls of circular houses, and a few of these (e.g. Moynagh Lough, Meath) are slightly larger in diameter.[68] The Toureen enclosure was unroofed, however, and was always open on the south side, as the merging of fences at the south-west and the fence terminals at the edge of Channel 3 at the south-east clearly indicate.

As has already been emphasized, larger-scale excavation is needed at one or more substantial Irish monasteries. On current evidence, however, it would seem that adaptations of local building forms are what we can usually expect to find at Irish monastic sites. After all, if monastic communities in Ireland chose to adopt more exotic building forms, Toureen was the sort of highly cosmopolitan site where we might expect to find them. If the little rectangular structure in Trench D really does have something to do with the site's Anglo-Saxon links (and this is far from certain), this would only underscore the very selective way in which monastic communities in Ireland chose to engage with building forms originating elsewhere, something that has already been noted in relation to their church buildings.[69] The contrast with the conscious material expression of *Romanitas* of contemporary Wearmouth, with its *porticus* with glass windows and *opus signinum* floor,[70] could hardly be starker, and yet, as we have seen, diligent adherence to Roman practices was an important part of the identity of the Toureen Peakaun community also. It must be emphasized, of course, that, even in the English context, Wearmouth and Jarrow were exceptional in this regard.

In the absence, in Ireland, and indeed at many other sites across Europe, of architectural forms that are sufficiently distinct and standardized for us to identify them as 'intrinsically' monastic (such as the cloister became for a time in the later Middle Ages, though even then it was far from ubiquitous), it is primarily by analysing the contexts, combinations and use-patterns of buildings and related features that we may be allowed to identify them as monastic. The fact that these monastic communities did not feel the need to adopt an architectural language, either for their religious or domestic buildings, that was substantially different from that encountered at non-monastic sites is significant. It suggests, perhaps, that they were not particularly interested in using architectural form (as distinct from architectural arrangements and combinations) to make a statement of difference: for example to express their separation from secular society, or how they differed from other forms of church settlement. Rather, it was primarily through their daily habitual routines – through embodied practice – that members of the community were inculcated with its core values, beliefs and identity. They were happy, it seems, to draw upon local building forms as long as they could be adapted (through new contexts for and combinations of existing forms) and developed (through modest alterations to and elaborations on existing forms) to structure such practices. At the same time, the use of regional building methods (for example drystone construction in peninsular Kerry from about the eighth century, wood and wattle further east) expressed how embedded monasteries were within local polities and traditions, and must have served to reinforce such important associations.[71] Identifying such monastic archaeology is, of course, only the first step. The real interest lies in considering, then, what this material culture, and the activities it was designed to structure, reveal about the specific ways in which monasticism was practised and experienced in the early Middle Ages.[72] There is no doubt that building form and materials contributed substantially to this experience and played a vital role in shaping the distinct identities of particular communities. Nevertheless, if we were to focus on how buildings and complexes were used, rather than how they looked, we would probably find that the contrasts between Ireland and her neighbours are not as marked as they might first appear.

## Acknowledgements

The Toureen Peakaun project was funded by the Royal Irish Academy with additional support from University College Cork. I would like to thank all of those who participated in the project (including over 200 University College Cork undergraduates) and who have been involved in writing up the results, especially Mick Monk, Aidan Harte, Bernadette McCarthy and Patrick Gleeson. Thanks also to the National Monuments Service and to the landowners, Billy, Bridget and James Bourke, for so graciously facilitating our work.

## Notes

1 Ó Carragáin forthcoming.
2 Thomas 2013.
3 See, for example, Sharpe 1984; Etchingham 1999.
4 See, for example, Ó Carragáin 2009; 2015b; Stout 2012.
5 Etchingham 1999, 457.
6 Ó Carragáin 2010, 215–25; McCarthy 2013.
7 Ó Carragáin 2013, 21.
8 Murray, McCormick and Plunkett 2004.
9 For example, Carver 2008, 119–25; Lowe 2008, 257–64.
10 Ó Carragáin 2015a, 11–12.
11 For example, Ó Carragáin 2010, 262–82.
12 Etchingham 1999, 413; McCarthy 2013, 31, 37–8; forthcoming.
13 O'Sullivan, McCormick, Kerr and Harney 2013, 143.
14 Hawkes 1954, 161–2.
15 Fogelin 2008.
16 For example, Ó Carragáin 2010, 175–8, 225–33.
17 O'Sullivan *et al.* 2013, 178; Ó Carragáin 2014b, vii.
18 See, for example, various contributions in Corlett and Potterton 2014.
19 Bolger 2008; Lehane and Delaney 2010; Stevens 2012.
20 Stevens 2012, 109–36.
21 *Ibid.*, 118, 129–30.
22 *Ibid.*, 126–31, fig. 8.13.
23 Young 2012; Ó Carragáin 2015a, 12.
24 Marshall and Walsh 2005; O'Sullivan and Ó Carragáin 2008; Bourke, Hayden and Lynch 2011; Scally 2014.
25 Murray *et al.* 2004; Hamilton-Dyer 2011; Murray and McCormick 2005, 77–8; McCarthy 2014, 261.
26 O'Sullivan and Ó Carragáin 2008, 237–8.

27 McCarthy 2013, 298–333; forthcoming.
28 For example, O'Sullivan and Nicholl 2011, 70–9.
29 Annals of Ulster: www.ucc.ie/celt/online/T100001A/
30 Stokes 1905, 126; Plummer 1910, 17; Ó Riain 2011, 93–4.
31 Ó Riain 2011, 93.
32 Moloney 1964, 103; Okasha and Forsyth 2001, 254.
33 Charles-Edwards 2002, 117–18.
34 *Ibid.*; Okasha and Forsyth 2001, 295.
35 MacCotter 2008, 156–8, 211–12, 214–16.
36 Gleeson 2014, 342–94; forthcoming.
37 Nicholls 1983.
38 MacCotter 2013; Gleeson 2014, 84–95.
39 Gottfried 1939, 133; McCarthy 2013, 221.
40 Gleeson and Ó Carragáin forthcoming; Gleeson 2014, 396–480.
41 Pickles 2011, 50–2; Arnold 2012.
42 Marshall and Walsh 2005, 81–6; Bourke *et al.* 2011, 373–90.
43 Lowe 2008, 257–64.
44 Manning 1991, 211–12.
45 Okasha and Forsyth 2001, 283.
46 UBA-16284: 1159 ± 22 BP: cal AD 779–93 (0.058), 802–901 (0.667), 916–66 (0.275) at ninety-five per cent probability level.
47 UBA-16283: 1088 ± 22 BP: cal AD 894–997 (0.969), 1004–13 (0.031) at ninety-five per cent probability level.
48 For example, UBA-7101: 1303 ± 32 BP: cal AD 658–730 (0.684), 735–69 (0.316) at ninety-five per cent probability level.
49 UBA-16281: 1305 ± 40 BP: cal AD 649–779 (0.992), 794–801 (0.008) at ninety-five per cent probability level.
50 For example, UBA-16280: 1255 ± 32 BP: cal AD 672–829 (0.931), 837–67 (0.069) at ninety-five per cent probability level.
51 Okasha and Forsyth 2001, 327.
52 Gleeson and Ó Carragáin forthcoming.
53 King 2009; Stevens 2012.
54 Ó Carragáin 2014a.
55 Gleeson 2014, 342–94; forthcoming; MacCotter 2008, 156–8, 211–12, 214–16.
56 Ó Carragáin 2009.
57 Ó Carragáin 2010, 211–13.
58 At Gortmakellis, County Tipperary (Moore, Stevens, Barker, Hardy and Green 2010), a sod-built circular house was appended to the exterior of an existing settlement enclosure, and that enclosure was redug and extended to surround the house in a manner somewhat reminiscent of the enclosure delimiting the circular fenced-off area in Trench D. The similarities and, just as importantly, the contrasts between the sites are explored in more detail elsewhere (Ó Carragáin forthcoming). I am grateful to Paul Stevens for bringing this site to my attention.
59 Annals of the Four Masters, 916: www.ucc.ie/celt/publish/T100005B
60 Gwynn and Purton 1911–12, § 7.
61 Plummer 1922, I, 141, II, 136–7.
62 Colgrave 1940, 97.
63 McCarthy 2013, 465–75.
64 *Pace* Lynn 1994.
65 Daniels 2007, 32–73; see also Hill 1997, 36, fig. 2.8.
66 Daniels 2007, 69–70, 203.
67 Daniels 2007, 72.
68 Bradley 1991, fig. 6.
69 Ó Carragáin 2010, 143–66.
70 Cramp 2005, 97–8.
71 Ó Carragáin 2010, 52–6.
72 See, further, McCarthy forthcoming.

## Bibliography


Arnold, E. 2012. *Negotiating the Landscape: Environment and Monastic Identity in the Medieval Ardennes*, Philadelphia: University of Pennsylvania Press.

Bolger, T. 2008. 'Excavations at Kilgobbin Church, Co. Dublin', *Jnl of Irish Arch.*, **17**, 85–112.

Bourke, E., Hayden, A. and Lynch, A. 2011. *Skellig Michael, Co. Kerry: The Monastery and South Peak: Archaeological Stratigraphic Report: Excavations 1986–2010*, Dublin: The Stationery Office.

Bradley, J. 1991. 'Excavations at Moynagh Lough, Co. Meath', *Jnl of the Royal Soc. of Antiquaries of Ireland*, **121**, 5–26.

Carver, M. 2008. *Portmahomack: Monastery of the Picts*, Edinburgh: Edinburgh University Press.

Charles-Edwards, G. 2002. 'The east cross inscription from Toureen Peacaun: some concrete evidence', *Jnl of the Royal Soc. of Antiquaries of Ireland*, **132**, 114–26.

Colgrave, B. (ed.) 1940. *Two Lives of Saint Cuthbert*, Cambridge: Cambridge University Press.

Corlett, C. and Potterton, M. (eds.) 2014. *The Church in Early Medieval Ireland in the Light of Recent Excavations*, Bray: Wordwell.

Cramp, R. 2005. *Wearmouth and Jarrow: Monastic Sites*, Vol. 1, Swindon: English Heritage.

Daniels, R. 2007. *Anglo-Saxon Hartlepool and the Foundations of English Christianity: An Archaeology of the Anglo-Saxon Monastery*, Hartlepool: Tees Archaeology.

Etchingham, C. 1999. *Church Organisation in Ireland, AD 650 to 1000*, Maynooth: Laigin Publications.

Fogelin, L. 2008. 'Delegitimizing religion: the archaeology of religion as … archaeology', in D. Whitley and K. Hays-Gilpin (eds.), *Belief in the Past. Theoretical Approaches to the Archaeology of Religion*, 129–41, California: Left Coast Press.

Gleeson, P. 2014. 'Landscapes of Kingship in Early Medieval Ireland', unpublished PhD thesis, University College Cork.

Gleeson, P. forthcoming. 'Defining the political landscape', in T. Ó Carragáin, *Toureen Peakaun: Insular Monasticism and Royal Patronage in the Glen of Aherlow, Co. Tipperary*, Dublin: Four Courts Press.

Gleeson, P. and Ó Carragáin, T. forthcoming. 'Ecclesiastical sites, burial monuments and landscape archaeology', in T. Ó Carragáin, *Toureen Peakaun: Insular Monasticism and Royal Patronage in the Glen of Aherlow, Co. Tipperary*, Dublin: Four Courts Press.

Gottfried, R. 1939. 'Irish geography in Spenser's view', *English Lit. Hist.*, **6(2)**, 114–37.

Gwynn, E. and Purton, W. (eds.) 1911–12. 'The monastery of Tallaght', *Proc. of the Royal Irish Acad.*, **29C**, 115–80.

Hamilton-Dyer, S. 2011. 'Bird and fish bones', in E. Bourke, A. Hayden and A. Lynch (eds.), *Skellig Michael, Co. Kerry: The Monastery and South Peak: Archaeological Stratigraphic Report: Excavations 1986–2010*, 437–49, Dublin: The Stationery Office.

Hawkes, C. 1954. 'Archaeological theory and method: some suggestions from the Old World', *American Anthropologist*, **56(2)**, 155–68.

Hill, P. 1997. *Whithorn and St Ninian: The Excavation of a Monastic Town, 1984–91*, Stroud: Sutton Publishing.

King, H. 2009. 'The economy and industry of early medieval Clonmacnoise: a preliminary view', in N. Edwards (ed.), *The Archaeology of the Early Medieval Celtic Churches*, 333–49, Leeds: Maney.

Lehane, J. and Delaney, F. 2010. *Final Archaeological Excavation Report: Owenbristy, Co. Galway. Cashel and Burial Ground*, Inishannon: Eachtra Archaeological Projects.

Lowe, C. 2008. *Inchmarnock: An Early Historic Island Monastery and its Archaeological Landscape*, Edinburgh: Society of Antiquaries of Scotland.

Lynn, C. 1994. 'Houses in rural Ireland, AD 500–1000', *Ulster Jnl of Arch.*, **57**, 81–94.

Manning, C. 1991. 'Toureen Peakaun: three new inscribed slabs', *Tipperary Hist. Jnl*, 1991, 209–14.

Marshall, J. W. and Walsh, C. 2005. *Illaunloughan Island: An Early Medieval Monastery in Co. Kerry*, Bray: Wordwell.

McCarthy, B. 2013. 'Monasticism and its Limits: Rematerialising Monastic Space in Early Medieval Ireland', unpublished PhD thesis, University College Cork.

McCarthy, B. forthcoming. *Disciplining Space, Transforming the Body. The Archaeology of Early Irish Monasticism*, Oxford: Archaeopress.

McCarthy, M. 2014. 'The faunal remains', in G. Scally, *High Island (Ardoileán), Co. Galway: Excavation of an Early Medieval Monastery*, 238–60, Dublin: The Stationery Office.

MacCotter, P. 2008. *Medieval Ireland: Territorial, Political and Economic Divisions*, Dublin: Four Courts Press.

MacCotter, P. 2013. 'Drong and Dál as synonyms of Óenach', *Peritia*, **22–3**, 275–80.

Moloney, M. 1964. 'Beccan's hermitage in Aherlow: the riddle of the slabs', *North Munster Antiquarian Jnl*, **9**, 99–107.

Moore, E., Stevens, P., Barker, L., Hardy, C. and Green, B. 2010. *M8/N8 Cullahill to Cashel Road Improvement Scheme: Archaeological Resolution Final Report A027/000 E2356 Site AR 1, Gortmakellis Townland, Co. Tipperary*, Unpublished Report, Valerie J. Keeley Ltd.

Murray, E. and McCormick, F. 2005. 'Environmental analysis and the food supply', in J. W. Marshall and C. Walsh, *Illaunloughan Island: An Early Medieval Monastery in Co. Kerry*, 67–80, Bray: Wordwell.

Murray, E., McCormick, F. and Plunkett, G. 2004. 'The food economies of Atlantic island monasteries: the documentary and archaeo-environmental evidence', *Environmental Arch.*, **9(2)**, 179–89.

Nicholls, K. 1983. 'A charter of John lord of Ireland in favour of Matthew Ua hÉannai, archbishop of Cashel 1192/3', *Peritia*, **2**, 267–76.

Ó Carragáin, T. 2009. 'Cemetery settlements and local churches in pre-Viking Ireland in light of comparisons with England and Wales', in J. Graham-Campbell and M. Ryan (eds.), *Irish/Anglo-Saxon Relations before the Vikings*, 239–61, Proceedings of the British Academy, 157, Oxford: Oxford University Press.

Ó Carragáin, T. 2010. *Churches in Early Medieval Ireland: Architecture, Ritual and Memory*, New Haven and London: Yale University Press.

Ó Carragáin, T. 2013. 'The view from the shore: perceiving island monasteries in early medieval Ireland', *Hortus Artium Medievalium. Journal of the International Research Center for Late Antiquity and the Middle Ages, Zagreb-Motovun*, **19**, 209–20.

Ó Carragáin, T. 2014a. 'The archaeology of ecclesiastical estates in early medieval Ireland', *Peritia*, **24–5**, 266–312.

Ó Carragáin, T. 2014b. 'Foreword', in C. Corlett and M. Potterton (eds.), *The Church in Early Medieval Ireland in the Light of Recent Excavations*, vii–ix, Bray: Wordwell.

Ó Carragáin, T. 2015a. 'Is there an archaeology of lay people at early Irish monasteries?', *Bulletin du Centre d'Études Médiévales d'Auxerre*, Hors-série No. 8, http://cem.revues.org

Ó Carragáin, T. 2015b. 'Churches and social power in early medieval Ireland: a case study of Fir Maige', in J. C. Sánches Pardo and M. Shapland (eds.), *Churches and Social Power in Early Medieval Europe*, 62–89, Turnhout: Brepols.

Ó Carragáin, T. forthcoming. *Toureen Peakaun: Insular Monasticism and Royal Patronage in the Glen of Aherlow, Co. Tipperary*, Dublin: Four Courts Press.

Okasha, E. and Forsyth, K. 2001. *Early Christian Inscriptions of Munster: A Corpus of the Inscribed Stones*, Cork: Cork University Press.

Ó Riain, P. 2011. *A Dictionary of Irish Saints*, Dublin: Four Courts Press.

O'Sullivan, A., McCormick, F., Kerr, T. and Harney, L. 2013. *Early Medieval Ireland, AD 400–1100: The Evidence from Archaeological Excavations*, Royal Irish Academy Monographs, Dublin: Royal Irish Academy.

O'Sullivan, A. and Nicholl, T. 2011. 'Early medieval settlement enclosures in Ireland: dwellings, daily life and social identity', *Proc. of the Royal Irish Acad.*, **111C**, 59–90.

O'Sullivan, J. and Ó Carragáin, T. 2008. *Inishmurray: Monks and Pilgrims in an Atlantic Landscape*, Cork: Collins Press.

Pickles, T. 2011. 'Anglo-Saxon monasteries as sacred places: topograhy, exegesis, vocation', in P. Thomas and J. Sterrett (eds.), *Sacred Text – Sacred Space*, 35–55, Leiden and Boston: Brill.

Plummer, C. 1910. *Vitae Sanctorum Hiberniae*, Oxford: Oxford University Press.

Plummer, C. 1922. *Bethada Náem nÉrenn*, Oxford: Oxford University Press.

Scally, G. 2014. *High Island (Ardoileán), Co. Galway: Excavation of an Early Medieval Monastery*, Dublin: The Stationery Office.

Sharpe, R. 1984. 'Some problems concerning the organization of the church in early medieval Ireland', *Peritia*, **3**, 230–70.

Stevens, P. 2012. 'Clonfad – an industrious monastery', in P. Stevens and J. Channing, *Settlement and Community in the Fir Tulach Kingdom: Archaeological Excavation on the M6 and N52 Road Schemes*, 109–36, Bray: Wordwell.

Stokes, W. (ed.) 1905. *Féilire Óengusso Célí Dé*, London: Henry Bradshaw Society.

Stout, M. 2012. 'The distribution of early medieval ecclesiastical sites in Ireland', in P. Duffy and W. Nolan (eds.), *At the Anvil. Essays in Honour of William J. Smyth*, 53–80, Dublin: Geography Publications.

Thomas, G. 2013. 'Life before the minster: the social dynamics of monastic foundation at Anglo-Saxon Lyminge, Kent', *Antiquaries Jnl*, **93**, 109–46.

Young, T. 2012. 'Metallurgical report', in P. Stevens (ed.), *N6 Kilbeggan to Kinnegad Dual Carriageway: Archaeological Resolution. Final Report. Site: Clonfad 3, Clonfad Townland, Co. Westmeath*, Vol. 2, Section 8.1, CD-ROM Appendices (no page numbers), in P. Stevens and J. Channing, *Settlement and Community in the Fir Tulach Kingdom: Archaeological Excavation on the M6 and N52 Road Schemes*, Bray: Wordwell.

Anglo-Saxon Studies in Archaeology and History 20, 2017

# The Anglian abbey of *Streonæshalch*-Whitby: new perspectives on topography and layout

Tony Wilmott

*Abstract*

*Between 1993 and 2014, Historic England (formerly English Heritage) conducted several archaeological projects at Whitby Abbey, the results of which provide the basis for a fundamental re-evaluation of the Anglian monastic landscape. Following the 1920s excavation of Sir Charles Peers, the pre-Viking monastery of Whitby was conceptualized as a small settlement on the cliff-top comprising a series of diminutive free-standing cells. This view was challenged in the 1970s by Philip Rahtz and Rosemary Cramp, but no new evidence was forthcoming until the recent work. Anglian-period archaeology has now been found across a very wide area of the headland, and it is apparent that much more has been lost to the sea. New findings include a major lay Christian cemetery, extensive 'domestic' settlement, evidence for high-status glass-working, and confirmation of a monastic cemetery situated in close proximity to the later abbey church. Most recently, in 2014, an Anglian-period boundary ditch was identified whose purpose may have been to cut off the headland from the River Esk to the North Sea. In advance of a full programme of analysis, this paper provides a provisional overview of these new remains and considers their implications for re-evaluating the extent and character of the Anglian monastic landscape on the Whitby headland.*

## Historical background

The historical aspects of the Anglian abbey at Whitby are well known, primarily from many references in Bede's *Historia ecclesiastica*. After the defeat of Penda of Mercia at the battle of the Winwaed in AD 655, King Oswiu of Bernicia dedicated his infant daughter Ælfflaed to the religious life in the monastery of Hartlepool then ruled by the Abbess Hild. He also gave twelve grants of land of ten hides each to found religious houses, six of which were to be in Deira and six in Bernicia. One of these was at a place called *Streonæshalch* where, in AD 657, ten hides were acquired by Hild to found a monastery.[1] Famous for her piety and wisdom, as well as her organizational skills, Hild was a confidante of many of the prominent churchmen of her day.[2] The monastery was apparently a double establishment of men and women; Bede refers to sisters, two abbesses and a prioress, and also to five men of the monastery who became bishops.[3] This period also saw the career of the vernacular poet Caedmon, a farmworker at Whitby who became a poet through divine inspiration.[4]

The event for which *Streonæshalch* is most celebrated by Bede is the great Synod held there in 664.[5] The kingdom of Northumbria was subject to opposing influences and tensions between the Continental Roman and the western Celtic churches. According to Bede, King Edwin had been baptized into the Roman church by Paulinus in AD 627.[6] He was killed at Hatfield in AD 633.[7] Edwin's successor Oswald (AD 634–42) had been exiled among the Scots along with his brother Oswiu, where both had been baptized in the Celtic tradition. On becoming king, Oswald brought Aidan from Iona and installed him at Lindisfarne as the base for his missionary activity.[8] On Oswald's death in battle in AD 642,[9] his brother Oswiu succeeded. Oswiu was married to Edwin's daughter Eanflæd, who kept the ways of Rome, particularly the Roman method of calculating Easter, from which Celtic practice differed. Bede paints a picture of a divided court, where Easter was observed twice the same year, the king celebrating the end of Lent while the queen and her people were still fasting.[10] The Synod was called to resolve the controversy. After long and detailed debate Oswiu famously judged in favour of Rome, as both parties agreed that St Peter had been granted the keys of heaven by Christ.[11] Bede's account concentrates on the ecclesiastical issues under debate, but it is clear that there was also an important political subtext. Oswiu's decision for Rome tied Northumbria into the mainstream of Continental Christianity, but also solved a potential political power struggle with his son Alhfrith.[12]

*Streonæshalch* became a burial place of the Northumbrian royal house, as Bede reports that Ælfflaed herself

**Fig. 1** Published plan of the 1924–5 excavations. The shaded areas are the buildings projected by Peers. (Society of Antiquaries of London.)

(who was abbess in succession to Hild and died at fifty-nine years of age), together with her father Oswiu, her mother Eanflæd, her mother's father Edwin and many other noble folk, was buried here.[13] The inclusion of Edwin in this list is at first sight odd, as he died twenty-four years before the monastery's foundation; however, in the *Life of St Gregory the Great*, written by an anonymous monk of Whitby, it is stated that Edwin's body was translated to Whitby by Ælfflaed.[14] Bede informs us that Ælfflaed and her mother Eanflæd jointly ruled the house when the Pictish bishop Trumwine sought refuge at *Streonæshalch* in 685. He, too, was buried there a few years later.[15]

The monastery was destroyed during the Danish invasions of 867, and in 944 the bones of St Hild, among those of other northern saints, were sent to Glastonbury by Edmund I.[16]

Thus far I have deliberately used the place-name *Streonæshalch* to refer to the site. This is because this is the name that appears in Bede, and also in two other contemporary sources, Stephen's *Life of Wilfrid*[17] and the *Life of Gregory the Great*.[18] The name is a problem in place-name studies,[19] and does not equate as Bede states,[20] to *fari sinus* or 'Bay of the lighthouse'.[21] Doubt has occasionally been expressed that Whitby was the location of the Synod, given the radical difference in place-name;[22] however, the identification of Whitby with *Streonæshalch* is secure. Bede states that the associated monastery of *Hacones* was 13 miles from *Streonæshalch*.[23] Hackness, where Anglian sculpture and an inscription which refers to an abbess have been found, lies just 13 miles from Whitby.[24] The Scandinavian name Whitby first appears in Domesday Book. It is probable that the name was applied to the port and town by the Esk by Scandinavian settlers, while the name *Streonæshalch* disappeared. The name *Prestbi*[25] may have been that applied to the ruins on the headland. Whitby as a place-name was first equated with Bede's *Streonaeshalch* by Symeon of Durham in his *Libellus de exordio* dating to 1104–7,[26] and also in a Whitby document dated to after 1177.[27] These sources refer to the refoundation of the monastery *c.* 1075 as a Benedictine house by Reinfrid, a monk of Evesham, having been granted the site by William de Percy. Reinfrid had been one of a group of Evesham monks led by Aldwin who had travelled north to discover ancient monasteries, guided by the works of Bede. They first settled at Jarrow, where remains of the earlier structures survived. There can be little doubt that the location of *Streonæshalch* was known and that Reinfrid would have had little trouble finding the place. It seems that the site of the monastery was still used for burials in the Anglo-Scandinavian period, as two cross fragments of this date have been found there.[28] The Whitby document states that there were 'as the old country people have told, nearly forty monasteries or oratories whose walls and altars remained empty and roofless on account of the destruction by pirate armies'.[29]

## Previous archaeology

The romantic ruin of the thirteenth-century abbey is now a flat and manicured site, but until the 1920s much of it was shrouded in its own collapse. It was cleared of rubble, and major excavations to the north of the thirteenth-century abbey church were conducted in 1924–5 by Sir Charles Peers. The report on these excavations was completed under very difficult circumstances during World War II, and published by Peers and Ralegh Radford in 1943. The report is specifically entitled *The Saxon Monastery of Whitby*.[30] As shown by the title, the report explicitly excludes consideration of any later archaeology. The single published site plan (Fig. 1) has been highly influential in discussion of the planning of early monastic sites. The plan

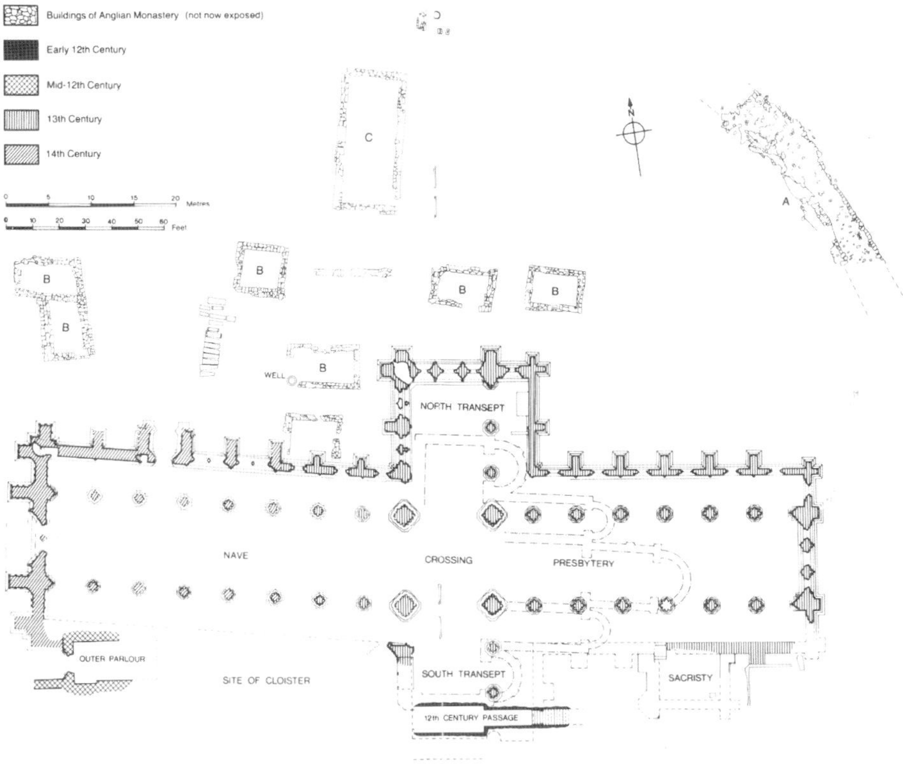


**Fig. 2** Plan of supposed Anglian 'phase' extracted from excavation plan by Clapham. (English Heritage.)

was apparently drawn by a surveyor with little knowledge of archaeology,[31] something of a double-edged sword, as although this is an objective record of stonework exposed, there is no indication of phasing. Despite this, the report's authors seem to have been able to identify medieval walls which are labelled and shown in outline only. These may well have been removed in excavation. The basis of the plan is an assumption that the stones depicted are Anglian. In the published report, seven individual square and rectangular structures were highlighted in red (shaded in Fig. 1), and these were interpreted by Radford as individual small buildings or cells. This interpretation was based in great part on Bede's description of the monastery of Coldingham[32] and also Reinfrid's '40 monasteries and oratories'[33] (although given that Reinfrid was following Bede in his quest for the Northumbrian holy places, the idea of oratories might itself have been an interpretation of the visible remains through the lens of Bede). These structures were later extracted from the overall plan and depicted separately from the rest of the walls, and interpreted as an Anglian 'phase' (Fig. 2), notably in Sir Alfred Clapham's guidebook to the site.[34] This 'phase plan' appeared in every edition of the guidebook from the Ministry of Works through the Department of Environment to English Heritage, until 1985. The selective extraction of apparent 'buildings' from the overall plan was condemned by Philip Rahtz, who said of it that 'it is difficult to imagine a better example of the misinterpretation of archaeological evidence'.[35] Rahtz's 1976 redraft and new interpretation of the plan showed that the 'cells' were more probably rooms in larger ranges of buildings, though the plan remains problematical.[36] At the same time, Rosemary Cramp attempted to refine knowledge of dating, phasing and finds distribution through an analysis of the finds registers. The results were patchy, partly because, until November 1924, no accurate finds location was undertaken (although we do have vague statements like 'north of the chancel' and 'north of the transept' to help). Thereafter, finds were at least collected in 40 ft grid squares, so some more accurate idea of location was possible (Fig. 8).[37]

The reconsiderations of the archaeology by Rahtz and Cramp, though rather lost as appendices in a larger volume,[38] remain the best modern assessments of the archaeology excavated in the 1920s. There was a limited amount of more recent work prior to 1992. In 1958, Rahtz had done small-scale excavation in the area north of the abbey, finding some Anglian material, and demonstrating that occupation of this date extended beyond the immediate area of the later abbey church.[39] A small evaluation spurred further reconsideration in the 1980s by Mark Johnson, although this was largely inconclusive.[40]

## Recent excavations: a summary of the results

In 1992, development and improvement plans for the abbey headland initiated a programme of archaeological work by English Heritage (now Historic England) that was to last intermittently for over twenty years (Fig. 3). Work began in 1992–5 with geophysical survey, and evaluation trenching carried out by this author over a wide area to the south of the abbey to establish whether a car park and visitor centre could be sited in the vicinity of Abbey Lands Farm. The only archaeology revealed in the area earmarked for the car park was the remnants of medieval

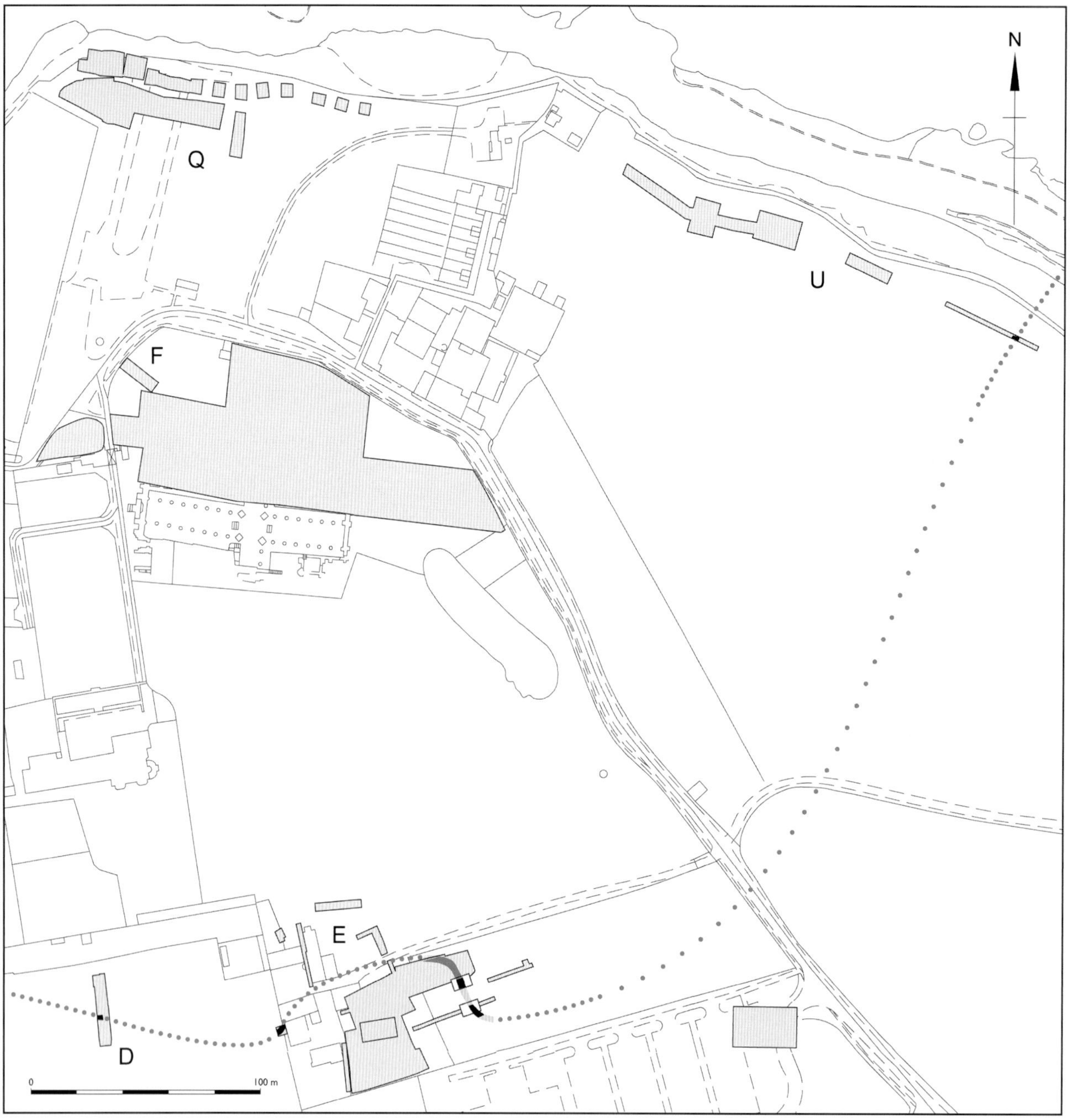


**Fig. 3** Map of the headland showing all trenches producing Anglian archaeology, and the projected line of the major Anglian boundary ditch. (Drawn by John Vallender, Historic England.)

ridge and furrow ploughing. In the area where the proposed visitor centre was to be sited, however, it was clear that a major Anglian focus had existed. This included stone-founded buildings, a previously unknown Anglian cemetery, and a series of substantial ditches, as well as indications of post-hole structures. Development here was cancelled. The cemetery, discovered only in evaluation trenches, was the subject of a major research excavation undertaken in 1999–2000 under the direction of Kath Buxton, and further research fieldwork in this area was undertaken by this author in 2014.

The development scheme was refocused in order to create a visitor centre in the former 'Banqueting House' of Abbey House, a scheme funded by the HLF. Peter 'Buzz' Busby ran the complex archaeological interventions, excavations and watching briefs necessitated by this work between 1997 and 2001. A great deal of new information on the medieval and post-medieval history of the site was recovered, but Anglian archaeology was only reached in the area immediately west of the medieval abbey. On 20 October 2000 a catastrophic cliff collapse took place. Busby immediately began an evaluation to establish the extent of damage to the archaeological remains. This soon developed into a salvage recording exercise, first exposing the archaeology with a long-reach machine, then grabbing the contents of cut features by machine and bringing them

**Fig. 4** Part of the Anglian palimpsest of features in Area Q. The kerbed burnt feature from which the archaeomagnetic date was secured is at the bottom of the shot. (Historic England.)

inland to be sorted. It was too dangerous to approach the cliff edge on foot. This heroic work revealed very intensive and important archaeological remains at the cliff edge. It was soon clear that the excavated features represented the curtilages of domestic buildings of Anglian date which are now lost to the sea, represented by structural remains, property boundaries and pits and wells. Mitigation work to excavate the archaeology under medium-term threat was undertaken by my late colleague Sarah Jennings and myself over the following years to 2008, and this revealed extensive Anglian structural archaeology to the north and north-east of the abbey. In order to come to some assessment of the volume of lost archaeology, a map regression exercise showed the pace of erosion since 1853.[41] This confirmed earlier conclusions on the mechanics of erosion and the speed of land attrition. The 2000 collapse was typical of the kind of episodic severe collapse that occasionally occurs at Whitby (the worst recorded took place in 1787, destroying homes and rendering 196 families destitute[42]), within a pattern of continuing gradual erosion.

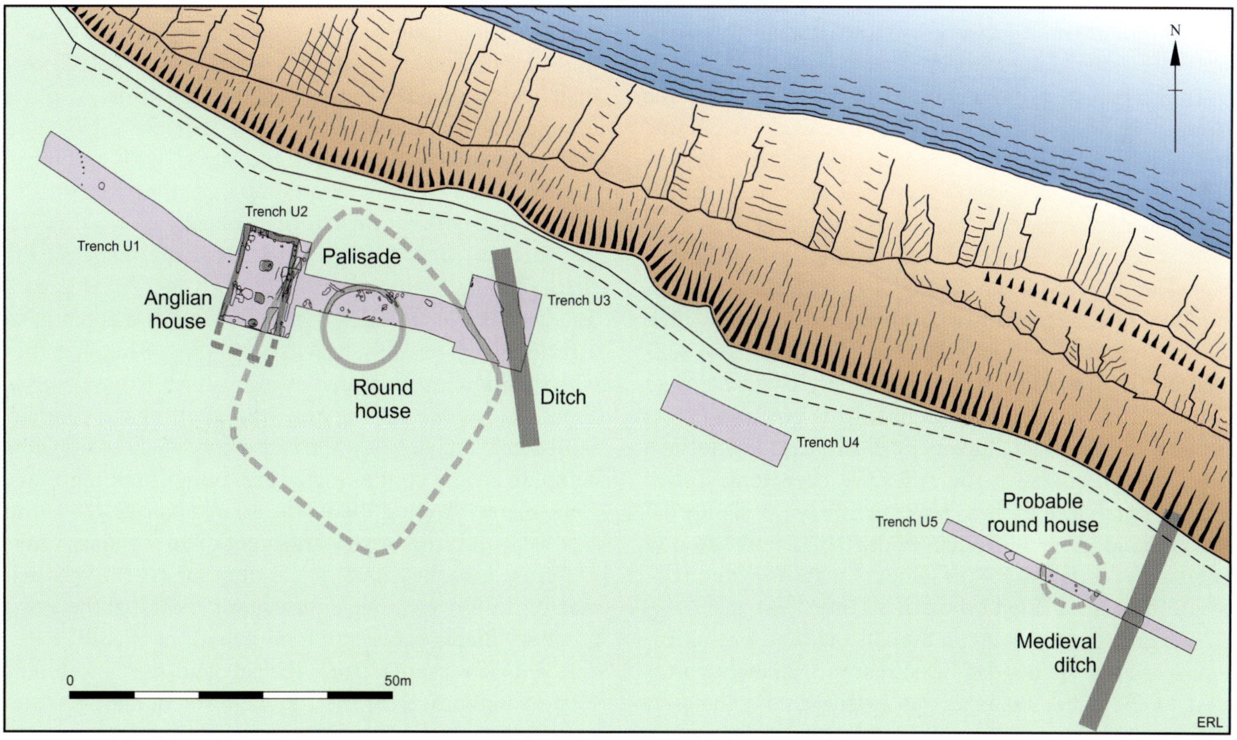


**Fig. 5** Simplified plan of trenches in the cliff-edge Area U. This shows the location of the Bronze Age round-house and the Anglian hall building. The 'medieval ditch' to the right is the feature postulated to be the end of the major southern boundary of the Anglian complex. (Historic England.)

**Fig. 6** The Anglian hall building in Area U. Site staff are standing along the side wall lines and in the central post-holes. (Historic England.)

All modern calculations show that loss is at a broadly consistent rate, and that some 450 m of land has been lost since the abbey's foundation.[43]

In the following discussion, I will briefly describe the Anglian archaeology unearthed by this work, beginning at the cliff edge and working southward, before considering the wider implications of these new discoveries for the interpretation of the Anglian monastic landscape.

It is highly likely on strategic grounds that a Roman 'signal station' was located at Whitby. These installations studded the East Yorkshire coast from Hartlepool to Filey. Whitby was not only central to the system, but also situated on the River Esk, which is the only navigable river between the Tees and the Humber.[44] Its position makes it likely that a larger Roman establishment was located here, though any such site will have been long lost to the sea. Archaeology has, however, shown a significant 'background noise' of Roman finds. Bede's translation of *Streonæshalch* as '*Fari Sinus*' (above) may, however, refer to a Roman installation extant in his time.[45]

The salvage excavation on the cliff edge and the mitigation work that followed showed that immediately northwest of the abbey there was an extensive and intensely occupied settlement (Area Q, Fig. 3). A few of the postholes appear to be parts of circular structures of possible prehistoric date, and certainly in Area U (Figs. 3 and 5). Bronze Age occupation was attested in the form of a round-house with associated pits and finds; however, the vast majority of the features present here represent a palimpsest of features of Anglian date. These included postbuilt rectangular structures recalling the plans of those found at the contemporary site at Hartlepool,[46] ditches and gullies (possibly water-control measures), wells and pits.[47] A kerbed area of burnt clay, rather large for a hearth, and never sufficiently heated to be a metalworking furnace, provided the best dating evidence for the phase in the shape of an archaeomagnetic date of AD 605–805 (Fig. 4).[48] The hearth overlay earlier large post-holes belonging to a rectangular, possibly hall-like, building. This, together with the complexity of intercutting features across the area, shows that we are dealing here with multi-phase, complex settlement archaeology. Stratigraphic analysis on this complex area is continuing at the time of writing. Finds were sparse. Among them was a large iron trivet found in a well, and from a pit a fragment of an Anglian funerary cross inscribed *orate pro* – pray for [...].[49] Although ceramic finds were not plentiful, it was clear that there was a pottery hiatus between the ninth and the twelfth centuries. This is repeated across the site, and seems to reflect total abandonment of the headland for domestic settlement following the Danish destruction of AD 867.

To the east of the cliff (Area U, Fig. 3), excavation revealed a large, rectangular, Anglian 'hall' type building measuring 6 m by at least 14 m (Figs. 5 and 6). This was of post-in-trench construction with an internal row of large post-holes, the former of which displayed further structural detail in the form of the *in situ* impressions of upright posts evident as patches of burnt clay. The wall trenches were flanked by the heavily truncated remains of possible eaves-drip trenches filled with burnt material.

Amongst the portable material culture recovered from this area, most significant were fragments of Anglian glass-working debris, previously published by Sarah Jennings.[50] This mainly consisted of raw glass in the form of small irregular-shaped 'beads'; however, there was also a single droplet and, most diagnostically of all, a twisted reticella cane of the same general type as the tiny twisted glass canes recovered from Peers' excavations used to make glass plaques to adorn book bindings[51] (Fig. 7). Frustratingly, it was not possible to associate this activity with the excavated building, and the site of the glass workshop represented by this waste material has yet to be positively identified.

As has been mentioned, the Peers excavation presents considerable problems of interpretation exacerbated

**Fig. 7** Anglian glass-working evidence from Area U. Right to left, a piece of glass-working waste, a bead of raw glass, and the twisted reticella cane. Five pence piece for scale. (Historic England.)

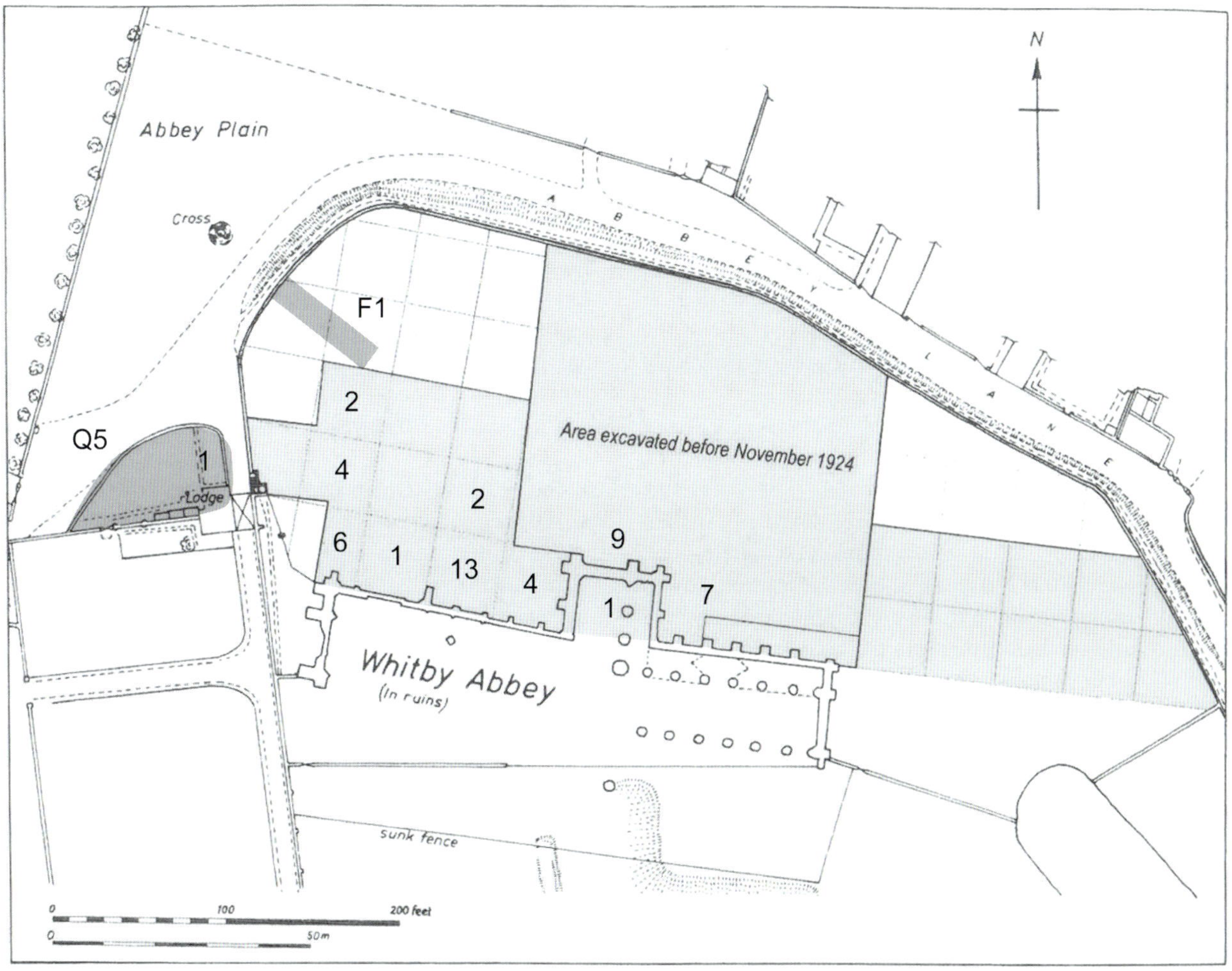


**Fig. 8** Plan locating Trenches F1 and Q5 with Peers' excavation area (in light shade). The 40 ft squares within which finds were located are marked. The bold numbers represent the grid locations of funerary crosses, inscriptions and grave covers found in 1924–5, with the cross head from Trench Q5 added. After Lang 1991. (Drawn by John Vallender, Historic England.)

**Fig. 9** Anglian burials in Trench Q5. (Historic England.)

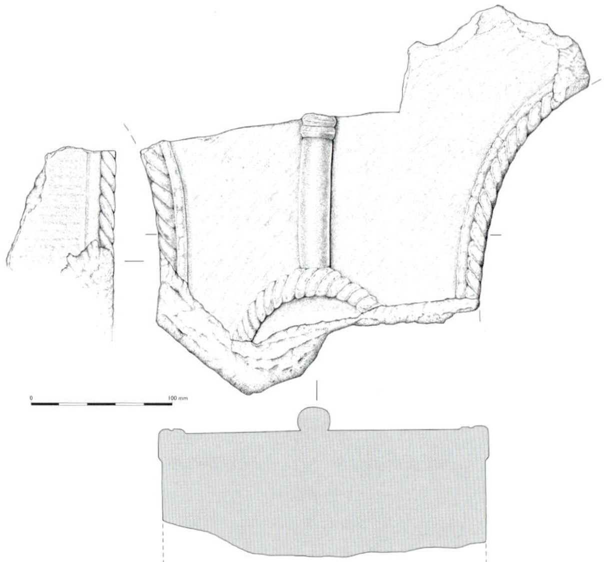

**Fig. 10** Anglian cross head found in Trench Q5. (Drawn by Chris Evans, Historic England.)

by the lack of surviving records beyond the plan, finds records, and a very few photographs, including those published in an early guidebook the originals of which are regrettably lost.[52] In an attempt to improve archaeological understanding of this previously investigated part of the site, two trenches were excavated in the area to the west of Peers' site (Fig. 8, F1 and Q5).

The first of these was extended to the very edge of Peers' area (Fig. 8, F1). Closest to the area excavated by Peers was an angle of what appears to have been a beam-slot. This was associated with a large sherd of Anglian pottery amounting to the whole profile of a cooking pot. The section of a much larger and later cut feature showed that the beam-slot was cut into an accumulation of some 1.1 m of archaeological deposits. Although only seen in section, these comprised very mixed and varied brown, black and red-brown soils, containing pottery, bone and very frequent flecks and lumps of burnt daub, with clear wattle impressions.[53] It seems certain that a major element in this material is the remains of burnt buildings whether *in situ* or dumped. Peers describes the structures he found as 'rough stone foundations laid in clay, and bits of fire-reddened clay, from a wattle-and-daub construction' and also mentions 'wattle and daub, hardened and reddened by fire'.[54] It seems likely that the deep dumps recorded in F1 comprise the material excavated away by Peers to reach the foundations he planned. Although medieval buildings are outlined in his plan, and were presumably removed by him, it is not known from what level their foundations were cut. In the absence of such evidence, we might conclude that the dumped material is debris from the destruction of the Anglian structures, which may have been stone founded with timber and wattle-and-daub superstructures (although there is also the possibility that the daub derives from earlier timber buildings). Though the burning was possibly in part due to the Danish sack, much of this material may have been moved in levelling for later church building. The feature in the section of which these deposits were observed seems to be associated with the construction of the eleventh-century church. At the north-western end of F1, these deposits seem to have been cut away by a later terrace. Such terracing elsewhere tends to belong to the period of construction of the thirteenth-century abbey. This terrace cut through the deposits of building debris to reveal, at a low level, a metalled road, scored with ruts which clearly belonged to the Anglian period, and which overlay earlier archaeology. The excavation of this trench clearly shows that the archaeology of this area is very complex indeed, but also suggests that the remains of the Anglian establishment survive, deeply buried by their destruction layers.

The second trench lay to the west of the abbey, in an area that has been greatly disturbed, largely in the post-Dissolution period (Fig. 8, Q5). Despite this, the lowest archaeological levels survived. These included a rutted road, probably the same as found in F1, as it lay at the same level, and some small, rectangular post-hole buildings which faced onto the road. It is worth speculating whether similar buildings existed under the debris layers in F1, and by extension whether there were timber buildings in the area excavated by Peers that were missed. The most important discovery in this area, however, was three east–west aligned graves (Fig. 9), and in a later pit in the same area a large fragment of an Anglian cross fragment (Fig. 10).[55]

**Fig. 11** Anglian cross head found in 1924–5 and associated with Acha, sister of Edwin. (Society of Antiquaries of London.)

**Fig. 12** Anglian stone building beneath thirteenth-century monastic terracing. (Historic England.)

The importance of this find in illuminating the work of Peers cannot be overstated. The different versions of his plan record many 'burials'; however, not only is there no record of any osteological remains from his work, but there is evidence that these burials, though recognized, were not excavated. One photograph, for instance, shows medieval graves, under grave slabs, remaining upstanding within the excavated area. These were left *in situ* and dug around. These are marked on the plan as 'medieval burials', as are a good many more. The grave slabs remain *in situ* today, and the graves beneath them remain intact. These were clearly cut through some of the early walls, and were thus cut from a high level through the accumulated demolition debris of the Anglian site which was observed in F1. In the area largely immediately north of the nave of the thirteenth-century abbey, a great many burials are just labelled 'burial'. These seem to have been recognized as grave cuts within the natural clay. Rahtz was the first to speculate whether 'some, if not most' of the burials on the plan were Anglian.[56]

The Peers excavations were noted for the large number of sculptural and epigraphic fragments found.[57] Some of these bear inscriptions which may pertain to the Northumbrian ruling house, though these interpretations are not without problems. A slab has long been associated with Aelfflaed,[58] and another with Cyneburg, the wife of Oswald.[59] A cross head inscribed '*ahhae*' (Fig. 11) has been identified with Acha, sister of Edwin and mother of Oswald, an interpretation which Lang finds the most convincing of the group.[60] Many of these fragments show sculptural decoration and fragmentary inscriptions. The funerary monuments divide into three categories: cross fragments (by far the largest group), inscriptions and grave covers. Thanks to the assessment of the finds register, first by Cramp and then by Lang,[61] it is possible to locate these objects within the 40 ft squares used to record finds (above). It is clear from Figure 8 that these objects, like the burials recorded on the Peers plan, are concentrated in the area immediately north of the thirteenth-century nave. The fact that both unexcavated burials and Anglian grave markers and monuments were found in exactly the same area would seem to indicate that the two groups of material are related. The excavation in Q5 shows just this relationship – Anglian burials in association with funerary sculpture in an extension of the same area. It would appear that this is the Anglian monastic cemetery within which high-status individuals were buried, and that the remains in Q5 are on the edge of this cemetery. By extension it can be argued that the area excavated by Peers was indeed the centre of the monastery where the cemetery and the (as yet unidentified) church would have been situated.

Some 140 m south of this focus, in Area E, was another very extensive concentration of Anglian material (Fig. 3). In a trench to the north of Area E was tantalizing evidence for a substantial Anglian stone building. In this area, within the thirteenth-century monastic boundary, the topography was completely altered by terracing. At this point, thirteenth-century terrace build-up sealed the footings of a substantial stone building, featuring an external buttress (Fig. 12). In the other evaluation trenches in this area, many linear features and post-holes were observed but not recorded. The fact that these features were well sealed beneath medieval terracing suggests that these, too, were Anglian in date.

To the west of Abbey Lands Farm, and first discovered in the 1994 evaluation, a large cemetery of unaccompanied east–west burials was extensively excavated in 1999–2000 under the direction of Kath Buxton (Figs. 3 and 13). Although 225 graves were excavated, the nature of the intensely acid natural clay meant that the bone was

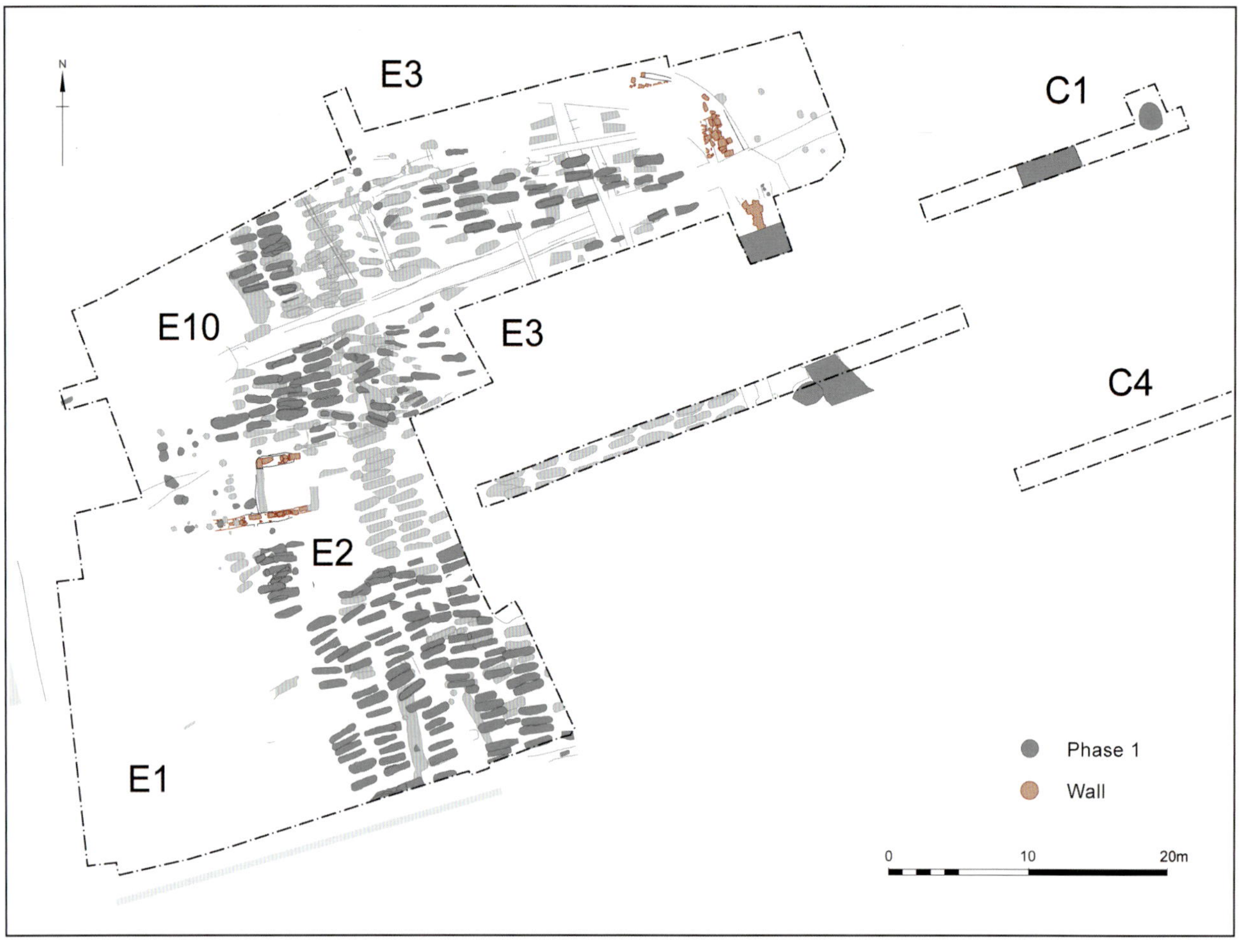


**Fig. 13** Plan of Phase 1 of the Anglian cemetery in Area E (Fig. 3), excavated in 1999–2000. (Drawn by Sharon Souter, Historic England.)

in extraordinarily poor condition and could not provide a radiocarbon date. One hundred and seventy-five adults, twenty-eight juveniles (aged 0–17) and twenty-two individuals of unidentifiable age and sex were recovered. Of the adults only sixteen inhumations could be sexed, eleven of which were men and five women. The majority could be aged.[62] The cemetery was well organized in clear rows, with little intercutting, though some discrete areas of intercutting may represent family plots. The earliest burial in this cemetery was a single human cremation. This produced a calibrated radiocarbon date of cal AD 610–80 (SUERC-24092) at ninety-five per cent probability level, giving a date of origin for the cemetery consistent with that of the foundation of the monastery by Hild. On the western side of the cemetery was an area, clear of burials, within which was a group of post-holes, linear features and walls. Re-excavation in 2014 revealed that among the post-holes was a small stone-founded building measuring 5 m square (Fig. 13). This, too, was primary to the cemetery as, though burials clustered around it on all sides, its walls neither cut, nor were cut by, any graves. It is interpreted as a small mortuary chapel. It was noticed that the stonework of the building was very similar in character to that of the building beneath the thirteenth-century terracing found in 1995, a further indication that this structure was of Anglian date.

During the early evaluation trenching, in 1994, a number of major ditches were found. To the west of Abbey Lands Farm, in Area D (Fig. 3), a segment of early ditch containing what appeared to be a collapsed fragment of stone wall was found, pre-dating the ditch and bank that formed the boundary of the thirteenth-century monastic precinct. This ditch contained no finds material except for a small assemblage of animal bone, characterized as 'high status Saxon'.[63] During the same exercise a morphologically identical ditch measuring 3.6 m wide and 1.45 m deep was found in the area of the cemetery (Fig. 13). At the time, this was interpreted as part of a 'major Anglian boundary'.[64] On the excavation of the cemetery in 1999–2000, it was shown that the latter ditch curved close around the north-east side of the cemetery, and it was thus interpreted as a cemetery boundary, and not part of the feature in Area D (Fig. 13). A problem in this interpretation was always that, although a substantial ditch seemed to enclose the cemetery on the north and west sides, there was no such feature on the south and east. The reason for this became clear during further work in 2015, when it was demonstrated that after skirting the cemetery corner the ditch broke eastwards, away from the cemetery and towards the sea coast (Fig. 3). This discovery allowed the association between this ditch and the segment in Area D to be reasserted. A further observation of the ditch between the cemetery and Area D reinforced this. In the immediate area of the cemetery, although finds from the ditch fill were few, it produced a large assemblage of animal bone, together with Anglian loom-weights and an Anglian coin. Crucially, nothing later was found in the fill of this feature. Immediately inside the ditch, on the opposite side to the cemetery, an evaluation trench produced a large pit containing a loom-weight and some metalworking waste.

Although dating evidence is sparse for the cemetery and ditch, the few hints that have been recovered give a good date spread. Within the cemetery the radiocarbon date for the beginning of the cemetery is AD 610–80, and the only datable object from a grave was a fourth-century Roman glass gaming piece, which is simply an aspect of the Roman 'background noise' found all over the site. A pit which cut a grave, and was conceivably for placing a grave marker, contained a Series E, Type 6 *sceatta* dated AD 700–40. The ditch contained a large number of loom-weights of Anglian date, and a coin of Eanbald II, Archbishop of York (AD 796–830) was recovered from its very top fill. These dates effectively span the period from the foundation of the monastery in AD 657 to its sack in AD 867.

During the mitigation work on the cliff edge, in Area U (Figs. 3 and 5), a segment of a ditch was found which shares most of the morphological features of the major boundary. It was V-shaped in profile, of similar dimensions, and had a large content of stone. Despite its distance from the other excavated segments of ditch, there is a strong possibility that it is part of the same feature. Geophysical survey in the area between the two observations undertaken in 1999 mostly showed medieval ridge and furrow, which always appears strongly in geophysics at Whitby.[65] Despite this, there is a trace of a feature beneath the ridge and furrow which may represent our ditch, a hypothesis which will be tested by further high-resolution geophysics and excavation. If it is a single feature, it would be of the first importance; an Anglian ditch, and later a wall, substantial enough to be a major boundary, potentially running from the River Esk to the North Sea, cutting off and bounding the headland, and defining the area of the Anglian monastic establishment. The various observations of this feature, and its possible course, are mapped in Figure 3.

## Provisional interpretations

Work towards the analysis of this wealth of new information has some way to go at the time of writing, but it is possible to draw some preliminary conclusions from the work. Firstly, and most obviously, the Anglian settlement at Whitby was extraordinarily extensive. The various archaeological trenches and area excavations shown in Figure 3 (with the exception of Peers' excavation) were not sited with a view to research, but to facilitating development and mitigation of coastal erosion, and yet every area produced Anglian archaeology. It is important to emphasize that all of the trenches on this plan have produced *in situ* structural or stratigraphic evidence – this is not a plot of random small finds, indeed such chance finds are non-existent on the headland. The persistent idea of the Whitby monastery comprising small individual cells set around a church on a windy and inhospitable headland, and the parallel of *Streonæshalch* with some of the Irish monasteries, must be emphatically rejected. The site excavated by Peers is not even on the end of the headland. The analysis of the pace of erosion shows that the monastic centre that Peers excavated was perhaps half a kilometre inland. Not only that, but the land rises gently from the site towards the coast. We have instead a centre that is well inland, in a sheltered hollow, and overlooking the fine harbour at the mouth of the Esk. This location has already been noted in reference to the possibility of Roman military occupation.

Major monastic foundations were sited at the mouths of all four of the navigable rivers on the coast of the kingdom of Northumbria. Hartlepool, on the Tees (founded AD 640s), was the first of these, followed by the daughter house of Whitby, on the Esk (founded AD 657), then, albeit under a different impetus, Monkwearmouth, on the Wear (founded AD 673) and Jarrow, on the Tyne (founded AD 682).[66] All were sited adjacent to sheltered harbours, and all were founded under royal aegis on land granted by successive kings. These sites must have been royal estates, themselves selected for their advantages for trading and communication. The access to sea routes and harbours, and probably also to royal authority, was clearly therefore a motive force in the establishment of these sites, rather than the desire for seclusion that was typical of the Irish tradition propagated by Aidan, though the site of Hartlepool may have been selected in part for its similarity to Lindisfarne.[67]

Given the location and royal connection of these sites, we might expect them to be extensive. Certainly the recent excavations at Hoddom have clearly demonstrated that the boundaries of an important monastic settlement of this period could enclose an area of considerable size.[68] A major problem in examining the layout and extent of such sites is the difficulty in locating boundaries. This was a theme returned to frequently during the Canterbury conference. Only by locating boundaries, and through extensive investigation within such boundaries, will it be possible to examine aspects of activity, and more particularly of the zoning of activity, within these settlements. This difficulty is compounded by the fact that a site such as Whitby, occupied by its monastic community for some two centuries, would experience change and development, with areas changing function over time, as, for instance, at Whithorn.[69] If it is accepted (or indeed proved by imminent work) that the southern ditch does cut off the headland and forms the boundary to the monastic settlement, it might be assumed that this solves the issue of the topographical limit to enquiry. This is spectacularly not so, however, as the large southern cemetery lies *outside* the ditch, as does an area of industrial pits of Anglian date which were excavated as part of the car park watching brief (Fig. 3, bottom right area). Furthermore, given the loss of some 450 m of land within the area bounded by the ditch, there is a huge area that we will never be able to sample.

Given these issues, what can we now say of topography, phasing and layout? As yet, our evidence for phasing is sparse. It is hoped that further analysis of the cliff-edge settlement evidence will allow some refinement in phasing. What we do not have is the phasing of buildings, with earlier structures built of timber and later buildings with stone footings that were recovered at Hartlepool, and we certainly may not assume a simple progression of this kind.[70] It seems reasonable to agree with Peers that the area he excavated is part of the main monastic centre, and that the original church must lie in this area, probably beneath the successive Romanesque and thirteenth-century church buildings. Work in Area Q5 has confirmed earlier suggestions that there was a cemetery of Anglian date to the north and west of the church, and that this cemetery was high status as attested by funerary sculpture. We have evidence from epigraphy to suggest that this was the cemetery in which important individuals were laid to rest, and to which Edwin and other members of his family were translated. We can contrast this with the southern cemetery, with its lack of any form of memorial; however, if the memorial stones are those of individuals such as Acha, the radiocarbon date from the southern cemetery would suggest the two burial places are contemporary. On the surface, this would seem to indicate that the church cemetery was for the royal and the religious, with the southern cemetery provided for the laity. The little stone-founded chapel in the southern cemetery was primary to the cemetery layout, and therefore again contemporary with the radiocarbon date. This shows that stone- founded buildings were being built from the earliest time for at least one religious building. If there is a stone building in this cemetery, it is unthinkable that contemporary buildings in the church area were not stone founded as well, so there is a possibility that some at least of Peers' buildings were primary.

The settlement on the cliff edge shows no evidence for stone construction, but does present a stratigraphic sequence of timber buildings and other features both predating and post-dating the archaeomagnetic date for the 'hearth'. A very stark difference between the centre and the cliff-edge settlement is the range of finds. Peers' work produced a richness and variety of finds, including finds connected with literacy and craft activity, while finds from the cliff-edge settlement produced virtually no Anglian small finds. The distinction between building type and finds distribution is stark, and somewhere between the two areas there must have been a significant boundary (it may be marked by the road observed in F1 and Q5). This would not necessarily be the boundary of the monastic settlement at large, however, but only a zone boundary between the monastic centre and a lay community associated with and serving the monastery, perhaps housing people like Caedmon.

It is impossible to judge the status of the timber 'hall' building in Area U, but it may be later in the life of the settlement, as it is apparently later than the attested glassworking. The glass works were surely a monastic enterprise, producing fine work for the monastery. Glass waste was found in the post-holes of the hall, as was a tiny strip of gold which must have come from a woven fabric. It seems likely that this was part of a zone of craft and industry.

The function and context of the stone-founded building just within the boundary are not known, but its construction alone suggests that it was important, and possibly some kind of ecclesiastical structure.

Finally we come to the conundrum of the major boundary ditch and its relationship with the southern cemetery. The ditch excludes the cemetery, but is diverted round it very closely on the north, east and west sides. The cemetery occupies a sort of embayment in the ditch line (Fig. 3). If the ditch marked the boundary of the land granted to Hild for the establishment of the monastery, and as the cemetery is contemporary with this in origin, then it was part of the primary scheme to accommodate the cemetery outside the boundary, but partly enclosed by it through a deliberate kink in the ditch line. If they were not contemporary, then the boundary was built deliberately to exclude the cemetery, its course dictated by the pre-existing burial ground. Whichever is the case, the result is the same – a cemetery excluded from the monastic precinct, but closely associated with it, as if partaking in the sanctity of the monastery. It is hard to believe that this cemetery was for the inhabitants of the cliff-edge settlement, as this is within the boundary. It seems more likely that this was the cemetery for the people of a township or settlement below the monastery, probably an original port settlement below the headland on the estuary. If such a settlement existed, it would surely have been part of the *raison d'etre* for the siting of the monastery.

This paper is very much a series of preliminary thoughts on the interpretation of the striking new evidence from Whitby. Work on the material continues towards eventual publication.[71] In the meantime, the author welcomes comments and suggestions from colleagues and scholars.

## Notes

1 Bede, *Historia ecclesiastica* III.24.
2 *Ibid.*, IV.23.
3 *Ibid.*
4 *Ibid.*, IV.24.
5 *Ibid.*, III.25.
6 *Ibid.*, II.14. An alternative British tradition given by Nennius, *Historia Brittonum* 63, that the baptism was by Rhun of Reghed has been discussed, with an attempt to reconcile the traditions, by Corning 2000, 5–15.
7 Bede, *Historia ecclesiastica* II.20.
8 *Ibid.*, III.3.

9 *Ibid.*, III.9.
10 *Ibid.*, III.25.
11 *Ibid.*
12 Abels 1983.
13 Bede, *Historia ecclesiastica* III.24.
14 Stephen of Ripon, *Vita Gregorii Magni* 18; Yorke 2003, 249.
15 Bede, *Historia ecclesiastica* IV.26.
16 William of Malmesbury, *De gestis pontificum Anglorum* II.9.
17 Anon., *Vita Wilfridi* 10.
18 Stephen of Ripon, *Vita Gregorii Magni* 18.
19 Gelling 1979, 189.
20 Bede, *Historia ecclesiastica* III.25.
21 Bell 1998, 308; Barnwell, Butler and Dunn 2003, 314.
22 The most recent discussion of this issue, pressing the claims of Strensall near York, but arriving at a compromise solution, is by Barnwell *et al.* 2003.
23 Bede, *Historia ecclesiastica* IV.23.
24 Lang 1991, 135–42.
25 Rahtz 1962, 605–6.
26 Symeon of Durham, *Libellus de exordio atque procursu istius, hoc est Dunhelmensis, ecclesie* III.22; Rollason 2000, xlii.
27 *Cartularium Abbathiae de Whitby*, Atkinson 1879–81, I, 1–10.
28 Lang 1991, 251, no. 32, 252, no. 35.
29 *Cartularium Abbathiae de Whitby*, Atkinson 1879–81, I, 1–10.
30 Peers and Radford 1943.
31 Rahtz 1976, 459.
32 Bede, *Historia ecclesiastica* IV.25.
33 *Cartularium Abbathiae de Whitby*, Atkinson 1879–81, I, 1–10.
34 Clapham 1952.
35 Rahtz 1976, 459.
36 Rahtz 1976; Cramp 1976a.
37 Cramp 1976a; 1976b; 1993.
38 Wilson 1976.
39 Rahtz 1962.
40 Johnson 1993.
41 Miller, Mills and Bryan 2008.
42 Anon. 1788, 49.
43 Hemingway 1958, 38; Agar 1960.
44 Wilson 1991.
45 Faull 1979, 36.
46 Daniels 2007.
47 Jennings, Muldowney and Wilmott 2002; 2003a; 2003b.
48 Linford 2001.
49 Lang 1991, 302.
50 Jennings 2005.
51 Peers and Radford 1943, 73, nos. 121, 122.
52 Hood 1950.
53 Wilmott 1996, 28.
54 Peers and Radford 1943, 29–30.
55 Lang 1991, 240–1, no. 19.
56 Rahtz 1976, 460.
57 Peers and Radford 1943, 33–46; Lang 1991, 231–67, 289–90, 302; Cramp 1992.
58 Lang 1991, 258–9, no. 47.
59 *Ibid.*, 259–60, no. 48.
60 *Ibid.*, 242–4, no. 21.
61 Cramp 1976b; 1992; Lang 1991, 232–4.
62 Vincent and Mays 2009.
63 Pers. comm., Sebastian Payne, 1996.
64 Wilmott 1996, 23.
65 Martin 1999.
66 Cramp 2005, 31.
67 Daniels 2007, 29.
68 Lowe 2006; see also Cramp, this volume.
69 Hill 1997, 93–140.
70 Daniels 2007, 163.
71 Wilmott forthcoming.

## Bibliography


Abels, R. 1983. 'The Council of Whitby: a study in early Anglo-Saxon politics', *Jnl of British Stud.*, **23(1)**, 1–25.

Agar, R. 1960. 'Post-glacial erosion of the North Yorkshire coast from the Tees estuary to Ravenscar', *Proc. of the Yorkshire Geological Soc.*, **32**, 409–28.

Anon. 1788. *The Universal Magazine of Knowledge and Pleasure*, **82(3)**, 49–50.

Atkinson, J. C. (ed.) 1879–81. *Cartularium Abbathiae de Whitby*, 2 vols., Publications of the Surtees Society, 69, 72, Durham: Andrews & Co.

Barnwell, P. S., Butler, L. A. S. and Dunn, C. J. 2003. 'The confusion of conversion: *Streanæshalch*, Strensall and Whitby and the Northumbrian church', in Carver, M. (ed.), *The Cross Goes North*, 311–26, York: York Medieval Press.

Bell, T. W. 1998. 'A Roman signal station at Whitby', *Arch. Jnl*, **155**, 303–22.

Clapham, A. 1952. *Whitby Abbey*, London: Ministry of Public Buildings and Works.

Colgrave, B. (ed. and trans.) 1985a. *The Earliest Life of Gregory the Great by an Anonymous Monk of Whitby*, Cambridge: Cambridge University Press.

Colgrave, B. (ed. and trans.) 1985b. *The Life of Bishop Wilfrid by Eddius Stephanus*, Cambridge: Cambridge University Press.

Colgrave, B. and Mynors, R. A. B. 1992. *Bede's Ecclesiastical History of the English People*, Oxford: Oxford University Press.

Corning, C. 2000. 'The baptism of Edwin, king of Northumbria: a new analysis of the British tradition', *Northern Hist.*, **36**, 5–15.

Cramp, R. J. 1976a. 'Monastic sites', in D. M. Wilson (ed.), *The Archaeology of Anglo-Saxon England*, 201–52, London: Methuen.

Cramp, R. J. 1976b. 'Appendix B; Analysis of the finds register and location plan of Whitby Abbey', in D. M. Wilson (ed.), *The Archaeology of Anglo-Saxon England*, 453–7, London: Methuen.

Cramp, R. 1992. *Studies in Anglo-Saxon Sculpture*, London: Pindar.

Cramp, R. J. 1993. 'A reconsideration of the monastic site at Whitby', in R. M. Spearman and J. Higgitt (eds.), *The Age of Migrating Ideas; Early Medieval Art in Northern Britain and Ireland*, 64–73, Stroud: National Museums of Scotland.

Cramp, R. J. 2005. *Wearmouth and Jarrow Monastic Sites*, Swindon: English Heritage.

Daniels, R. 2007. *Anglo-Saxon Hartlepool and the Foundations of English Christianity; An Archaeology of the Anglo-Saxon Monastery*, Tees Archaeological Monograph, 3, Hartlepool: Tees Archaeology.

Faull, M. L. 1979. 'Place-names and past landscapes', *Jnl English Place-Name Soc.*, **11**, 24–46.

Gelling, M. 1979. *Signposts to the Past*, London: Dent.

Hemingway, J. E. 1958. 'The geology of the Whitby area', in G. H. J. Daysh (ed.), *A Survey of Whitby and the Surrounding Area*, 1–47, Windsor: Shakespeare Head Press.

Hill, P. 1997. *Whithorn and St Ninian; The Excavation of a Monastic Town 1984–91*, Stroud: Alan Sutton.

Hood, P. 1950. *Whitby Abbey*, Middlesbrough: Hood & Co.

Jennings, S. 2005. 'Evidence for Anglian glass working at Whitby', *AIHV Annales*, **16**, 207–9.

Jennings, S., Muldowney, E. and Wilmott, T. 2002. 'Work on the East Cliff at Whitby, 2002', *Whitby Lit. and Philosophical Soc. Ann. Report 2002*, 25–7.

Jennings, S., Muldowney, E. and Wilmott, T. 2003a. 'Excavation and evaluation on the East Cliff at Whitby, 2002', *CBA Yorkshire Forum 2003*, 32–4.

Jennings, S., Muldowney, E. and Wilmott, T. 2003b. 'Excavation and evaluation at Whitby, 2002', *Eng. Heritage Centre for Arch. News*, **4**, 2–4.

Johnson, M. 1993. 'The Saxon monastery at Whitby: past, present, future', in M. O. H. Carver (ed.), *In Search of Cult: Archaeological

*Investigations in Honour of Philip Rahtz*, 85–8,Woodbridge: Boydell Press.

Lang, J. T. 1991. *Corpus of Anglo-Saxon Sculpture*, 3. *York and East Yorkshire*, Oxford: Oxford University Press.

Linford, P. 2001. *Whitby Abbey Cliff, Whitby, North Yorkshire: Archaeomagnetic Dating Report*, Centre for Archaeology Report, 94/2001, Portsmouth: English Heritage.

Lowe, C. 2006. *Excavations at Hoddom, Dumfriesshire: An Early Ecclesiastical Site in South-west Scotland*, Edinburgh: Society of Antiquaries of Scotland.

Martin, L. 1999. *Abbey Lands Farm, Whitby, North Yorkshire. Report on Geophysical Survey, April 1999*, Ancient Monuments Laboratory Report Series, 40/99, Portsmouth: English Heritage.

Miller, P., Mills, J. and Bryan, P. 2008. 'Scanning for change: assessing coastal erosion at Whitby Abbey headland', *Eng. Heritage Research News*, **9**, 4–7.

Peers, C. R. and Radford, C. A. R. 1943. 'The Saxon monastery at Whitby', *Archaeologia*, **89**, 27–88.

Rahtz, P. A. 1962. 'Whitby 1958', *Yorkshire Arch. Jnl*, **40(4)**, 604–8.

Rahtz, P. A. 1976. 'Appendix C; The building plan of the Anglo-Saxon monastery of Whitby Abbey', in D. M. Wilson (ed.), *The Archaeology of Anglo-Saxon England*, 459–62, London: Methuen.

Rollason, D. (trans.) 2000. *Libellus de exordio atque procursu istius hoc est Dunelmensis ecclesie*, by Symeon of Durham, Oxford: Oxford University Press.

Vincent, S. and Mays, S. 2009. *Osteological Analysis of Human Remains from Whitby, Whitby Abbey Headland Project: Southern Anglian Enclosure 1999–2000*, English Heritage Research Report Series, 27-2009, Portsmouth: English Heritage.

Wilmott, T. 1996. *Whitby Abbey, North Yorkshire: Archaeological Evaluation Assessment Report*, unpublished report, Central Archaeology Service, English Heritage.

Wilmott, T. forthcoming. *Whitby Abbey and its Headland from Prehistory to 1916*, Historic England.

Wilson, D. M. (ed.) 1976. *The Archaeology of Anglo-Saxon England*, London: Methuen.

Wilson, P. R. 1991. 'Aspects of the Yorkshire signal stations', in V. A. Maxfield and M. J. Dobson (eds.), *Roman Frontier Studies 1989: Proceedings of the 15th International Congress of Roman Frontier Studies*, 142–7, Exeter: University of Exeter.

Yorke, B. 2003. *Nunneries and the Anglo-Saxon Royal Houses*, London: Continuum.

# Part III

## From tribal centre to royal monastery:

## Anglo-Saxon Lyminge explored through its archaeology

# Monasteries and places of power in pre-Viking England: trajectories, relationships and interactions

Gabor Thomas

*Abstract*

*Recent archaeological studies conducted at different scales, from the level of site through to landscapes and regions, have focused critical attention on the connections and interactions existing between secular and religious realms of life in Anglo-Saxon England. Settlement archaeology has made an important contribution to this re-evaluation by drawing attention to a series of high-status residences of the seventh–ninth centuries* AD *whose trajectories and lifestyle blur the boundaries between monastic and secular aristocratic culture in pre-Viking England. Recent excavations in the Kentish village of Lyminge extend an appreciation of this theme into a region which has hitherto suffered from a deficit of Anglo-Saxon settlement archaeology. Originally conceived to improve archaeological understanding of a documented pre-Viking monastery, the Lyminge Project has subsequently gone on to uncover the remains of a separate and spatially distinct royal focus – a rare example of a seventh-century 'great hall complex' – grafted onto an earlier fifth–sixth-century settlement. A provisional interpretation of these results was published in 2013, but it is now possible to offer a more nuanced and richly textured account in the light of more recent findings and radiocarbon dating. This paper draws upon these new insights to reassess the settlement sequence and to evaluate Lyminge's wider contribution to relevant debates in early medieval studies.*

## Introduction

Three seasons of excavation have passed since the last synthetic overview of the Lyminge Archaeological Project was submitted for publication in 2012.[1] This was written when the ink was barely dry on the first campaign in a new scheme of excavation designed to channel the momentum of previous fieldwork into the investigation of a large, centrally located open space within the village known as Tayne Field (Figs 1 and 3). The conclusions put forward in this earlier paper were necessarily provisional and, in a strong measure, predictive – hypothesizing what might be found in future years on the then available evidence. As a consequence, it is hardly surprising that parts of the synthesis advanced in 2012 require revision in the light of new archaeological discoveries and changes in perspective. With the final campaign of excavations now at an end, this contribution takes the opportunity to review what new evidence has been found and to evaluate its wider significance for Anglo-Saxon studies. The first part of the discussion reviews the evidence for two successive, but chronologically distinct, phases of Anglo-Saxon occupation unearthed on Tayne Field, together offering vital evidence for Lyminge's embryonic development and consolidation as a theatre of royal power. This is followed by a concluding discussion which draws out the key strands of interpretation and examines their implications for future analysis and wider research agendas.

## Establishment and consolidation: Lyminge before the seventh century AD

In 2012, it was already possible to make some clear statements on Lyminge's early, pre-Christian, development based upon fresh archaeological discoveries. At that point in the project, domestic settlement remains of characteristic early Anglo-Saxon type had been identified at two sites within the village: a cluster of four sunken-featured buildings and a rectangular ground-level building of post-hole construction at the bottom of Rectory Lane, and a fifth sunken-featured building investigated as part of the inaugural season on Tayne Field (Figs 2 and 3). The wide separation of these two sites suggested that occupation of this period formed a spatially diffuse sprawl straddling the headwater of the River Nailbourne. While the structural remains seemed fairly typical of the period, albeit if evincing some regional tendencies, the rich cultural assemblages recovered from the backfilled remains of the sunken-featured buildings clearly marked

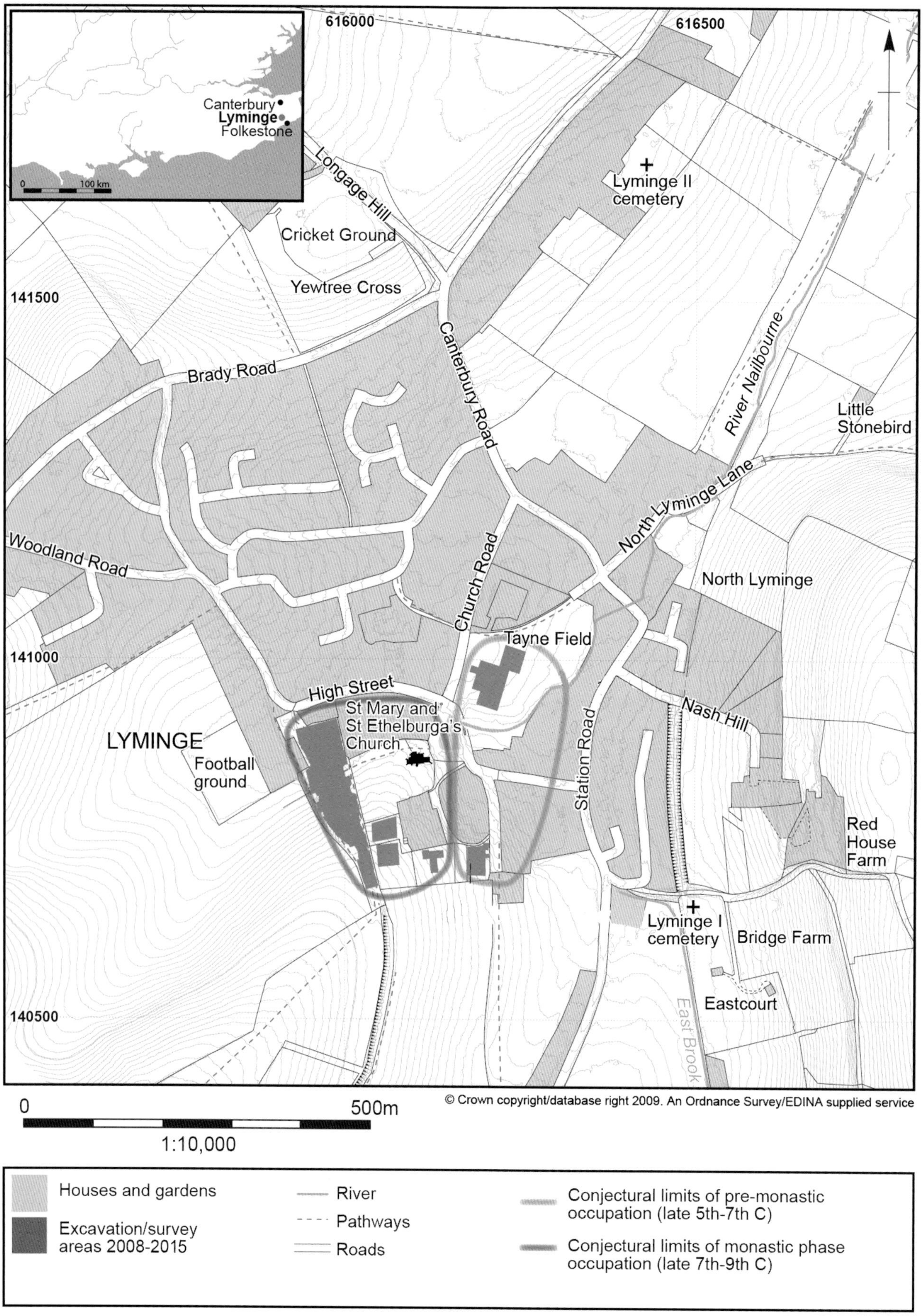


**Fig. 1** Map showing location of excavations in relation to the modern-day topography of Lyminge village.

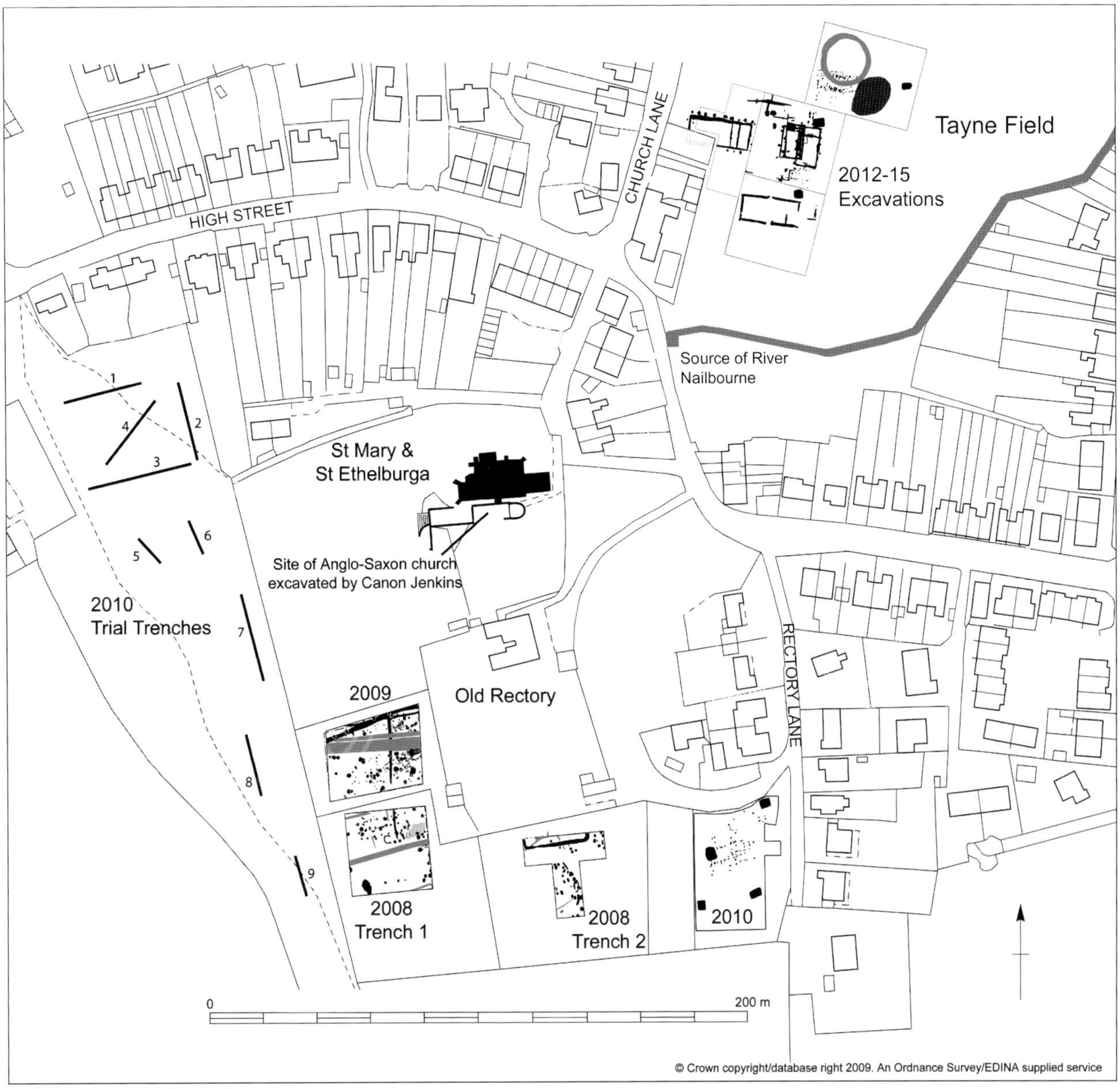


**Fig. 2** Map showing different phases of excavation with Anglo-Saxon archaeology highlighted in bold.

sixth–seventh-century Lyminge out as a prosperous and socially pre-eminent community.[2]

The results of the ensuing three seasons of excavation add significant new detail and texture to this basic sketch. It is almost certain that the plateau of Tayne Field, a spur projecting into the main axis of the valley of the River Nailbourne, and directly overlooking its source, formed the epicentre of the early Anglo-Saxon settlement as well as its longest-lived component. The discovery of significant prehistoric activity in this same locale has also opened up a new vista for exploring the relationship between antecedent landscape features and Lyminge's emergent identity as a place of early medieval power and authority.

To understand the substance behind these statements, it is necessary to provide a brief summary of the newly unearthed evidence. For convenience, this can be broken down into features of, respectively, structural, and non-structural, character (Fig. 4); typological and radiocarbon dating indicates that these various components belong to a single, contemporaneous phase of occupation centring on the sixth century AD, pre-dating the site's subsequent redevelopment as a 'great hall complex' in the seventh century (Table 1).[3] Of the former, there were a further three sunken-featured buildings and one clearly identifiable ground-level building of post-hole construction of greater scale and architectural pretentions than that excavated in 2010 and displaying clear evidence for multiple constructional phases (Fig. 5). Non-structural features were present in two categories, both of which produced prodigious volumes of dumped midden material: a spatial cluster of three pits located at the western end of Tayne Field which shared large dimensions and carefully cut vertical sides and flat bases (Fig. 6), and, some 30 m to the north-west, a substantial

**Fig. 3** View across Tayne Field looking south-west, with the 2014 excavation trenches in the foreground and the chalk promontory capped by the parish church beyond. The clump of trees in front of the church marks the source of the River Nailbourne.

infilled hollow, with plan dimensions of *c.* 18 m north–south by 12 m east–west.

It is possible to gain an enriched understanding of Tayne Field as the likely ancestral cult focus of Anglo-Saxon Lyminge by drawing attention to the considerable body of prehistoric archaeology unearthed in the 2012–15 excavations. Particularly germane to the current discussion is a previously unidentified Bronze Age barrow located on the north-east edge of the Tayne Field plateau, investigated as part of the 2014 excavation campaign (Figs. 4 and 5). It seems highly probable that this prehistoric monument influenced the layout and spatial development of the early Anglo-Saxon settlement on the grounds that the southern arc of the ring-ditch was directly superimposed by the aforementioned post-built hall representing the most significant structural component of the fifth–sixth-century occupation. Although this proposal lies beyond stratigraphic proof, it nevertheless falls into a coherent pattern of prehistoric monument reuse identified on fifth–seventh-century Anglo-Saxon

**Table 1** Selected radiocarbon dates from the Tayne Field Anglo-Saxon settlement sequence.

| Context | Sample number | Radiocarbon age (BP) | Calibrated 68% confidence | Calibrated 95% confidence |
|---|---|---|---|---|
| **Dates for pre-hall-complex occupation** | | | | |
| Primary infill of midden-filled solution hollow | OxA-31785 | 1598±26 | cal AD 414–534 | cal AD 405–537 |
| Primary infill of midden-filled solution hollow | OxA-31786 | 1602±26 | cal AD 410–533 | cal AD 401–537 |
| Primary fill of pit [6118] | OxA-31719 | 1629±27 | cal AD 388–527 | cal AD 347–535 |
| Secondary fill of pit [6134] | OxA-31720 | 1634±27 | cal AD 385–506 | cal AD 343–535 |
| Secondary fill of pit [6788] | OxA-31721 | 1602±26 | cal AD 410–533 | cal AD 401–537 |
| **Dates for hall complex** | | | | |
| Hall A | OxA-31717 | 1479±27 | cal AD 560–613 | cal AD 544–640 |
| Hall sequence B Phase 2 | OxA-31726 | 1409±35 | cal AD 615–656 | cal AD 579–668 |
| Hall sequence B Phase 3 | SUERC-50221 | 1269±42 | cal AD 681–770 | cal AD 662–870 |
| Hall sequence C Phase 3 | OxA-31788 | 1259±26 | cal AD 673–764 | cal AD 663–770 |

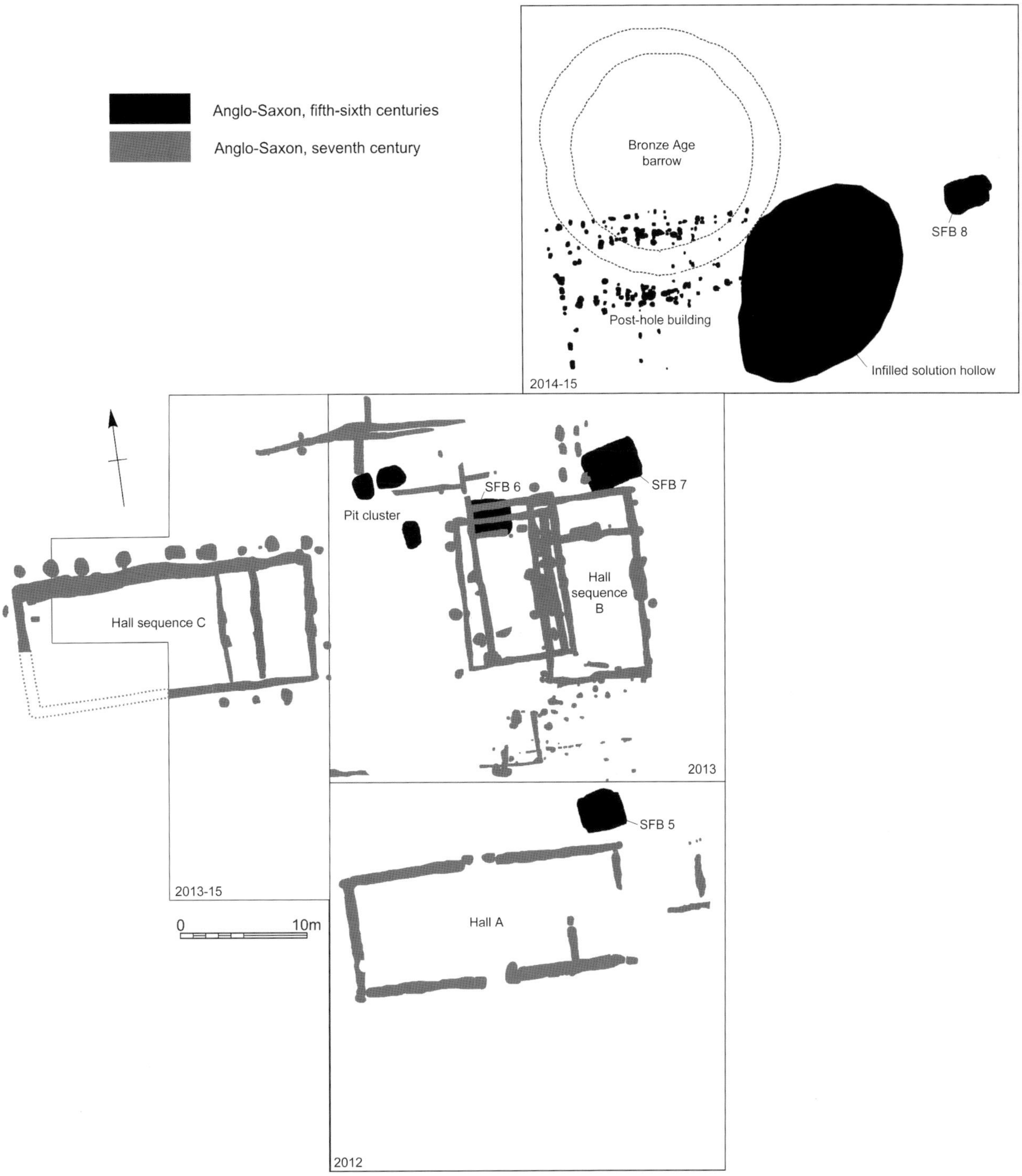


**Fig. 4** Plan of Tayne Field excavations showing features relating to the two main phases of Anglo-Saxon occupation.

settlements echoing similar practices in contemporary funerary contexts.[4]

This interpretation can be developed further by taking into consideration clues that the hall concerned enjoyed focal or special significance within the settlement. It has previously been noted that this structure had a complex and extended structural biography reflected in a palimpsest of overlapping wall alignments which is unusual at this early period.[5] In addition, two pieces of Anglo-Saxon metalwork – an annular brooch and a delicate dress-pin measuring 120 mm long – were recovered from the foundations of this building, the former from a doorpost marking a principal entrance aligned on the mound of the barrow. According to the latest research examining the theme of 'special deposits' on Anglo-Saxon settlements, it is exceptionally rare to find metalwork deposited in association with halls and the Lyminge building is almost certainly unique in having a pair.[6] While somewhat earlier in date, it can be noted that the depositionary treatment of these items has clear affinities with articulated human/animal remains

**Fig. 5** Vertical view of the post-hole building in relation to the Bronze Age ring-ditch and infilled solution hollow.

**Fig. 6** The largest of the three pits from the western pit-cluster.

placed within the structural foundations and thresholds of major seventh-century Anglo-Saxon halls at the aristocratic sites of Cowdery's Down, Hampshire (Building C12) and Yeavering, Northumberland (Building D2).[7]

Any assessment of the influence of the antecedent landscape over Lyminge's formative development must also take into account the barrow's conspicuous neighbour: the large midden-filled hollow sampled in 2014–15 (Fig. 5). The current hypothesis is that this feature represents the infilled remnants of a prehistoric sink-hole or 'doline', the original formation of which pre-dated the construction of the neighbouring barrow.[8] While unusual in a valley bottom setting, juxtapositions of a similar kind have been identified in preserved tracts of prehistoric downland such as the Dorset ridgeway, attracting the theory that Bronze Age peoples attached particular cosmological significance to natural sink-holes as portals to the Otherworld.[9]

The key significance of the hollow for current purposes, however, is that it appears to have enjoyed a significant secondary life synchronous with the embryonic development of the Anglo-Saxon settlement. The earliest evidence for this early medieval appropriation comprised a 2-m-wide flint ramp which descended from the northern lip of the hollow to an interior depth of 2 m at a consistent 26 degree gradient (Fig. 7). This feature is difficult to explain, but may have been constructed to aid the extraction of fine quality clay which, according to cores extracted from the hollow's lower stratigraphic horizons, accumulated under natural erosional processes during later prehistory. The ramp was subsequently buried by the first of an extended sequence of dumped deposits representing the systematic disposal of midden material generated by intense and sustained occupation and industrial activity. The process of infilling appears to have been punctuated by specific events of intense burning and a longer period of stabilization when the hollow, by then no more than a shallow bowl, was exploited as a setting for industrial activity represented by *in situ* hearths and associated deposits of metalworking slag and furnace lining (Fig. 8).

The thick 'layer-cake' of stratigraphic superimposition within the hollow implies a relatively lengthy period of deposition which is to some extent confirmed by available dating evidence. Diagnostic dress-accessories indicate that the core period of infilling occurred in the period AD 500–70 and that the hollow had been completely infilled by the close of the sixth century at the latest (Fig. 9).[10] There are some indications that the earliest phases of the hollow's use, represented by the flint ramp and the midden deposits lying in direct superimposition, may date back into the fifth century. This is supported by clear differences in the material cultural signatures derived from relevant contexts: on the one hand, these lacked the diagnostic metalwork and vessel glass frequent in later levels, and on the other, produced a pottery assemblage characterized by a distinct admixture of Late Romano-British and early 'Germanic' forms. It may be further noted that a fifth-century inception can be safely accommodated within the

**Fig. 7** A view of the flint ramp exposed beneath the Anglo-Saxon midden deposits contained within the prehistoric solution hollow.

error ranges associated with radiocarbon determinations from these same contexts (Table 1).

There is one final point that needs to be made in evaluating the influence of the antecedent cultural landscape on Lyminge's early medieval trajectory: the fact that the multi-period archaeology uncovered on Tayne Field was totally devoid of *in situ* Romano-British occupation. This chronological gap, mirrored in all recent interventions within the village, takes on particular significance in light of the long-established tradition that a Romano-British villa was sited at the end of the chalk ridge later inhabited by the Anglo-Saxon church and its medieval successor. Many commentators have accepted this tradition at face value with the result that Lyminge is frequently cited in the literature as an Anglo-Saxon centre displaying strong and direct continuity with the Romano-British past.[11] This notion seems increasingly untenable in light of the chronological gap noted above: if there was indeed a Romano-British presence in this locale it was most unlikely to have matched the scale or economic significance of a villa and a smaller, perhaps ritual, focus is the more likely scenario given Lyminge's springhead location.

It remains to make some provisional and necessarily selective observations on the economy and social identity

**Fig. 8** North-facing section across the infilled solution hollow showing the complex depositionary sequence as revealed by excavation in 2014. The in situ hearth shows up as black and orange banding at roughly the mid-point of the picture with more extensive burnt horizons below towards the right-hand edge of the section. An exposed portion of the flint ramp appears at the bottom of the sequence, part of which has been removed for sampling. Depth of section approximately 2 m.

**Fig. 9** A selection of the sixth-century gilded dress-accessories recovered from the infilled solution hollow.

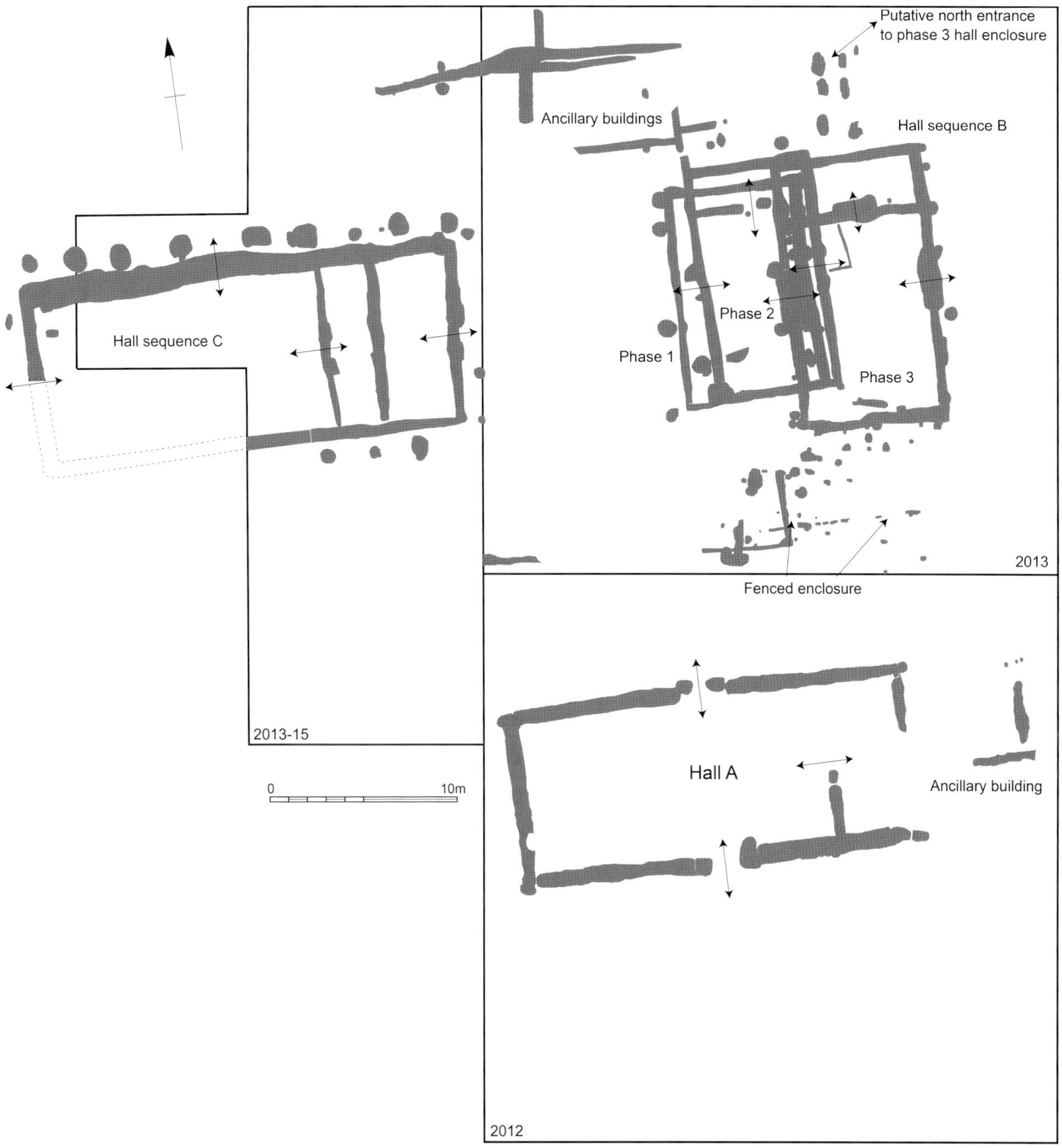


**Fig. 10** Plan of the seventh-century great hall complex; arrows mark the position of entrances.

of the early settlement gleaned from the large cultural assemblages recovered over 2013–15. First is the strong imprint made by ironworking reflected in large quantities of smelting and smithing slag and furnace lining recovered from the cluster of pits identified in the western sector of Tayne Field and from the infilled solution hollow. This evidence anticipates by over a century a charter reference dated AD 689 attesting that the royal vill (*cors*) of Lyminge enjoyed proprietorship of an iron mine.[12] By the time this charter was issued, it would thus appear that Lyminge's involvement in iron production was already long established. The co-occurrence of smelting and secondary smithing debris at this early period is particularly significant as evidence for the centralization of the production process as a means of controlling the conversion of iron ore into finished products.[13]

A second point is that early Anglo-Saxon Lyminge played host to not one, but a multiplicity of specialist technologies. This extended to the manufacture of bronze artefacts employing both cast and wrought technology, the former attested by mould and crucible fragments, and the latter by a miscellany of sheet and wire offcuts, rivets and other attachments from composite objects. More tantalizing is the possibility that such specialization extended to the production of glass vessels. Standing at around 600 sherds, Lyminge has produced, by a considerable margin, the

**Fig. 11** View across Hall sequence B looking west.

largest assemblage of vessel glass from a rural settlement in early Anglo-Saxon England. Preliminary analysis has highlighted clues strongly suggestive of on-site production: a significant quantity of Roman glass intended for recycling and waste products in the form of raw/molten glass, accompanied by possible moils from the glass-blowing process.[14] In the absence of more emphatic evidence in the form of glass furnaces and crucibles, confirmation for on-site production must ultimately await the results of detailed scientific analysis as a key priority of the post-excavation programme. Regardless of the final outcome of this analysis, however, it is the scale of *consumption* of glass vessels which deserves attention: in the period under review, one has to look to high-status fortified enclosures and monastic settlements in Celtic-speaking regions of Britain to find a comparable assemblage from a settlement context.[15]

Much more could be said on the wide range of portable material culture from this early period, but it is interesting to consider what is poorly represented. Textile manufacturing equipment is an immediate case in point: no loom-weights or shears were recovered from the 2013–15 excavations, and pin-beaters and spindle whorls were found in only limited numbers. This under-representation demands some explanation given the vast quantities of midden material sifted in these campaigns and the general ubiquity of textile manufacturing equipment on early Anglo-Saxon settlements. Since textile production appears to have been a female-gendered activity closely associated with the domestic sphere, the paucity of such objects might be interpreted as a reflection of Tayne Field's special status as a ritual/ceremonial focus of the settlement.[16]

## Royal appropriation: delineating an Anglo-Saxon great hall complex

2012 marked a key turning-point in the Lyminge Project with the unexpected unearthing of a major timber hall at the southern edge of the Tayne Field plateau. Its large dimensions (21 m × 8.2 m), combined with a distinctive method of planked-wall construction, immediately placed this building (Hall A) within an Anglo-Saxon architectural tradition synonymous with what have become known in the literature as 'great hall complexes', first subjected to detailed archaeological examination at Yeavering, Northumberland, and subsequently at Cowdery's Down (Hampshire).[17] On the basis of these excavated parallels, it was conjectured that the Lyminge hall was likely to be accompanied by further buildings of comparable scale and sophistication.[18] Such was proven to be the case when the ground-plans of several further, spatially articulated, halls, displaying multiple phases of construction, were unearthed over 2013–15 (Fig. 10). It seems likely on the basis of the coherent layout of these halls that a greater part of the nucleus of the Lyminge complex has been successfully delineated; a brief description of the new structures follows, leading to some more general reflections concerning layout and chronology.

**Fig. 12** A view of the western entrance of Hall sequence B (Phase 3) showing structural detail at the base of the massive entrance pit. The rectangular planks of the two doorposts can clearly be seen in the configuration of stone packing material. Vertical scale = 1 m.

*Hall sequence B*

Excavation in 2013 identified an overlapping sequence of three north–south structures constructed on a site 15 m to the north of Hall A (Fig. 11). It is clear from stratigraphic superimposition that the order of construction of the halls progressed from west to east and that each new hall was built on a larger scale than its predecessor (the largest measuring 13.60 m by 7.40 m and the smallest 11.0 m by 6.0 m). In spite of these and other variations in ground-plan, the three halls shared the same basic constructional technique: a foundation trench displaying a single row of plank uprights set towards the outside edge of the trench, flanked by external raking posts. The second- and third-phase halls had partition walls at their northern ends and, in all cases, opposed entrances were situated centrally in the long-walls of the buildings. One notable divergence between the third-phase hall and its predecessors related to the construction of the entrances: in the latter case, doorposts were founded in separate pits delineated from the main length of wall-trench, whereas in the former case, both doorposts were held in a single elongated pit of massive proportions (Fig. 12).[19] In all cases where timber impressions survived, the doorposts comprised larger versions of the cut planks used for the main walls.

It was possible to adduce additional architectural details for these halls from the excavated ground-plan evidence. Considerable quantities of fired daub were contained in the wall-trenches of the third-phase hall indicating that panels of wattle and daub filled the spaces between each of the plank uprights in accordance with 'C9 type' wall construction identified at the site of Cowdery's Down.[20] The same contexts also contained redeposited material derived from preceding constructional phases, indicating a surprisingly high level of interior finish for the Phase 1 and 2 halls. This included numerous fragments of *opus signinum* derived from internal flooring and slabs of walling material whitewashed on both surfaces to give a plaster-like appearance (Fig. 13).[21]

**Fig. 13** Fragments of *opus signinum* recovered from the foundations of Hall sequence B.

**Fig. 14** Vertical view of Hall sequence C with modern playground (bottom right) and the foundations of World War II structures (top right) including an associated drain-block cut through the southern long-wall of the Anglo-Saxon hall.

### *Hall sequence C*

A further major timber hall of east–west alignment was identified at the western extremity of Tayne Field and excavated sequentially over 2013–15. The evidence for this hall and its constituent phases was less than ideal: its south-west corner extended under a modern playing ground and the exposed portion of the ground-plan was disturbed by a cluster of Saxo-Norman pits and intrusive features associated with a World War II canteen (Fig. 14). As with Hall sequence B, there were obvious signs of sequential rebuilding, but with a notable divergence: whereas in the former case, the same general construction style was maintained throughout the sequence, each phase of rebuilding here was accompanied by a change in technique. It is also possible to demonstrate that there was a selective reuse of certain wall-trenches from one phase to the next which introduces complexities for interpreting how the building developed architecturally. With these complications in mind, the following reconstruction can be tentatively attempted.

The first hall to occupy this site employed double-planked wall construction of the same general type featured by Hall A to the south-east. This was replaced by a second structure sharing the same constructional style as Hall sequence B (i.e. single-plank wall construction with exterior raking posts). This building reused the southern long-wall trench of its predecessor, but was repositioned slightly on its east–west axis and extended in length and width to give recorded dimensions of *c.* 24 m by 9.0 m. Much greater uncertainty concerns the third and final developmental phase of this hall, the evidence being confined to an alignment of regularly spaced post-pits which cut through the northern long-wall of the second-phase hall, perhaps suggesting that the northern façade was replaced while the remainder of the structure was still standing.

As well as being the largest structure on this site, the second-phase hall also displayed divergences in internal layout and the arrangement of doorways. Unlike its predecessor, it was furnished with an interior partition wall, as in the case of Hall A, located towards the eastern end of the building; it is also unique amongst the Lyminge halls in having two pairs of opposed entrances through both the long- and short-walls, the latter set on precise alignment with the doorway through the internal partition wall (Fig. 10).

### *Other constructional elements*

On the evidence of Yeavering and Cowdery's Down, fenced boundaries and internal enclosures seem to be a recurrent expression of the formalized planning exhibited by Anglo-Saxon great hall complexes.[22] Unfortunately, evidence for such at Lyminge has largely been destroyed by the severe ground-truncation caused by medieval ploughing. A small portion of a north–south fence-line was, however, identified to the south of Hall sequence B and could conceivably have formed part of a continuous circuit designed to enclose one or more of its constructional phases (Fig. 10). Of possible further relevance were three pairs of oval post-pits extending in an axial alignment beyond the northern wall of the third-phase hall, which might tentatively be suggested to represent a formal, passaged, entrance into the same enclosure.

More certain is the observation that the main range of halls at Lyminge was surrounded by a series of more lightly built structures of post-in-trench construction (Fig. 10). A portion of one of these smaller ancillary buildings was identified to the west of Hall A, with fragmentary remains of another, or potentially a range of interconnected structures, extending beyond the north-west corner of Hall Complex B. Both examples were clearly laid out on the principal site axis so must have formed an integrated part of the overall layout and conception of the complex. One can only speculate as to their function, but stables or storehouses immediately suggest themselves as necessary infrastructural components for a site of periodic royal residence and assembly.[23]

In stark contrast to the underlying phase of sixth-century occupation, no pits or features associated with storage or the regulated disposal of domestic refuse were found in association with the great hall complex. As a consequence, the quantity of material culture directly attributable to the occupation and use of the complex is small, practically all of the relevant objects being derived from structural features (wall-trenches and post-pits) relating to the halls themselves. On the other hand, the diminutive tally does include survivals redolent of the aristocratic cultural milieu of the Anglo-Saxon mead hall, including a delicately crafted bone gaming piece of a type replicated in the princely burial from Taplow (Buckinghamshire), and a selection of vessel glass fragments again representative of elite burial assemblages of the later sixth–seventh centuries AD (Fig. 15).[24]

**Fig. 15** Bone gaming piece recovered from the foundations of Hall sequence B.

### *Layout and chronology*

Lyminge follows other examples of Anglo-Saxon great hall complexes in displaying a high degree of spatial formality described in the relevant literature as 'ritual symmetry'.[25] The constructional precision underlying this symmetry is particularly evident in the relative positioning of Hall sequences B and C whose entrances fall on an intersecting alignment (Fig. 10). Although clearly forming an integral part of the complex, it may be noted that the entrances of Hall A do not appear to have articulated with those of adjacent structures and it is also the only hall within the complex *not* to display evidence for major episodes of rebuilding, other than the replacement of its long-wall entrances while the building was still standing. Notwithstanding these internal divergences, it is possible to propose a hypothetical model for the evolution of the complex informed by a comparable structural sequence from Cowdery's Down.[26] In this reading, the original kernel of the complex took the form of a small and quite modest north–south hall (Hall sequence B, Phase 1) which was then rebuilt on a larger scale as part of a massively more ambitious and architecturally sophisticated arrangement incorporating Halls A and C.

Hall complexes of Lyminge type are generally dated to the later sixth to seventh centuries AD on the basis of the site chronologies constructed for Yeavering and Cowdery's Down, but the quality of the underpinning dating evidence is in both cases deficient and problematic.[27] While better chronological precision is clearly required, opportunities are constrained by the scarcity of diagnostic material culture produced by such sites and, more generally, by the problem of artefact residuality endemic to Anglo-Saxon settlement archaeology. Lyminge exemplifies these issues well. With the obvious exception of the bone gaming piece, very few closely datable objects were recovered from the foundations of the halls and one of these – a sixth-century bridle fitting recovered from Hall A – was almost certainly an heirloom when consigned to the ground.[28]

In light of these limitations, an attempt has been made to exploit radiocarbon dating as a tool for placing the Lyminge complex on a more refined chronological footing. This objective has had to contend with the key constraint of an absence of preserved timbers and other samples (e.g. articulated animal disposals) that can be proven to be contemporary with the construction or occupation of the halls. To overcome this constraint, multiple samples of animal bone from each constructional phase were submitted as a strategy for isolating contemporary 'events' from residual background noise.[29] This exercise has confirmed that a significant proportion of the disarticulated animal bone recovered from the foundations of the halls is indeed derived from earlier phases of the settlement: in the case of Hall A, this extended to as many as four out of the five submitted samples. When these residual dates are taken out of the equation, one is left with four determinations which, notwithstanding their wide chronological bandwidths, embrace some part of the seventh century, placing them within the expected target range (Table 1). Of these four dates, particular attention should be drawn to the pair relating to the ultimate phases of Hall sequences B and C: providing a constructional *terminus post quem* of the AD 660s, these determinations demonstrate that the complex is very likely to have endured into the final third of the seventh century and conceivably as late as AD 700.[30]

## Discussion

On superficial reading, the detailed summary of pre-Christian remains provided above would seem to be of no more than peripheral interest to Lyminge's historically documented life as a royal monastery and, by extension, the core themes examined in this volume. In strictly chronological terms, it is true to say that the most recent campaign of excavation has added barely a scrap of new evidence relating to Lyminge's 'monastic phase' archaeology which previous investigative mapping has shown is restricted to high ground to the south and west of the churchyard, where the remains of a seventh-century church and potentially further contemporary masonry structures were uncovered by antiquarian excavations in the mid-nineteenth century.[31] On the other hand, there are very good reasons why the earlier temporal perspective provided by the results of the Tayne Field excavations deserves considered treatment in this publication. Lyminge is unique among the small corpus of excavated Anglo-Saxon monastic sites from pre-Viking England in possessing a continuous and tightly phased sequence of antecedent settlement extending deep into the pre-Christian era. As such, it is well placed to contribute to wider research agendas fixing attention on how the twin processes of Christianization and monastic foundation were negotiated in relation to landscapes of power and political authority.[32] The concluding discussion evaluates Lyminge's contribution to this sphere of understanding, commencing with the rapid and dynamic changes of the seventh century, followed by an examination of the antecedent landscape and its role in shaping Lyminge's long-term evolution as a theatre of royal power.

### *The creation of a monumental royal landscape: Lyminge in the seventh century AD*

A large part of Lyminge's distinctiveness as one of a small and geographically disparate corpus of excavated royal centres dating to the pre-Viking era rests on the fact that a rare example of a 'great hall complex' has been unearthed in strikingly close proximity to the cult focus of a documented monastery. What significance can be attached to this near spatial convergence? At a general level, it exemplifies the magnetic influence of pre-existing geographies of power over the locations of pre-Viking monastic houses: as detailed topographic research has shown, monasteries were frequently established in close proximity to *villae regales*, typically within a radius of 2 to 3 miles – a clear expression of the agency of ruling dynasties in spearheading the Christianization of the Anglo-Saxon kingdoms.[33] While parallels for the spatial contiguity seen at Lyminge seem to represent the exception rather than the rule in most parts of Anglo-Saxon England, there do appear to be some regional anomalies, including east Kent, where the unusual preponderance of such cases has attracted repeated comment in the literature.[34] Depending upon which perspective is taken, this localized pattern can be interpreted as a reflection of a local kingship taking especially keen interest in the control of family monasteries as a dynastic strategy,[35] or, alternatively, as a manifestation of the long-term locational stability of royal vills within their dominion.[36] One of the key results of the Lyminge Project is that it has created a platform for examining how the monumental core of one of these centres evolved over the course of the seventh century in response to sustained royal investment; the following provides an appraisal of the relevant evidence leading to some wider reflections on the interplay between royal and ecclesiastical monumentality in Anglo-Saxon England.

The most recent phases of excavation on Tayne Field have reinforced the interpretation laid out in the previously published project synthesis that Lyminge's early medieval trajectory spans a transition between two spatially distinct foci – the earlier evidenced by fifth–seventh-century occupation inhabiting low-lying terrain overlooking the headwater of the River Nailbourne, and the later by eighth–ninth-century occupation sited on elevated ground surrounding the churchyard (Fig. 1).[37] This spatial reconfiguration was clearly influenced by two key events in Lyminge's evolution as monumental royal landscape: the abandonment of the Tayne Field great hall complex and the construction, on an adjacent site, of a masonry church in the Romanizing architectural style of the Augustinian mission.[38] Like other examples of its type, the former constituted a relatively short-lived, albeit architecturally extravagant, statement of royal power and ambition, the final demise of which marked the cessation of the long-established ancestral focus.[39] Conversely, the construction of the church created a new and enduring gravitational focus which structured the long-term development of the settlement throughout and well beyond its documented period as a royal monastery in the eighth and ninth centuries.

Although we can be reasonably confident of the general sequence underpinning Lyminge's seventh-century development, less certain is the precise temporal relationship between the great hall complex and the church: did one replace the other or was there a period of co-existence? Here we come up against major ambiguities surrounding the dating and chronological development of the 'monastic' core unearthed by the antiquarian Canon Jenkins and differing views on the historical timeframe for the establishment of royal nunneries in Kent.[40] While there can be no definitive resolution of this issue without re-examination of the relevant area of the churchyard, it is not inconceivable that the church started life as an adjunct to the Tayne Field royal complex either in the role of a private oratory or funeral chapel.[41] Such a scenario would certainly be consistent with expected patterns of church foundation in east Kent as a 'Frankish-influenced aristocratic milieu',[42] while also according with evidence, albeit slender, for the existence of churches at other English great hall sites.[43]

A further piece of evidence which has relevance to the current argument, if only indirectly, is the striking discovery that certain phases of Lyminge's monumental timber halls were floored internally with pseudo *opus signinum* – a tantalizing glimpse of an active architectural dialogue between hall complexes and masonry churches in seventh-century Kent. This style of flooring is generally recognized as a diagnostic feature of the earliest extant generation of Anglo-Saxon churches in England, including such members of the so-called 'Kentish' group as SS Peter and Paul, and St Pancras, Canterbury, and St Mary's, Reculver.[44] Frequently overlooked, however, is evidence from excavated Anglo-Saxon levels at Dover demonstrating a parallel vernacular context: specifically two seventh–eighth-century timber halls forming part of a spatially articulating complex closely comparable to that excavated at Lyminge.[45] Crucially, extensive spreads of flooring at Dover were preserved *in situ* as a result of deep urban stratification, indicating that the redeposited fragments of *opus signinum* recovered from Lyminge are almost certainly derived from the sequence of halls rather than representing reused Romano-British building material.[46] Taken in conjunction, the evidence from Lyminge and Dover indicates that certain royal halls in conversion-period Kent were provided with elaborate terracotta-coloured floors inspired by the same 'Romanizing' architectural tendencies displayed by contemporary churches.[47]

This new perspective on royal architectural practice in conversion-period Kent offers an interesting contrast to Northumbria, the one kingdom of Anglo-Saxon England where it has been previously possible to make informed intra-regional comparisons between vernacular and ecclesiastical building traditions over the seventh–eighth centuries AD. For here, in a reversal of the direction of influence seen in Kent, ecclesiastical stone buildings, whether small bicameral churches of Escomb type or larger 'monastic' buildings exemplified by structures A and B at Jarrow, appear to have borrowed aspects of their architectural design and layout from Yeavering's monumental timber repertoire.[48] While following divergent pathways, Kent and Northumbria seem to be united in displaying evidence for hybrid architectural forms embodying a fusion between vernacular and ecclesiastical architectural traditions, a comparative insight which chimes well with other creative forms of monumental investment reproduced across the nascent kingdoms of seventh-century England.[49]

### *The ancestral background*

Lyminge is by no means unique in providing firm evidence for the superimposition of a great hall complex on a pre-existing settlement. The monumental phases of Yeavering and Cowdery's Down appear to have been laid out across portions of earlier settlements of more modest character featuring smaller buildings organized in less formalized and theatrical configurations.[50] The most apt comparison, however, is with Sutton Courtenay (Oxfordshire). Here the great hall complex was implanted within the limits of an expansive and spatially diffuse settlement of the later fifth to sixth centuries featuring sunken-featured buildings some of which, in a manner identical to Lyminge, had been cut through by the seventh-century halls.[51] How should we characterize the antecedent phases of great hall sites given this recurrent pattern of appropriation? It would be very easy to dismiss these precursors as 'ordinary' on the grounds that they conform to observed tendencies in the fifth–sixth-century settlement record usually equated with the absence of a recognizable settlement hierarchy – loosely articulated layouts, relatively small, undifferentiated buildings and a lack of functional specialization.[52] In light of what we know of their later trajectories, however, one might legitimately ask if there was anything special or different about these places which might explain why they were exploited as focal points of royal power in the later sixth and seventh centuries AD. This question has been difficult to address robustly hitherto because the quality of the archaeological evidence for these phases is often ephemeral, incomplete and poorly recorded. But in the case of Lyminge we can draw upon a diversity of archaeological indicators which converge to show that it was functioning as a centre of power and regional authority significantly earlier than AD 600 in spite of lacking recognizably high-status architecture.[53] To draw out the relevant strands, it is necessary briefly to revisit the summary of the excavated remains given in the first part of this paper.

An obvious place to start is with the evidence for conspicuous consumption and ritualized feasting most likely conducted in connection with social gatherings and public assembly. The exceptionally large assemblage of fifth–sixth-century vessel glass immediately stands out in this regard as does the copious quantity of animal bone characterizing the majority of the midden deposits sampled from this phase of the occupation. While displaying much less of an emphasis on marine resources than the faunal assemblage associated with the later monastic-phase settlement, outlying coastal environments were clearly being exploited at some intensity during this period and it is notable that the contemporary fish assemblage includes evidence for the consumption of sturgeon as a potential luxury food with high-status connotations.[54] A potential further material expression of such activities (and of tenurial centrality more generally) is the cluster of large pits identified at the western extremity of Tayne Field. The capaciousness of these features combined with their carefully sculpted interiors suggests that they are likely to have functioned as receptacles for the centralized storage of grain or other types of food render.[55]

A further strand crucial to understanding Lyminge's character at this early period is the practice of specialist craft technologies. Early Anglo-Saxon Kent has long been celebrated for the quality and distinctiveness of its jewellery and other native artefacts richly represented in contemporary furnished cemeteries, but previous archaeological evidence directly attesting to sites of manufacture has been all but non-existent.[56] The various forms of production identified at sixth-century Lyminge – the smelting and working of iron, the manufacture of a range of copper-alloy objects and less certainly the fabrication of glass vessels – help to fill this gap in knowledge while at the same time demonstrating that the patronage of specialist technologies was no less important to the identity of power centres in early medieval Kent as it was to their counterparts in other regions of the early medieval northern world.[57] Iron production deserves special consideration in this context given the strong indications from Kent and elsewhere that the distribution of iron, both in its refined state and as fabricated products, is likely to have been strictly controlled as a currency of power and important component of the tribute economy in early Anglo-Saxon England.[58] The desire to regulate this versatile and vital resource might explain why ironworking at Lyminge was seemingly sited within the ancestral core of the settlement in close proximity to contemporary buildings.[59] Given the mythological connotations of smiths in contemporary society and the symbolic meanings attached to smelting and smithing as 'processes of transformation', this strategy can only have added to the ritual and cultic aura of this particular setting.[60]

A final theme that helps to focus attention on Lyminge's embryonic development as a place of power is that of prehistoric monument reuse enshrined in the multi-period palimpsest unearthed on Tayne Field. Lyminge provides an interesting contrast to other excavated great hall complexes in this regard because here appropriation of the prehistoric backdrop occurs very early in the occupation sequence, long before the site reached its seventh-century zenith.[61] Valuable comparisons can, however, be made with a growing repertoire of fifth–sixth-century settlements attesting this practice, typically exemplified by the superimposition of sunken-featured buildings, and less commonly ground-level halls, on Bronze Age barrows.[62] Semple has argued that these settlements can be conceived as 'places of emergent power where connections were being made with the supernatural or ancestral and where access to this powerful resource was managed' which were engaged in the process of 'confirming identity and signalling territorial power at small scales'.[63]

Viewed against the regional backdrop, it is perhaps unsurprising that Lyminge should display evidence consistent with an identity as a regional centre of power and authority at such a precociously early date. The evidence provided by Kentish laws, place-names and other topographic sources indicates that the historic heartland of the Anglo-Saxon kingdom possessed a sophisticated territorial structure by AD 600 which went on to influence later administrative arrangements enshrined in the Kentish lathes.[64] This structure was underpinned by a network of royal vills originating as head settlements within river/springhead estates embedded within wider resource networks encompassing coastal marshlands and Wealden 'dens'.[65] Recent archaeological studies exploiting old cemetery archives in combination with modern metal-detector finds have shed new light on the life of these places as focal points of power and cult in the pre-Christian landscape.[66] The significance of Lyminge is that it extends our comprehension of these phenomena into the sphere of the living and a complementary nexus of social practices offering their own unique perspective on emerging power structures during the prehistory of the Kentish kingdom.

## Conclusion

The material reviewed in this contribution provides graphic witness to the continuity and locational stability of regional centres of power and governance in Anglo-Saxon Kent: Lyminge was clearly functioning as a 'politico-religious' centre within its immediate locality by the mid-sixth century and continued to serve as a focal point for confirming royal power and authority in its wider region over several successive centuries. Masked beneath this apparent immutability, however, is a complex layering of transformations, each of which referenced and appropriated Lyminge's past, while simultaneously drawing new meaning, purpose and expression from changing social, political and ideological circumstances.

The Lyminge palimpsest invites consideration of a number of themes of wider relevance to the role played by places of power in processes of kingdom formation and Christian conversion in Anglo-Saxon England. The earliest horizon of early medieval activity encountered on the Tayne Field plateau offers significant new perspectives on the material and symbolic basis of power in early Anglo-Saxon Kent, while providing pointers on how we might begin to recognize similar tendencies in a broader spectrum of settlements of the fifth–sixth centuries AD lacking formalized layouts and high-status buildings. The argument made in this contribution is that this phase of Lyminge's occupation sequence deserves to be interpreted on its own terms as a vital stage in the crystallization of a regional power centre which determined its future trajectory as a theatre of kingship down through subsequent centuries.

By extending our appreciation of the great hall phenomenon to Kent, Lyminge highlights the widespread uniformity of the tradition and its underlying architectural principles: the simultaneous replication of this tradition across several kingdoms bespeaks of the social proximity between emergent hereditary dynasties and pervasive modes of aristocratic self-expression which transcended political boundaries. Simultaneously, the Lyminge evidence alerts our attention to regional variations within the monumental idiom. Unlike their counterparts in Wessex and Northumbria, a proportion of great halls in Kent appear to have shared the interior flourishes of contemporary masonry churches, indicating that this was a regional context where the active proclamation of *Romanitas* through the medium of monumental display permeated the boundary between vernacular and ecclesiastical architectural traditions.

The short-lived trajectory of great hall sites provides a clear embodiment of the fragility of power in the seventh century as well as the fluid cultural basis of contemporary rulership: Lyminge and its like represent a transient experiment in the discourse of Anglo-Saxon kingship that soon passed into monumental history. Whereas other known sites seem to have fallen into obscurity relatively quickly, Lyminge displays a uniquely attested 'afterlife' as a royal monastery.[67] Aspects of how the transition from royal power centre to royal monastery played itself out in the seventh-century landscape remain obscure, but there are two good reasons why we should resist polarizing Lyminge's hypothesized monumental development into two separate and chronologically discrete phases, the earlier secular and the later ecclesiastical. Firstly, such a dichotomization fails to acknowledge the religious dimension of English great hall sites and analogous expressions of 'hall culture' in other parts of the early medieval North Sea world, attested most conspicuously within the Scandinavian/Viking sphere.[68] Secondly, it is difficult to reconcile this scenario with the complex conversion narratives of the Anglo-Saxon royal dynasties themselves, not least that of the native Kentish royal house, which readily exemplifies the twists and turns involved in what was a multi-generational, and indeed reversible, process.[69]

This contribution was written with the aim of offering a comprehensive re-evaluation of the Lyminge excavations based upon the assimilation of new results generated between 2013 and 2015. While the foregoing account is more comprehensive and nuanced than its predecessor, the underpinning research is still very much a work in progress. A large and complex programme of post-excavation analysis lies ahead and the interpretive landscape is currently shifting under the impetus of a spate of new research into sites of royal residence across early medieval Britain.[70] Further modifications and refinements to the Lyminge narrative can be expected in future publications.

## Acknowledgements

I should like to express my gratitude to Sarah Lambert-Gates, Simon Maslin and Dana Goodburn-Brown for assistance with the production of some of the illustrations appearing in the paper, and to Helena Hamerow and John Blair for supplying me with constructive feedback on a previous version of the text.

## Notes

1 Thomas 2013.

2 *Ibid.*, 123–4.

3 More detailed descriptions of these features can be found in Thomas and Knox 2014 and 2015.

4 Crewe 2012; Semple 2013. A strikingly similar spatial relationship between an Anglo-Saxon building and prehistoric ring-ditch is seen at the seventh-century great hall complex of Sutton Courtenay (Oxfordshire): Hamerow and Brennan 2015.

5 Hamerow 2010, 64; 2012, 34.

6 Hamerow 2006; Sofield 2012; Sofield, pers. comm. As far as the author is aware, Yeavering is the only Anglo-Saxon settlement with comparable evidence for this practice: Hamerow 2006, 26, note 108.

7 *Ibid.*, 11–12.

8 The archaeological significance of dolines is well established in Palaeolithic studies, e.g. White 1997; Delagnes and Ropars 1996, and a number of investigated examples in the chalklands of east Kent have produced material of this date, e.g. Halliwell and Parfitt 1993. The origins of the Lyminge example appear to be considerably later on the testimony of a small assemblage of later prehistoric flint recovered from its lower horizons.

9 Tilley 1999, 225–9.

10 This attribution is based upon the typological dating of metalwork (specifically brooch types) following the periodization of female grave assemblages by Brugmann (1999); the forms present straddle Phase I (AD 500–530/40) and Phase II (AD 530/40–560/70) of her chronology.

11 Chadwick Hawkes 1982; Everitt 1986, 102, 244, 75; Kelly 2006, 99.

12 S 12, *Charters of St Augustine's and Minster-in-Thanet*, no. 8, Kelly 1995, 33–6. The unnamed mine is often assumed to have lain in the Weald, but Harrington and Welch (2014, 116) have argued that ore deposits in the vicinity of Lyminge could have been viably exploited. Future analysis of the ironworking residues should be able to determine between these two sources.

13 The Middle Saxon ironworking site of Ramsbury (Wiltshire) offers a good comparison for centralized production under the control of a *villa regalis*, see Haslam 1980.

14 See Broadley, this volume.

15 Alcock 2003, 87–9; Campbell 2007. One might expect a similar scale of domestic consumption at other Kentish political/administrative centres associated with glass-rich cemeteries (e.g. Faversham), but the settlement archaeology for these places has proved to be stubbornly elusive.

16 Walton Rogers 2007.

17 Hope-Taylor 1977; Millett and James 1983; for the most up-to-date overview of the phenomenon, see Hamerow 2012, 102–9.

18 Thomas 2013, 127.

19 The third-phase hall also had shallower wall-trenches than its predecessors and much more substantial external raking posts, suggesting a rather different structural solution for counteracting the outward thrust of the walls.

20 Millett and James 1983, 228–33.

21 For comparable evidence for the use of white lime-plastered walls in relation to great halls at Yeavering and Sutton Courtenay, see Hope-Taylor 1977, 53, 140, and Hamerow and Brennan 2015.

22 Reynolds 2003, 105; Hamerow 2012, 102–5.

23 The character of the evidence accords well with the expectation, hitherto unsubstantiated, that the ceremonial cores of

contemporary royal vills are likely to have been surrounded by a 'penumbra of subsidiary occupation' (Blair 2005, 276).

24 See Webster 2007 for a review of the finds from the Taplow burial (Buckinghamshire) and Broadley, this volume, for the glass.

25 Reynolds 2003, 104–6; Hamerow 2012, 102–5.

26 Millett and James 1983, 197–200.

27 For a critique and reassessment of Hope-Taylor's phasing of Yeavering, see Scull 1991; the radiocarbon dating for Cowdery's Down lacks the precision of modern calibration techniques and also relies on 'best estimates' based upon the statistical correction of determinations returned from charred wood samples: Millett and James 1983, 197–200.

28 The bridle fitting is discussed and illustrated in Thomas 2013, 127.

29 A similar dating strategy was employed at the Anglo-Saxon settlement of Yarnton (Oxfordshire): Bayliss and Hey 2004, 259.

30 One would have to make special pleading for a date much later than AD 700; none of the portable material culture recovered from sealed contexts associated with the hall complex conforms to recognized 'Middle Saxon' types and the same is true of unstratified background noise associated with this sector of the settlement.

31 Thomas 2013, 128–32.

32 For various archaeological perspectives on this theme, see Carver 2003; Pestell 2004; Turner 2006; Semple 2013; Sánchez-Pardo and Shapland 2015.

33 Foot 2006, 77; Blair 2005, 186–8, 275–9.

34 Everitt 1986, 187–96; Tatton-Brown 1988.

35 Yorke 2003 and this volume.

36 Blair 2005, 278.

37 As explored in the 2013 article, this rupture in the occupation sequence also finds expression in other aspects of the archaeological record including a diachronic shift in dietary regime consistent with the adoption of Christian/monastic food regulations. See Knapp, this volume, for an updated zooarchaeological assessment of this shift.

38 The relevant evidence was recovered in a series of investigations by Canon R. C. Jenkins in the 1850s (Jenkins 1874; 1876; 1889). A useful summary of Jenkins' discoveries and their subsequent re-evaluation by modern scholarship can be found in Kelly 2006, 99–100.

39 On the temporary character of Anglo-Saxon royal vills, see Blair 2005, 204–12, 281–5; Hamerow 2012, 109.

40 Kelly 2006, 99–100; Cambridge 1999. For contrasting opinions on the dating of Kentish nunneries, see contributions by Wood and Yorke in this volume.

41 Such a suggestion (i.e. a purpose-built funerary chapel attached to a royal vill) has previously been entertained by Kelly (2006, 104) as one possible way of explaining Lyminge's early foundation date of AD 633. A number of Frankish sites, including the royal nunnery of Chelles, offer precedents for this hypothesized developmental sequence; see York, this volume, for Chelles.

42 Blair 2005, 70.

43 For Yeavering, see Hope-Taylor 1977, 72–8 and Petts, this volume; Shapland (2015, 497–500, 511–12) provides a more general survey of churches represented on great hall complex sites with the acknowledgement that further excavation is required to determine whether the apsidal-ended buildings represented at Foxley (Wiltshire), Hatton Rock (Warwickshire) and Sprouston (Roxboroughshire) might be churches.

44 For the use of *opus signinum* flooring in Kentish churches, see Dowker 1878, 259 (St Mary's, Reculver); St John Hope 1902, 232 (St Pancras, Canterbury); and Gem 1997, 97 (SS Peter and Paul, Canterbury). Gittos (2013, 157) highlights that the former two churches make use of such flooring as part of eighth-century alterations. Frustratingly, no direct mention of flooring material is made in Canon Jenkins' published accounts of the early church at Lyminge, though such seems highly probable in light of his mention of other, clearly Romanizing, tendencies such as the heavy reuse of Romano-British brick and tile for the surviving lower courses of the walls (Jenkins 1874; 1876; 1889).

45 Philp 2003, 46, 65 (Structures S10 and S14). The larger of the two structures, S14, is described as a church in the original excavation report but the striking similarities with Lyminge favour a secular interpretation as previously advocated by Welch 2007, 202–3.

46 The evidence will be examined in greater detail as part of a comparative examination of the great hall phenomenon in Anglo-Saxon Kent (Thomas forthcoming).

47 The white plastered walls noted at Lyminge may have similarly taken their inspiration from contemporary church architecture, but the evidence is less clear-cut than it is for *opus signinum* flooring because the use of lime wash to 'weatherproof' the exterior of timber buildings is fairly widely attested in the Anglo-Saxon settlement record.

48 Fernie 1983, 59; Blair 2005, 199–200; Cramp 2005, 352–4, 359; Gittos 2013, 72–3; see, also, Cramp, this volume.

49 Carver 2001; Blair 2005, 51–65; Semple 2013, 106–7, 207–9.

50 Hope-Taylor 1977, 154–8; Scull 1991; Millett and James 1983, 192–5.

51 Hamerow, Hayden and Hey 2007, 183–90. It is worth noting that some of the sunken-featured buildings at Sutton Courtenay forming the portion of the settlement excavated by E. T. Leeds were in use into the seventh century and thus were probably contemporary with (though some distance from) the great hall complex. A similar relationship may have existed at Lyminge given that one of the sunken-featured buildings excavated at the bottom of Rectory Lane is securely dated to the first half of the seventh century on the basis of radiocarbon dates and diagnostic material culture: see Thomas 2013.

52 Reynolds 2003, 130; Hamerow 2012, 70–2; Ulmschneider 2011, 159; Loveluck 2013, 105–8. Scull (1991, 60) describes the relevant phase of Yeavering as a 'modest farming settlement'; this rather dismissive view can be contrasted with Blair (2005, 57) who places emphasis on Yeavering's long-standing significance as a site of public assembly/cult observance as a context for its subsequent appropriation as a place of royal residence.

53 Thomas (2013, 116) provides an examination of contextual and place-name evidence attesting to Lyminge's importance as a pre-Christian centre of authority. Exciting new discoveries made at Rendlesham (Suffolk) suggest that the *villa regalis* here enjoyed a similarly early and significant ancestry to Lyminge (Scull, Minter and Plouviez 2014).

54 Loveluck 2013, 70, 131. See Knapp, this volume, for a more detailed examination of diachronic trends in the faunal assemblage.

55 Although accorded a different function as water-storage features, the scale of the pits compares favourably with those at the eighth–ninth-century settlement at Lake End, Dorney (Buckinghamshire), interpreted as an open-air assembly site: Hiller, Petts and Allen 2002, 57–72.

56 Faversham is frequently invoked in the literature as a likely manufacturing centre for elite jewellery and glassware on the basis of its place-name (= **OE** 'the village of the smith') combined with the material richness of the King's Field cemetery (Thomas 2011, 410–11).

57 Bayley 1991; Alcock 2003, 297–335; Hedeager 2011, 144–50.

58 Loveluck 1996; Harrington and Welch 2014, 104–21.

59 A similar spatial context for metalworking (both iron-smithing and the casting of copper-alloy) is repeated at the sixth–seventh-century settlement at Carlton Coalville (Suffolk) (Lucy, Tipper and Dickens 2009, 372–81).

60 Hinton 2003; Hedeager 2011, 139–40.

61 For this dimension of great hall complex phenomenon, see Semple 2013, 96–7, 207–11.

62 Crewe 2012; Semple 2013, 95–9.

63 *Ibid.*, 98.

64 On the origins of the Kentish lathes, see Brooks 1989; Brookes 2011.

65 Everitt 1986.

66 See Dickinson, Fern and Richardson 2011 for an application of this approach to Eastry, and Thomas 2013, 116–20, for a reconsideration of the cemetery evidence for Lyminge in the light of this pioneering study.

67 See Loveluck (2013, 110–11) for comparative settlement sequences

involving the monasticization of secular estate centres in a seventh-century Frankish milieu.

68 Walker (2010) provides a stimulating interrogation of the religious character of Yeavering interpreted against a wider backdrop of Scandinavian hall sites. A recent overview of the latter, examined as part of a broader continuum of sacred places/ritual landscapes, is provided in Fabech and Näsman 2013.

69 For reflections on the complex conversion narratives of the Anglo-Saxon royal houses, see Yorke 1999.

70 This new research is being pulled together in an academic network funded by the Arts and Humanities Research Council entitled 'Monumentalising Kingship: Places of Royal Residence and the Making of Early Medieval British Kingdoms AD 500–800'. For further information, see: http://royalresidencenetwork.org/

# Bibliography


Alcock, L. 2003. *Kings and Warriors, Craftsmen and Priests in Northern Britain AD 550–850*, Edinburgh: Society of the Antiquaries of Scotland.

Bayley, J. 1991. 'Anglo-Saxon non-ferrous metalworking: a survey', *World Arch.*, **23**, 115–30.

Bayliss, A. and Hey, G. 2004. 'Scientific dating', in G. Hey, *Yarnton: Saxon and Medieval Settlement and Landscape*, 255–66, Thames Valley Landscapes Monograph, No. 20, Oxford: Oxford Archaeology.

Blair, J. 2005. *The Church in Anglo-Saxon Society*, Oxford: Oxford University Press.

Brookes, S. 2011. 'The lathes of Kent: a review of the evidence', in S. Brookes, S. Harrington and A. Reynolds (eds.), *Studies in Early Anglo-Saxon Art and Archaeology: Papers in honour of Martin G. Welch*, 156–70, BAR British Series, 527, Oxford: Archaeopress.

Brooks, N. 1989. 'The creation and early structure of the kingdom of Kent', in S. Bassett (ed.), *The Origins of the Anglo-Saxon Kingdoms*, 55–74, Leicester: Leicester University Press.

Brugmann, B. 1999. 'The role of Continental artefact-types in the sixth-century Kentish chronology', in J. Hines, K. Høilund Nielsen and F. Siegmund (eds.), *The Pace of Change: Studies in Early-Medieval Chronology*, 37–50, Oxford: Oxbow Books.

Campbell, E. 2007. *Continental and Mediterranean Imports to Atlantic Britain and Ireland, AD 400–800*, Council for British Archaeology Research Report, 157, York: CBA.

Cambridge, E. 1999. 'The architecture of the Augustinian mission', in R. Gameson (ed.), *St Augustine and the Conversion of England*, 202–36, Stroud: Sutton Publishing.

Carver, M. 2001. 'Why that, why there, why then? The politics of early medieval monumentality', in H. Hamerow and A. MacGregor (eds.), *Image and Power in Early Medieval British Archaeology: Essays in honour of Rosemary Cramp*, 1–22, Oxford: Oxbow Books.

Carver, M. (ed.) 2003. *The Cross Goes North: Processes of Conversion in Northern Europe, AD 300–1300*, Woodbridge: Boydell.

Chadwick Hawkes, S. 1982. 'Anglo-Saxon Kent c.425–725', in P. E. Leach (ed.), *Archaeology in Kent to AD 1500*, 65–6, Council for British Archaeology Research Report, 48, York: CBA.

Cramp, R. 2005. *Wearmouth and Jarrow Monastic Sites*, Vol. 1, Swindon: English Heritage.

Crewe, V. 2012. *Living with the Past: The Reuse of Prehistoric Monuments in Anglo-Saxon Settlements*, BAR British Series, 573, Oxford: British Archaeological Reports.

Delagnes, A. and Ropars, A. (eds.) 1996. *Paléolithique moyen en pays de Caux (Haute-Normandie)*, Paris: Éditions de la Maison des Sciences de l'Homme.

Dickinson, T. M., Fern, C. and Richardson, A. 2011. 'Early Anglo-Saxon Eastry: archaeological evidence for the beginnings of a district centre in the kingdom of Kent', *ASSAH*, **17**, 1–86.

Dowker, G. 1878. 'Reculver church', *Arch. Cantiana*, **12**, 248–68.

Everitt, A. 1986. *Continuity and Colonization: The Evolution of Kentish Settlement*, Leicester: Leicester University Press.

Fabech, C. and Näsman, U. 2013. 'Ritual landscapes and sacred places in the first millennium AD in south Scandinavia', in S. Nordeide and S. Brink (eds.), *Sacred Sites and Holy Places: Exploring the Sacralization of Landscape through Time and Space*, 53–110, Turnhout: Brepols.

Fernie, E. 1983. *The Architecture of the Anglo-Saxons*, London: B. T. Batsford.

Foot, S. 2006. *Monastic Life in Anglo-Saxon England, c.600–900*, Cambridge: Cambridge University Press.

Gem, R. 1997. 'The Anglo-Saxon and Norman churches', in R. Gem (ed.), *St Augustine's Abbey, Canterbury*, 90–122, London: B.T. Batsford/English Heritage.

Gittos, H. 2013. *Liturgy, Architecture, and Sacred Places in Anglo-Saxon England*, Oxford: Oxford University Press.

Halliwell, G. and Parfitt, K. 1993. 'Non-river gravel Lower and Middle Palaeolithic discoveries in east Kent', *Kent Arch. Rev.*, **114**, 80–9.

Hamerow, H. 2006. 'Special deposits on Anglo-Saxon settlements'. *Medieval Arch.*, **50**, 1–30.

Hamerow, H. 2010. 'Herrenhöfe in Anglo-Saxon England', *Siedlungs- und Küstenforschung im Südlichen Nordseegebiet*, **33**, 59–67.

Hamerow, H. 2012. *Rural Settlements and Society in Anglo-Saxon England*, Oxford: Oxford University Press.

Hamerow, H. and Brennan, N. 2015. 'An Anglo-Saxon great hall complex at Sutton Courtenay/Drayton, Oxfordshire: a royal centre of early Wessex?', *Arch. Jnl*, **172**, 325–50.

Hamerow, H., Hayden, C. and Hey, G. 2007. 'Anglo-Saxon and earlier settlement near Drayton Road, Sutton Courtenay, Berkshire', *Arch. Jnl*, **164**, 109–96.

Harrington, S. and Welch, M. 2014. *The Early Anglo-Saxon Kingdoms of Southern Britain AD 450–650: Beneath the Tribal Hidage*, Oxford: Oxbow Books.

Haslam, J. 1980. 'A Middle Saxon iron smelting site at Ramsbury, Wiltshire', *Medieval Arch.*, **24**, 1–68.

Hedeager, L. 2011. *Iron Age Myth and Materiality: An Archaeology of Scandinavia AD 400–1000*, London: Routledge.

Hiller, J., Petts, D. and Allen, T. 2002. 'Discussion of the Anglo-Saxon archaeology', in S. Foreman, J. Hiller and D. Petts, *Gathering the People, Settling the Land: The Archaeology of a Middle Thames Landscape: Anglo-Saxon and Medieval*, 57–72, Oxford: Oxford Archaeological Unit.

Hinton, D. A. 2003. 'Anglo-Saxon smiths and myths', in D. Scragg (ed.), *Textual and Material Culture in Anglo-Saxon England*, 261–82, Cambridge: D. S. Brewer.

Hope-Taylor, B. 1977. *Yeavering: An Anglo-British Centre of Early Northumbria*, London: Her Majesty's Stationery Office.

Jenkins, R. C. 1874. 'The basilica of Lyminge: Roman, Saxon and medieval', Arch. *Cantiana*, **9**, 205–23.

Jenkins, R. C. 1876. 'Remarks on the early Christian basilicas, in connection with recent discoveries at Lyminge', *Arch. Cantiana*, **10**, ci–ciii.

Jenkins, R. C. 1889. 'Observations on the remains of the basilica of Lyminge', *Arch. Cantiana*, **18**, 46–54.

Kelly, S. (ed.) 1995. *Charters of St Augustine's Abbey, Canterbury and Minster-in-Thanet*, Anglo-Saxon Charters, 4, Oxford: Oxford University Press.

Kelly, S. 2006. 'Lyminge minster and its early charters', in S. Keynes and A. P. Smyth (eds.), *Anglo-Saxons; Studies presented to Cyril Hart*, 98–113, Dublin: Four Courts Press.

Loveluck, C. 1996. 'The development of the Anglo-Saxon landscape, economy and society "On Driffield", East Yorkshire, 400–750 AD', *ASSAH*, **9**, 25–48.

Loveluck, C. 2013. *Northwest Europe in the Early Middle Ages, c. AD 600–1150: A Comparative Archaeology*, Cambridge: Cambridge University Press.

Lucy, S., Tipper, J. and Dickens, A. 2009. *The Anglo-Saxon Settlement and*

*Cemetery at Bloodmoor Hill, Carlton Colville, Suffolk*, East Anglian Archaeology, **131**, Cambridge: Cambridge Archaeological Unit.

Millett, M. and James, S. 1983. 'Excavations at Cowdery's Down, Basingstoke, Hampshire, 1978–81', *Arch. Jnl*, **140**, 151–279.

Pestell, T. 2004. *Landscapes of Monastic Foundation*, Woodbridge: Boydell.

Philp, B. 2003. *The Discovery and Excavation of Anglo-Saxon Dover*, Ninth Report in the Kent Monograph Series, Dover: Kent Archaeological Rescue Unit.

Reynolds, A. 2003. 'Boundaries and settlements in later sixth to eleventh-century England', *ASSAH*, **12**, 98–139.

Sánchez-Pardo, J. and Shapland, M. (eds.) 2015. *Churches and Social Power in Early Medieval Europe: Integrating Archaeological and Historical Approaches*, Turnhout: Brepols.

Scull, C. 1991. 'Post-Roman Phase 1 at Yeavering: a reconsideration', *Medieval Arch.*, **35**, 51–63.

Scull, C., Minter, F. and Plouviez, J. 2014. 'Rendlesham rediscovered', *British Arch.*, **137**, 50–5.

Semple, S. 2013. *Perceptions of the Prehistoric in Anglo-Saxon England: Religion, Ritual, and Rulership in the Landscape*, Oxford: Oxford University Press.

Shapland, M. 2015. 'Palaces, churches, and the practice of Anglo-Saxon kingship', in J. Sánchez-Pardo and M. Shapland (eds.), *Churches and Social Power in Early Medieval Europe: Integrating Archaeological and Historical Approaches*, 495–522, Turnhout: Brepols.

Sofield, C. M. 2012. 'Placed Deposits in Early and Middle Anglo-Saxon Rural Settlements', unpublished DPhil thesis, University of Oxford.

St John Hope, W. H. 1902. 'Excavations at St Austin's Abbey, Canterbury I. The Chapel of St Pancras', *Arch. Cantiana*, **25**, 222–37.

Tatton-Brown, T. 1988. 'The churches of Canterbury diocese in the eleventh century', in J. Blair (ed.), *Minsters and Parish Churches: The Local Church in Transition 950–1200*, 105–18, Oxford University Committee for Archaeology Monograph, 18, Oxford: Oxford University Committee for Archaeology.

Thomas, G. 2011. 'Overview: craft production and technology', in H. Hamerow, D. A. Hinton and S. Crawford (eds.), *The Oxford Handbook of Anglo-Saxon Archaeology*, 405–22, Oxford: Oxford University Press.

Thomas, G. 2013. 'Life before the minster: the social dynamics of monastic foundation at Anglo-Saxon Lyminge, Kent', *Antiquaries Jnl*, **93**, 109–45.

Thomas, G. forthcoming. 'Hall culture and kingship in Anglo-Saxon Kent: new archaeological perspectives on sites of royal residence in pre-Viking England', *Early Medieval Europe*.

Thomas, G. and Knox, A. 2014. *Lyminge Excavations 2013: Interim Report on the University of Reading Excavations at Lyminge, Kent*, http://www.reading.ac.uk/web/FILES/archaeology/Lyminge_2013_interim.pdf

Thomas, G. and Knox, A. 2015. *Lyminge Excavations 2014: Interim Report on the University of Reading Excavations at Lyminge, Kent*, http://www.reading.ac.uk/web/FILES/archaeology/Lyminge_2014_Interim.pdf

Tilley, C. 1999. *Metaphor and Material Culture*, Oxford: Blackwell.

Turner, S. 2006. *Making a Christian Landscape: The Countryside of Early Medieval Cornwall, Devon and Wessex*, Exeter: Exeter University Press.

Ulmschneider, K. 2011. 'Settlement hierarchy', in H. Hamerow, D. A. Hinton and S. Crawford (eds.), *The Oxford Handbook of Anglo-Saxon Archaeology*, 156–71, Oxford: Oxford University Press.

Walker, J. 2010. 'In the hall', in M. Carver, S. Semple and A. Sandmark (eds.), *Signals of Belief in Early England: Anglo-Saxon Paganism Revisited*, 83–102, Oxford: Oxbow Books.

Walton Rogers, P. 2007. *Cloth and Clothing in Early Anglo-Saxon England, AD 450–700*, Council for British Archaeology Research Report, 145, York: CBA.

Webster, L. 2007. 'Taplow', *Reallexikon der Germanischen Altertumskunde*, **35**, 69–72.

Welch, M. 2007. 'Anglo-Saxon Kent to AD 800', in J. H. Williams (ed.), *The Archaeology of Kent to AD 800*, 187–250, Woodbridge: Boydell.

White, M. J. 1997. 'The earlier Palaeolithic occupation of the Chilterns (southern England): reassessing the sites of Worthington G. Smith', *Antiquity*, **71**, 912–31.

Yorke, B. 1999. 'The reception of Christianity at the Anglo-Saxon royal courts', in R. Gameson (ed.), *St Augustine and the Conversion of England*, 152–73, Stroud: Sutton Publishing.

Yorke, B. 2003. *Nunneries and the Anglo-Saxon Royal Houses*, London: Continuum.

# Preliminary observations on the Anglo-Saxon glass from Lyminge

Rose Broadley

*Abstract*

*The Lyminge excavations have produced the largest and most diverse assemblage of vessel and window glass yet recovered from a rural settlement in Anglo-Saxon England. The assemblage is unique in embracing a typo-chronological progression of vessel glass from Early through to Middle Saxon forms and also includes the first collection of Anglo-Saxon window and vessel glass from a monastic context in the kingdom of Kent. The fifth–sixth-century glass assemblage is of particular significance in providing the first evidence for large-scale vessel consumption within a settlement context in early Anglo-Saxon England and for the provisional identification of glass-working waste and raw materials, potentially associated with the production of glass vessels. This contribution provides a preliminary overview of the assemblage and evaluates its research potential for Anglo-Saxon glass studies.*

## Scale and diversity

The current number of glass finds from the project stands at 682. This total is dominated by early Anglo-Saxon vessel glass of the fifth–seventh centuries AD which accounts for over eighty per cent of the assemblage (572 sherds), followed by Middle Saxon (eighth–ninth century) vessel and window glass (fifty sherds), Romano-British glass (forty-two sherds) and molten droplets, moils and fragments of raw glass recovered from stratified early Anglo-Saxon contexts (thirteen fragments) (Table 1).

The most striking feature of Lyminge in a national context is the large size of its early Anglo-Saxon assemblage given that settlements of this period, even extensively excavated sites such as Mucking (Essex), West Stow and Carlton Colville (Suffolk), typically produce no more than a handful of sherds. For comparably sized glass assemblages from a settlement context one has to cast the net either forwards in time to include densely occupied Middle Saxon *wics* (of which only the assemblage from *Hamwic* is larger than Lyminge) or beyond England to include high-status/monastic sites in Celtic-speaking regions of early medieval Britain (Table 2).[1]

Lyminge's distinctiveness as an Anglo-Saxon glass assemblage is further underlined by the fact that it includes a uniquely wide chronological distribution of vessel types spanning both Early and Middle Saxon forms and associated changes in the art and technology of glass-making. While the size of the latter assemblage falls some way short of other excavated Middle Saxon rural settlements from England, including Brandon (Suffolk) and Jarrow (Tyne and Wear) (Table 2), it nevertheless deserves close attention as the first significant collection of vessel and window glass yet recovered from a documented monastic context in Anglo-Saxon Kent.

**Table 1** Numbers of glass finds from Lyminge by artefact type and date.

| | Vessel | Window | Unclassified | Droplets, moils and raw glass |
|---|---|---|---|---|
| 10th–12th century | 3 | 2 | · | · |
| 8th–9th century | 31 | 19 | · | 2 |
| 7th century | 14 | · | · | · |
| 5th–6th century | 558 | · | · | 11 |
| Romano-British | 19 | 8 | 15 | · |
| **Totals** | **625** | **29** | **15** | **13** |

**Table 2** Numbers of Anglo-Saxon vessel glass sherds from the largest settlement assemblages in England.

| Site | Numbers of Anglo-Saxon vessel glass sherds |
|---|---|
| Hamwic (Southampton) | 1675 |
| **Lyminge** | **603** |
| Ipswich, Suffolk | 335 |
| Brandon, Suffolk | 171 |
| London | 154 |
| York | 113 |
| Jarrow | 79 |

**Fig. 1** Early Anglo-Saxon cone beaker sherds from Lyminge: left to right, two rims with opaque white trailed decoration; the loop of a vertical self-coloured trail and a large fragment from a base; a series of horizontal trails from the top of a cone beaker and a plain rim.

## Fifth- to sixth-century vessel glass

Preliminary analysis of the fifth- to sixth-century Anglo-Saxon vessel glass indicates a form profile focused strongly on cone beakers (Figs 1 and 2), with claw beakers as the second largest group (Fig. 3) and very few other identifiable vessel forms.

Sherds from Kempston cone beakers are particularly well represented in this period. Named after a vessel found in a grave at Kempston (Bedfordshire), this type features fine horizontal self-coloured trails below the rim and vertical trails covering the remainder of the body, looped across at the top and bottom (see the looped trail sherd and sherd with horizontal self-coloured trails in Figure 1). Dated by grave assemblages from the second half of the fifth to the first half of the sixth centuries AD, it has a widespread distribution covering France, Belgium, the Netherlands, Germany and the former Czechoslovakia,[2] but the highest find-concentrations come from England and the Rhine valley.[3] Lyminge now surpasses the cremation cemetery of Spong Hill (Norfolk), as the most productive English site for the discovery of Kempston cone beaker fragments,[4] and includes a range of decorative variants in olive green, pale green, blue-green and colourless glass.

Amongst the variants in coloured glass is a particularly fine group of olive green sherds made from high quality metal (Fig. 2, centre row) paralleled locally at the Kentish cemeteries of Buckland, Dover (graves 22 and 297), Mill Hill, Deal (grave 70 (a)), and Howletts, Littlebourne (graves 18 and 30).[5] Another sub-type comprises sixteen sherds in either olive green or pale blue-green glass present in two decorative variants: opaque white decoration in an arcaded pattern characteristic of Evison's '*Haillot*' sub-type and represented locally at the cemeteries of Buckland, Dover (grave 432) and Bifrons;[6] and a more standard form of white trailed decoration (see the two rims on the left of Figure 1) paralleled locally at Buckland (graves 254 and 347) and Milton-next-Sittingbourne.[7] According to Evison, both manifestations are likely to represent Continental imports of the late fifth–sixth centuries, the former deriving from one or more centres of manufacture located in either Belgium or northern France and the latter from the Meuse and Rhine valleys.

The range of cone beakers in coloured glass extends to more unusual and localized variants, including blue-green glass fragments featuring distinctive diagonally ribbed decoration (Fig. 2, bottom row) for which there is a good parallel at Buckland, Dover (grave 38).[8] There are also three sherds in a 'smoky' green glass with dark swirls through the metal for which an exact parallel is yet to be found (Fig. 2, top row).

The cone beaker assemblage is augmented by a significant quantity of colourless sherds. This includes thirty-five fragments representing at least eight vessels, from a sunken-featured building excavated in 2010.[9] This collection forms an extraordinary contextual group that has no

**Fig. 2** Three early Anglo-Saxon cone beaker sherd groups: top to bottom, 'smoky' green sherds, olive green sherds with self-coloured horizontal trails, and pale blue diagonally ribbed sherds.

exact parallels in Anglo-Saxon England, and will provide a fascinating opportunity for compositional batch analysis to establish whether all beakers were made from the same batch of glass or same campaign of production, perhaps as matching sets.

Claw beakers form the second largest group based on preliminary observation. Amongst the most distinctive sherds in this group are four claw fragments in pale olive green glass where the claws have been deliberately flicked up, or 'feathered', at the point where they meet the body of the vessel (Fig. 3, left-hand group). While no exact parallel for this particular decorative feature has been identified to date, the overall style is reminiscent of glass beakers belonging to Evison's types 3a and 3b, which she assigns to the period AD 475–525.[10] The similarities with type 3a are particularly significant given its representation in a number of local cemeteries, including Lyminge itself (grave 41), Buckland, Dover (graves 20 and 372) and Sarre, which has encouraged the view that the type represents a local Kentish product.[11]

Lyminge has also produced several glass sherds classifiable as type 3c claw beakers which Evison has dated to the middle of the sixth century and which are represented locally in the Kentish cemeteries at Howletts (grave 37), Littlebourne and Sittingbourne.[12] This includes five near-identical olive claws with amber swirls in the metal which must be derived from the same vessel or a matching set (Fig. 3, right-hand group), and five further fragments in a deeper amber colour (Fig. 3, centre group).

In contrast to the glass recovered from the nearby cemeteries at Buckland, Dover, and Mill Hill, Deal, no bell beakers, bowls or globular beakers have yet been firmly identified within the fifth–sixth-century assemblage, although there are a few sherds from vessels of 'globular' form and at least one pale green cavity rim that may be from a bowl form. It would be unwise to read too much

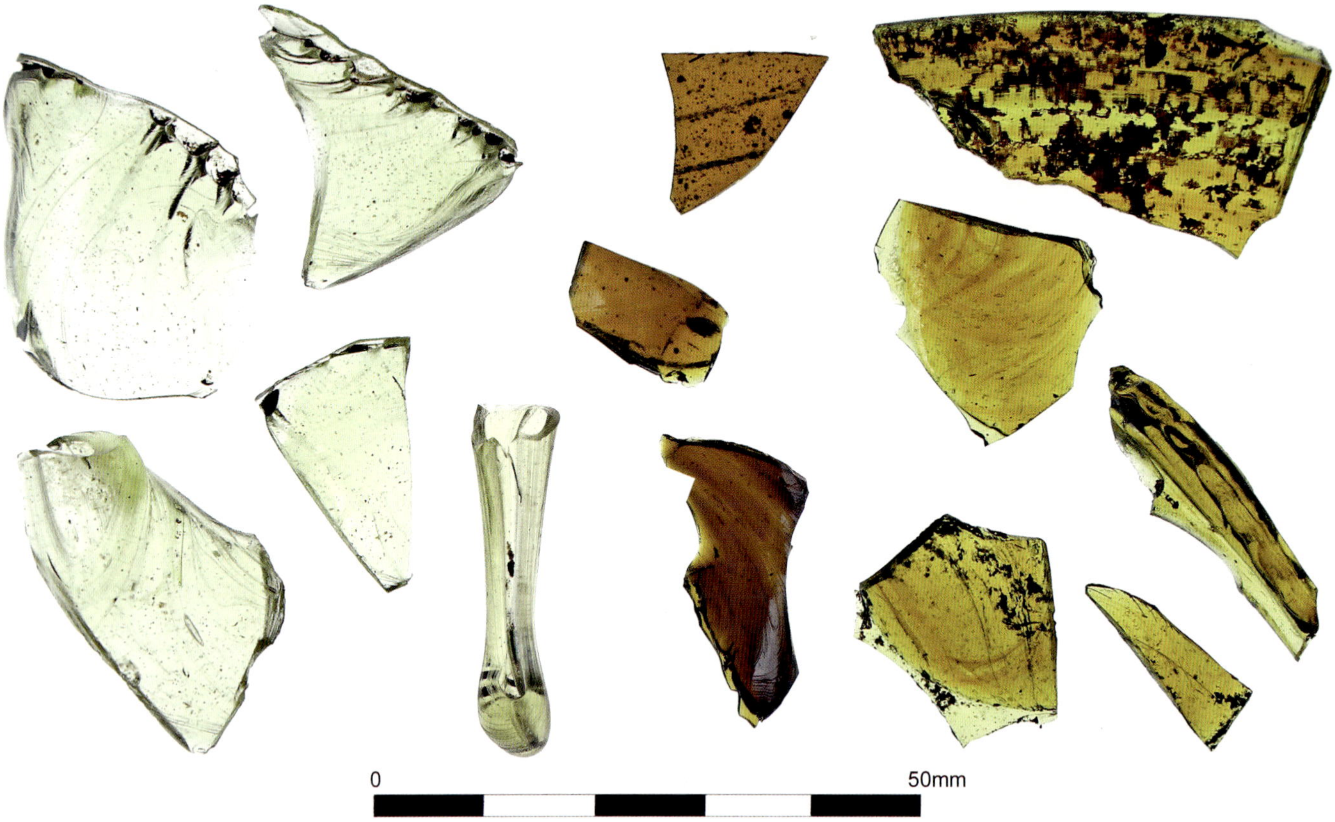


**Fig. 3** Early Anglo-Saxon claw beaker sherds from Lyminge, including three sherd groups: left to right, pale olive green twisted claws, amber-brown fragments, and olive green sherds with amber swirls in the metal.

into these apparent absences given that it can be very hard to distinguish the presence of these particular vessel forms from highly fragmentary settlement assemblages; bell beakers, for example, are impossible to identify unless a distinctive base or pattern of trailed decoration survives. On the other hand, it seems plausible that coastal communities such Dover and Deal may have consumed a greater portion of imported glass than inland sites such as Lyminge, resulting in genuinely different form profiles: bell beakers might be relevant here given that the type is attributed to a Continental source of production, most likely located in northern France, Belgium or potentially Germany.[13] The provisional picture overall, however, is that the majority of the early Anglo-Saxon glass from Lyminge comprises forms which are likely to be of sixth-century English manufacture, with a smaller component of imported Continental glass.

Before leaving this component of the Lyminge assemblage, a preliminary and very conservative assessment of the minimum number of vessels can be given to underline its scale and significance. For the Tayne Field area (excavation seasons 2012–14, minus the *c.* 200 sherds recovered in 2015) the glass represents a *minimum* of twenty-nine cone beakers and five claw beakers, to which can be added a further fifteen vessels (again mostly cone beakers) recovered from the 2010 excavation area, making a total of forty-nine vessels. In considering this total, it is important to remember that over three-quarters of the assemblage of fifth–sixth-century vessel glass was recovered from a single feature – the midden-infilled solution hollow located on Tayne Field[14] – only an estimated five to ten per cent of which has been excavated. Given that glass fragments are fairly evenly distributed through this feature, the overall total is likely to number several hundreds of vessels.

## Late sixth- to seventh-century glass

Amongst the glass recovered from contexts directly associated with, or in close proximity to, Lyminge's seventh-century 'great hall complex' were a number of fragments in deep blue and turquoise (Fig. 4). While few in number, these sherds form an important chronological marker given that these colours were not introduced in the technological repertoire of Anglo-Saxon glass production until the turn of the seventh century.[15] They thus represent one of the few object categories that can be independently dated to the period of the occupation of the hall complex itself, bearing in mind that much of the material recovered from these contexts was residual from underlying, fifth–sixth-century occupation.

Two vessel sherds in particular deserve further comment for their elite connotations. The first is a fragment of a deep blue globular beaker characterized by applied trailed decoration in a lattice formation (Fig. 4, left).[16] Vessels belonging to this distinctive series have often been described in the past as 'princely' owing to

**Fig. 4** Two examples of the seventh-century deep blue vessel glass found at Lyminge, from a 'princely' globular beaker decorated with a thick lattice trail (left) and a claw beaker (right).

their discovery in very well furnished graves dating to the late sixth to seventh centuries AD; indeed, part of the significance of the Lyminge discovery is that it is the first time that evidence for one of these luxury products has been found in an unambiguously royal settlement context.[17] The distribution of the type is confined to the northern and southern fringes of the Thames estuary in Kent and Essex: a complete pair was found in the elite burial at Prittlewell in Essex, and one complete vessel each in burials from Broomfield, Essex, and Aylesford and Deal, Kent.[18]

Compositional analysis of this group, including the Lyminge sherd, has shown very similar chemical profiles across the board, with the pair from Prittlewell being a 'batch pair' – i.e. made as a pair at the same time from the same batch of glass. The whole group was made using the same type of glass, using the same cobalt source and very little recycled Roman glass, reinforcing the impression that they emanate from a single de-luxe workshop located somewhere in south-east England.[19]

The second noteworthy fragment is the claw from a deep blue claw beaker recovered from the foundation trench of Hall sequence C, which belongs to Evison's type 4c, dated by her to the late sixth to seventh centuries AD (Fig. 4, right).[20] The type is well represented in richly furnished graves from Kent, including at the cemeteries of Wickhambreaux, Buckland, Dover (grave 353), and Faversham,[21] and also makes a limited appearance on the Continent in elite contexts, including on the Swedish island of Gotland and Nettersheim, Germany.[22]

## Eighth- to ninth-century vessel glass

The smaller number of Middle Saxon sherds were all recovered from sites excavated between 2007 and 2009 which targeted Lyminge's monastic focus.[23] Some of the individual sherds are of high quality, typifying the distinctive palette and polychrome techniques of vessel glass of the eighth–ninth centuries AD: for example, pale green cavity rims encasing opaque yellow trails, and a large turquoise base fragment including a swirl of deep red (Fig. 5, lower right and centre). The form profile of the Middle Saxon glass also offers clear points of contrast with the fifth–seventh-century assemblage as it is dominated by globular beakers, with possible representatives of palm cups and the palm-funnel form series.[24]

One individual discovery deserving special mention for its quality and rarity is a small sherd originally decorated with an intricate pattern of applied gold foil (Fig. 6).[25] It is a small fragment of very pale blue glass, measuring 12 × 8 mm. No actual gold foil survives, only the adhesive used, which reveals a delicate pattern comprising a row of lozenges set between two parallel lines. This style of decoration is matched on the famous funnel beaker from Borg, Norway, and one of the glass vessels found at Dorestad, in the Netherlands.[26] Only three other examples of this decorative variant are known from England, all from the Middle Saxon *wic* of Ipswich.[27] The combined weight of evidence suggests that the Lyminge vessel was a high quality import which emanated from a workshop located in the Rhineland area of modern Germany.

## Anglo-Saxon window glass

Alongside the vessel glass, nineteen sherds of middle Anglo-Saxon window glass were found within the monastic settlement (Fig. 5).[28] These sherds are particularly noteworthy because until recently, in spite of a number of important excavations on sites of major pre-Viking

**Fig. 5** A range of middle Anglo-Saxon vessel and window glass. Four sherds of window glass to the left, four sherds of vessel glass centre and right, including a cavity rim enclosing opaque yellow trails and the base of a pale blue globular beaker featuring red streaks.

monastic institutions, including St Augustine's Abbey, no Anglo-Saxon window glass had been recorded from Kent.[29] Almost all the sherds from Lyminge are plain pale blue (twelve), or pale green (five), with the exception of one colourless sherd and one of deep emerald green colour (Fig. 5). In other words, most of the Lyminge window glass can be regarded as 'colourless', in the sense that the pale blues and greens result from impurities in the raw materials rather than deliberately added colourants. This is similar to the assemblage from Brandon, Suffolk,[30] where there were also very few deeply coloured sherds of window glass, in contrast with the highly coloured glass from the monastic site of Jarrow (Tyne and Wear). Cramp has observed that glass of the former category would have been ideal for transmitting light into buildings, 'a characteristic particularly praised in contemporary Anglo-Saxon literature', and that its employment on certain English sites may represent 'a separate tradition' to the highly coloured one seen at Jarrow.[31]

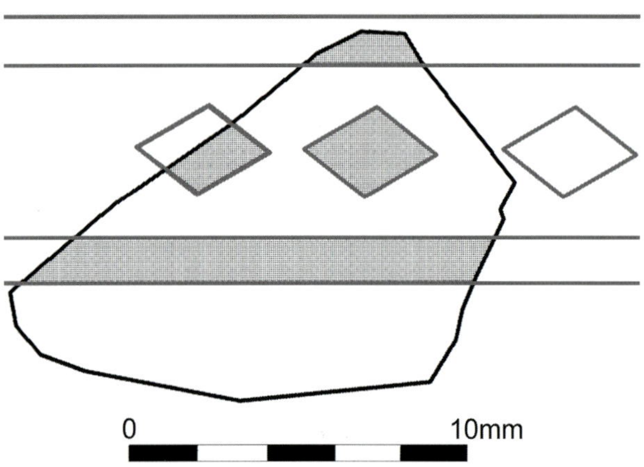


**Fig. 6** The gold-foil-decorated sherd from Lyminge.

Five of the Lyminge sherds have original edges surviving, three of which are grozed and two of which are fire rounded, the latter being indicative of cylinder blown glass. These fragments of window glass may have been mounted in lead cames, which are thought to have been in regular use from the ninth century onwards.[32] Another possibility, particularly where there is no evidence specifically to indicate leading, is a system of mounting in a frame constructed entirely from wood, as suggested by Cramp for the timber buildings at the Northumbrian monastic site of Whithorn (Dumfries and Galloway).[33]

Lyminge joins a growing corpus of Middle Saxon rural settlements of high-status/monastic character to have produced window glass which have recently been reviewed by Cramp.[34] Lyminge falls within middle-ranking sites on the basis of sherd count, below superabundant assemblages such as Whithorn, (Dumfries and Galloway), Brandon (Suffolk) and Wearmouth and Jarrow (Tyne and Wear) which have in excess of 100 sherds, and above sites such as Escomb (County Durham) and Brixworth (Northamptonshire) with only a couple; other sites in the middle-ranking group include Repton (Derbyshire) with thirty, Dacre (Cumbria) with twenty-two, Beverley

(Yorkshire) with twenty, Glastonbury (Somerset) with nineteen and Flixborough (Lincolnshire) with seventeen.

One of the significant conclusions to emerge from Cramp's evaluation of these assemblages is that it cannot be assumed that window glass at this period was exclusively used in association with mortared stone buildings; indeed, it is almost certainly the case that the glass recovered from Whithorn, Brandon and possibly Flixborough derives from wooden buildings. This has clear implications for Lyminge given that the relevant finds were recovered over 100 m away from the stone church lying at the core of the monastic settlement: while this structure remains the likeliest source, one cannot discount the possibility that the glass derives from a glazed wooden building located within the domestic sector of the monastery identified by the recent excavations.[35]

## Manufacturing evidence

The equipment required for glass-working and the resulting waste products remained remarkably consistent from the Romano-British period up until the nineteenth century. At a basic level, glass blowing, which could be used to create glass vessels or cylinder blown window glass, required cullet or raw glass to melt, a crucible or tank to contain the molten glass, a furnace in which to heat it, and an iron blow pipe with which to gather molten glass to inflate and shape. Blowing glass vessels usually also involved the use of a pontil rod, to which the vessel can be attached during the manufacturing process, usually for rim shaping and finishing. The process of blowing glass vessels might leave behind remnants of any of the above, and also droplets, trails, fragments of overblow and moils (excess glass surrounding the end of the blowpipe that remains attached to it when the vessel is removed, which is detached and discarded separately).[36] The key archaeological finds for the identification of glass vessel manufacture are crucible or furnace fragments with glass adhering, moils, and raw glass ingot fragments.

Nearly all of the relevant finds from Lyminge were recovered from securely stratified contexts dating to the sixth century, the greatest constituent deriving from the midden deposits contained within the prehistoric solution hollow sampled in the 2014–15 excavations (Fig. 7).[37] The material comprises five potential moil fragments containing characteristic flakes of iron from the blowpipe, in pale/olive green, blue-green and colourless glass; several unmelted chunks of pale blue glass provisionally identified as the crushed remains of imported glass ingots; three fragments of melted waste, one pale green and two olive green; several small fragments of fired clay with what appears to be melted glass adhering to their internal surfaces; and over forty fragments of Roman glass, mainly consisting of thick sherds of bottle and window glass ideally suited for recycling.

To appreciate the potential significance of these remains, it is necessary to draw attention to the glass-working evidence from Glastonbury Abbey (Somerset) which has recently been re-evaluated as the earliest site of glass blowing in Anglo-Saxon England. Originally recovered by Radford's excavations in the 1950s, the glass-working evidence from Glastonbury Abbey has received considerable academic attention over the years on account of the unprecedented survival of *in situ* remains comprising at least three (and perhaps as many as five) glass furnaces combined with a wide array of associated waste material, including numerous crucible fragments, ingot chunks, droplets, pulls, moils and vessel glass fragments.[38] A major impetus towards a reassessment of these remains and their wider significance has come with newly commissioned radiocarbon dates which place the glass-working activity into the later seventh century AD, several centuries earlier than Radford's original 'Late Saxon' dating derived from stratigraphic evidence.[39]

This redating firmly situates the glass-working operation within the pre-Viking phases of the Abbey, specifically in connection with providing window glass for the first stone church constructed on the site *c.* AD 700, as well as vessels for use by members of the early community.[40] Exploiting the Glastonbury evidence as a springboard, and integrating comparable glass-working evidence from other documented monastic sites such as Barking (Essex), Monkwearmouth (Tyne and Wear) and Whithorn (Dumfries and Galloway), Willmott and Welham have argued that the spread of the pre-Viking Church provided the key stimulus for the development of glass-working in Anglo-Saxon England, with the conscription of Frankish glaziers by monastic founders forming an integral part of the process.[41]

This clear horizon of Middle Saxon glass-working activity can readily be contrasted with the much more meagre evidence for glass production during the fifth–seventh centuries AD, limited to (according to one recent assessment by Wilmott) 'some melted cullet in western areas and … crucibles from Buckden (Cambridgeshire), probably related to the making of beads and coloured inlays'.[42] Influenced by this chronological disparity, Wilmott has asserted that there is 'as yet no evidence that [vessel glass] was produced domestically' in the early Anglo-Saxon period and that the concentration of early Anglo-Saxon glass vessels in Kent 'indicates that all vessels from the fifth to seventh century were imported'.[43]

This is clearly a conservative viewpoint given that Insular manufacture has long been accepted by Anglo-Saxon archaeologists on the basis of the high quantity and morphological consistency of glass vessels placed in Kentish graves.[44] While Lyminge currently lacks watertight evidence in the form of *in situ* furnaces and crucibles, the manufacturing evidence reviewed in this paper (in particular the moils and crushed glass ingots) points strongly in the direction of on-site glass vessel manufacture during the sixth century AD, a period in which a variety of other specialist high-temperature crafts were being practised within the settlement.[45] This hypothesis

**Fig. 7** Glass-working waste: two moils on the left, two droplets and two chunks of 'raw' glass ingots on the right.

will need to be tested and refined through future compositional analysis and consultation with leading specialists, but there is a good possibility that Lyminge may soon supplant Glastonbury as the earliest site of glass vessel production in Anglo-Saxon England.

## Conclusion

While still at a preliminary stage of analysis, there can be no doubt that the glass assemblage from Lyminge is of international importance. It is the only settlement assemblage from Anglo-Saxon England to embrace a typo-chronological progression from Early through to Middle Saxon vessel forms and associated glass-working traditions. Eclipsing the meagre collections typifying excavated rural settlements of the fifth–seventh centuries AD, the early Anglo-Saxon constituent provides the first clear demonstration of how glass vessels were used and consumed within a high-status domestic context in Anglo-Saxon Kent, offering a complementary perspective to well-studied cemetery assemblages from the same region. The middle Anglo-Saxon window and vessel glass groups are somewhat smaller and less representative, but nonetheless provide an important first glimpse of patterns of glass use within a monastic context in the kingdom of Kent. Amplifying the significance of the assemblage is a range of waste materials certainly associated with glass-working and very possibly with the production of glass vessels. If verified through future analysis and study, the latter will constitute the earliest evidence for glass blowing in Anglo-Saxon England and provide long-awaited confirmation that Kent was indeed home to an indigenous and vibrant glass industry during the pre-Christian era. Overall, these preliminary observations clearly demonstrate the outstanding importance of the glass from Lyminge and the strong potential for future research.

## Acknowledgements

I would like to express my gratitude to John Piddock for producing the photographs for my paper and to Emily Harwood for her assistance in refining Figure 6 for publication. I would also like to thank Gabor Thomas for his many useful suggestions for improving my paper.

## Notes

1 Hunter and Heyworth 1998; Campbell 2007. Different sampling strategies must be acknowledged when making basic numerical comparisons of this type. Lyminge's high glass count can partly be explained as a product of intensive screening whereby 100% of stratified early medieval contexts were dry-sieved using a 5 mm mesh. This does not alter the underlying significance of the Lyminge total, however, which far exceeds other early Anglo-Saxon settlement assemblages.

2 Evison 2012, 139.

3 Evison 1997, 242.

4 *Ibid.*

5 Evison 2012, 139, fig. 10.29; 1997, 241–2, fig. 40; 2008, nos. 36–42.

6 Evison 2012, 139, fig. 10.66; 2000, group 21, 1–3.

7 Evison 2012, 138–9, fig. 10.16; 2008, nos. 31, 32; 2008, nos. 29, 30.

8 *Ibid.*, no. 25. The type is dated to the sixth to seventh centuries, and the Buckland grave specifically to AD 575–625, based on associated grave goods.

9 The sunken-featured building in question (SFB 2) formed part of the early Anglo-Saxon settlement complex investigated at the bottom of Rectory Lane described in Thomas 2013, 120–2. For a catalogue and summary discussion of the glass finds, see Scull 2011, 8–10.

10 Evison 1982, 47–8.

11 Warhurst 1955, 7–8, pl. XI; Evison 1987, 96–7, 221, fig. 13, 16; 2000, group 35, 3; 2012, 139.

12 Evison 2008, 67, 69.

13 Evison 1997, 240, 242–3, figs. 28, 50; 2012, fig. 10.63.

14 See Thomas, this volume, for a description of this feature.

15 Evison 2008, 3.

16 The fragment was recovered from a small pit located directly outside the footprint of one of the major structures (Hall A) from the seventh-century great hall complex: see Thomas 2013 for a discussion of this specific structure and Thomas, this volume, for an updated overview of the hall complex.

17 Evison 2000, 69, fig. 3.17; 2008, 18, catalogue nos. 150, 151, 152 and cover photograph.

18 *Ibid.*, 151.

19 I would like to thank Ian Freestone for sharing the results of this unpublished analysis with me.

20 Evison 1982, 51.

21 Evison 1982, 51, 70, pl. XIIIb; *ibid.*, 70, nos. 52, 53, fig. 12f.

22 Evison 2012, 140.

23 Broadley 2011.

24 Evison 2000, 78–80.

25 The relevant sherd was recovered from a residual 'Saxo-Norman' context on Tayne Field. See Broadley 2016 for further discussion of this piece.

26 Henderson and Holand 1992, fig. 6; Baumgartner and Krueger 1988, 66, fig. 8.

27 Broadley 2016.

28 Broadley 2011.

29 Cramp 2000, 105. See Broadley 2015 for recent evaluation of four sherds of eighth-century window glass recovered during excavations by the Canterbury Archaeological Trust within the grounds of Canterbury Christ Church University, neighbouring the site of St Augustine's Abbey. They are all larger than those from Lyminge, and remain in very good condition. Three of the four join, and together form a very large portion of a window pane in colourless glass featuring swirls of a deep red colour in the metal.

30 Cramp 2014, 139–42.

31 *Ibid.*, 140.

32 Cramp 2009, 161. It may be noted that no lead cames were recovered from the excavations.

33 Cramp 1997, 329.

34 Cramp 2014, 139–40.

35 The relevant evidence is discussed in Thomas 2013, 128–32.

36 Wilmott 2005, 12–14, especially figs. 2, 3; Gudenrath 1991, 213–41 for a step-by-step photographic guide.

37 See Thomas, this volume, for a discussion of the relevant contexts and their dating.

38 Willmott and Welham 2015; 2013.

39 Willmott and Welham 2013, 74.

40 Willmott and Welham 2015, 236.

41 Willmott and Welham 2015, 235–7.

42 Wilmott 2005, 35.

43 *Ibid.*, 33.

44 Harden 1956, 146–7; Evison 2008, 6–8.

45 See Thomas, this volume, for an assessment of the relevant manufacturing evidence.

## Bibliography


Baumgartner, E. and Krueger, I. 1988. *Phönix aus Sand und Asche; Glas des Mittelalters*, München: Klinkhardt and Biermann.

Broadley, R. 2011. *Lyminge Glass: Assessment Report*, unpublished University of Reading report, http://www.reading.ac.uk/web/FILES/archaeology/Anglo-Saxon_glass_assessment_report._Broadley_2011.pdf

Broadley, R. 2015. 'Windows', in A. Hicks, *Destined to Serve: Use of the Outer Grounds of St Augustine's Abbey, Canterbury, before, during and after the Time of the Monks. Canterbury Christ Church University Excavations, 1983–2007*, 277–80, Canterbury Archaeological Trust Occasional Paper, 11, Canterbury: Canterbury Archaeological Trust.

Broadley, R. 2016. 'Gold foil decorated glass vessels in Anglo-Saxon England', in I. Riddler, J. Soulat and L. Keys (eds.), *Ce que livre les objets: Studies in honour of Professor Vera Evison*, 155-162, Autun, France: Editions Mergoil.

Campbell, E. 2007. *Continental and Mediterranean Imports to Atlantic Britain and Ireland, AD 400–800*, Council for British Archaeology Research Report, 157, York: CBA.

Cramp, R. 1997. 'The early medieval window glass', in P. Hill, *Whithorn and St Ninian: The Excavation of the Monastic Town*, 326–32, Stroud: Sutton.

Cramp, R. 2000. 'Anglo-Saxon window glass', in J. Price (ed.), *Glass in Britain and Ireland AD 350–1100*, 105–19, British Museum Occasional Paper, 127, London: British Museum Press.

Cramp, R. 2009. 'Window glass and lead cames', in D. H. Evans and C. Loveluck (eds.), *Life and Economy at Early Medieval Flixborough, c. AD 600–1000: The Artefact Evidence*, 159–64, Oxford: Oxbow.

Cramp, R. 2014. 'Window glass', in A. Tester, S. Anderson, I. Riddler and R. Carr, *Staunch Meadow, Brandon, Suffolk: A High Status Middle Saxon Settlement on the Fen Edge*, 139–42, East Anglian Archaeology, 151, Bury St Edmunds: Suffolk County Council Archaeological Service.

Evison, V. I. 1982. 'Anglo-Saxon glass claw beakers', *Archaeologia*, **107**, 43–76.

Evison, V. I. 1987. *Dover: The Buckland Anglo-Saxon Cemetery*, Historic Buildings and Monuments Commission for England Archaeological Report, 3, London: English Heritage.

Evison, V. I. 1997. 'The glass vessels', in K. Parfitt and B. Brugmann, *The Anglo-Saxon Cemetery on Mill Hill, Deal, Kent*, 240–3, Society for Medieval Archaeology Monograph Series, 14, London: SMA.

Evison, V. I. 2000. 'Glass vessels in England AD 400–1100', in J. Price (ed.), *Glass in Britain and Ireland AD 350–1100*, 47–104, British Museum Occasional Paper, 127, London: British Museum Press.

Evison, V. I. 2008. *Catalogue of Anglo-Saxon Glass Vessels in the British Museum*, British Museum Research Publication, 167, London: British Museum Press.

Evison, V. I. 2012. 'Glass vessels', in K. Parfitt and T. Anderson, *Buckland Anglo-Saxon Cemetery, Dover, Excavations 1994*, 138–41, Archaeology of Canterbury New Series, Vol. 6, Canterbury: Canterbury Archaeological Trust.

Gudenrath, W. 1991. 'Techniques of glassmaking and decoration', in H. Tait (ed.), *Five Thousand Years of Glass*, 213–41, Philadelphia: University of Pennsylvania Press. Rev. ed. 2004.

Harden, D. B. 1956. 'Glass vessels in Britain and Ireland, A.D. 400–1100', in D. B. Harden (ed.), *Dark-Age Britain: Studies presented to E.T. Leeds*, 132–67, London: Methuen.

Henderson, J. and Holand, I. 1992. 'The glass from Borg, an early medieval chieftain's farm in northern Norway', *Medieval Arch.*, **36**, 29–58.

Hunter, J. and Heyworth, M. P. 1998. *The Hamwic Glass*, Council for British Archaeology Research Report, 116, York: CBA.

Scull, C. 2011. *Assessment of Material Culture Assemblages (Copper-Alloy,*

*Bone/Antler and Vessel Glass) from SFBs 1, 2 and 3*, unpublished University of Reading report, http://www.reading.ac.uk/web/FILES/archaeology/Scull_2011_-_2010_small_finds.pdf

Thomas, G. 2013. 'Life before the minster: the social dynamics of monastic foundation at Anglo-Saxon Lyminge, Kent', *Antiquaries Jnl*, **93**, 109–45.

Warhurst, A. 1955. 'The Jutish cemetery at Lyminge', *Arch. Cantiana*, **69**, 1–40.

Willmott, H. 2005. *A History of English Glassmaking AD 43–1800*, Stroud: Tempus Publishing.

Willmott, H. and Welham, K. 2013. 'Late seventh-century glassmaking at Glastonbury Abbey', *Jnl of Glass Stud.*, **55**, 71–83.

Willmott, H. and Welham, K. 2015. 'Anglo-Saxon glass furnaces', in R. Gilchrist and C. Green, *Glastonbury Abbey Archaeological Excavations 1904–79*, 218–38, London: Society of Antiquaries of London.

Anglo-Saxon Studies in Archaeology and History 20, 2017

# Seeds and status: the archaeobotany of monastic Lyminge

Mark McKerracher

*Abstract*
*The excavations at Lyminge have produced an archaeobotanical assemblage of exceptional size, scope and variety for the Anglo-Saxon period. Plant remains representing both an Early Saxon royal vill and a Middle Saxon monastery have been retrieved, alongside prehistoric and medieval material. This paper reviews the potential of this large, well-preserved assemblage to elucidate changes in diet and cultivation practices at this uniquely important site. In particular, drawing upon the results of the author's doctoral research, it argues that the plant remains from Lyminge's monastic phase have a distinctive élite character, an archaeobotanical signature echoed at other ecclesiastical and high-status sites of this period. This signature, chiefly characterized by an unusual diversity and abundance of plant remains, betokens the special botanical interests of Middle Saxon élite settlements.*

## Archaeobotany at Lyminge

Even royal minsters were rooted firmly in the soil. Around the great halls and smoking hearths of monastic Lyminge lay the rolling fields of its estate: great engines of food and fuel. We cannot understand Anglo-Saxon life at Lyminge without considering the plants, both wild and cultivated, upon which it depended. This is true of all settlements of the period. Anglo-Saxon England was fundamentally an agricultural society, so the archaeology of its flora is a crucial field of study. Yet in most excavation reports, the verdict is uninspiring. Arable farming is framed as a site's cursory background, rather than the crux of rural life that it surely was. The reader is informed that 'wheat and barley were grown', or simply that 'cereals were important'. Archaeobotanists are not to blame for this brevity. The strictures of time and finance in contract archaeology, or else the paucity of organic preservation, limit the scope for in-depth botanical investigation at a great many Anglo-Saxon sites.[1]

But Lyminge is different. Blessed with good organic preservation in a comparatively undisturbed village core location, and with a strong sampling strategy for environmental remains, the Lyminge Archaeological Project has reaped a tantalizingly rich harvest of archaeobotanical data. In each season of excavation from 2008 to 2014, bulk soil samples have been taken from the majority of excavated contexts, with bioarchaeological remains extracted by the process of flotation. Plant remains, especially charred cereal grains, are chief among the items thus obtained. Material was packaged on site, and kept for later sorting and analysis in laboratory conditions. At the time of writing, post-excavation analysis has yet to commence in earnest. Preliminary assessments have, however, already begun to indicate the unique importance of Lyminge's botanical remains.[2] For example, alongside the charred seeds, grains and chaff which are the mainstay of British archaeobotany, the Lyminge assemblage also includes mineral-replaced and waterlogged items. Such material is exceptionally rare at Anglo-Saxon rural settlements; it is subject to very different biases from those incurred through charring and it affords a breadth of perspective seldom possible for this period.[3]

Besides the sheer size and inherent quality of Lyminge's archaeobotanical assemblage, it is also uniquely important in representing an Early Saxon (fifth- to seventh-century) royal centre and its Middle Saxon (seventh- to ninth-century) monastic successor, as well as Bronze Age and Saxo-Norman activity. Few sites of these kinds have yielded so rich a botanical record, and none has produced a comparably rich, extended occupation sequence to that preserved at Lyminge. Some of the sampled features at Lyminge are unprecedented for the period, and especially relevant to the study of agrarian production and consumption, including a probable midden of sixth-century date, and what appears to be a barn and threshing floor complex belonging to the Middle Saxon phase.[4] In addition, Lyminge has produced a vast and informative assemblage of animal bones (as discussed by Knapp in this volume), and perhaps the most significant agricultural artefact ever discovered in Anglo-Saxon archaeology: an iron plough coulter, representing a heavy mouldboard plough, in a uniquely early context for England (early seventh century).[5] All of these factors render Lyminge an ideal case-study for exploring a popular but largely speculative hypothesis: that Middle Saxon ecclesiastical estate centres were especially important to agrarian development in early medieval England.[6]

## Research context

The international significance of Lyminge and its archaeobotanical material is thus clear: no other site has such potential to elucidate the relationship between Early and Middle Saxon central places and their agricultural hinterlands. A wealth of botanical information remains to be accessed when post-excavation work proceeds. This paper presents only a partial and preliminary foray into the material, offering some provisional interpretations of Lyminge's preserved plant life. It draws upon the three assessment reports prepared so far for the Lyminge Archaeological Project, which together consider material from all phases of occupation.[7] These assessments, as advised in national guidelines, are broad, inclusive and generalizing. They assess the informative *potential* of samples, but do not entail full analysis at any level.[8] To date, only ten of the samples from Lyminge have been fully analysed, all representing the Middle Saxon monastic phase, and all but one representing the putative agricultural processing zone with its barn and threshing floor.

This work was undertaken as part of my doctoral research, by kind permission of project director Dr Gabor Thomas; further details on methodology and results are available in an archive report and in my thesis.[9] The doctoral project was undertaken between 2010 and 2013 at the University of Oxford, funded by the Arts and Humanities Research Council. Through an archaeological investigation of agricultural change between the fifth and ninth centuries AD in southern Britain, my research identified a suite of agrarian innovations that developed through the seventh and eighth centuries, especially at sites of high status, including Lyminge.

By way of context, I will first offer a general outline of Anglo-Saxon archaeobotany and crop husbandry in the fifth to ninth centuries: the typical botanical background against which the distinctive plant remains of Lyminge – and other contemporary élite sites – are thrown into higher relief. In some respects, this is still a very shadowy period of agricultural history, even though recent work has done much to advance debate. Particularly enigmatic are the fate and legacy of Romano-British farming beyond the early fifth century. Under Roman rule, British crop husbandry had been dominated by spelt wheat (*Triticum spelta* L.) and hulled barley (*Hordeum vulgare* L.), besides which staples a wide variety of other crops had been grown. Arable farming had been sufficiently intensive and high-yielding to support towns and military garrisons, as well as providing exports to the Continent.[10]

From the early fifth century onwards, however, in tandem with changes in material culture and settlements, archaeobotanical evidence paints a very different picture of crop husbandry. While hulled barley remained commonplace, the Roman preference for spelt wheat gave way – apparently quite abruptly – to an Anglo-Saxon emphasis upon bread wheat (*Triticum aestivum* L.), which has prevailed in English wheat cultivation ever since. Well-dated remains of Anglo-Saxon spelt are gradually becoming more common in the archaeobotanical record, but the present dominance of bread wheat (or other similarly free-threshing varieties) is far from being seriously challenged. For the great majority of excavated fifth- to ninth-century sites in southern Britain, hulled barley and bread-type wheat are the prevalent, definitive cereal crops.[11] While oat (*Avena* L.) and rye (*Secale cereale* L.) seem to have become more important from the seventh century onwards, at least in some regions, wheat and barley nonetheless remained the ubiquitous staples.[12]

Non-cereal crops are not much in evidence for this period. To judge from the archaeobotanical record, plant foods contributed little variety to the Anglo-Saxon diet. However, non-cereal crops will be inherently under-represented in a predominantly charred dataset, and especially in such a relatively meagre dataset as that from Anglo-Saxon England.[13] With a few exceptions (considered below), Anglo-Saxon plant remains are literally much thinner on the ground than their Iron Age and Romano-British predecessors or later medieval successors: samples from Anglo-Saxon contexts tend to produce far fewer botanical items per litre of soil.[14] In comparison with other periods, the early medieval archaeobotanical record appears much diminished and, along with a similar paucity of evidence for granaries and mills, this could well suggest a relatively low level of arable production across much of the Anglo-Saxon countryside.[15]

## Intimations of innovation

Such is a simplified account of Anglo-Saxon plants and crop husbandry as revealed by archaeobotany. How does the Lyminge assemblage compare? In some ways, the material from Lyminge conforms very well to this general profile. When discussing the earlier Anglo-Saxon samples from Lyminge (sixth to seventh centuries), all three assessment reports concur: charred grain tends to occur only sparsely or sporadically, and is often poorly preserved. Hulled barley and bread-type wheat are always the principal – if not the only – crop species, individually or collectively. Other plant remains apart from charred grain are extremely rare or absent. Cereal remains from seventh-century contexts sometimes appear more abundant than their sixth-century precursors, but the overall distribution for this early period is still parsimonious.[16] Even in some of the later samples from monastic Lyminge (eighth to ninth centuries), quantities of plant macrofossils are low, and mostly characterized by hulled barley and bread-type wheat.[17] All of this material is still useful and holds great informative potential – especially when contextualized with other archaeological data – but it is not, in itself, hugely distinctive. However, this appearance of conformity is misleading. Lyminge's plant remains, most especially those from the monastic phase, in fact exhibit several remarkable features.

Perhaps most striking from even a casual perusal of the assessment reports, as well as my preliminary analysis, is the presence at monastic Lyminge of several relatively unusual plant species. As discussed above, Anglo-Saxon archaeobotany as a whole is fairly monotonous in character. Evidence of fruits, vegetables, herbs and spices is minimal in the extreme, and compares very poorly with the panoply of exotic introductions in the Romano-British record, a disparity not entirely attributable to differential preservation biases.[18] The repeating wallpaper of charred bread-type wheat and hulled barley is indeed the botanical backdrop to many Anglo-Saxon sites. Yet while cereals inevitably dominate the assemblage from monastic Lyminge, they are here accompanied by an unusual diversity of other possible taxa – edible, medicinal or otherwise useful – which are either absent or exceedingly rare elsewhere in this period. True, there are stray occurrences of Celtic bean (*Vicia faba* L.) and garden pea (*Pisum sativum* L.) in seventh-century contexts at Lyminge.[19] But it is the eighth and ninth centuries that herald a veritable feast of variety: flax (*Linum usitatissimum* L.), apple/pear (*Malus* L./*Pyrus* L.), plum/sloe (*Prunus* L.), elder (*Sambucus nigra* L.), blackberry (*Rubus fruticosus* L. agg.), cherry (*Prunus avium* L.), opium poppy (*Papaver somniferum* L.), hemlock (*Conium maculatum* L.), and tentative identifications of black mustard (*Brassica nigra* L.), damson (*Prunus domestica* ssp. *insititia* (L.) Bonnier & Layens) and grape (*Vitis vinifera* L.).[20] Such botanical diversity places Lyminge within a select group of Middle Saxon rural sites excavated at Yarnton and Eynsham (Oxfordshire), Dorney (Buckinghamshire), Abbots Worthy (Hampshire), Brandon (Suffolk), Forbury House (Reading, Berkshire), Addenbrooke's Hospital (Cambridge), Harston Mill (Cambridgeshire), Flixborough (Lincolnshire), Bishopstone (Sussex), Hartlepool (County Durham) and Whithorn (Dumfriesshire).[21] While the precise set of species present at each site varies, there genuinely appears to be a set of rare taxa, such as grape and poppy, whose distribution was restricted to a small number of rural sites in the Middle Saxon period.

Before considering the significance of this pattern, we should note a further, special instance of rare species occurring at Lyminge, a case which may prove controversial. Spelt wheat (*Triticum spelta* L.), and probably also emmer wheat (*Triticum dicoccum* Schübl.), occur in Lyminge's monastic assemblage. Both are hulled wheats which, unlike bread-type wheat, remain encased in tightly adhering chaff even after threshing. They require an additional processing stage, dehusking, before culinary preparation. Spelt, far and away the dominant wheat of Roman Britain, is usually understood to have fallen out of favour in the early fifth century, for reasons which have never adequately been addressed; while emmer, a minority or volunteer (self-seeding) crop since the Iron Age, has seldom been considered part of the Anglo-Saxon flora.[22] It is true that the remains of spelt and emmer so far identified at monastic Lyminge, by Campbell and myself, are very few and far between.[23] Such low quantities warn against assuming that these crops were necessarily cultivated and harvested at Lyminge. Nonetheless, the grain and chaff remains are well preserved and derive from apparently undisturbed contexts: they seem genuinely to belong to the monastic phase. Again, these highly unusual occurrences place Lyminge in a select group of contemporary rural sites excavated at Yarnton, Dorney, Harston Mill, Bishopstone, Abbots Worthy, Addenbrooke's, Ely (Cambridgeshire), Great Wakering (Essex), Thetford (Norfolk) and Newton Bewley (near Hartlepool), all of which have yielded evidence of spelt and/or emmer.

Before offering an interpretation of these emerging patterns, I would like to raise two additional points. Firstly, taken as a whole, the material from monastic Lyminge bucks the diminutive trend of most Anglo-Saxon assemblages. The greater richness of Lyminge's eighth- to ninth-century samples, compared with those from earlier phases at the site, is clearly marked in Campbell's assessment.[24] This observation fits well within a wider pattern in this period, one which can be illustrated quantitatively. A popular measure of quantitative richness in archaeobotany is *average density*: the number of preserved items per litre of soil processed. This method allows for the different volumes of soil which may be extracted from different contexts, and it can be standardized by including only a selected suite of common and readily quantified plant parts such as seeds/grains and straw nodes.[25] In this way, I calculated the average density of the ten charred samples from monastic Lyminge which I analysed in my doctoral work, as well as 182 comparative charred samples from fifth- to ninth-century sites across central and southern England. The general pattern among the latter samples is immediately striking: high-density samples are largely a phenomenon of the eighth to ninth centuries (Fig. 1). Two samples of this period, from Yarnton and Brandon respectively, are so dense that they have been omitted from Figure 1 so as not to obscure the main trend. The ten samples so far analysed from monastic Lyminge accord well with this trend. Four have a density higher than thirty items per litre, two higher than 100 items per litre, placing them in the premier league of dense charred samples from Middle Saxon England (Table 1).[26]

Not all Middle Saxon sites produce such dense samples, however. A certain select group of sites in fact contributes most of the denser samples in my doctoral dataset, and some of these will by now be familiar to the reader: Yarnton (Oxfordshire), Dorney (Buckinghamshire),

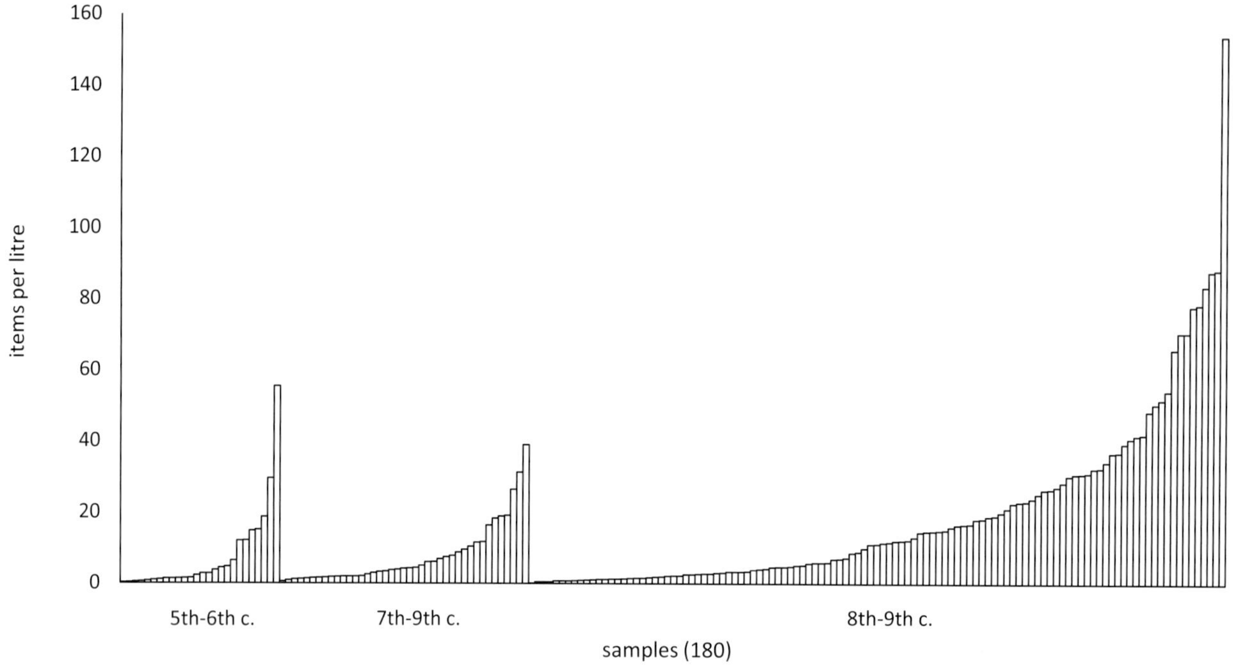


**Fig. 1** Average density of charred plant remains in Anglo-Saxon samples, grouped chronologically.

Ely (Cambridgeshire), Brandon (Suffolk), Harston Mill, Addenbrooke's (Cambridgeshire), Forbury House, Pennyland (Buckinghamshire), Cherry Hinton (Cambridgeshire), Lackford Bridge Quarry (Suffolk), Walpole St Andrew and Ingleborough (Norfolk).[27]

Interpretation of this trend is not straightforward but, in brief, I contend that the eighth and ninth centuries witnessed a behavioural change in the production and processing of crops whose legacy is a distinctively rich archaeobotanical record at certain sites, including Lyminge. Put simply, the most economical interpretation of the pattern is that certain settlements in Middle Saxon England were producing and depositing more charred crop remains than had been produced and deposited hitherto. It seems likely, therefore, that these communities were either producing or else mobilizing greater crop surpluses. This simple model is somewhat similar to that offered by Jones and van der Veen for grain-rich assemblages in the Iron Age,[28] and finds support in Lyminge's exceptional evidence for a barn and threshing floor in the monastic phase. The archaeobotanical evidence also offers some clues as to how such greater surpluses might have been attained. To pursue this line of enquiry, we must consider both crop remains and their associated arable weeds, whose ecological preferences can offer a sensitive proxy for contemporary arable environments and crop husbandry strategies.[29]

**Table 1** Average density of charred plant remains in selected samples from Lyminge (2008 excavations).

| Sample | Botanical items per litre (to 1 d.p.) |
|---|---|
| <02> | 19.5 |
| <03> | 29.6 |
| <05> | 31.8 |
| <08> | 27.8 |
| <24> | 477.9 |
| <26> | 20.0 |
| <30> | 160.1 |
| <42> | 11.0 |
| <53> | 49.3 |
| <518> | 11.8 |

This is a complex field of study, and here I propose only a simplified, provisional interpretation. I have argued elsewhere that Middle Saxon crop husbandry was often specifically attuned to local environmental conditions, to obtain optimal productivity on a given geology, and that this was a means of increasing crop surpluses in this period.[30] Thus, for example, crop deposits in the sandy Breckland of East Anglia are heavily dominated by rye and barley, taxa which are tolerant of such dry, poor soils, while in clayey regions, such as the peat fens and East Anglian plain, bread-type wheat is much more prominent, in accordance with its oft-perceived preference for heavier, richer soils.[31] The immediate hinterlands of Lyminge are variegated. The village sits in an area of Lower Chalk, which is overlain in places by silts, clays, sands and gravels. To the north and west rise chalk downlands at the northern fringe of the High Weald, once a heavily wooded zone, which is characterized by sandstones and clays.[32] The main crop patterns, as represented in the charred samples, are similarly variegated. Of the ten samples so far analysed, three are dominated by bread-type wheat, three by barley, two jointly by wheat and barley, and one each – albeit more narrowly – by rye and oat (Table 2).

What about the arable weeds? These represent a particularly challenging subject of research for the Anglo-Saxon period, the majority of whose samples represent clean, processed grain, largely devoid of weed seeds. Nonetheless, my doctoral research highlighted a notable increase in the presence and abundance of Stinking Chamomile (*Anthemis cotula* L.) seeds in the Middle Saxon period, particularly in wheat-rich samples from Ely and Yarnton. This species is a key indicator not only of rich, heavy, clayey soils but also, according to Jones' interpretation of seed dormancy strategies, of heavy ploughing and thus of a more intensive mode of agriculture.[33] Given the discovery of a coulter from such a heavy plough at Lyminge, we might expect Stinking Chamomile to be similarly well represented in Lyminge's charred assemblage. Seeds of this odoriferous weed are certainly present in the samples so far analysed, but not in such great proportions as to indicate a competitive advantage in Lyminge's arable fields. On the contrary, far better represented at monastic Lyminge are Cleavers (*Galium aparine* L.) and Brome (*Bromus hordeaceus/secalinus* L.), species which Jones specifically associates with lighter ploughing, and thus less intensive agriculture.[34] I would therefore suggest that the surpluses flowing into Lyminge were attained less through intensive, fine-tuned mono-cropping than through extensive diversification, with a variety of staples grown on the varied geological patchwork of the Kentish hinterland to ensure that at least one crop might yield a successful harvest.

**Table 2** Relative proportions of free-threshing cereal grain in selected samples from Lyminge.

| | % Free-threshing cereal grain | | | | |
|---|---|---|---|---|---|
| **Sample** | **Barley** | **Wheat** | **Rye** | **Oat** | **Total no.** |
| <02> | 9.7 | 77.8 | · | 12.6 | 207 |
| <03> | 76.0 | 15.0 | 1.0 | 8.0 | 100 |
| <05> | 18.7 | 71.6 | 0.3 | 9.5 | 729 |
| <08> | 56.3 | 40.5 | · | 3.2 | 126 |
| <24> | 15.6 | 20.9 | 14.1 | 49.4 | 2437 |
| <26> | 78.7 | 14.6 | · | 6.7 | 89 |
| <30> | 17.7 | 21.2 | 34.4 | 26.7 | 1331 |
| <42> | 16.7 | 77.8 | · | 5.6 | 18 |
| <53> | 80.5 | 13.6 | 0.3 | 5.6 | 734 |
| <518> | 48.8 | 41.9 | · | 9.3 | 43 |

## Landed interests in Middle Saxon England?

The preceding section has outlined a series of related archaeobotanical patterns. It is time now to weave these threads together and offer an interpretation. I have suggested that the Middle Saxon plant remains from monastic Lyminge are marked in particular by three distinctive characteristics: (i) the occurrence of unusual, useful, non-cereal species such as opium poppy and various fruits; (ii) the rare occurrence of the hulled wheats spelt and emmer; (iii) the presence of rich, dense samples suggesting the production and/or mobilization of substantial crop surpluses. Lyminge is not the only site whose assemblage displays such characteristics, some or all of which are paralleled at a select set of rural sites across Middle Saxon England (Table 3).

In terms of geography, preservation, and extent of excavation (or sampling), this is a diverse group of sites. The botanical data represent the work of a variety of archaeobotanists and excavation teams, both commercial and research-led. The sites span southern England, East Anglia, the Thames Valley, the Fens, north-eastern England and south-western Scotland. They represent a range of geologies, including chalk, sands, gravels and clays. Some sites have very few excavated Middle Saxon features, such as the two pits at Forbury House, while at others, such as Yarnton and Brandon, much more substantial areas of settlement have been revealed. Larger excavated areas of settlement do not, however, necessarily guarantee rich archaeobotanical assemblages: the comparative scarcity of plant remains at Flixborough, for instance, was not for want of excavated settlement features.[35] In short, there is no obvious, extrinsic, taphonomic bias which can explain entirely the restricted distribution of these archaeobotanical patterns at this specific set of sites. We are left with the possibility that these traits – this nascent archaeobotanical signature – represent a genuine historical pattern.

Thus, it is surely significant that a thread of ecclesiastical and/or high status can be traced through Table 3. For several of these sites, there is evidence of ecclesiastical and/or high status – evidence which, importantly, is wholly independent of the archaeobotanical evidence. The sites at Lyminge, Ely, Eynsham, Great Wakering, Hartlepool and Whithorn can all be plausibly associated with documented minsters, and artefactual evidence at Brandon and Flixborough suggests that these settlements are also likely to have had ecclesiastical phases.[36] Bishopstone's settlement remains have been persuasively interpreted as those of an estate centre.[37] Imported Continental pottery at Dorney and Ingleborough could suggest high-status connections, likewise the presence at Harston Mill, Yarnton and Pennyland of large planned ditch systems and Ipswich Ware pottery.

Admittedly, this high status hypothesis does not account for all of the sites in Table 3. No specific interpretation is forthcoming for the sites at Addenbrooke's, Forbury House, Thetford, Cherry Hinton, Walpole St Andrew, or Lackford Bridge Quarry. There is little or nothing to suggest that these sites were particularly high or low, ecclesiastical or lay, in status. On the other hand, these more obscure sites are in a definite minority in this group; the archaeobotanical traits still seem to be most concentrated at sites with indications of high and/or ecclesiastical status. Indeed, one could argue that the very exclusivity of these archaeobotanical traits would be consistent with their perceived special status. If status indicators can be sought in the remains of butchered animals, as at Flixborough, why not also in the botanical record? It is a central tenet of the Flixborough zooarchaeological

**Table 3** Summary of archaeobotanical patterns across settlements discussed in the text.

| Sites | Rare taxa | Emmer/spelt | Dense samples | References |
|---|---|---|---|---|
| Lyminge | X | X | X | |
| Ely | · | X | X | Ballantyne in Mortimer, Regan and Lucy 2005. |
| Whithorn | X | · | · | Hill 1997. |
| Eynsham | X | · | · | Pelling in Hardy, Dodd and Keevill 2003. |
| Hartlepool | X | X | · | Daniels 2007. |
| Great Wakering | · | X | · | Fryer in Dale, Maynard, Tyler and Vaughan 2010. |
| Flixborough | X | · | · | Dobney, Jacques, Barrett and Johnstone 2007. |
| Brandon | X | · | X | Murphy in Tester, Anderson, Riddler and Carr 2014. |
| Bishopstone | X | X | · | Ballantyne in Thomas 2010. |
| Dorney | X | X | X | Pelling in Foreman, Hiller and Petts 2002. |
| Pennyland | · | · | X | M. Jones in Williams 1993. |
| Yarnton | X | X | X | Stevenson and Robinson in Hey 2004. |
| Addenbrooke's | X | X | X | Roberts in Evans, Mackay and Webley 2008. |
| Harston Mill | · | X | X | Scaife in O'Brien 2016. |
| Forbury House | X | · | X | Vaughan-Williams 2005; Edwards 2008. |
| Thetford | · | X | · | Fryer in Atkins and Connor 2010. |
| Cherry Hinton | · | · | X | Roberts in Mortimer 2003. |
| Walpole St Andrew | · | · | X | Murphy in Crowson, Lane, Penn and Trimble 2005. |
| Ingleborough | · | · | X | Murphy in Crowson et al. 2005. |
| Lackford Bridge | · | · | X | Murphy in West 1985; Tipper 2007. |

report that secular and monastic estate centres of this period 'drew upon and utilised resources on a scale and of a diversity that reflected their "special" status' – a model which might reasonably be extended to floral as well as faunal resources.[38]

So much for general consistency; the *specific* implications of my proposed signature traits also fit well within a special status model. Greater diversity of useful non-cereal plants, for instance, would be unsurprising at monastic or lay estate centres. Grapes, which may but need not have been imported from the Continent, very likely represent a luxury foodstuff in this period, access to which required (and displayed) wealth and status. The various fruits and herbs represented at Lyminge and other sites, which may well have been gathered rather than cultivated, added further variety to the available plant food diet – although we cannot necessarily discount their consumption at humbler Anglo-Saxon settlements. The chemical properties of plants such as opium poppy and hemlock, if they were utilized at all, could be consistent with medicinal preparation in the Classical milieu of Saxon monasticism – a theme explored in detail by Fowler.[39]

The special status of emmer and spelt is still more contentious, but a case can be made. It is not inconceivable, for example, that spelt retained some prestigious Roman associations – if not remembered locally, then perhaps rediscovered through Continental contacts. More functionally, hulled wheats, spelt and emmer, benefit from greater natural protection against spoilage whilst in storage, because of their adherent chaff. This might have offered a serious advantage when transporting and storing bulk surpluses at estate centres.[40] This brings us to the third element in my proposed archaeobotanical signature, the dense crop deposits, which I have interpreted as an artefact of the handling of large crop surpluses. I have argued, on independent grounds, that different estate centres achieved their surpluses through different arable strategies: a more intensive, specializing tendency at Yarnton and Ely, a more risk-averse diversification at Lyminge. Either way, the production or mobilization, storage and processing of large crop surpluses must have been a crucial characteristic of estate centres, secular or monastic, with their non-agrarian residents, retainers and visitors to feed.

In short, there are sound reasons for supposing that ecclesiastical and high-status sites in Middle Saxon England utilized plant resources in distinctive ways, and the archaeobotanical record at such sites is entirely consistent with this view. Deductive and inductive approaches alike support a real connection between seeds and status.

## Conclusion

This paper has reviewed the informative potential of a remarkable archaeobotanical assemblage from Anglo-Saxon Lyminge, and offered some provisional interpretations. It is also the third in a 'bread-keeper' trilogy of papers, arguing for the importance of agricultural production in the emergence of later Anglo-Saxon lordship. The first of these papers considered the evidence for grain ovens, the second proposed a model of crop surplus production which has been reiterated briefly here.[41] Hence, both are ultimately concerned with staple food production, which is the inevitable focus of most Anglo-Saxon archaeobotanical studies to date. A small number of outstanding assemblages, however, such as that preserved at

Lyminge, allow us to take a broader view of plants and people in Anglo-Saxon society. The preserved plant life of Early Saxon Lyminge, unlike its artefactual and faunal counterparts, is unexceptional; but the succeeding monastic phase, in botanical terms, belongs in an exclusive group which embodies a genuine association between seeds and status in Middle Saxon England. A greater abundance and diversity of useful plants – cultivated, imported or gathered – could well have characterized lay and monastic estate centres of this period. Such is the hypothesis outlined in this paper. It is a preliminary and provisional interpretation of a complex interim dataset. It remains to be tested and contested, revised and refined as the national archaeobotanical dataset continues to grow, and as more of the Lyminge assemblage is analysed. At the very least, however, the Lyminge assemblage promises a unique and vital contribution to Anglo-Saxon archaeobotany, a view beyond wheat and barley – a story of seeds and status.

## Acknowledgements

I am grateful to the Arts and Humanities Research Council for providing the funding for my doctoral research. I wish to thank Gabor Thomas for his invitation and encouragement to present and publish this paper; and, along with Alexandra Knox and Simon Maslin (University of Reading), for so generously sharing material and information from the Lyminge Archaeological Project. My involvement with the project has been a pleasure and a privilege. I must also thank Helena Hamerow and Amy Bogaard (University of Oxford), exemplary mentors and supervisors of my doctorate. Finally, I offer my thanks to Ruth Pelling and Gill Campbell (Historic England) for assisting with my work on the Lyminge material; to Peter Murphy and Leonora O'Brien who kindly shared data from Brandon and Harston Mill respectively in advance of publication, and to the many units and specialists whose unpublished work has been drawn upon in my research.

## Notes

1 van der Veen, Hill and Livarda 2013, 169–71.
2 Campbell 2012.
3 Green 1982; Moffett 2011, 347–8.
4 Thomas 2013; McKerracher 2015.
5 Thomas, McDonnell, Merkel and Marshall 2016.
6 Blair 2005, 251–61.
7 Campbell 2012; Ballantyne 2014; McKerracher 2015.
8 Campbell, Moffett and Straker 2011, 7–8.
9 McKerracher 2013; 2014a, 521–47.
10 Booth, Dodd, Robinson and Smith 2007, 280–99.
11 McKerracher 2014a, 228–50; Banham and Faith 2014, 22–7.
12 McKerracher 2016.
13 Green 1982.
14 Campbell *et al.* 2011, 33.
15 Hamerow 2012, 151–5: the few excavated Anglo-Saxon mills and granaries are impressive but scarce.
16 Campbell 2012, 2–3; Ballantyne 2014, 2–5; McKerracher 2015, 2–3.
17 Campbell 2012, 5.
18 van der Veen *et al.* 2013, 160–4; van der Veen, Livarda and Hill 2008.
19 Ballantyne 2014, 4.
20 Campbell 2012, 4–6; McKerracher 2013, 13.
21 McKerracher 2014a, 194–8, 370–5.
22 Pelling and Robinson 2000; Pelling 2003; Moffett 2011, 348–9.
23 Campbell 2012, 8; McKerracher 2013, 12–13.
24 Campbell 2012, 5–6.
25 McKerracher 2014a, 77.
26 McKerracher 2014a, 217–27.
27 McKerracher 2014a, 226.
28 van der Veen and Jones 2006.
29 G. Jones 2002.
30 McKerracher 2016.
31 For example, M. Jones 1981, 107.
32 Trueman, Whittow and Hardy 1971, 89–105.
33 McKerracher 2014a, 251–75; M. Jones 2009.
34 M. Jones 2009.
35 Dobney, Jacques, Barrett and Johnstone 2007, 40–1.
36 Blair 2005, 206.
37 Thomas 2010.
38 Dobney *et al.* 2007, 217.
39 Fowler 2002, 242–5.
40 McKerracher 2014a, 369.
41 Respectively, McKerracher 2014b and 2016.

## Bibliography

Atkins, R. and Connor, A. 2010. *Farmers and Ironsmiths: Prehistoric, Roman and Anglo-Saxon Settlements beside Brandon Road, Thetford, Norfolk*, Bar Hill: Oxford Archaeology East.

Ballantyne, R. 2014. *Assessment of Charred and Mineral-replaced Biota from Lyminge (LYM12 LYM13)*, unpublished report for University of Reading.

Banham, D. and Faith, R. 2014. *Anglo-Saxon Farms and Farming*, Oxford: Oxford University Press.

Blair, J. 2005. *The Church in Anglo-Saxon Society*, Oxford: Oxford University Press.

Booth, P., Dodd, A., Robinson, M. and Smith, A. 2007. *The Thames through Time. The Archaeology of the Gravel Terraces of the Upper and Middle Thames. The Early Historical Period: AD 1–1000*, Oxford: Oxford Archaeology.

Campbell, G. 2012. *Assessment of Charred and Mineral-replaced Macroscopic Plant Remains from Excavation at Lyminge, Kent, 2008–10*, unpublished report for University of Reading.

Campbell, G., Moffett, L. and Straker, V. 2011. *Environmental Archaeology. A Guide to the Theory and Practice of Methods, from Sampling and Recovery to Post-excavation*, 2nd edit., Swindon: English Heritage.

Crowson, A., Lane, T., Penn, K. and Trimble, D. 2005. *Anglo-Saxon Settlement on the Siltland of Eastern England*, Sleaford: Heritage Trust of Lincolnshire.

Dale, R., Maynard, D., Tyler, S. and Vaughan, T. 2010. 'Carved in stone: a late Iron Age and Roman cemetery and evidence for a Saxon minster, excavations near St Nicholas' church, Great Wakering 1998 and 2000', *Essex Soc. for Arch. and Hist.*, **1**, 194–231.

Daniels, R. 2007. *Anglo-Saxon Hartlepool and the Foundations of English Christianity. An Archaeology of the Anglo-Saxon Monastery*, Hartlepool: Tees Archaeology.

Dobney, K., Jacques, D., Barrett, J. and Johnstone, C. 2007. *Farmers, Monks and Aristocrats: The Environmental Archaeology of Anglo-Saxon Flixborough*, Oxford: Oxbow.

Edwards, C. 2008. 'Saxon archaeology and medieval archaeology at Forbury House, Reading', *Berkshire Arch. Jnl*, **77**, 39–44.

Evans, C., Mackay, D. and Webley, L. 2008. *Borderlands. The Archaeology of the Addenbrooke's Environs, South Cambridge*, Cambridge: Cambridge Archaeological Unit.

Foreman, S., Hiller, J. and Petts, D. 2002. *Gathering the People, Settling the Land. The Archaeology of a Middle Thames Landscape: Anglo-Saxon to Post-medieval*, Oxford: Oxford Archaeology.

Fowler, P. J. 2002. *Farming in the First Millennium AD: British Agriculture between Julius Caesar and William the Conqueror*, Cambridge: Cambridge University Press.

Green, F. 1982. 'Problems of interpreting differentially preserved plant remains from excavations of medieval urban sites', in A. Hall and H. Kenward (eds.), *Environmental Archaeology in the Urban Context*, 40–6, London: Council for British Archaeology.

Hamerow, H. 2012. *Rural Settlements and Society in Anglo-Saxon England*, Oxford: Oxford University Press.

Hardy, A., Dodd, A. and Keevill, G. D. 2003. *Ælfric's Abbey: Excavations at Eynsham Abbey*, Oxford: Oxford Archaeology.

Hey, G. 2004. *Yarnton: Saxon and Medieval Settlement and Landscape. Results of Excavations 1990–96*, Oxford: Oxford Archaeology.

Hill, P. 1997. *Whithorn and St Ninian: The Excavation of a Monastic Town, 1984–91*, Stroud: Sutton Publishing.

Jones, G. 2002. 'Weed ecology as a method for the archaeobotanical recognition of crop husbandry practices', *Acta Palaeobotanica*, **42**, 185–93.

Jones, M. 1981. 'The development of crop husbandry', in M. Jones and G. Dimbleby (eds.), *The Environment of Man: The Iron Age to the Anglo-Saxon Period*, 95–127, BAR British Series, 87, Oxford: British Archaeological Reports.

Jones, M. 2009. 'Dormancy and the plough: weed seed biology as an indicator of agrarian change in the first millennium AD', in A. Fairbairn and E. Weiss (eds.), *From Foragers to Farmers. Papers in honour of Gordon C. Hillman*, 58–63, Oxford and Oakville: Oxbow.

McKerracher, M. 2013. *Charred Plant Remains from Lyminge: Analysis and Interpretation of Ten Selected Samples from the 2008 Excavations*, unpublished report for University of Reading.

McKerracher, M. 2014a. 'Agricultural Development in Mid Saxon England', unpublished DPhil thesis, University of Oxford.

McKerracher, M. 2014b. 'Landscapes of production in Mid Saxon England: the monumental grain ovens', *Medieval Settlement Research*, **29**, 82–5.

McKerracher, M. 2015. *Assessment of Macroscopic Plant Remains from the 2014 Excavations at Lyminge, Kent*, unpublished report for University of Reading.

McKerracher, M. 2016. 'Bread and surpluses: the Anglo-Saxon "bread wheat thesis" reconsidered', *Environmental Arch.*, **21**, 88–102.

Moffett, L. 2011. 'Food plants on archaeological sites: the nature of the archaeobotanical record', in H. Hamerow, D. A. Hinton and S. Crawford (eds.), *The Oxford Handbook of Anglo-Saxon Archaeology*, 346–60, Oxford: Oxford University Press.

Mortimer, R. 2003. *Rosemary Lane, Church End, Cherry Hinton*, unpublished report by Cambridge Archaeological Unit.

Mortimer, R., Regan, R. and Lucy, S. 2005. *The Saxon and Medieval Settlement at West Fen Road, Ely: The Ashwell Site*, Cambridge: Cambridge Archaeological Unit.

O'Brien, L. 2016. Bronze Age Barrow, Early to Middle Iron Age Settlement and Burials, and Anglo-Saxon Settlement at Harston Mill, Cambridgeshire. Bury St Edmunds: Archaeological Solutions.

Pelling, R. 2003. 'Early Saxon cultivation of emmer wheat in the Thames Valley and its cultural implications', in K. A. Robson Brown (ed.), *Archaeological Sciences 1999. Proceedings of the Archaeological Sciences Conference, University of Bristol, 1999*, 103–10, BAR International Series, 1111, Oxford: British Archaeological Reports.

Pelling, R. and Robinson, M. 2000. 'Saxon emmer wheat from the Upper and Middle Thames Valley, England', *Environmental Arch.*, **5**, 117–19.

Tester, A., Anderson, S., Riddler, I. and Carr, R. 2014. *Staunch Meadow, Brandon, Suffolk: A High Status Middle Saxon Settlement on the Fen Edge*, Bury St Edmunds: Suffolk County Council Archaeological Service.

Thomas, G. 2010. *The Later Anglo-Saxon Settlement at Bishopstone: A Downland Manor in the Making*, York: Council for British Archaeology.

Thomas, G. 2013. 'Life before the minster: the social dynamics of monastic foundation at Anglo-Saxon Lyminge, Kent', *Antiquaries Jnl*, **93**, 109–45.

Thomas, G., McDonnell, G., Merkel, J. and Marshall, P. 2016. 'Technology, ritual and Anglo-Saxon agrarian production: the biography of a seventh-century plough coulter from Lyminge, Kent', *Antiquity*, **90**, 742–758.

Tipper, J. 2007. *West Stow, Lackford Bridge Quarry (WSW 030). A Report on a Rescue Excavation Undertaken in 1978–9*, unpublished report by Suffolk County Council Archaeological Service.

Trueman, A. E., Whittow, J. B. and Hardy, J. R. 1971. *Geology and Scenery in England and Wales*, revised edit., London: Penguin Books.

van der Veen, M., Hill, A. and Livarda, A. 2013. 'The archaeobotany of medieval Britain (c AD 450–1500): identifying research priorities for the 21st century', *Medieval Arch.*, **57**, 151–82.

van der Veen, M. and Jones, G. 2006. 'A re-analysis of agricultural production and consumption: implications for understanding the British Iron Age', *Vegetation Hist. and Archaeobotany*, **15**, 217–28.

van der Veen, M., Livarda, A. and Hill, A. 2008. 'New plant foods in Roman Britain – dispersal and social access', *Environmental Arch.*, **13**, 11–36.

Vaughan-Williams, A. 2005. 'Report on the plant remains from Forbury House, Reading', in C. Edwards and S. Adams (eds.), *Forbury House, Reading, Berkshire. Archive Report*, 44–8, unpublished report by AOC Archaeology Group.

West, S. E. 1985. *West Stow. The Anglo-Saxon Village*, Ipswich: Suffolk County Council.

Williams, R. J. 1993. *Pennyland and Hartigans. Two Iron Age and Saxon Sites in Milton Keynes*, Aylesbury: Buckinghamshire Archaeological Society.

# Changing tastes: farming, feasting and fasting at Lyminge

Zoe Knapp

*Abstract*

*The study of human–animal relationships in their myriad forms has the potential to answer some of the most fundamental questions relating to human behaviour and cultural identity. The well-dated zooarchaeological assemblage from Anglo-Saxon Lyminge offers an exceptional opportunity to examine how these relationships were shaped and reconfigured by key processes encapsulated by the settlement's 400-year occupation sequence, including the emergence of a Kentish social elite and the conversion to Christianity. Drawing upon the results from the author's doctoral research, this paper argues for a more nuanced approach to the interpretation of Anglo-Saxon zooarchaeological assemblages acknowledging that the consumption, management and perception of animals in the past was always subject to local and regional variability.*

## Introduction

Due to a paucity of excavated Anglo-Saxon rural settlements, our understanding of the exploitation and perception of animals in early medieval Kent remains limited in comparison to other regions of England. As the first large and well-stratified excavated faunal assemblage from Anglo-Saxon Kent, Lyminge provides a long-awaited opportunity to redress this geographical imbalance through detailed zooarchaeological study. Yet the importance of the Lyminge faunal assemblage extends far beyond purely local or regional concerns. Accompanied by rich collections of portable material culture and complementary categories of bioarchaological information derived from well-dated contexts, the data examined in this paper provide an opportunity to place animal-human relationships at the heart of interpreting Lyminge's wider significance as a centre of Anglo-Saxon royal power inextricably bound with the process of Christianization and the growth of monastic culture in England.

This paper highlights the importance of adopting a regionally and contextually sensitive approach to the interpretation of Anglo-Saxon zooarchaeological assemblages. Too often, the findings from Anglo-Saxon zooarchaeological assemblages are taken out of their regional context and applied to generalized discussions of animal consumption and husbandry.[1] Whilst nationwide synthesis of Anglo-Saxon zooarchaeological assemblages have enabled us to see the 'big picture' in terms of broad scale diachronic change, they have arguably masked other types of patterning influenced by localised and regional variations in the way in which animals were managed, consumed and exploited.[2]

An approach sensitive to these issues not only necessitates placing an assemblage like Lyminge in its regional Kentish context, but also paying consideration to the site's more localized significance as a centre of long-standing territorial and political significance in the early medieval landscape. Strategically sited at the head of the valley of the River Nailbourne, a natural 'funnel' between the south coast and Canterbury, Lyminge formed a hub within a radiating web of routeways and droveways[3] which enabled it to extract a spectrum of outlying resources spanning downland, Wealden and coastal marshland environments, all of which might be expected to leave their impression in the zooarchaeological record.[4] Interpretation should also acknowledge the close cultural connections which existed between Kent and the Frankish world during the Anglo-Saxon period, as evidenced in a range of historical and archaeological sources.[5] While the impact of these Continental connections on dietary fashions and attitudes towards animals would have varied across Kent depending upon location and social scale, we might expect such influences to be strongly registered at Lyminge given that it enjoyed relatively convenient access to the coast, sat at the apex of the local settlement hierarchy, and was exploited as a centre of royal authority and identity.

This paper presents the results of a detailed programme of zooarchaeological analysis undertaken as part of the

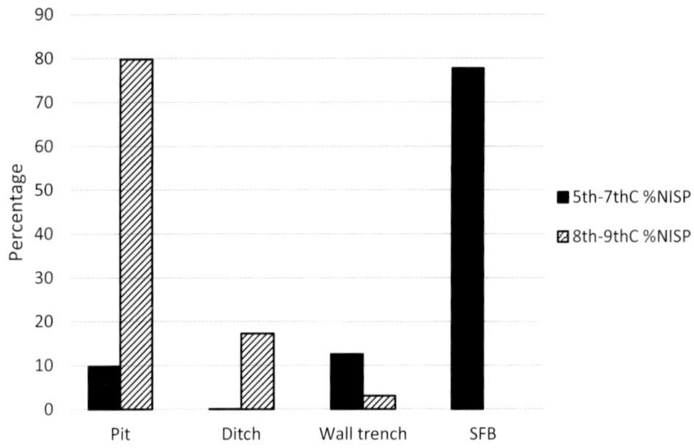


**Fig. 1** Graph showing percentage number of identified specimens (NISP) by context type. The NISP from the sunken-featured buildings (SFB) have been combined.

author's doctoral research at the University of Reading. While this research is still ongoing at the time of writing, my analysis has identified clear temporal trends within the assemblage embodying important changes in the way in which animals were consumed, exploited and managed over Lyminge's 400-year occupation sequence. The potential meaning of these changes will be explored through examination of comparative zooarchaeological assemblages from Kent and further afield and through broader reflections on the cultural trajectory of Anglo-Saxon Kent informed by historical sources.

## Sampling, methods and taphonomy

This research is based upon the animal bone recovered from excavations in the modern village of Lyminge conducted in 2008–13. The analysis includes a previously assessed assemblage derived from the 2008–10 excavations and more recent material recovered from the first two seasons of fieldwork on the site of Tayne Field, the overwhelming majority of which dates to the early Anglo-Saxon period.[6] The assemblage breaks down into two broad chronological groups, the earlier derived from later fifth–seventh-century occupation present on Tayne Field and a further site examined at the end of Rectory Lane in 2010 (hereafter referred to as Phase I), and the later derived from eighth–ninth-century occupation (contemporary with Lyminge's documented existence as a royal monastery) sampled in land to the south of the churchyard in 2008–9 (hereafter referred to as Phase II).[7] Whilst justification could be made for conducting the analysis at a more refined chronological level, this is constrained by a combination of limited stratigraphic phasing and high degrees of residuality particularly affecting the Phase I assemblage.[8] This explains why it has not been possible, for example, to isolate animal bone from the seventh-century great hall complex as a distinct chronological component of the assemblage.

The Lyminge Project employed a rigorous sampling strategy in order to maximize the recovery of bioarchaeological and zooarchaeological remains. In addition to an intensive environmental sampling strategy employing on-site flotation, all sealed Anglo-Saxon contexts were dry-sieved in the field using a 5 mm mesh. By boosting the recovery of small/fragile bones, particularly associated with fish, birds and small mammals, this strategy has resulted in a far more representative sample of data than obtainable by hand collection alone.[9]

The Lyminge assemblage was too large to record in its entirety using a detailed methodology. As such, recording and quantification methods broadly follow Davis 1992, a method which focuses on recording those bones that are more accurately identifiable and that provide the most useful information on the basis of a select suite of elements.[10]

In general, the bones from Lyminge were extremely well preserved, with the majority of the material from both the Phase I and II assemblages displaying either 'excellent' or 'good' levels of preservation and with less than three per cent falling into the 'medium' to 'bad' categories. Unsurprisingly, given the detailed recovery strategy employed at Lyminge, both phases displayed high levels of fragmentation, with Phase I registering the higher of the two. This variance can be accounted for by differences in the main feature types from which the animal bone was collected (Fig. 1): whereas nearly eighty per cent of the Phase I assemblage was recovered from sunken-featured buildings, the majority of the Phase II assemblage (again at the eighty per cent level) derived from pits. Previous research has shown that, on abandonment, sunken-featured buildings were often infilled with redeposited material derived from surface middens, the artefactual constituents of which are characterized by high levels of fragmentation and weathering.[11] While the depositional history of pits represented across the Anglo-Saxon settlement spectrum displays considerable diversity and complexity, it is nonetheless relatively common to encounter distinct horizons of 'primary' refuse dumped in a relatively fresh, unweathered state within such features, and this practice was widely attested in the 100 or so pits excavated at Lyminge.[12]

### *Associated bone groups (ABGs)*

A total of three ABGs are represented in the Phase I assemblage, with as many as fifty being recorded in Phase II. A number of these ABGs were recorded during excavation, whereas others were noticed during the analysis of the faunal material. The species represented included cattle, sheep, pig, horse, chicken, cat, dog, roe deer, chicken, corvids and a single human foetus. Pig was the only species represented in the first phase, and the most frequently represented species in the second phase were chickens and dogs (Table 1). Many of these ABGs were partial skeletons and articulated limbs, and a number of neonates were recorded. These ABGs were recovered from a number of contexts including pits, sunken-featured buildings (SFBs) and ditches. Conforming to Morris's nationwide study,

**Table 1** ABGs from both phases of Lyminge with brief description of content.

| Year | Fill no. | Context type | ABG species | Date |
|---|---|---|---|---|
| LYM10 | 2293 | SFB2 | Neonatal pig – partial skeleton | 5th–7th century |
| LYM10 | 2690 | SFB2 | Associated pig scapula, humerus and radius | 5th–7th century |
| LYM13 | 6119 | Pit | Juvenile pig – complete | 5th–7th century |
| LYM08 | 12 | Pit | Sheep/goat – partial | 8th–9th century |
| LYM08 | 12 | Pit | Dog – partial neonate (MNI 4) | 8th–9th century |
| LYM08 | 197 | Pit | Cat – almost complete | 8th–9th century |
| LYM08 | 243 | Pit | 2 partial neonatal sheep/goat | 8th–9th century |
| LYM08 | 273 | Pit | Chicken and sheep/goat | 8th–9th century |
| LYM08 | 313 | Pit | Dog – partial neonates (MNI 5) | 8th–9th century |
| LYM08 | 520 | Pit | Cat – almost complete | 8th–9th century |
| LYM08 | 580 | Pit | Cat – almost complete | 8th–9th century |
| LYM08 | 628 | Pit | 2 chickens – almost complete | 8th–9th century |
| LYM08 | 641 | Pit | Sheep/goat articulating feet bones | 8th–9th century |
| LYM08 | 645 | Pit | Cat – articulating feet bones | 8th–9th century |
| LYM08 | 656 | Pit | Cat – almost complete | 8th–9th century |
| LYM08 | 658 | Pit | Sheep/goat articulated vertebrae | 8th–9th century |
| LYM08 | 679 | Pit | Red sea bream | 8th–9th century |
| LYM08 | 680 | Pit | Chicken – partial | 8th–9th century |
| LYM08 | 744 | Pit | Chicken – partial | 8th–9th century |
| LYM09 | 1312 | Pit | Chicken – partial | 8th–9th century |
| LYM09 | 1333 | Pit | Chicken – partial | 8th–9th century |
| LYM09 | 1333 | Pit | Cat – almost complete | 8th–9th century |
| LYM09 | 1340 | Pit | Juvenile domestic fowl, cf. chicken – partial | 8th–9th century |
| LYM09 | 1491 | Ditch | 2 juvenile pigs – partial | 8th–9th century |
| LYM09 | 1506 | Pit | Juvenile corvid – partial | 8th–9th century |
| LYM09 | 1506 | Pit | Juvenile domestic fowl – partial | 8th–9th century |
| LYM09 | 1506 | Pit | Cat – partial | 8th–9th century |
| LYM09 | 1506 | Pit | Dog – partial, neonate | 8th–9th century |
| LYM09 | 1506 | Pit | Roe deer – articulated radius and ulna | 8th–9th century |
| LYM09 | 1552 | Pit | Juvenile tarsometatarsi of domestic fowl | 8th–9th century |
| LYM09 | 1566 | Pit | Juvenile domestic fowl | 8th–9th century |
| LYM09 | 1571 | Pit | Cow – 1–7 months old, not complete | 8th–9th century |
| LYM09 | 1571 | Pit | Cat – almost complete | 8th–9th century |
| LYM09 | 1596 | Pit | 2 neonatal dogs | 8th–9th century |
| LYM09 | 1600 | Pit | Cat – almost complete | 8th–9th century |
| LYM09 | 1667 | Pit | Cow – partial | 8th–9th century |
| LYM09 | 1667 | Pit | Dog – almost complete | 8th–9th century |
| LYM09 | 1672 | Pit | cf. chicken, and neonatal human | 8th–9th century |
| LYM09 | 1730 | Pit | Chicken | 8th–9th century |
| LYM09 | 1730 | Pit | Sheep/goat – partial | 8th–9th century |

the overwhelming majority of ABGs were derived from pits.[13] The recovery of ABGs from a wide range of contexts in Anglo-Saxon settlements has been noted elsewhere, and there does not appear to be any correlation between species and context type.[14]

Whilst it is possible that these ABGs are a result of primary butchery waste, the possibility that they also represent specific and ritualized domestic behaviours must also be considered.[15] These deposits are often deemed as 'special', as they are distinct from the 'normal' fragmented animal bone recovered from excavations.[16] Research has shown that 'ritual' and 'functional' aspects behind the creation of such deposits are inseparable;[17] thus, these ABGs are a result of complex human actions and motives that would have been guided by the values held within the community.[18]

## Results

A total of 6908 animal bones were identified to species from both phases of the site: 2448 animal bones from Phase I and 4460 from Phase II (Table 2).[19] As is common in most Anglo-Saxon assemblages, the main domesticates of cattle, pig and sheep dominated the mammal NISP counts, accounting for over fifty per cent of the animal

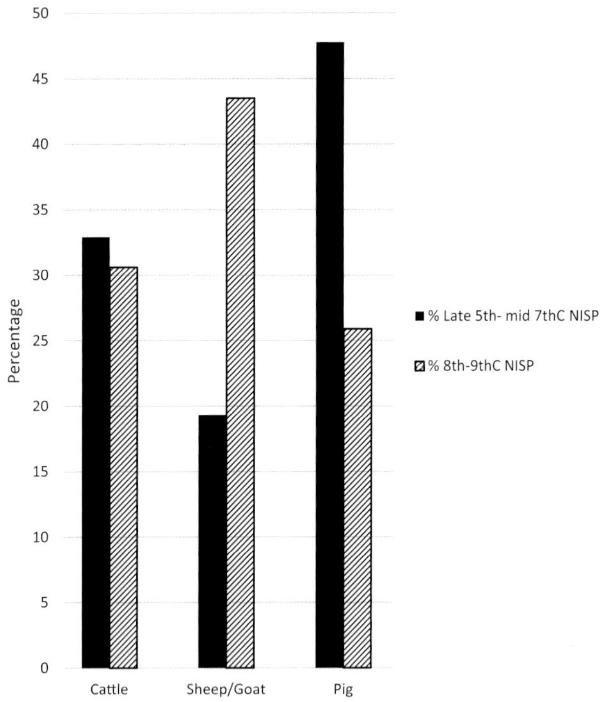


**Fig. 2** Graph showing the changing relative percentage of cattle, sheep/goat and pig between the two phases.

bone in both phases.[20] As highlighted in a provisional statement of the material collected in 2008–10, however, the proportions of these species vary significantly between the two phases, revealing important changes in the exploitation and consumption of animal resources over time (Fig. 2).[21] The detailed analysis conducted as part of this research has both amplified and refined the diachronic trends identified in this previous examination while at the same time extending insights into new areas such as animal husbandry practices. The following section elucidates the key patterns, commencing with domesticated mammals and followed by other mammals and birds.

### *The domestic mammals*

#### Cattle

Compared with the other main domesticates, cattle seems to have been exploited at a more consistent level over time at Anglo-Saxon Lyminge, as reflected in a minor decline between the two phases from thirty-three to thirty-one per cent (Fig. 2). Mandible wear stages show that the majority of cattle were being culled in adulthood and old adulthood (Fig. 4), with very few being kept alive into their 'senile' years, suggesting that at the end of their working lives they were killed and eaten. Calving occurred on site, as indicated by the presence of a small number of very young individuals, and it is likely that some animals were killed in their first year obviating the need for overwintering. The low number of very young individuals suggests that dairying did not play an important role in cattle husbandry practices.

**Table 2** Number of identified specimens (NISP) table of both phases showing all identified taxa.

| Taxa | Phase I (Late 5th–mid 7thC NISP) | Phase II (8th–9thC NISP) |
|---|---|---|
| **Mammals** | | |
| Cattle | 636 | 719 |
| Sheep/Goat | 324 | 909 |
| Sheep | 48 | 109 |
| Goat | 1 | 4 |
| Pig | 922 | 607 |
| Equid sp. | 5 | 21 |
| Dog | 2 | 35 |
| Canid sp. | 8.6 | 51 |
| Fox | 3 | 0 |
| Cat | 7 | 47 |
| Roe deer | 3 | 32 |
| Red deer | 3 | 0 |
| Hare | 1 | 1 |
| Badger | 1 | 0 |
| Pole cat/Pine martin | 1 | 0 |
| **Birds** | | |
| Chicken | 380 | 1662 |
| Chicken/Pheasant | 37 | 198 |
| Goose | 19 | 8 |
| Anser sp. | 0 | 10 |
| **Wild birds** | | |
| Mallard duck | 13 | 11 |
| Black-headed gull | 0 | 2 |
| Common gull | 1 | 4 |
| Oystercatcher | 2 | 0 |
| Coot | 2 | 0 |
| Common moorhen | 1 | 0 |
| Gannet | 1 | 0 |
| Golden plover | 2 | 0 |
| Plover | 1 | 1 |
| Crane | 2 | 0 |
| Curlew | 1 | 4 |
| Lapwing | 3 | 0 |
| cf. Lapwing | 1 | 0 |
| Plover/Lapwing family | 1 | 0 |
| Snipe | 1 | 0 |
| Heron | 0 | 1 |
| Woodcock | 2 | 0 |
| cf. Woodcock | 0 | 2 |
| Stock dove | 0 | 1 |
| Woodpigeon | 1 | 1 |
| Jay | 0 | 7 |
| cf. Jay | 0 | 1 |
| Raven | 1 | 0 |
| Magpie | 1 | 0 |
| Jackdaw | 0 | 7 |
| Goshawk | 2 | 0 |
| Peregrine falcon | 1 | 0 |
| cf. Sparrowhawk | 0 | 1 |
| Buzzard | 1 | 0 |
| Red kite | 2 | 0 |
| Turnidae sp. | 1 | 1 |
| Wader sp. | 0 | 3 |
| Accipitridae family | 1 | 0 |
| **Fish** | | |
| Sturgeon | 1 | 0 |
| **Total** | 2448 | 4460 |

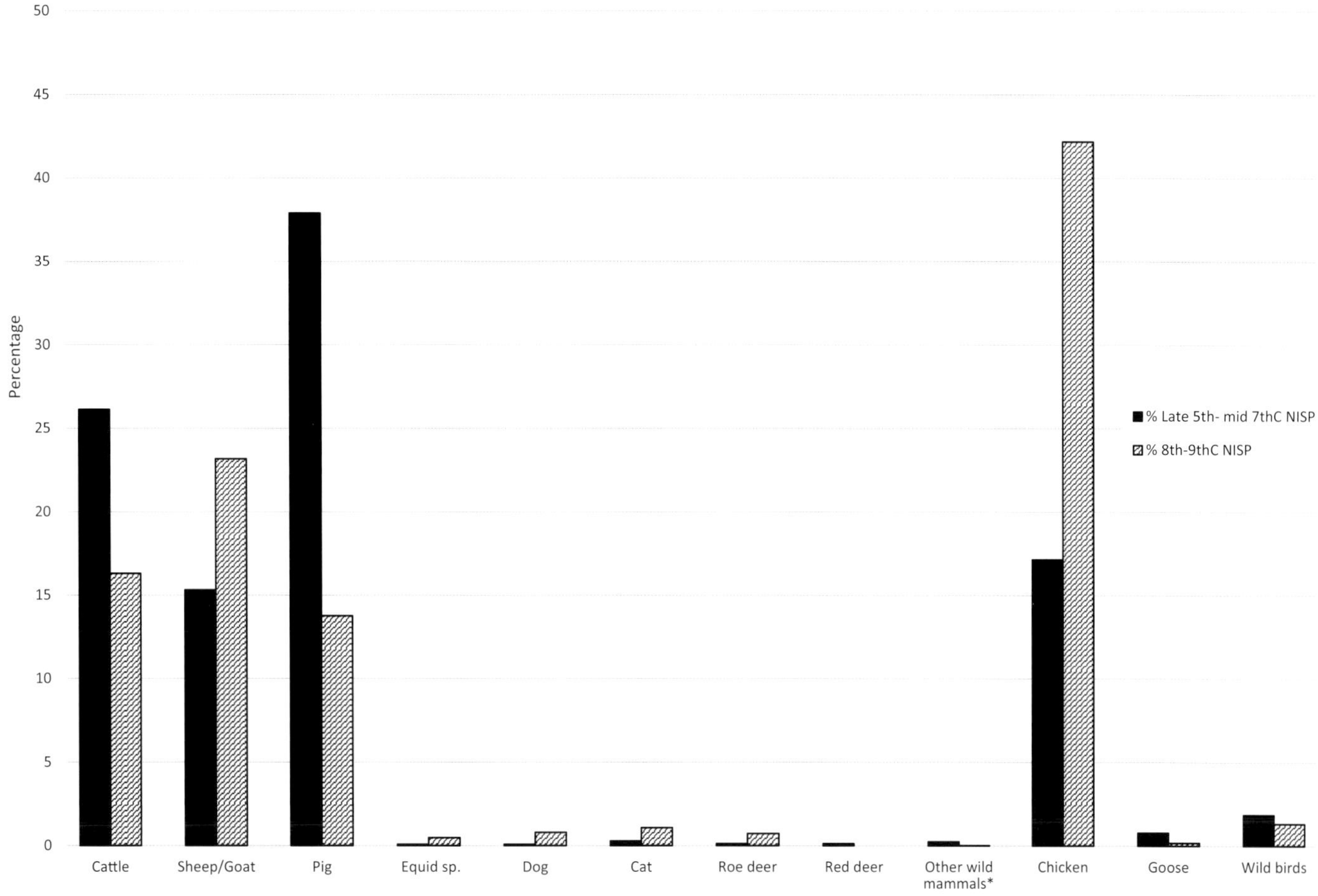


**Fig. 3** Graph showing the percentage NISP of all identified taxa in both phases; *'other wild mammals' include hare, badger, pole cat/pine martin and fox.

The peak in age-at-death at two and a half to three years of age in Phase I suggests that more cattle were being kept purely for their meat at this period. In spite of this difference, there are significant numbers of elderly cattle in both assemblages, indicating that their main purpose was for secondary functions/products. Analysis revealed a significant increase in the number of cattle-related pathologies within the Phase II assemblage including exostosis and ankylosed bone, all located on the distal end of metacarpals and the first and second phalanges.[22] There was also evidence from one horn core for possible cattle yoking, indicated by a ring-like depression at the base of the horn core.[23] The higher number of older cattle present in the Phase II assemblage, combined with an increased presence of pathological indicators, suggests that a greater reliance was placed on cattle for traction in the eighth–ninth centuries than in the sixth–seventh. Given that other aspects of Lyminge's archaeology attest to a shift towards arable farming at the same period,[24] it is possible that this zooarchaeological trend is specifically linked to increased ploughing activity and conceivably the introduction of heavy plough technology for which there is uniquely early evidence from Anglo-Saxon Lyminge.[25]

### Caprines

The number of sheep/goat relative to the other main domesticates registers a significant increase over the two phases, from just over nineteen per cent in Phase I to forty-four per cent in Phase II (Fig. 2).

The sheep/goat mandible wear data associated with the Phase I assemblage indicate that most of the caprines were being killed by four to six years of age (Fig. 5), pointing towards a husbandry regime focused on meat consumption during this period. In both phases there is a peak in the number of caprines dying at six to twelve months, most likely as a result of annual culls designed to mitigate the need for overwintering. There are some significant changes in the Phase II assemblage, however, demonstrating a stronger reliance on caprines for dairy during this period: this includes a higher number of sheep being culled at two to six months (Fig. 5) and an elevated incidence of depressions in sheep horn cores as a recognized pathological indicator of intensive dairying. The Phase II assemblage also registers a higher proportion of animals surviving beyond their fourth year which is consistent with an intensification in wool production in the eighth–ninth centuries, although it should be noted that the trend is not as pronounced as at other Middle Saxon sites such as

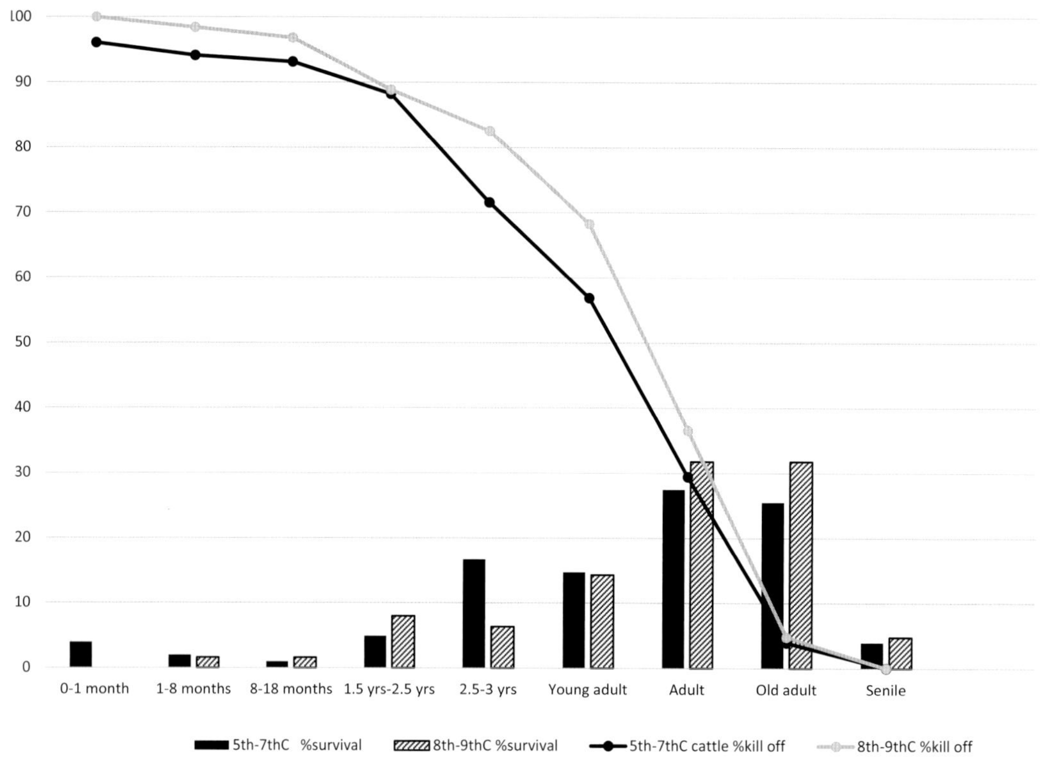


**Fig. 4** Graph showing cattle age-at-death patterns based on mandible data and percentage of age survival in both phases; dental ageing from Legge 1992.

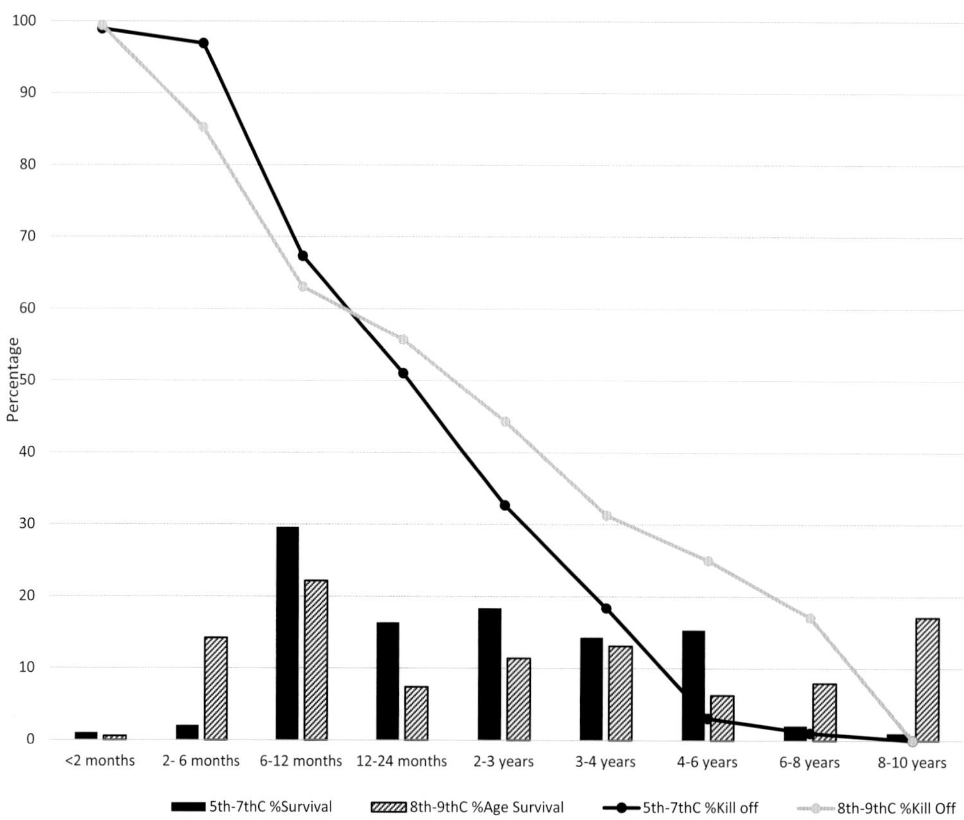


**Fig. 5** Graph showing caprine age-at-death patterns based on mandible data and percentage of age survival in both phases; dental ageing from Payne 1973.

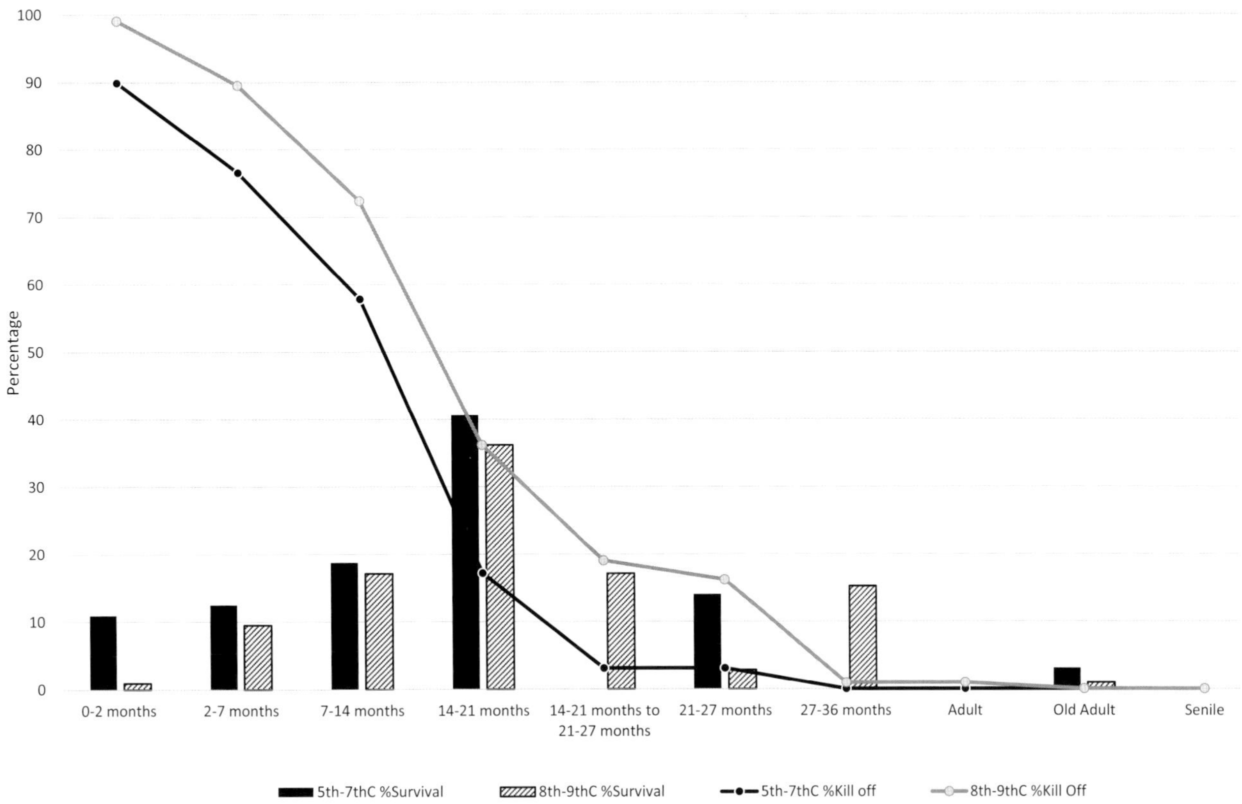


**Fig. 6** Graph showing pig age-at-death patterns based on mandible data and percentage of age survival in both phases; dental ageing from Hambleton 1999.

Brandon (Suffolk) and Flixborough (Lincolnshire) where specialized wool production has been inferred.[26] Broadly speaking, there appears to have been a mixed husbandry regime for caprines in both phases of the site, with some minor specialization in primary products (i.e. meat) in the fifth to seventh centuries and a higher reliance on dairy and wool in the eighth to ninth centuries.

Sheep are thrifty animals to keep as they are very low maintenance and can be grazed on almost any terrain.[27] With the shift towards arable farming in the eighth century, sheep would have been the ideal type of livestock to keep, as they could have been grazed on harvested and fallow fields, providing valuable fertilizing manure in the process.[28]

## Pig

Pig displays a diachronic shift similarly marked to that of sheep/goat, but in this case the trend over time is one of decline, specifically from forty-eight per cent in the Phase I assemblage down to twenty-six per cent in Phase II (Fig. 2).

A comparison of the pig age-at-death profiles for the two phases of the settlement indicates that the majority of animals were culled between the ages of fourteen and twenty-two months, which is consistent with a meat-orientated regime (Fig. 6). The management of breeding stocks throughout the occupation of the settlement is indicated by the presence of a small number of older animals as well as neonatal and young piglets in both phases (Fig. 6). The one clear temporal distinction highlighted by the analysis is that far fewer animals survived beyond the age of twenty-one months in Phase I; combined with the notable peak in the 0–2 months category, this suggests a preference for suckling pig during this phase of the settlement.

### *Other mammals*

Other mammals, both domesticated and wild, are present in small numbers, their combined contribution representing some two to three per cent of the entire assemblage (Table 2). Horse, cat and dog all register significant increases in Phase II, as does roe deer, although red deer is only present in Phase I and in a very low proportion (Fig. 3).

### *Birds*

While some goose is present in the assemblage, chicken (*Gallus gallus*) represents the dominant domestic species of bird in both phases.[29] The analysis demonstrates that the incidence of this species more than doubles in Phase II. Comprising over forty per cent of the dataset, the remains of chicken outnumber all other species of domesticated animal during this phase (Fig. 3), a highly significant total given that chicken typically comprises only ten to twenty per cent of other contemporary zooarchaeological assemblages.[30] The ageing and sexing data indicate that chickens at this period were kept for both meat and eggs; at

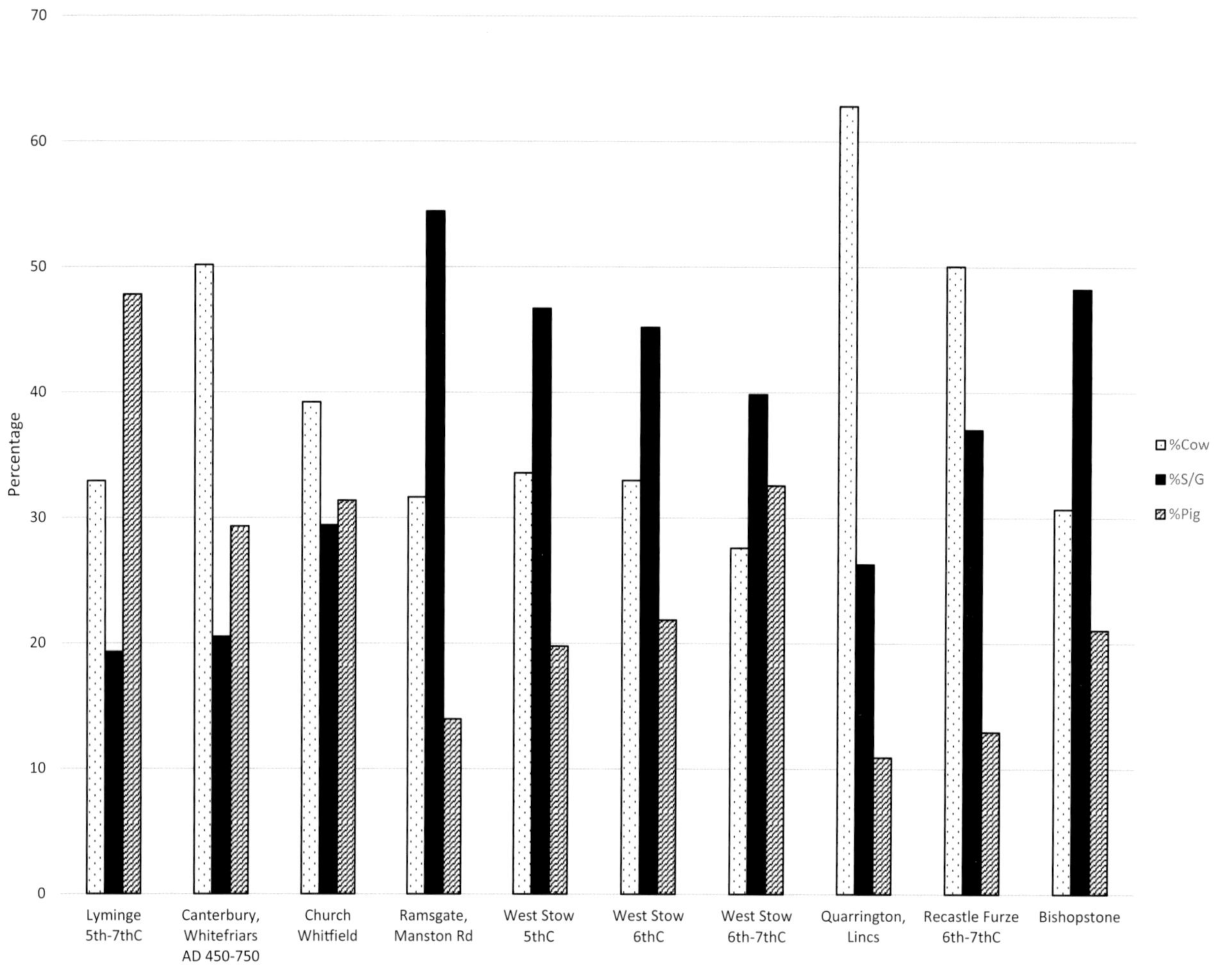


**Fig. 7** Graph comparing the numbers of cattle, sheep/goat and pig from the fifth- to seventh-century phase of Lyminge to contemporary sites.

seventy-five per cent, female birds dominate the Phase II assemblage and the majority of the male population at this period were slaughtered for meat as young cockerels.

A high frequency of pathologies was recorded in the Phase II chicken assemblage, the dominant indicator being osteophytes, a symptom of osteoarthritis which, as with humans, tends to occur in older individuals.[31] The majority of these osteoarthritic chickens were females, suggesting that hens were being kept and cared for beyond an 'economically useful' age (i.e. well beyond the optimal age for egg laying and meat provision).

Although occurring in much smaller proportions than chicken, a wide variety of wild bird species are present in both assemblages (Table 2). Sea birds and inhabitants of coastal marshland environments (e.g. mallard duck, gull, oystercatcher, curlew, crane etc.) are well represented in both phases of the site, demonstrating Lyminge's long-term dependence upon these ecological zones. However, there is a slight increase in the proportion and diversity of wild birds between the two phases, the Phase I assemblage being notable for the presence of a variety of raptors including goshawk, peregrine falcon, red kite and buzzard which were most likely kept as hunting birds.

## Discussion

### *Phase I: fifth to seventh centuries*

When the relative percentages of cattle, sheep/goat and pigs from Lyminge are compared with a range of other contemporary sites in Kent and other regions, some interesting patterns emerge. One of the most noticeable zooarchaeological aspects of Lyminge at this period is the high proportion of pig, given that this species typically ranks third amongst the three main domesticates at most other sites of this period (Fig. 7).[32] Although the number and quality of contemporary zooarchaeological assemblages from Kent is far from satisfactory, a similar pattern of pig dominance is seen at the sites of Cheriton, Folkestone and Keston,[33] while pig constitutes the middle ranking of the three domesticates at the sites of Linacre Garden and Whitefriars in Canterbury and Church Whitfield, Dover.[34] While there are some exceptions to this pattern (e.g. Manston Road, Ramsgate), the cumulative weight of the evidence suggests that pig was farmed and consumed more intensively in Kent than in most other regions of early Anglo-Saxon England.

The reasons for this regional preference are likely to be multiple, first and foremost being the physical environment, the influence of which – as highlighted in a recent study – has been somewhat overlooked in the interpretation of early medieval and medieval zooarchaeological assemblages.[35] As one of the most heavily wooded regions of Anglo-Saxon England, boasting extensive forested tracts not only in the Weald but also in the Blean to the north of Canterbury, the natural environment of Kent lent itself to the pannage of pigs.[36] The presence of Wealden 'dens' acting as swine pasture combined with their attendant transhumance routes[37] has long been recognized as a key feature of the economy of Anglo-Saxon Kent. As documented in detail by scholars such as Witney and Everitt, this pig-orientated regime had a long-term influence on territorial development and the structure of landholding within the region.[38] The indication of this research is that the everyday human–animal, and in this specific case human–pig, interactions gave shape and meaning to the physical world in Early Anglo-Saxon Kent.[39] While the physical environment of Kent was no less important than other regions of early medieval England in structuring the character of animal bone assemblages,[40] it is crucial to take into account the influence of cultural and social factors, especially in the case of Lyminge which has a distinctive identity in this period as a regional centre subsequently appropriated as a site of royal residence during the seventh century.[41]

While there has been some debate about the social connotations of pig during the Anglo-Saxon period,[42] the evidence from Lyminge reinforces the link between feasting and pig consumption in a high-status Anglo-Saxon cultural milieu characterized by a suite of complementary archaeological indicators for elite practices and social display.[43] Given the significant level of cultural exchange which existed between Kent and the Frankish world at this period,[44] it is also relevant to note that Lyminge subscribes to a broader pattern of elevated pig consumption at elite sites in the southern part of the North Sea Basin. As registered in other fields of social discourse such as personal adornment, these Continental connections are very likely to have impacted on dietary fashions and attitudes towards animals amongst the native Kentish elite.[45]

Although it is difficult to identify contextually discrete feasting events or deposits in the archaeology of early Anglo-Saxon Lyminge, the pig assemblage holds cumulative evidence for such practices in the relatively high percentage of suckling pig represented at this phase in comparison to the eighth–ninth centuries. Descriptions of Anglo-Saxon feasts do not detail the species that were consumed;[46] however, well-known ethnographic studies conducted in Papua New Guinea provide vivid testimony to the exploitation of pig as a ceremonial feasting food.[47]

There are aspects of the contemporary cattle assemblage that point in the same direction, for more animals were being killed at a younger, prime meat-bearing age in this period than in the eighth–ninth centuries. Given the amount of meat a single cattle carcass can provide, these beasts would have made a substantial contribution to the table, presenting an opportunity for the community to come together, most likely to feast at specific points in the year.[48]

Another perspective on elite social practices at early Anglo-Saxon Lyminge is provided by the notable diversity of birds of prey represented in this phase of the assemblage. While such species as peregrine falcon, goshawk, buzzard and red kite are sometimes encountered in zooarchaeological collections derived from excavated Anglo-Saxon rural settlements, they are very infrequent before the Middle Saxon period and they very rarely occur in such a wide combination as at Lyminge on pre-Conquest sites.[49] The significance of the Phase I assemblage in this regard is further underlined by the fact that it includes peregrine falcon, the earliest find of this raptor in Anglo-Saxon England.[50] The natural habitat of peregrine falcons is cliffs and uplands; thus, the Lyminge specimen most likely represents a captive bird employed in falconry, the elite social associations of which are well attested in Anglo-Saxon historical sources and, from an earlier period, in visual culture and iconography.[51]

### *Phase II: eighth to ninth centuries*

As we have seen, this period is associated with a range of changes in the exploitation of animal resources. In terms of the relative importance of different species, the most dramatic transformations include the steep decline in the proportion of pig combined with a marked increase in chicken which, as highlighted by Reynold's analysis of the fish assemblage, is mirrored by a similarly pronounced upturn in the consumption of marine fish, particularly deep-water species such as cod (Fig. 2).[52] Taken in combination, these patterns can be interpreted as the reflection of the influence of Christian attitudes on dietary practices, as might be expected at Lyminge as a high-status monastic milieu. As indicated by the decline in pig, however, Lyminge's dietary reorientation was more than simply a process of adopting new patterns of consumption, but also of turning away or creating distance from 'old' types of food perhaps tainted by lingering associations from the pre-Christian past.[53]

Given that the period under review saw the widespread expansion of monastic culture across the Anglo-Saxon kingdoms,[54] it is unsurprising that the Rule of St Benedict is often invoked to explain and interpret excavated zooarchaeological assemblages of the eighth–ninth centuries, whether the site in question is a documented monastery or must be characterized, as in the case of Flixborough or Brandon, on purely archaeological terms.[55] The Benedictine Rule was one of the most influential monastic rules in north-west Europe during this period.[56] The Rule ordained strict periods of fasting and that brethren should 'abstain from the meat of four-footed animals, except for the weak and the sick'.[57] Fish are postulated to have been a valuable source of protein during times of abstinence on the technicality that they were not quadrupeds;[58] similarly, hen's eggs would also have provided an ideal source of protein in an otherwise strictly vegetarian diet.

There is, however, no evidence to suggest that Anglo-Saxon monastic houses followed a single, all-encompassing rule at this early period.[59] Indeed, it is likely to be the case that a greater proportion of pre-Viking monastic institutions adhered to a *regula mixta* – a selection of different traditions governing daily routines, not only for the ordained but also for secular guests.[60] There is also no indication that fish were considered to be an acceptable fasting food; in fact, it has been argued that the opposite was true on the basis that fish were regarded as a delicacy until the later medieval period, and thus would have been unsuitably decadent for periods of fasting.[61]

Whilst the Christian practice of fasting is extremely difficult to identify in the archaeological record,[62] historical documents reveal that fasting took place from an early stage in Kent. Fasting appears to have been enforced in both monastic and secular contexts, as indicated by the laws of King Wihtred (AD 695), which state that: 'if anyone gives meat to his household in time of fasting, he is to redeem both freeman and slave with *healsfang*' and 'if a slave eat it of his own accord [he is to pay] six shillings or be flogged'.[63] In religious communities, fast days could take place for up to 200 days of the year including Lent, Advent and holidays.[64] To eat animal flesh during a period of fasting may have been seen as impure, not as a result of the foodstuff but because of the season within which it was being consumed.[65]

Frantzen argues that King Wihtred's laws reveal the influence of Theodore's *Penitential* which was circulated in England by Irish missionaries in the seventh and eighth centuries.[66] Handbooks of penance show a preoccupation with fasting and food purity, and the literal interpretation of the concept that 'you are what you eat' is a resounding theme throughout.[67] The largest category of penitentials concerns the use of animals and contamination by animals, with a particular focus on how these animals lived and died, and whether or not it then made them unfit for human consumption.[68] The existence of such sentiments encourages a more nuanced view of the role played by the consumption of marine fish in the process of Christian conversion. While the significance of fish as a penitential food cannot be ignored in a documented monastic context such as Lyminge, the deeper meanings of this species also need to be acknowledged, not least given its core position within the symbolic vocabulary of early Christianity. One must also bear in mind the particular meanings and associations which the teachings of humeral theory attributed to the consumption of fish as against other forms of meat,[69] and acknowledge the possibility that in certain social contexts fish consumption may have come to signify an elite taming of the wild. All of the above would have been desirable attributes for individuals living within a monastic community or an educated elite wishing to proclaim their adherence to a new Christian ideology.

The analysis has also drawn out subtler diachronic transformations in the Phase II assemblage, which shed further light on changing attitudes to animals at this time. Amongst the wild species, the increase in the prevalence of roe deer is worthy of note given that it has previously been observed that this species is well represented on ecclesiastical sites of the Anglo-Saxon period.[70] It is possible that this association has some symbolic/religious basis given that roe deer were regarded as chaste, faithful and abstemious creatures in later medieval sources.[71]

Another notable feature of the Phase II assemblage is an increased proportion of cats and dogs, the practical value of which would have extended to a variety of functions including hunting, herding, killing vermin and providing furs.[72] It is difficult to adduce a single causal factor for this increase, but in the case of the former species it is impossible to ignore clear evidence for the intensified processing and conversion of arable surplus in the monastic phase of the settlement which would have placed a higher demand on cats to control the vermin population. More speculatively, the increase in dogs may have been linked with changes in animal husbandry, particularly the herding of larger flocks of sheep.[73]

The extent to which the cats and dogs represented within the Lyminge assemblage were kept as pets in the more modern sense of the term is debatable. Some commentators have argued that there would have been little room for such sentiments in Anglo-Saxon England following the conversion on the basis that the Christian cosmos was ordered around a sharp human–animal dichotomy.[74] Saint Augustine's writings taught that animals were 'irrational, soulless and created only for Men's utility, consumption and dominion';[75] thus, it was acceptable for Christians to show care towards animals, but not to express the same levels of affection towards them as they would give people.[76]

Animal pathology provides an alternative means of addressing the question of the degree to which Christian teachings – in particular the view promulgated through Genesis that humankind was granted dominion over all beasts of nature[77] – influenced attitudes towards cats and dogs in conversion period England. At Lyminge, pathologies present in cats and dogs are almost entirely confined to the Phase II assemblage: examples include healed rib and leg fractures/breaks, and in the case of one unfortunate dog, severely irregular tooth wear on the right side as a result of a missing first molar and alveolar resorption on the left side. Undoubtedly these pathologies are a result of trauma and it is clear that a proportion of the affected animals survived well into adulthood following significant injuries. More difficult to determine, however, is the extent to which the healing and rehabilitation of these animals was the result of direct human care and intervention.[78]

The Middle Anglo-Saxon period is commonly associated with new husbandry practices on rural estate centres and ecclesiastical sites, geared towards specialized sheep husbandry for wool production.[79] Such patterns can be seen at the rural centre of Brandon, probably part of a monastic estate, and the monastic sites of Eynsham (Oxfordshire) and Hartlepool (Tyne and Wear) (Fig. 8). The trend is not so clear-cut at Lyminge, however, for whilst the ratio of

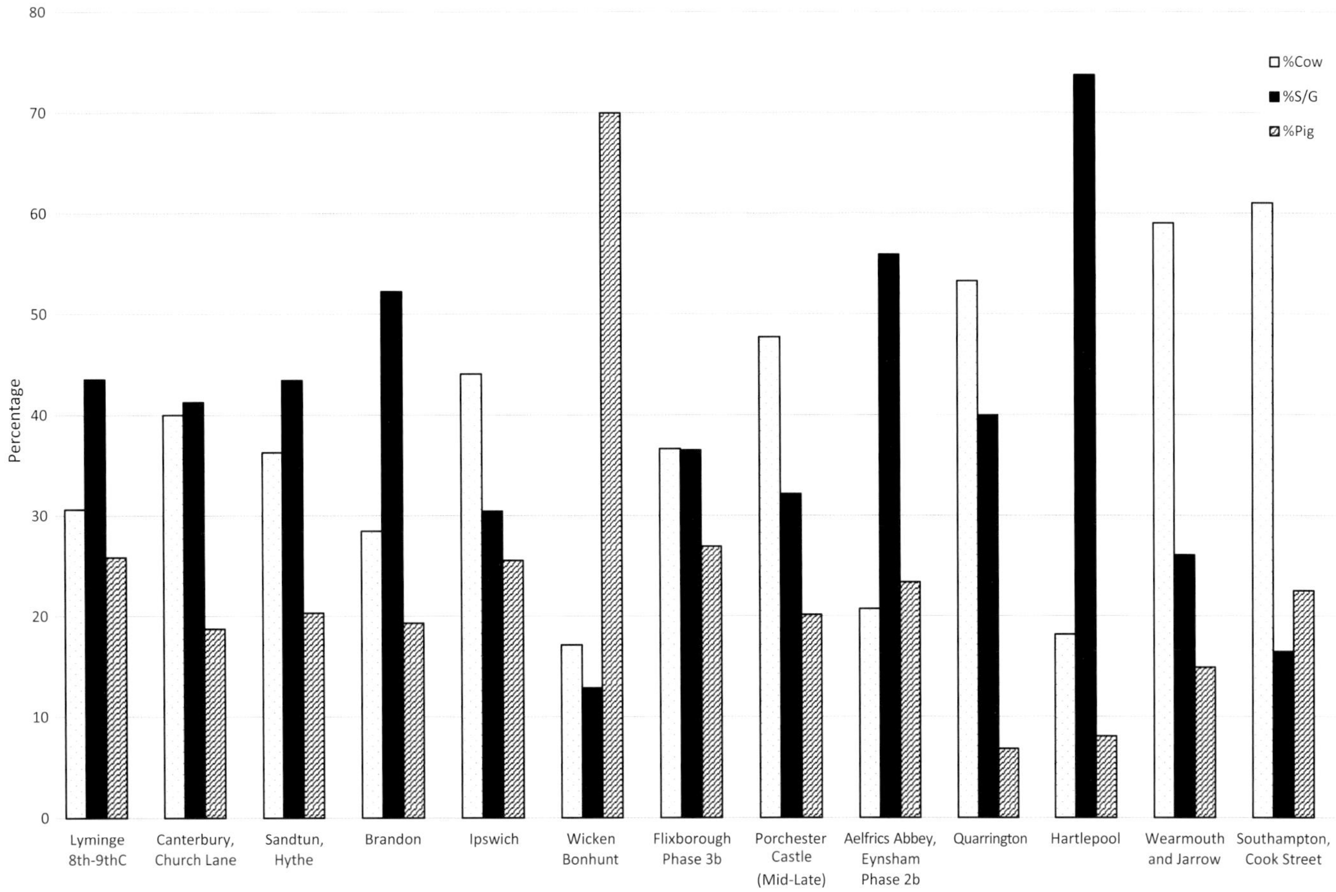


**Fig. 8** Graph comparing the numbers of cattle, sheep/goat and pig from the eighth- to ninth-century phase of Lyminge to contemporary sites.

caprines to the other main livestock does increase slightly in Phase II, the ageing evidence does not suggest that monastic husbandry practices were exclusively or mainly guided by highly specialized wool production.

The ratio of the three main domesticates at Lyminge during this phase has much in common with other caprine-dominated assemblages from Anglo-Saxon Kent, including the coastal settlement of *Sandtun*, West Hythe, and Church Lane, Canterbury, both of which had recorded connections with Lyminge during this phase (Fig. 8).[80] It is difficult to make generalisations on the basis of such a small number of assemblages, but the Kentish data do appear to hint towards a regional shift in farming practices during the eighth to the ninth centuries consistent with the expansion of a cereal-based agrarian regime accompanied by an abatement in pastoralism driven towards meat production. This suggestion receives strong support from Lyminge itself, both in relation to the increased number of cattle traction pathologies and multiple palaeobotanical indicators for an intensification in arable production.[81]

## Conclusion

The zooarchaeological assemblage from Lyminge offers the basis for a refined examination of how cultural attitudes to the consumption and exploitation of animals changed over the Anglo-Saxon period. My research has identified a series of diachronic trends in species representation and, in the case of domesticated animals, management strategies, which are synchronous with Lyminge's transformation from a pre-Christian royal vill into a flourishing monastic community closely entwined with the dynastic strategies of the Kentish royal house. While observed in microcosm, these transformations reflect wider changes in the cultural practices, religious affiliations and economic strategies of the Kentish elite during a key period in the formation of Christian kingdoms within Anglo-Saxon England at large. The study of zooarchaeological assemblages clearly has an important role to play in teasing out the complexities of how these changes unravelled in different localities under the influence of varying cultural influences and social trajectories.

One of the most important implications raised by my research is that past attempts to identify different 'signatures' in the Anglo-Saxon zooarchaeological record in relation to rigidly categorising sites as either 'monastic' or 'secular' has had a constraining influence over the interpretation of faunal assemblages. My paper has emphasised the need for zooarchaeological data to be interpreted within a local and regional framework grounded in the particularities of early medieval communities and their place within landscapes and cultural networks.

## Acknowledgements

This article was based on the author's AHRC-funded PhD research being carried out at the University of Reading as part of the wider Lyminge Archaeological Project. Many thanks go to all of those who offered assistance and advice, with particular thanks to the Lyminge Project excavation team, the Chicken Project, Rebecca Reynolds, Simon Maslin, Alexandra Knox and James Westoby. A special thanks must go to Gabor Thomas who commented on an early version of this paper and made many suggestions for its improvement.

## Notes

1 Sykes 2007; Poole 2010; Holmes 2014.
2 Rippon, Wainwright and Smart 2014, 201.
3 Brookes 2007.
4 Thomas 2013; Brooks 1989; Kelly 2006; Brooks and Kelly 2013; Thomas 2016.
5 Kelly 1992, 19.
6 Thomas 2013.
7 Thomas, this volume.
8 See Thomas, this volume.
9 For the purpose of this paper only animal bone recovered from hand collection and dry-sieving has been included in the analysis.
10 Recorded elements follow Davis 1992, with the addition of the atlas and axis as well as the proximal articulation of the ulna (trochlear notch and coronoid process) following Baker 1998. Horn cores and antler pedicles were also recorded, but have not been included in the overall fragment counts. Other 'non-countable specimens' were recorded as 'other' but were also not included in the overall fragment counts. Proximal articulations were recorded in cases where the distal articulation was not present in the same context. The criteria of Zeder and Lapham (2010) have been used to differentiate between the bones of sheep and goat; where this was not possible the bones were recorded as sheep/goat. In both phases of the site, goats were in the minority, and it is probable that the majority of sheep/goat bones derive from sheep.
11 Tipper 2004.
12 Thomas 2010, 70–1.
13 Morris 2008; 2011.
14 Hamerow 2006, 12.
15 Poole 2010, 157.
16 Morris and Jervis 2011, 68.
17 Knox 2012; see pp. 227–57 for a detailed discussion of the significance of animal deposition in burials and settlements.
18 Morris and Jervis 2011, 69–70.
19 The large quantity of fish bones that have been recovered from Lyminge were not included within this analysis. Any discussion of other Lyminge fish remains within this paper will be drawn from Reynolds' (2015) analysis of the 2008 and 2013 Lyminge fish assemblage.
20 Wherever possible, sheep and goat were distinguished morphologically to their individual species. In both phases, the majority of those fragments identified to individual species were sheep, a pattern reflected at many contemporary sites. For the purposes of this paper I will be referring to the combined total NISP of sheep and goat under the term 'sheep/goat' or 'caprines'. Owing to the difficulty in separating horse (*Equus caballus*) from ass (*Equus asinus*) most skeletal fragments were recorded under 'Equid sp.'. It is possible to separate cheek teeth based on their enamel folds (Eisenmann 1986), so the few horse teeth that were recovered were recorded as 'horse like'. Small numbers of horse were recovered from both phases of the site, with larger numbers being recorded in the eighth to ninth centuries.
21 See Thomas 2013, 132–7.
22 Bartosiewicz 2013, 108–9.
23 *Ibid.*, 132; Traction-related pathologies were absent in the Phase I assemblage, but constitute thirteen of the nineteen pathologies identified in the Phase II assemblage.
24 Thomas in press; McKerracher, this volume.
25 Thomas, McDonnell, Merkel and Marshall 2016.
26 Crabtree 2012. This pattern accords with an abundance of textile manufacturing equipment recovered from the eighth–ninth-century settlement focus (Thomas 2013).
27 Banham and Faith 2014, 92.
28 *Ibid.*, 92.
29 Owing to the similarities in skeletal make-up, this constituent of the assemblage includes a proportion of specimens which could only be identified as chicken/pheasant (*Gallus/Phasianus*), but which have been accepted as chicken on the basis of the general rarity of pheasant in the Anglo-Saxon period.
30 Holmes 2014.
31 Bartosiewicz 2013.
32 See Higbee 2009, 286–91, table 5.15, for consideration of a broader range of comparative assemblages.
33 Bendry 2002; Harman 1973.
34 Driver 1990; Bendry 2014, 171.
35 Rippon *et al.* 2014.
36 Harrington and Welch 2014, 43–5.
37 Banham and Faith 2014, 154.
38 Everitt 1986, 34; Hooke 2012, 34.
39 Sykes 2014, 99.
40 Rippon *et al.* 2014, 214; also see table 3.
41 Hamerow 2002, 133.
42 Hamerow 2002, 131; 2012, 162.
43 See Thomas, this volume.
44 Welch 2007, 220–3; Harrington and Welch 2014, 174–205.
45 Roymans 1996, 56; Doll 1999; Hamerow 2002, 16; Loveluck 2013, 132.
46 Banham and Faith 2014, 98; Magennis 1999.
47 Banham and Faith 2014, 98.
48 Fiddes 1991, 13; Lee 2007, 41.
49 Dobney and Jacques 2002, 17; Holmes 2014, 47.
50 The only other Anglo-Saxon identification of peregrine falcon known to the author derives from the Middle Saxon settlement of Brandon (Suffolk) (Crabtree and Campana 2014, 309).
51 *Ibid.*, 309.
52 Thomas 2013; Reynolds 2015.
53 Fiddes 1991, 5.
54 Blair 2005.
55 Dobney, Jacques, Barrett and Johnstone 2007; Barrett, Locker and Roberts 2009; Holmes 2014.
56 Ervynck 1997, 71.
57 Ervynck 1997, 73.
58 Frantzen 2014, 233.
59 Foot 2006, 6.
60 Foot 2006, 52.
61 Dembińska 1986, 155; Frantzen 2014, 238–9.
62 Ervynck 1997, 75.
63 Whitelock 1979, 397.
64 Dembińska 1986, 152–4.
65 Frantzen 2014, 178.
66 *Ibid.*, 207.
67 *Ibid.*, 182.
68 *Ibid.*, 190–3.
69 Sykes, 2014, 154-55.
70 Sykes 2007, 68; Poole 2010, 278.
71 *Ibid.*
72 Poole 2010, 178.
73 Poole 2014, 866; Crabtree 2015.

74 Poole 2014, 870–1; Serpell 1986; Serpell and Paul 1994.
75 Clark 1998; Fern 2010, 148.
76 Fern 2010, 148.
77 Bulliet 2005, 47.
78 Bartosiewicz 2013, 178.
79 Crabtree 2012.
80 Brooks and Kelly 2013.
81 McKerracher, this volume.

## Bibliography


Baker, P. 1998. *The Vertebrate Remains from Scole-Dickleburgh, Excavated in 1993 (Norfolk and Suffolk), A140 and A143 Road Improvement Project*, Ancient Monuments Laboratory Report, 29/98, London: English Heritage.

Banham, D. and Faith, R. 2014. *Anglo-Saxon Farms and Farming*, Oxford: Oxford University Press.

Barrett, J. H., Locker, A. M. and Roberts, C. M. 2009. '"Dark Age Economics" revisited: the English fish-bone evidence 600–1600', in L. Sicking and D. Abreu-Ferreira (eds.), *Beyond the Catch: Fisheries of the North Atlantic and the North Sea and the Baltic 900–1850*, 31–61, Leiden: Koninklijke Brill.

Bartosiewicz, L. 2013. *Shuffling Nags, Lame Ducks: The Archaeology of Animal Diseases*, Oxford and Oakville: Oxbow Books.

Bendry, R. 2002. 'The Animal Bones from Excavations at the Channel Tunnel Terminal at Cheriton, Folkestone', unpublished report for the Canterbury Archaeological Trust.

Bendry, R. 2014. 'Animal bone', in P. Bennett, K. Parfitt and J. Rady (eds.), *Prehistoric and Anglo-Saxon Discoveries on the East Kent Chalklands: Investigations along the Whitfield-Eastry By-pass 1991–1996*, 159–72, Canterbury: Canterbury Archaeological Trust Ltd.

Blair, J. 2005. *The Church in Anglo-Saxon Society*, Oxford: Oxford University Press.

Brookes, S. J. 2007. *Economics and Social Change in Anglo-Saxon Kent AD 400–900: Landscapes, Communities and Exchange*, BAR British Series, 431, Oxford: Archaeopress.

Brooks, N. 1989. 'The creation and early structure of the kingdom of Kent', in S. Bassett (ed.), *The Origins of the Anglo-Saxon Kingdoms*, 55–74, London: University of Leicester Press.

Brooks, N. and Kelly, S. 2013. *Charters of Christ Church Canterbury*, Vol. 1, Oxford: Oxford University Press.

Bulliet, R. W. 2005. *Hunters, Herders and Hamburgers: The Past and Future of Human–Animal Relationships*, New York: Columbia University Press.

Clark, G. 1998. 'The fathers and the animals: the rule of reason?', in A. Linzey and D. Yamamoto (eds.), *Animals on the Agenda: Questions about Animals for Theology and Ethics*, 67–79, Illinois: Illinois University Press.

Crabtree, P. J. 2012. *Middle Saxon Animal Husbandry in East Anglia*, Bury St Edmunds: Suffolk County Council.

Crabtree, P. J. 2015. 'A note on the role of dogs in Anglo-Saxon society: evidence from East Anglia', *International Jnl of Osteoarchaeology*, **25**, 976–80.

Crabtree, P. J. and Campana, D. 2014. 'Animal bone', in A. Tester, S. Anderson, I. Riddler and R. Carr (eds.), *Staunch Meadow, Brandon, Suffolk: A High Status Middle Saxon Settlement on the Fen Edge*, 296–312, Bury St Edmunds: Suffolk Archaeological Service.

Davis, S. J. M. 1992. *A Rapid Method for Recording Information About Mammal Bones from Archaeological Sites*, Ancient Monuments Laboratory Report, 19/92, London: English Heritage.

Dembińska, M. 1986. 'Fasting and working monks: regulations of the fifth to the eleventh centuries, in A. Fenton and E. Kisbán (eds.), *Food in Change: Eating Habits from the Middle Ages to the Present Day*, 152–60, Edinburgh: John Donald.

Dobney, K. and Jacques, D. 2002. 'Avian signatures for identity and status in Anglo-Saxon England', *Acta Zoologica Cracoviensia*, **45**, 7–21.

Dobney, K. D., Jacques, J., Barrett, J. H. and Johnstone, C. 2007. *Farmers, Monks and Aristocrats: The Environmental Archaeology of Anglo-Saxon Flixborough*, Oxford: Oxbow Books.

Doll, M. 1999. 'Im Essen jedoch connote er nicht enthalstam sein: Fleischverzehr in der Karolingerzeit', in C. A. W. Stiegemann and M. Wemhoff (eds.), *Kunst und Kultur de Karolingerzeit*, 445–9, Mainz: Philip von Zabern.

Driver, J. C. 1990. 'Faunal remains', in J. C. Driver, J. Rady and M. Sparks (eds.), *Excavations in the Cathedral Precincts, 2 Linacre Garden, 'Meister Omers', and St Gabriel's Chapel*, 228–57, Archaeology of Canterbury Monograph, 4, Maidstone: Canterbury Archaeological Trust.

Eisenmann, V. 1986. 'Comparative osteology of modern and fossil horses, half-asses, and asses', in R. H. Meadow and H.-P. Uerpmann (eds.), *Equids in the Ancient World*, 67–116, Wiesbaden: Reichert.

Ervynck, A. 1997. 'Following the rule? Fish and meat consumption in monastic communities in Flanders (Belgium)', in G. de Boe and F. Verhaeghe (eds.), *Environment and Subsistence in Medieval Europe*, 67–81, Rapporten, 9, Zellick: Instituut voor het Archeologisch Patrimonium.

Everitt, A. 1986. *Continuity and Colonization: The Evolution of the Kentish Settlement*, Leicester: Leicester University Press.

Fern, C. 2010. 'Early Anglo-Saxon horse burial of the fifth to seventh century AD', in M. Carver, A. Sanmark and S. Semple, *Signals of Belief in Early England: Anglo-Saxon Paganism Revisited*, Oxford: Oxbow Books.

Fiddes, N. 1991. *Meat: A Natural Symbol*, London: Routledge.

Foot, S. 2006. *Monastic Life in Anglo-Saxon England, c. 600–900*, Cambridge: Cambridge University Press.

Frantzen, A. J. 2014. *Food, Eating and Identity in Early Medieval England*, Woodbridge: Boydell Press.

Hambleton, E. 1999. *Animal Husbandry Regimes in Iron Age Britain: A Comparative Study of Faunal Assemblages from British Iron Age Sites*, Oxford: Archaeopress.

Hamerow, H. 2002. *Early Medieval Settlements: The Archaeology of Rural Communities in Northwest Europe, AD 400–900*, Oxford: Oxford University Press.

Hamerow, H. 2006. 'Special deposits in Anglo-Saxon settlements', *Medieval Arch.*, **50**, 1–30.

Hamerow, H. 2012. *Rural Settlements and Society in Anglo-Saxon England*, Oxford: Oxford University Press.

Harman, M. 1973. 'The mammalian bones from the Saxon hut at Keston', in B. Philp (ed.), *Excavations in West Kent 1960–1970*, 160–1, Kent Research Report, 2, Dover: West Kent Border Archaeological Group by the Kent Archaeological Rescue Unit.

Harrington, S. and Welch, M. 2014. *The Early Anglo-Saxon Kingdoms of Southern Britain AD 450–650: Beneath the Tribal Hidage*, Oxford and Philadelphia: Oxbow Books.

Higbee, L. 2009. 'Mammal and bird bone', in S. Lucy, J. Tipper and A. Dickens, *The Anglo-Saxon Settlement and Cemetery at Bloodmoor Hill, Carlton Colville, Suffolk*, 279–304, East Anglian Archaeology, 131, Cambridge: Cambridge Archaeological Unit.

Holmes, M. 2014. *Animals in Saxon and Scandinavian England: Backbones of Economy and Society*, Leiden: Sidestone Press.

Hooke, D. 2012. 'Wood pasture in early medieval England', in S. Turner and B. Sylvester (eds.), *Life in Medieval Landscapes: People and Places in the Middle Ages: Papers in Memory of H.S.A Fox*, 32–49, Oxford: Windgather Press.

Kelly, S. 1992. 'Trading privileges from eighth century England', *Early Medieval Europe*, **1**, 3–28.

Kelly, S. 2006. 'Lyminge minster and its charters', in S. Keynes and A. P. Smyth (eds.), *Anglo-Saxons: Studies Presented to Cyril Roy Hart*, 98–113, Dublin: Four Courts Press.

Knox, A. 2012. 'The Sacred and the Secular: Investigating Anglo-Saxon Ritual Action and Belief Systems through a Holistic Study of Settlements and Cemeteries in the Seventh to Ninth Centuries AD', unpublished PhD thesis, University of Reading.

Lee, C. 2007. *Feasting the Dead: Food and Drink in Anglo-Saxon Burial Rituals*, Woodbridge: Boydell Press.

Legge, E. T. 1992. *Excavations at Grimes Graves, Norfolk, 1972–1976*, Fascicule 4, *Animals, Environment and the Bronze Age Economy*, London: British Museum Press.

Loveluck, C. 2013. *Northwest Europe in the Early Middle Ages, c. AD 600–1500: A Comparative Archaeology*, Cambridge: Cambridge University Press.

Magennis, H. 1999. *Anglo-Saxon Appetites: Food and Drink and their Consumption in Old English and Related Literature*, Bodmin: Four Courts Press.

Morris, J. 2008. 'Re-examining Associated Bone Groups from Southern England and Yorkshire, *c.*4000 BC to AD 1550', unpublished PhD thesis, Bournemouth University.

Morris, J. 2011. *Investigating Animal Burials; Ritual, Mundane and Beyond*, BAR British Series, 535, Oxford: Archaeopress.

Morris, J. and Jervis, B. 2011. 'What's so special? A reinterpretation of Anglo-Saxon "special deposits"', *Medieval Arch.*, **55**, 66–81.

Payne, S. 1973. Kill-off patterns in sheep and goats: the mandibles from Asvan Vale. *Anatolian Stud.*, **23**, 281–303.

Poole, K. 2010. 'The Nature of Society in England, *c.* A.D. 410–1066', unpublished PhD thesis, University of Nottingham.

Poole, K. 2014. 'The contextual cat: human–animal relations and social meaning in Anglo-Saxon England', *Jnl of Arch. Method and Theory*, **22**, 857–82.

Reynolds, R. 2015. 'Food for the Soul: The Dynamics of Fishing and Fish Consumption in Anglo-Saxon England: *c.* A.D. 410–1066', unpublished PhD thesis, University of Nottingham.

Rippon, S., Wainwright, A. and Smart, C. 2014. 'Farming regions in medieval England: archaeobotanical and zooarchaeological evidence', *Medieval Arch.*, **58**, 195–255.

Roymans, N. 1996. 'The sword or the plough: regional dynamics in the Romanisation of Belgic Gaul and the Rhineland area', in N. Roymans (ed.), *From the Sword to the Plough*, 9–126, Amsterdam: Amsterdam University Press.

Serpell, J. 1986. *In the Company of Animals. A Study of Human–Animal Relationships*, Oxford: Blackwell.

Serpell, J. and Paul, E. 1994. 'Pets and the development of positive attitudes to animals', in A. Manning and J. Serpell (eds.), *Animals and Human Society: Changing Perspectives*, 127–44, London: Routledge.

Sykes, N. 2007. *The Norman Conquest: A Zooarchaeological Perspective*, BAR International Series, 1656, Oxford: Archaeopress.

Sykes, N. 2014. *Beastly Questions*, London: Bloomsbury.

Thomas, G. 2010. *The Later Anglo-Saxon Settlement at Bishopstone: A Downland Manor in the Making*, Council for British Archaeology Research Report, 163, York: CBA.

Thomas, G. 2013. 'Life before the minster: the social dynamics of monastic foundation at Anglo-Saxon Lyminge, Kent', *Antiquaries Jnl*, **93**, 109–45.

Thomas, G. 2016. 'Downland, marsh, and weald: monastic foundation and rural intensification in Anglo-Saxon Kent', in R. Flechner and M. Ní Mhaonaigh (eds.), *Converting the Isles: The Introduction of Christianity into the Early Medieval Insular World*, 349–376, Brepols: Turnhout.

Thomas, G., McDonnell, G., Merkel, J. and Marshall, P. 2016. 'Technology, ritual and Anglo-Saxon agrarian production: the biography of a seventh-century plough coulter from Lyminge, Kent', *Antiquity*, **90**, 742–58.

Tipper, J. 2004. *The Grubenhaus in Anglo-Saxon England*, Yedingham: Landscape Research Centre.

Welch, M. 2007. 'Anglo-Saxon Kent to AD 800', in J. H. Williams (ed.), *The Archaeology of Kent to AD 800*, 187–250, Woodbridge: Boydell Press.

Whitelock, D. 1979. *English Historical Documents c.500–1042*, London: Eyre Methuen.

Zeder, M. A. and Lapham, H. A. 2010. 'Assessing the reliability of criteria used to identify post-cranial bones in sheep (Ovis) and goats (Capra)', *Jnl of Arch. Science*, **37**, 2887–905.